A
GUIDE TO PANJABI

A
GUIDE TO PANJABI

B. JAWAHIR SINGH

SECOND EDITION

GYAN

Published by

GYAN

Gyan Publishing House
5, Ansari Road
Daryaganj, New Delhi-110002
Phone: 011-47034999, 9811692060
E-mail: books@gyanbooks.com

Distribution Network
gyanbooks.com
India, USA, Canada, UK, Australia, France

ISBN : 978-81-212-4409-1 (PB)
First Published, 1902

2nd Impression 2020

Printed at: Gyan Press, Delhi.

A
Guide to Panjabi
Author: B. Jawahir Singh

PREFACE.

TO THE STUDENT.

1. In submitting this new edition of the Punjábí Guide, I would beg to state that it has been made as clear and as simple as possible in the hope that those who reside at great distances from any practical munshi may find it almost a self teacher.

2. Many new words and rules have been added and old ones more simply explained, and I hope that it will meet with as cordial a reception as the first edition.

In conclusion I would give the student the following few words of advice :—

First ; when learning words by heart, without which a knowledge of the language cannot be obtained, I should advise pupils to be specially careful in writing down all words resembling one another such as ਛੁਟੀ *chhuṭṭī* = leave ਚਿਠੀ *chiṭṭhī* = letter ਚੇਤਾ *chetā* = recollection ਛੇਤੀ *chhetī* = quickly ਚਿੰਤਾ *chintā* = anxiety ਚਿਤਾ *chitā* = pyre ਦਿੱਤਾ *dittā* = gave ਡਿੱਠਾ *diṭhā* = saw ਮਿੰਨਤ *minnat* = entreaty ਮਿਹਨਤ *mihnat* = labour (work) ਸਲਾਹ *slāh* = advise ਸੁਲਾ *sulā* = peace ਟੋਟਾ = *ṭoṭā* = piece ਤੋਤਾ *totā* = parrot ਗਲ *gal* = a word ਗਲ੍ਹ *galh* = check &c. &c.

Secondly ; when a word comes under notice find out all other words connected with, it write them down, and learn thoroughly.

FOR EXAMPLE.

If the word is ਘੋੜਾ *ghoṛā* = a horse the words to be learnt are ; ਕਾਠੀ *kāṭhī* = saddle ਲਗਾਮ *lagām* = bridle ਰਕਾਬ *rakāb* = stirrup ਤਬੇਲਾ *tabelā* = stable &c.

In this way a thorough and lasting knowledge of the words in most common use will be obtained.

Thanking all those who have patronised the book in the past and those who take up the present work.

I Remain,
Your obedient servant.
JAWAHIR SINGH.

PUNJABI EXAMINATION.

HIGHER STANDARD.

The following are the text books for the examination, Punjábí dialogues by Pandit Sardhá Rám and the *Sikhāṅ-dè-Rāj-dī Vithyā*, omitting Part II and Section 19 and 20 of Part IV

T e following are the tests laid down for this examination :—

I.—Constructing, with readiness and accuracy, from the prescribed text-books.

II.—Translating accurately, and with correctness of idioms and grammar, not less than half an ordinary octavo page of plain English into Punjábí.

III.—Reading fairly and translating readily and correctly manuscripts in the language of examination.

These manuscripts may be selected from the proceedings of a case in Court, from reports and petitions addressed to civil or military authorities, from letters passing between natives of India in the ordinary course of business or from private correspondence. They should not be written with clearness of a printed book nor yet in a very cramped or crabbed hand; but in such a manner as fairly and honestly to represent the written characters generally employed.

IV.—*Viva voce* translation into the language of a paper of English sentences, and conversing with the Examiners, or in their presence with person selected by them, with fluency and such correctness of pronunciation, grammar and idiom as to be at once intelligible.

Committees for Examination in the Punjabi language are assembled half yearly at Mian Meer on the 10th January and 10th July (not being Sunday), and are composed of the three members, one an officer of the Civil Service, or other person selected by the Government of the Punjáb as being well acquainted with the Punjábí language, and two military officers who have passed an examination in that language. The character to be employed is Gurmukhi. Applications for examination will be forwarded to the District Staff Office, Lahore District one month prior to the dates above given.

The proceedings of the Committee, with the certificate of the president and that of each candidate will be sent to the Staff Officer of the Station.

The station committee will decide upon the exercise, as well as upon the oral subjects of examination, and will complete and sign C2, which is the form to be used for this examiniation.

The Staff Officer of the station will then forward the proceedings to the District Staff Office, where the procedure detailed in para 64 will be taken (same as lower standard, Persian.

Obligatory Punjābī.

The following rules for the examination of officers of the staff corps in the languages chiefly spoken by the men of the regiments to which they may be permanently posted are pnblished.

Punjābī.—In the 12th, 16th and 18th Bengal Cavalry, 14th, 15th, 23rd, 29th, 30th, 31st, 32nd, 34th, 35th, 36th, 27th, 38th, and 45th Bengal Infantry and 29th, 30th, 31st and 32nd Madras Infantry.

(*a*).—Reading and translating at sight page of some easy text book except in the case of Khaskura for which at present there is no text book.

(*b*).—Reading the written character, a either letter or an urzi actually received in the Adjutant's Office if available and vernacular order books, care being taken to select those plainly written.

(*c*). *Colloquial.*—The candidate to be given orders, instructions, &c, to translate to the native soldier or civilian ordered to attend for the purpose of conversation, and to ask the man questions about himself, or to translate into the vernacular, at sight, the evidence given by a witness before the Court Enquiry or Court Martial.

Examinations will be held for the present as required, under the orders of the Officer Commanding at all military stations where there are candidates :—

The proceedings of the board of examination will be drawn up on Army form a2 and are to be transmitted through the prescribed channel to the Deputy Adjutant General of the Command. The proceedings are not subject to review by the Boards of Examiners in Calcutta, Madras or Bombay. The result will be published in Command Orders. If a candidate fails to satisfy the Board the President will inform him of the fact.

An allowance of Rs. 100 will be granted to each officer on passing the examination in any one of the languages.

All officers now serving below the rank of substantive field officer or who, at date of issue of this army circular are not permanent wing or squadron commmanders, will be required to pass within two years ; and in future all officers entering the native army will be required to pass with in two years from date of permanent appointment to a regiment ; this period to exclude any period spent on leave out of India or on field service. An officer permanently transferred from one regiment, to another will be required to pass in the lauguage spoken by the men of his new regiment, with in two years whether transferred for his own convenience or on account of the exigencies of the services unless he holds field rank or is transferred as permanent wing or squadron commander.

SPECIMEN OF COPIES OF TESTIMONIALS.

PUNJABI EXAMINATION.

Undersigned begs to offer his services as Teacher in Native Languages, *i. e.* Hindustani, Punjábi, &c., (especially in Punjábi b ing his Native Language,) d has passed several Civil and Military Officers from whom he has obtained extraordinary chits.

He can also correct Exercise through correspondence.

JAWAHIR SINGH, R. H. A. MUNSHI,

Author of " Punjābī Guide " " English to Punjābī Vocabulary."

" Urdu Teacher."—" Aid to candidates." " Translator of Punjābī Bātchīt Sikhān-de-Raj-dī-Vithyā, and selection from the Bagh-o-Bahar, with Vocabulary.

---

* New and Second hand Books for Sale and Purchase or exchange.

Umballa, 1st February 1887.

I worked Punjábí with Munshi Jawahir Singh, R. H. A., for four months, at the end of which time on 10th January 1887, passed ; I previously knew nothing of the language. I consider him a very capable Munshi. He has a good system of teaching knows English well, and is exceedingly painstaking. I recommend him strongly.

(Sd.) C. F. MINCIN, LIEUT.,
1st Punjab Cavalry, P. F. E.
Attached 2nd D. Gds. Queen's Bays.)

Umballa, 15th October 1817.

I studied Punjábí with Munshi Jawahir Singh for six months, and successfully passed the examination held on 11th July 1887. I consider him very painstaking and proficient in Punjabi.

(Sd). G. H. UNDERDOWN,
SCHOOL MASTER,
2nd Drāgoon Guards.

Munshi Jawahir Singh taught me for the space of four months in the Punjabi Language, at the end of which time I passed the Higher Standard successfully.

I consider him a very good Punjabi Munshi he is attentive, punctual and painstaking in preparing candidates for examination.

UMBALLA,
23rd August 1888.

(Sd.) A. GOTT,
SCHOOL MASTER,
7th Dragoon Guards.

I worked with Munshi Jawahir Singh for one week before going up for Punjábí Examination which I passed successfully, there was very little time, but he taught me a great deal, and from what I have seen of him, I consider him the only really good. Pnujabi Munshi I knew, he has thorough knowledge of English which is in my opinion most important.

UMBALLA, 23rd August 1888. (Sd.) M. COWPER, LIEUT., *10th Bengal Lancers.*

Munshi Jawahir Singh taught me Punjabi for 2½ months, but owing to illness I could not continue working with him in order to pass in January 1890. He is very painstaking and knows English very well. He is by far the best Munshi for Punjabi in this station.

UMLALLA, 5th December 1889. (Sd.) F. TWEEDELL, LIEUT., *28th P. I.*

I read Punjabi with Munshi Jawahir Singh about four months passing the examination at Lahore, in January 1890, (in which only his pupils passed.) I consider him in every respect a first class Munshi for the Punjabi Language.

(Sd.) LCE.-CORPL. ALLEYNE,

Umballa 1890. *The Queen's,*

Munshi Jawahir Singh taught me in the Punjábí Language for a period of six months, after which I passed the prescribed examination at Meean Meer on 10th January 1890, at the same examination, thirteen candidates were present out of which only two were successful, and they were pupils of Munshi Jawahir Singh.

This man is known through the Punjábí as the best Munshi and that his pupils never or very seldom fail, he is also a very steady hard working and respectful man, and I with pleasure recommend him to any one that wishes to learn the Native languages.

UMBALLA, 10 February 1890. (Sd.) V. DUNNE, SERGT., *C. D.*

Jawahir Singh Munshi, taught me Punjábí for some months. He did not pass me as I had to leave the station. He is a good and intelligent Munshi, and speaks English well.

UMBALLA, 19th August 1890. (Sd.) R. C. LYE, LIEUT., *23rd Pioneers.*

Munshi Jawahir Singh has passed me for the Punjabi examination, I worked with him for the last 2 months and found him of the greatest service and very zealous in his work, I can thoroughly recommend him to any one who wishes to read Gurmukhi.

UMBALLA, 15th July 1890. (Sd.) E. ST. A. WAKE, LIEUT., *10th Bengal Lancers.*

I read Punjabi with Jawahir Singh, R. H. A. Munshi, for one month and was successful. I consider him an excellent teacher, and he takes a great deal of trouble, at the same examination, (July 10th 1895,) one canidate passed who prepared himself by correspondence with Jawahir Singh.

I found the book (which he is preparing for the Press) invaluable.

(Sd.) H. E. COTTERILL, LIEUT.,

4th September 1895. *The Queen's.*

Jawahir Singh, Munshi, R. H. A , Umballa, gave me lessons, by post in Punjabi for 4 or 5 months. His style of training was excellent, and his papers from the book he is published were so well selected that I passed successfully in the Examination in July 1895. He was painstakiug and considerate in the price, he charged for tuition and I can recommend him to any one requiring a really good Muushi.

B. D. CANAL, MADHOPUR. *6th October 1895.* (Sd.) E. HOME PURVES. *Temporary Engineer.*

I worked at Punjabi for 3 months with Jawahir Singh R. H. A. Munshi, and at the end of that period passed successfully in the July 1896 Examination.

I should think he is quite one of the best Munshi for Punjabi that can be got and the Grammar that he was publishing at the time and which is the first thing of its kind gave me infinite help.

NOWSHERA, *2nd October 1896.* (Sd.) J. L. STEWART, 2ND LIEUT., *11th (P. W. O.) Bengal Lancers.*

I certify that Jawahir Singh, R. H. A. Munshi, Umballa, taught me Punjábí for about 5 months, after which I successfully passed the examination held at Meean Meer on the 10th July 1896. His style of teaching was very good and most of lessons were taken from his Punjábí Guide which was then in Press, and which in my opinion is an excellent book not only for those preparing for the Punjábí Examination, but for others also, and I can thoroughly recommend to it any one wishing to study the language.

PESHAWAR, *1st September 1896.* (Sd.) F. LAMBERT, PRIVATE, *1st Devon. Regiment.*

I worked with Munshi Jawahir Singh for 2 months before going up for the Punjabi Examination, and was successful in passing after this short period. It is owing to Munshi Jawahir Singh's knowledge of the language, method of teaching and acquaintance with English that so many of his pupils are successful.

UMBALLA, 8th March 1897. } (Sd.) H. F. A. PEARSON, LIEUT., *23rd Pioneers.*

I strongly recommend Jawahir Singh, R. H. A. Munshi, Umballa, to any one working up for Punjabi Examination. I consider his Punjábi Guide an invaluable aid and I think any one could pass the Punjabi obligatory by reading it himself without a Munshi to teach him.

UMBALLA, 18th October 1899. } (Sd.) G. GILBERT, CAPT. *34th Punjab Infantry.*

I worked with Munshi Jawahir Singh for about a month through the post before going up for the July 1897, Punjábi examination. His system of teaching is excellent. He has a very good "Guide," which is a thorough tutor to the language.

(Sd.) R. G. MUNN, LIEUT.,

25th March 1898. *36th Sikhs.*

I have much pleasure in recommending Munshi Jawahir Singh's Guide to Punjábi, to all learners of that language who wish to acquire a thorough knowledge of the same within a very short time. it is a book which really reflects great credit and honor on the author. Besides this I worked with Munshi Jawahir Singh in correspondence, and became quite competent for the H. S. within three weeks time. I can recommend Munshi Jawahir Singh to all who require a genuine and expert tutor in that language He has my best wishes as I am transferred to Bengal Command, I will be glad to hear of his invariable success in life.

UMBALLA, 22nd October 1897. } (Sd.) W. M. McMILLON, *Assistant Surgeon, I. M. S.*

Jawahir Singh, Munshi, R. H. A. Umballa, gave me lessons by post in Punjábi for 2½ months, his style of training was excellent, and his papers from the book which has published are so well selected that I passed successfully the examination in January 1897. He was painstaking and considerate in the price he charged for tuition, and I can recommend him to any one requiring a really good Munshi.

(Sd.) M. BEDEL, ASST, SURGEON, *I. M. S.*

I worked with Munshi Jawahir Singh personally for 1½ months, and by correspondence for another two months, and then gave up the language (Punjábi) owing to want of leisure. He seems to be most painstaking and intelligent, so that I can confidendtly recommend him.

MARDAN, 18th August 1900 } (Sd.) I. VAN. BATTYE, LIEUT., *Guides.*

Certified that I worked with Munshi Jawahir Singh for the H. S. Punjabi which I passed in July last. I consider his mode of teaching by correspondence all that could be desired.

CALCUTTA,
17th September 1898.

(Sd.) L A. WATSON, LIEUT.,
31st P. I.

Munshi Jawahir Singh taught me by correspondence for about three months in Punjabi and enabled me to pass the examination satisfactorily. He teaches very well and takes great pains to make his pupils proficient. I can thoroughly recommend him.

JULLUNDER,
29th January 1898

(Sd.) A. WARD, LIEUT.,
30th P. I.

Jawahir Singh, R H. A. Munshi, Umballa, taught me a great deal by correspondence in 2 and half months for the H. S. Punjabi Examination. His corrections to my exercises and explanations to a large number of question as to Grammar, &c., which I put him through the post were most explicit and satisfactory.

I was throughly pleased with him and add my recommendation to his already long list of testimonials

EDWARDESABAD,
11th March 1899.

(Sd). S. W. ROBINSON, LIEUT., R. A.,
No. 2 (Derajat M. Battery.)

Munshi Jawahir Singh coached me by correspondence for the H. S. Punjabi for less than 3 months at the end of which time I passed successfully. I had only two days personal tuition Four out of five of his pupils passed at the same examination all of whom had been coached by correspondence ; which seems to say a good deal for his method.

LUDHIANA,
7th August 1898.

(Sd.) A. SKEEN, LIEUT.,
24th P. I.

My Dear Munshi.

I attribute my success to your systematic, instruction without which. I am sure my labours would have been in vain. I am indeed thankful to you for the trouble you took with my exercise and I shall recommend you to any one who is desirous of taking up Punjábi. I have already, secured for you a good pupil of whom I contrain the strongest at the next Punjábi Examination in July.

60 Church Road,
RAWALPINDI,
20th January 1902.

G. M. TURNER,

I have pleasure in stating that I consider Jawahir Singh a good and capable Munshi, I worked with him by post for six months and then passed the Punjábi Higher standard previously knowing nothing of the language.

AMRITSAR,
6th Marc h1902.

H. A. HAINES,
MAJOR,
R. A. M. C.

The following Gentlemen are working for the H. S. Punjabi by correspondence :—

QR.-MR.-SERGT.
MOORE,
District Staff Office.
Rawalpindi.

LT. J. Y. TANCRED,
19th Punjab Infantry.

PART 1.

THE ALPHABET.

The *Panjābī* or *Gurmukhī* Alphabet consists of thirty-five letters and is therefore called *Paiṅtī* (thirty-five).

The letters are written from left to right, as in English.

1.—*Consonants*—

FORM.	NAME.	POWER.
ਉ	*ūṛā*	U in put.
ਅ	*aiṛā*	U „ but.
ੲ	*iṛī*	I „ pit.
ਸ	*sassā*	S „ sun.
ਹ	*hāhā*	H „ hot.
ਕ	*kakkā*	K „ king.
ਖ	*khakhā*	K (aspirated).
ਗ	*gaggā*	G in go.
ਘ	*ghaggā*	G (aspirated).
ਙ	*ngangā*	Ng in king (seldom used).
ਚ	*chachā*	Ch. in church.
ਛ	*chhachhā*	Ch. (aspirated).
ਜ	*jajjā*	J in jag.
ਝ	*jhajjā*	J (aspirated).
ਞ	*naiyāṅ*	Ny. (seldom used).
ਟ	*ṭaiṅkā*	Ṭ in tight (hard)
ਠ	*ṭhaṭṭhā*	Ṭ (aspirated) („)
ਡ	*ḍaḍḍā*	Ḍ in dog („)
ਢ	*ḍhaḍḍā*	Ḍ (aspirated) (hard)
ਣ	*ṇāṇā*	N in now (soft.)
ਤ	*tattā*	T „ town („)
ਥ	*thaththā*	Th. „ think („)
ਦ	*daddā*	Th. in that („)
ਧ	*dhaddā*	D (aspirated), („)
ਨ	*ṇannā*	Ṇ in not (hard)
ਪ	*pappā*	P „ push.
ਫ	*phaphā*	P (aspirated).
ਬ	*babbā*	B in ball.
ਭ	*bhabbā*	B (aspirated).
ਮ	*mammā*	M in mat.
ਯ	*yayyā*	Y „ you.
ਰ	*rārā*	R „ right (soft).
ਲ	*lallá*	L „ long.
ਵ	*wawwā*	V „ vow. *
ੜ	*rāṛā*	Ṛ „ rogue, (hard).

* It also gives the sound of *w.*

The *Punjābī* characters have some connection with each other as shewn below, with the exceptions of the last five letters.

p kh dh th b w t ḍ bh m s sh h r g j ṛ k d ch ph ḍh ng
ਪ ਖ ਧ ਥ ਬ ਵ ਤ ਡ ਭ ਮ ਸ ਸ਼ ਹ ਰ ਗ ਜ ੜ ਕ ਦ ਚ ਫ ਢ ਙ

ṭ ṭh ṇ ny i jh gh a y n chh l u
ਟ ਠ ਣ ਞ ੲ ਝ ਘ ਅ ਯ ਨ ਛ ਲ ੳ

The compound letters are :—

ਤ੍ਰ *tr* ਪ੍ਰ *pr* ਸ੍ਨ *sn* ਸ੍ਚ *sch* ਗ੍ਯ *gy* ਸ੍ਵ *sw* ਸ੍ਥ *sth* ੜ੍ਹ *ṛh*

As there are no *Panjābī* characters equal in power to *sh, f, z,* or *kh* (*urdū* خ) they are denoted by the following :—

sh by ਸ਼, *f by* ਫ਼, *z by* ਜ਼, and *kh by* ਖ਼

Note.—When written in Roman character hard letters are distinguished by a dot underneath ;

Examples. ਕੁੜੀ = *kuṛī*, girl ਘੋੜਾ = *ghoṛā*, a horse. ਘੰਟਾ = *ghanṭā*, an hour

II.—Vowels.—

LETTER.	INITIAL, OR WHEN PRECEDED BY A VOWEL.	WHEN PRECEDED BY A CONSONANT.	POWER.
a	ਅ	(see note a)	u in but.
ā	ਆ	ਾ	a „ dart.
i	ਇ	ਿ (see. b).	i „ pit
ī	ਈ	ੀ	ee „ bee.
u	ਉ	ੁ	u „ put.
ū	ਊ	ੂ	oo „ fool.
e	ਏ	ੇ	a „ mate.
ai	ਐ	ੈ	ai „ kaisar.
o	ਓ	ੋ	o „ mote.
au	ਔ	ੌ	ow „ fowl.

In addition to the above, the following symbols are in common use :—

(ਂ) *bindī*, and (ੰ) *tippī*. When either is placed over a letter, that letter is to be followed by a nasal *n* ;

Examples ਮਾਂਦਾ, *māṅdā*, sick. ਮੁੰਡਾ, *muṅḍā*, boy.

(ੱ) *adhak*, denotes that the following letter is to be doubled.

Examples ਕੁੱਤਾ *kuttā*, a dog. ਸੱਦਣਾ *saddṇā*, to call.

(।) or (॥) Denotes a period.

Notes.—(*a*) short a (ਅ) is not written after a consonant, in *punjābī*, but is to be understood. Example, ਮਨੁਖ = *manukh*, a man.

(*b*) short *i* (ਿ) is written before a consonant but is pronounced after it

Examples, ਗਿਆ = *giā*, gone. ਪਿਉ = *piu*, father.

(*c*) Tippí (ੰ) is used with short vowels, *bindī* (ਂ) with long vowels, except long *ū* (ਊ) which takes tippí.

Examples, ਅੰਦਰ = *aṅdar*, inside. ਮਾਂ = *māṅ*, mother. ਤੂੰ = *tūṅ*, Thou.

(*d*) The nasal *n*, in Roman character is denoted by placing a dot above it.

Examples. ਮੈਂ = *maiṅ*, I ਤੰਬੂ = *taṅbū* tent.

THE NOUN.

I.—*Number and case.*

In *punjābī* there are two numbers Singular and Plural.

There are seven cases, one Nominative and six oblique. The latter is formed by the use of the following particles with the Nominative :—

CASE.	PARTICLE.		MEANING,
	Punbābī.	*Roman.*	
Genitive	ਦਾ,ਦੇ,ਦੀ,ਦੀਆਂ	*dā, de, dī, dīāṅ* (c)	of, or belonging to.

Dative and Accusative	ਨੂੰ	*nūṅ*	to.
Ablative	ਤੇ,ਕੋਲੋਂ,ਥੋਂ	*te, koloṅ,* or *thoṅ*	from.
Locative	ਵਿਚ, ਉੱਤੇ,ਤੀਕ	*wichch, utte, tīk*	in, on, up to.
Instrumental	ਨੇ	*ne* (*b*)	by.
Vocative	ਓ, ਓਏ	*o, oe, &c.* (*a*)	(form of address.)

Notes.—(*a*) The Vocative is not regular and must be learned by practice.

(*b*) The Instrumental is only used with the Past, Perfect, and Pluperfect Tenses, When used with the 1st and 2nd Person the ਨੇ is omitted

(*c*) dā is followed by a Noun, sing : Masc ;

de	Do.	do.	plu :	„	
diāṅ	Do.	do.	„	„	(Obl).
dī	Do.	do.	sing Fem :		
dīāṅ	Do.	do.	plu :	„	

Example.

ਮਨੁੱਖ ਦਾ ਕੁੱਤਾ	*manukh dā kuttā*	The man's dog.
ਮਨੁੱਖ ਦੇ ਕੁੱਤੇ	*manukh de kutte*	The man's dogs.
ਮਨੁੱਖ ਦਿਆਂ ਕੁੱਤਿਆਂ ਨੂੰ	*manukh diāṅ kuttiāṅ nūṅ*	To the man's dogs.
ਮਨੁੱਖ ਦੀ ਕੁੱਤੀ	*manukh dī kuttī*	The man's bitch.
ਮਨੁੱਖ ਦੀਆਂ ਕੁੱਤੀਆਂ	*manukh dīāṅ kuttīāṅ*	The man's bitches.
ਮਨੁੱਖ ਦੀਆਂ ਕੁੱਤੀਆਂਨੂੰ	*mānukh dīāṅ kuttiāṅ nūṅ*	To the man's bitches.

For declension, as to number and case, the Nouns may be divided into five groups These groups with all necessary changes are :—

1st, Masculine Nouns ending in Á.

To form oblique cases sing : change ਆ ā into ਏ e.

„ Nom : „ plu : „ ਆ ā „ ਏ e.

„ Obl : „ „ „ ਆ ā „ ਇਆਂ iāṅ.

Note.—The following Nouns do not inflect to form the Obl : cases, sing ; or Nom : plu :—

ਤਲਾ	*talā*	tank.	ਖ਼ੁਦਾ	*khudā*	God.
ਬਚਾ	*bachā*	defence.			
ਦਰਿਆ	*dariā*	river.	ਭਰਾ	*bharā*	brother.

2nd—ALL OTHER MASCULINE NOUNS.

To form Obl : cases plu : , add *āṅ*.

3rd.—FEMININE NOUNS ENDING IN ā

To form Obl : cases plu : add *wāṅ*.

4th.—FEMININE NOUNS ENDING IN *u* or *uṅ*.

To form all cases plu : change *u* or *uṅ* into *wāṅ*.

5th.—ALL OTHER FEMININE NOUNS.

To form all cases plu : add *āṅ*.

Note.—Cases and numbers not mentioned above do not require any change fc Nominative.

EXAMPLES.

	Singular.				Plural.		
	Panjābí.	Roman.	Meaning.		Panjābí.	Roman.	Meaning.
N.	ਘੋੜਾ	*ghoṛā*	a horse.	N.	ਘੋੜੇ	*ghoṛe*	horses.
G.	ਘੋੜੇਦਾ, ਦੇ, ਦੀ, ਦੀਆਂ	*ghoṛe dā, de, dī, diāṅ.*	of a horse	G.	ਘੋੜਿਆਂ ਦਾ	*ghoṛiāṅ dā, &c.*	of „
D & A.	ਘੋੜੇ, ਨੂੰ	*ghoṛe nūṇ*	to „	D & A.	ਘੋੜਿਆਂ ਨੂੰ	*ghoṛiāṅ nūṅ*	to „
Ab.	ਘੋੜੇ ਤੇ, ਕੋਲੋਂ, ਥੋਂ	*ghoṛe te, kolon, thoṅ*	from „	Ab	ਘੋੜਿਆਂ ਤੇ	*ghoṛiāṅ te, &c.*	from „
L.	ਘੋੜੇ, ਵਿਚ	*ghoṛe wichch*	in „	Loc.	ਘੋੜਿਆਂ ਵਿੱਚ	*ghoṛiāṅ wichch*	in „
	ਘੋੜੇ, ਉਤੇ	*ghoṛe utte*	on „		ਘੋੜਿਆਂ ਉੱਤੇ	*ghoṛiāṅ utte*	on „
	ਘੋੜੇ,ਤੀਕ	*ghoṛe tīk*	np to „		ਘੋੜਿਆਂ ਤੀਕ	*ghoṛiāṅ tīk*	up to „
I.	ਘੋੜੇ,ਨੇ	*ghoṛe ne*	by „	I.	ਘੋੜਿਆਂ ਨੇ	*ghoṛiāṅ ne*	by „
V.	ਓਏ ਘੋੜੇ	*oe ghoṛe*	o „	V.	ਓਏ ਘੋੜਿਓ	*oe ghoṛio*	oh „

Note.—On [ੋਂ] and *in* (ਾਂ) are often used for the affixes *thoṅ* and *wichch* respectively.

Example ਘਰੋਂ = *gharoṅ*, from the house | ਘਰੀਂ = *gharīṅ*, in the house.

II.—Gender.

In Panjābi there are only two Genders, Masculine, and Feminine, but there are no fixed rules by which these can be determined.

All names of Masculine and Feminine objects are Masculine and Feminine Gender respectively.

The following is a rough guide to the Gender of other Nouns :—

Nouns ending in ਆ *ā* are generally Masculine.

" " " ਈ *ī* " " Feminine.

The principal exceptions to these two rules are :—

(1) Feminine Nouns ending in *ā* (ਆ) *

ਜਗਾ	*jagā*	a place.	ਸਿੱਖਾ	*sañthā*	lesson.
ਦੁਨੀਆ	*duniā*	world.	ਵਾ	*wā*	air.
ਦੁਆ	*duā*	medicine.	ਰਜਾ	*rajā*	furlough.
ਆਗਯਾ	*āgyā*	order.	ਬਵਾ	*bawā*	an epidemic.
ਸੈਨਾ	*sainā*	an army.	ਚਿਖਾ	*chikhā*	funeral pyre.
ਕਿਰਪਾ	*kirpā*	kindness.	ਅਧੀਨਤਾ	*adhīntā*	obedience.
ਦਯਾ	*dyā*	mercy.	ਹਤਿਆ	*hatiā*	murder.
ਸੁਲ੍ਹਾ	*sulhā*	peace.	ਸਜਾ	*sajā*	punishment.
ਖਿਮਾਂ	*khimāṅ*	patience.	ਭੇਟਾ	*bheṭā*	sacrifice.
ਵਿਦਿਆ	*widiā*	knowledge.	ਈਰਖਾ	*īrkhā*	malice.
ਜਾਤ੍ਰਾ	*jātrā*	shrine.	ਸੂਰਮਤਾ	*sūrmtā*	bravery.
ਗੁਫਾ	*guphā*	cave.	ਮਾਯਾ	*māyā*	wealth.
ਲਜਿਆ	*lajiā*	shame.	ਸੇਵਾ	*sewā*	service.
ਅਵਗਿਆ	*awagiā*	fault.	ਧਰਮਸਾਲਾ	*dharmsālā*	religious meeting house for *Sikhs*.

* Feminine Nouns never change in oblique cases singulars.

2.—Masculine Nouns ending in ī (ੀ).

ਮੋਤੀ	*motī*	a pearl.	ਕਿਰਤੀ	*kirtī*	a workman.
ਪਾਣੀ	*pāṇī*	water.	ਹਿਤਕਾਰੀ	*hitkārī*	a benefactor.
ਜੀ	*jī*	the mind.	ਸ਼ੈਹਿਰੀ	*shaihrī*	a citizen.

The following Feminine Nouns should also be noted :—

ਫੌਜ	*phauj*	an army.	ਮੰਡਲੀ	*maṇḍlī*	crowd of fakirs.
ਪਲਟਨ	*pulṭaṇ*	a regiment.	ਸਰਕਾਰ	*sarkār*	government.
ਪੁਲਸ	*pulas*	police.	ਭੀੜ	*bhīṛ*	a crowd.
ਸੰਗਤ	*saṅgat*	society (religious).	ਲੁਕਾਈ	*lukāī*	people.

Some rules for forming the Feminine from the Masculine.

(a) Change final ā to ī Example ; ਘੋੜਾ *ghoṛā* a horse. ਘੋੜੀ *ghoṛī* a mare.

(b) „ „ ī „ n „ ਧੋਬੀ *dhobī* a washerman. ਧੋਬਨ *dhoban* a washerwoman.

(c) Some are formed by adding ī to the last letters as :—

ਪਠਾਨ *paṭhān* an Afghan. ਪਠਾਨੀ *paṭhānī* an Afghan woman

THE ADJECTIVE.

I.—Formation.

The following are the chief ways in which Adjectives are formed :—

(a) By adding ī (ੀ) to a Noun.

Ex.—ਜੰਗਾਲੀ *jaṅgālī* rusty, from ਜੰਗਾਲ *jaṅgāl* rust.

ਗੁਲਾਬੀ *gulābī* rosy „ ਗੁਲਾਬ *gulāb* rose.

(b) By adding wān (ਵਾਨ) to a Noun.

Ex.—ਭਾਗਵਾਨ *bhāgwān* fortunate from ਭਾਗ *bhāg* fortune.

ਦਯਾਵਾਨ *dyāwān* merciful „ ਦਯਾ *dyā* mercy.

(c) By prefixing *an* (ਅਨ) to the past tense of a Verb.

Ex.—ਅਨਸਿਖਿਆ *ansikhiā*, unlearned, from ਸਿਖਣਾ *sikhnā*, to learn.

II.—Declension.

All Adjectives ending in ā (ਆ) are declinable, and follow the same rules, for inflection, as Nouns.

Ex.—ਵੱਡਾ ਮਨੁਖ	*waḍḍā manukh*	a great man.
ਵੱਡੇ ਮਨੁਖ ਦਾ	*waḍḍe manukh dā*	of a great man.
ਵੱਡੇ ਮਨੁਖ	*waḍḍe manukh*	great men.
ਵਡਿਆਂ ਮਨੁਖਾਂ ਦਾ	*waḍḍiāṅ manukhāṅ dā*	of great men.
ਵੱਡੀ ਕੁੜੀ	*waḍḍī kuṛī*	a big girl.
ਵੱਡੀ ਕੁੜੀ ਦਾ	*waḍḍī kuṛī dā*	of a big girl.
ਵੱਡੀਆਂ ਕੁੜੀਆਂ	*waḍḍīāṅ kuṛīāṅ*	big girls.
ਵੱਡੀਆਂ ਕੁੜੀਆਂ ਦਾ	*waḍḍīāṅ kuṛīāṅ dā*	of big girls.

Exception.

ਦਨਾ	*danā*	wise.

III.—Comparison.

The Comparative degree is formed by means of the postposition *te* (ਤੇ) meaning from.

Ex.:—ਇਹ ਪੋਥੀ ਉਸ ਪੋਥੀ ਤੇ ਚੰਗੀ ਹੈ = *Ih pothī us pothī te changī hai.* This book is better than that.

The Superlative degree is formed by using ਸਭ ਤੇ, *sabh te*, ਸਭਨਾਂ ਤੇ, *sabhnāṅ te*, or ਸਾਰਿਆਂ ਤੇ, *sāriāṅ te*, meaning from all.'

Ex.:—ਇਹ ਪੋਥੀ ਸਭ ਤੇ ਚੰਗੀ ਹੈ = *Ih pothī sabh te changī hai.* This book is the best of all.

Note.—*koloṅ* (ਕੋਲੋਂ) and *nāloṅ* (ਨਾਲੋਂ) are sometimes used instead of *te* (ਤੇ)

Ex.:—ਇਹ ਘੋੜੀ ਉਸ ਕੋਲੋਂ ਚੰਗੀ ਹੈ *Ih ghoṛī us koloṅ changī hai*, This mare is better than that.

The affix *iā* (ੀਆ) is frequently found added to the name of a place and its meaning is 'belonging to.'

Ex.—Sing.: ਲਹੌਰੀਆ *lahauriā* a man of Lahore.

Plu.: ਲਹੌਰੀਯੇ *lahauriye* people of Lahore.

The word *ku* (ਕੁ) is often prefixed to a Noun and gives a sense of badness.

Ex.:—ਕੁਰਾਹੀ = *kurāhi*, a wanderer from the right path, (religious sense). See *Sikhān de rāj di vithyā* page 6 line 19.

The particle *hori* (ਹੋਰੀ) or *horāṅ* (ਹੋਰਾਂ) is used in *panjābi* as a term of respect. *Hori* is the Nom. form and *horāṅ* the Inflected form.

Ex.:—Nom. ਮੇਰੇ ਚਾਚੇ ਹੋਰੀ ਆਏ ਹਨ = *mere chāche hori ā-e han*, my respected uncle has come.

Infl. See *Punjābi Bāt chit*, page 28 line 11.

The particle *sārā* (ਸਾਰਾ) when added to an Adjective gives a sense of 'much.'

Ex.—ਬਹੁਤ ਸਾਰਾ ਦੁਧ *bahut sārā dudh*, plenty of milk.

The particle *jihā* (ਜਿਹਾ) gives a sense of 'like,' or when added to an Adjective a sense of diminution. It is Inflected in the ordinary way.

Ex.:—*Punjābi Bāt chit*, page 68, line 4.

" " " " 22 " 4.

To give a sense of 'each, an Adjective is repeated or the figure 2(੨) placed after it; for example:—

Give five pice to each man = ਇਕ ੨ ਮਨੁਖ ਨੂੰ ਪੰਜ ੨ ਪੈਸੇ ਦੇ = *ik ik manukh nūṅ panj panj paise de.*

or

This rule also applies to other classes of words besides Adjectives.

Ex:—ਘਰ ੨ ਵਿੱਚ ਲੋਕ ਮਾਂਦੇ ਪਏ ਹਨ *ghar ghar wichch lok māṅde pa-e han.* In every house people are lying sick.

The following are a few of the most common Adjectives:—

ਚੰਗਾ *chaṅgā*, good.	ਮੰਦਾ, ਬੁਰਾ *maṅdā, burā*, bad.
ਕਾਲਾ *kālā*, dark.	ਗੋਰਾ *gorā*, fair.
ਸਯਾਨਾ *sayānā*, wise.	ਨਯਾਨਾ *nayānā*, ignorant.
ਬੁੱਢਾ *buḍhḍhā* old.	ਜੁਆਨ *juān*, young.
ਛੋਟਾ *chhoṭā*, small.	ਵੱਡਾ *waḍḍā*, large.
ਸੋਹਣਾ *sonnā*, handsome.	ਕੋਝਾ *kojhā*, ugly.
ਤੰਗ *taṅg*, tight.	ਢਿੱਲਾ *ḍhillā*, loose.
ਸਿੱਧਾ *sidhdhā*, straight.	ਵਿੰਗਾ *wiṅgā*, crooked.
ਕਮਲਾ *kamlā*, foolish.	ਅਕਲ ਵਾਲਾ *akulwālā*, sensible.
ਤਕੜਾ *takṛā*, healthy.	ਰੋਗੀ *rogī*, sickly.
ਚੁਸਤ *chust*, active.	ਜਿੱਲ੍ਹਾ *jillhā*, lazy.
ਉੱਚਾ *uchchā*, high.	ਨੀਵਾਂ *niwāṅ*, low.
ਲੰਮਾ *laṅmā*, long.	ਚੌੜਾ *chauṛā*, broad.
ਬੋਲਾ *bolā*, deaf.	ਗੁੰਗਾ *guṅgā*, dumb.
ਸੁਜਾਖਾ *sujākhā*, seeing, having power to see.	ਅੰਨ੍ਹਾ *aṅnhā*, blind.

In *punjābī*, when we wish to show the material of which a thing is made, we reverse the statement ; Ex. ਪਿਤਲ ਦੀ ਤੋਪ = *pital dī top*, a brass gun, lit : brass of gun

ਸੋਨੇ ਦੀ ਵਾਲੀ = *sone dī wālī*, a gold earing, lit. earing of gold.

THE PRONOUN.

	1ST PERSON. Singular.			1ST PERSON. Plural.		
Nom.	ਮੈਂ	*maiṅ*	I.	ਅਸੀਂ	*asiṅ*	we.
Gen.	ਮੇਰਾ &c.	*merā &c.*	my, mine.	ਅਸਾਡਾ &c.	*asāḍā &c.*	our, ours.
D & A.	ਮੈਂ ਨੂੰ	*maiṅ nūṅ*	to me.	ਅਸਾਂ ਨੂੰ	*asāṅ nūṅ*	to us.
Abl.	ਮੈਂ ਤੇ &c.	*maiṅ te &c.*	from me.	ਅਸਾਂ ਤੇ &c.	*asāṅ te &c.*	from us.
Loc.	ਮੇਰੇ ਵਿਚ	*mere wichch*	in me.	ਅਸਾਡੇ ਵਿੱਚ	*asāḍe wichch*	in us.
	ਮੇਰੇ ਉੱਤੇ	*mere utte*	on me	ਅਸਾਡੇ ਉੱਤੇ	*asāḍe utte*	on us.
	ਮੇਰੇ ਤੀਕ	*mere tik*	up to me.	ਅਸਾਡੇ ਤੀਕ	*asāḍe tik*	up to us.

Note.—(1). In oblique cases plural *sā* (ਸਾ) may be used in place of *asā* (ਅਸਾ)

Ex. ਸਾਡਾ ਘਰ *sādā ghar*, our house.

2. Another form (uninflected) in use amongst villages for the plural is *āpāṅ* ਆਪਾਂ meaning ' we,' ' us.' This is used by those people speaking the *mālwā* dialect.

ਆਪਾਂ ਭਲਕੇ ਲਹੌਰ ਨੂੰ ਜਾਂਵਾਂਗੇ *āpāṅ bhalke lahore mūṅ jāwāṅ ge* tomorrow we will go to Lahore.

2ND PERSON.

	Singular.			Plural.		
Nom.	ਤੂੰ	*tūṅ*	Thou.	ਤੁਸੀਂ	*tusīṅ*	you.
Gen.	ਤੇਰਾ ਤੇਰੇ ਤੇਰੀ	*terā tere, terī*	thy, thine.	ਤੁਸਾਡਾ &c.	*tusādā &c.*	your, yours.
				ਤੁਸਾਂਨੂੰ	*tusāṅ nūṅ*	to you.
D & A.	ਤੈਂਨੂੰ	*taiṅ nūṅ*	to thee	ਤੁਸਾਂ ਤੇ	*tusāṅ te*	from you.
Abl.	ਤੈਂਤੇ or ਤੇਤੇ	*taiṅ te or te te*	from thee.	ਤੁਸਾਡੇ ਵਿੱਚ	*tusāḍe wichch*	in you.
Loc.	ਤੇਰੇਵਿੱਚ	*tere wichch*	in thee.	ਤੁਸਾਡੇ ਉੱਤੇ	*tusāḍe utte*	on you.
	ਤੇਰੇਉੱਤੇ	*tere utte*	on thee.	ਤੁਸਾਡੇ ਤੀਕ	*tusāde tīk*	up to you.
	ਤੇਰੇ ਤੀਕ	*tere tīk*	up to thee.			

Note.—In oblique cases plural *tuhā* (ਤੁਹਾ) is commonly used in place of *tusā.* (ਤੁਸਾਂ) Ex. ਮੈਂ ਤੁਹਾ ਨੂੰ ਪੰਜ ਰੁਪੈ ਦੇਵਾਂਗਾ = *maiṅ tuhānūṅ panj rupae dewāṅ gā.* I shall give you Rs. 5.

3rd person (Remote).

	Singular.			Plural.		
Nom.	ਉਹ *uh* or ਓਹ	*oh*	he, she, it, that.	ਓਹ *oh* or ਉਹ	*uh*	they, those
Gen.	ਉਸਦਾ &c.	*us dā &c.*	his &c.	ਉਨ੍ਹਾਂਦਾ &c.	*unhāṅ dā &c.*	their, theirs.
D & A.	ਉਸ ਨੂੰ	*us nūṅ*	to him	ਉਨ੍ਹਾਂ ਨੂੰ	*unhāṅ nūṅ*	to them.
Abl.	ਉਸ ਤੇ &c.	*us te &c.*	from him.	ਉਨ੍ਹਾਂ ਤੇ &c.	*unhāṅ te &c.*	from them.
Loc.	ਉਸ ਵਿੱਚ	*us wichch*	in him.	ਉਨ੍ਹਾਂ ਵਿਚ	*unhāṅ wichch*	in them.
	ਉਸ ਉੱਤੇ	*us utte*	on him.	ਉਨ੍ਹਾਂ ਉੱਤੇ	*unhāṅ utte*	on them.
	ਉਸ ਤੀਕ	*us tīk*	up to him.	ਉਨ੍ਹਾਂ ਤੀਕ	*unhāṅ tīk*	up to them.
Inst.	ਉਸਨੇ	*us ne*	by him.	ਉਨ੍ਹਾਂ ਨੇ	*unhāṅ ne*	by them

Note,—(1). The Genitive affixes in the 1st and 2nd Persons are spelt with a hard *ḍ* (ਡ). In all other places they take *d* soft (ਦ).

(2). In the 3rd person *oh* ਓਹ does not change. Ex. ਉਹਤੇ, *oh te* ਓਹ ਦਾ *oh dā*.

(3). A common usage of the people is to express the Inst : case by ਉਨ *un* or ਓਨ *on* instead of ਉਸਨੇ *us ne* or ਉਹਨੇ *oh ne* This also applies to the Pronoun ਇਹ *ih* or ਏਹ, *eh* but these forms cannot be used with Nouns.

NEAR DEMONSTRATIVE.

	Singular.			Plural.		
Nom.	ਇਹ	*ih* or ਏਹ *eh*	this.	ਇਹ	*ih* or ਏਹ *eh*	these.
Gen.	ਇਸਦਾ &c	*isdā &c.*	of this.	ਇਨ੍ਹਾਂ ਦਾ &c.	*iṇhāṅ dā &c.*	of these.
D & A.	ਇਸ ਨੂੰ	*is ṇūṅ*	to this.	ਇਨ੍ਹਾਂ ਨੂੰ	*iṇhāṅ nūṅ*	to these.
Abl.	ਇਸ ਤੇ &c.	*is te &c.*	from this.	ਇਨ੍ਹਾਂ ਤੇ &c,	*iṇhāṅ te &c.*	from these.
Loc.	ਇਸ ਵਿੱਚ	*is wichch*	in this.	ਇਨ੍ਹਾਂ ਵਿੱਚ	*iṇhāṅ wichch*	in these.
	ਇਸ ਉੱਤੇ	*is utte*	on this.	ਇਨ੍ਹਾਂ ਉੱਤੇ	*iṇhāṅ utte*	on these.
	ਇਸ ਤੀਕ	*is tīk*	up to this.	ਇਨ੍ਹਾਂ ਤੀਕ	*iṇhāṅ tīk*	up to these
Inst.	ਇਸਨੇ	*is ne*	by this	ਇਨ੍ਹਾਂ ਨੇ	*iṇhāṅ ne*	by these.

INTERROGATIVE.

	Singular.			Plural.		
Nom.	ਕੌਨ,	*kaun,* ਕੀ *kī*	who ?, what ?.	ਕੌਨ,	*kaun,* ਕੀ *kī*	who ?, what.
Gen.	ਕਿਸ ਦਾ &c.	*kis dā &c.*	of whom &c.	ਕਿਨ੍ਹਾਂ ਦਾ &c.	*kiṇhāṅ dā &c.*	as in singular
D & A.	ਕਿਸ ਨੂੰ	*kis ṇūṅ*	to whom &c.	ਕਿਨ੍ਹਾਂ ਨੂੰ	*kiṇhāṅ nūṅ*	do.
Abl.	ਕਿਸ ਤੇ &c.	*kis te &c.*	from whom.	ਕਿਨ੍ਹਾਂ ਤੇ	*kiṇhāṅ te*	do.
Loc.	ਕਿਸ ਵਿੱਚ	*kis wichch*	in whom &c.	ਕਿਨ੍ਹਾਂਵਿੱਚ	*kiṇṇāṅ wichch*	do.
	ਕਿਸ ਉੱਤੇ	*kis utte*	on whom &c.	ਕਿਨ੍ਹਾਂ ਉੱਤੇ	*kiṇhāṅ utte*	do.
	ਕਿਸ ਤੀਕ	*kis tīk*	up to whom &c.	ਕਿਨ੍ਹਾਂ ਤੀਕ	*kiṇhāṅ tīk*	do.
Inst.	ਕਿਸ ਨੇ	*kis ne*	by whom &c.	ਕਿਨ੍ਹਾਂਨੇ	*kiṇhāṅ ne*	do.

RELATIVE AND CO-RELATIVE.

Nom.	ਜੋ *jo* ਸੋ	*so*	he &c. who.	ਜੋ *jo* ਸੋ	*so*	they, who.
Infl:	ਜਿਸ	*jis*	Do.	ਜਿਨ੍ਹਾਂ	*jinhāṅ*	

ਸੋ (so) has no inflected form.

Example ਜੋ ਚਾਹੇਂ ਸੋ ਕਰ = *jo chaheṅ so kar*, do as you like.

INDEFINITE.

Nom. ਕੋਈ *koī*, ਕੁਝ *kujh* some, any }
Infl. ਕਿਸੇ *kise* ਕੁਝ *kujh*. } Singular and plural.

Note.—(1). The Genitive affix, *de* (ਦੇ or ਡੇ), *de* where used in the preceding with another affix, is often omitted.

Ex. ਕਿਸ ਵਿੱਚ *kis wichch*, in whom.

(2). Another form of the Relative and Interrogative pronouns is ਜਿਹੜਾ *jihṛā* or ਜੇਹੜਾ *jehṛā* and ਕਿਹੜਾ *kihṛā* or ਕੇਹੜਾ *kehṛā* Ex. ਜੇਹੜਾ ਮਨੁਖ ਕਲ੍ਹ ਆਇਆ ਆਸੀ *jehṛā manūkh kal āiā sī* The man who came yesterday ਓਹ ਕੇਹੜਾ ਘਰ ਹੈ *oh kehṛā ghar hāi* which is that house ?

ਆਪ (*āp*) in *panjābī* is used to express 'self,' as ਅਸੀਂ ਆਪ ਜਾਵਾਂਗੇ= *asiṅ āp jāwāṅge*, we shall go ourselves.

It is also used, nowadays, as a term of respect, as, ਆਪਦੀ ਚਿਠੀ ਪਹੁੰਚੀ= *āp dī chiṭhī pahuṅchī*. I received your letter.

ਆਪਨਾ is used in a Possessive sense and signifies 'own' as ਆਪਨਾ ਘੋੜਾ ਲਿਆ = *āpnā ghoṛā liā*, bring your own horse.

ਤੁਸੀਂ (*tusiṅ*) is used when addressing an equal or a superior, and ਤੂੰ (*tūṅ*) when speaking to an inferior. But *túṅ* is often used in ordinary conversation without any meaning of inferiority.

ADVERBS.

TIME.

ਕਦ	*kad*	when ?
ਜਦ	*jad*	when.
ਹੁਣ	*hun*	now.
ਕਦੀ	*kadī*	ever.
ਕਦੀ ਨਹੀਂ	*kadī nahīṅ*	never.
ਤਦ	*tad*	then.
ਕਦੀ ਕਦੀ	*kadī kadī*	sometimes.
ਕਦੀ ਨਾ ਕਦੀ	*kadī nā kadī*	sometime or other.
ਕਿੰਨੀ ਵਾਰੀ	*kinnīṅ wārī*	how often ?
ਜਿੰਨੀ ਵਾਰੀ	*jinnīṅ wārī*	as often.
ਓਨੀਂ ਵਾਰੀ	*onīṅ wārī*	so often
ਅਚਾਨਕ	*achāṇk*	suddenly.
ਹੁਣੇ	*hune*	soon.
ਚਿਰਕਾ	*chirkā*	late.
ਕਿੰਨਾ ਚਿਰ	*kinnā chir*	how long
ਵਾਲਾ	*wālā*	about (with verb).

ਇੱਕ ਵਾਰੀ	*ikk wārī*	once.
ਵਾਰੀ ਵਾਰੀ	*wārī wārī*	alternately.
ਫੇਰ	*pher*	again.
ਕਲ	*kal*	yesterday.
ਅਜ	*aj*	to-day.
ਕਲ, ਭਲਕੇ	*kal, bhalke*	to-morrow,
ਸਦਾ, ਨਿੱਤ	*sadā, nitt*	always.
ਦਿਨੋਂ ਦਿਨ	*dinoṅ din*	day by day.
ਅਜੇ ਨਹੀਂ	*aje nahīṅ*	not yet.
ਓੜਕ ਨੂੰ	*oṛak nūṅ*	at last.
ਸਭਥੋਂ ਪੈਹਲਾਂ	*sabh thoṅ pahilān*	at first.
ਅੰਤ ਨੂੰ	*aṅt nūṅ*	at length.
ਤੁਰਤ	*turt*	at once.
ਸਵਖਤੇ	*sawakhte.*	early.
ਅਕਸਰ	*aksar*	often.

Note.—When ਜਦ ਤੀਕ *jad tik*, is used in the sense of 'as long as' it is expressed affirmatively, but if it carries the meaning 'until' it must be expressed negatively.

Ex. :—ਜਦ ਤੀਕ ਮੈਂ ਕੰਮ ਕਰਦਾ ਰਿਹਾ ਓਹ ਚੁਪ ਕੀਤਾ ਰਿਹਾ=*jad tīk main kam kardā rihā oh chup kītā rihā*, as long as I worked he kept quiet.

ਜਦ ਤੀਕ ਮੈਂ ਨਾ ਆਵਾਂ ਤੂੰ ਇਥੇ ਰਹੁ = *jad tīk maiṅ nā āwāṅ tūṅ ithe rahu*, until I (do not) come back, remain here.

PLACE.

ਕਿੱਥੇ	*kiththe*	where ?	ਅੰਦਰ	*aṅdar*	within.
ਜਿੱਥੇ	*jiththe*	where.	ਬਾਹਰ	*bāhar*	without.
ਏਥੇ	*ethe*	here.	ਇਸ ਪਾਸੇ	*is pāse*	on this side.
ਓਥੇ	*othe*	there.	ਓਸ ਪਾਸੇ	*os pāse*	on that side.
ਕਿਤੇ ਨਾ ਕਿਤੇ	*kite nā kite*	somewhere or other.	ਹਰ ਥਾਂ	*har thāṅ*	everywhere.
ਹੋਰ ਕਿਤੇ	*hor kite*	elsewhere.	ਦੋਹੀਂ ਪਾਸੀਂ	*dohīṅpāsīṅ*	on both sides.
ਕਿੱਥੋਂ	*kiththoṅ*	} whence.	ਕਿਤੇ ਨਹੀਂ	*kite nahīṅ*	} nowhere.
ਜਿੱਥੋਂ	*jiththoṅ*		ਕਿਧਰੇ ਨਹੀਂ	*kidhre nahīṅ*	
ਨੇੜੇ	*neṛe*	near.	ਕਿਧਰਨੂੰ	*kidhar nūṅ*	whither
ਦੂਰ	*dūr*	far.	ਇਸ ਪਾਸੇ	*is pāse*	in this direction
ਅੱਗੇ	*agge*	forward.	ਉਸ ਪਾਸੇ	*us pāse*	in that direction.
ਪਿੱਛੇ	*pichhe*	backward.			

MANNER.

ਕਿਸਤ੍ਰਾਂ	*kis trāṅ*	how ?	ਇਸਤ੍ਰਾਂ	*is trāṅ*	in this manner
ਛੇਤੀ	*chhetī*	quickly.	ਉਸਤ੍ਰਾਂ	*us trāṅ*	in that manner
ਛੇਤੀ ਨਾਲ	*chhetī nāl.*	"	ਬਿਲਕੁਲ	*billkul*	entirely.
ਹੌਲੀ ਹੌਲੀ	*haulī haulī*	slowly.	ਜਾਨ ਬੁਝਕੇ	*jān bujhke*	knowingly.
ਖਾਹ ਮ ਖਾਹ	*khāh makhāh*	enlene veleae.	ਦੀਨਤਾਨਾਲ	*dīntā nāl*	humbly,
ਇਸ ਤ੍ਰਾਂ	*is trāṅ*	thus.	ਪਰਸੰਤਾ ਨਾਲ	*parsaṅtā nāl*	gladly.
ਕਿਸੇਨਾਕਿਸੇਤ੍ਰਾਂ	*kise nā kise trāṅ*	somehow or other,	ਕੱਲਾ	*kallā*	alone.
ਉਲਟ ਪੁਲਟ	*ulṭ pulṭ*	topsy turvy	ਤੁਰਤ	*turt*	all at once.
ਮੂਧਾ	*mūdhā*	upside down	ਅਚਾਨਕ	*achānk*	suddenly.

The Verb ਚਲਿਆ *chaliā* (gone) is often used to give a sense of 'nearly'.

Ex. :—ਮੈਂ ਮਰ ਚਲਿਆ ਹਾਂ = *maiṅ mar chaliā hāṅ.* I am nearly dead.

ਜਦ ਸੰਦੂਕ ਖਾਲੀ ਹੋ ਚਲਿਆ ਸੀ = *jad sandūk khālī ho chaliā sī* when the box was nearly empty.

MISCELLANEOUS.

ਹਾਂ	*hān*	yes,	ਸੱਤ ਬਚਨ	*satt bachaṇ*	alright.
ਨਹੀਂ	*ṇahīṅ*	no.	ਨਿਰਾ	*nirā*	only.
ਕਿੱਨਾਂ	*kiṇṇāṅ*	how much ?	ਬਸ	*bas*	enough.
ਇਨਾਂ	*eṇāṅ*	so much.	ਅਕਸਰ	*aksar*	generally.
ਓਨਾਂ	*oṇnāṅ*	that much.	ਕਿਉਂ	*kiuṅ*	why ?
ਜਿੱਨਾਂ	*jiṇnāṅ*	so much.	ਡਾਢਾ	*ḍāḍhā*	very.
ਗਲਤ	*galt*	wrong.	ਠੀਕ	*ṭhīk*	right.
ਭਰ	*bhar*	whole ful (written after noun.)	ਜਿਹਾ	*jihā*	rather (affix,-ish).

Note.—ਨਾ is used with the conditional or Imperative mood in place of ਨਹੀ

The word ਮੂਲੋਂਹੀ gives the meaning of 'quite' or 'at all.'

Ex :—ਗੁਰਾਂ ਦੇਈ ਤੇ ਮੂਲੋਂ ਹੀ ਨਿਆਣੀ ਹੈ = *gurāṇ deī te mūloṅ hī niyāṇī hai*, Gurandei is quite child-like.

ਓਹ ਚੀਜ ਮੂਲੋਂ ਹੀ ਖਰਾਬ ਹੈ ; *on chīj mūloṅ hī ḳharāb hai*, that thing is no good at all.

Some Adverbs such as ਬਿਨਾਂ *bināṅ* (without) and ਨੇੜੇ *neṛe* (near) when used as Prepositions do not inflect.

Ex. :— ਮੈਂ ਤੇਰੇ ਬਿਨਾਂ ਨਹੀਂ ਜਾ ਸਕਦਾ = *maiṅ tere bināṅ nahīṅ jā sakdā*, I cannot go without you.

ਮੇਰਾ ਘਰ ਤੁਹਾਡੇ ਨੇੜੇ ਹੈ = *merā ghar tuhāḍe neṛe hai*, my house is near yours.

PREPOSITIONS.

All Prepositions, except those given in the declensions of Nouns and Pronouns, given previously, require a Genitive affix to connect them with the Noun they govern.

They may be divided into two groups ;

1.—Those taking the affix *de* (ਦੇ).

ਅੱਗੇ	*agge*	before.	ਸੰਗ,ਨਾਲ	*sang, ṇāl*	with.
ਅਨੁਸਾਰ	*aṇusār*	according to.	ਸਬਬ	*sabab*	on account of.
ਅੰਦਰ	*andar*	within.	ਹੇਠ	*heṭhan*	below.
ਅੰਦਰੋਂ	*andaroṅ*	from within.	ਕੋਲ	*kol*	by, near.
ਉੱਤੇ,ਉੱਪਰ	*utte, uppar*	above.	ਕੋਲੋਂ	*koloṅ*	from near.
ਉੱਪਰੋਂ	*upparoṅ*	from above.	ਕਾਰਨ	*kāran*	on account of.
ਸਮੇਤ, ਸਣੇ	*samet, sane*	together with.	ਗਿਰਦ	*gird*	around.
ਸਾਹਮਣੇ	*sāhmne*	before, in front.	ਗੱਭੇ	*gabhe*	in the midst of
ਇਰਦੇ ਗਿਰਦੇ	*irde girde*	round about.	ਪਿਛੇ	*pichhe*	behind, after.
ਨੇੜੇ	*neṛe*	near.	ਪਰਲੇਪਾਸੇ	*parle pāse*	beyond.
ਬਾਹਰ	*bāhar*	outside.	ਬਿਨਾ	*biṇā*	except.

2.—Those taking the affix *dī* (ਦੀ).

ਬਾਬਤ	*bābat*	concerning.	ਲਈ (ਦੇ *de* or ਦੀ *dī*)	*laī*	for.
ਵੱਲ	*wall*	towards.	ਖਾਤ੍ਰ	*khātr*	for the sake of.

CONJUNCTIONS.

ਅਥਵਾ	*athwā*	or.	ਜੇ,ਜੇਕਰ	*je, jekar*	if.
ਕਿਉਂਜੋ	*kioṅ jo*	because.	ਇਸਕਰਕੇ	*is karke*	therefore.
ਭਾਵੇਂ	*bhāweṅ*	although.	ਸਗਵਾਂ, ਸਗੋਂ	*sagwāṅ, sagoṅ*	moreover.
ਅਤੇ,ਤੇ,ਅਰ	*ate, te, ar*	and.	ਤਾਂ	*tāṅ*	then. (but even).
ਪਰ	*par*	but.	ਨਾਲੇ	*ṇāle*	also.
ਕੀਕਨ	*kīkaṅ*	how.	ਤਾਂਵੀ	*tāṅwī*	nevertheless, still unless.
ਕਦਾਚਿਤ	*kadāchit*	perhaps.	ਬਗੈਰ	*bagair*	without

Note.—ਭਾਵੇਂ *bhāweṅ* (although) and ਪਰ *par* (but) are co-relative ; as also are ਜੇ *je* or ਜੇਕਰ *je kar* (if) and ਤਾਂ *tān* (then).

Ex. :—ਭਾਵੇਂ ਓਹ ਨੇ ਪੰਜ ਰੋਟੀਆਂ ਖਾਧੀਆਂ ਪਰ ਤਾਂ ਵੀ ਭੁਖਾ ਰਿਹਾ *bhāweṅ oh ne panj rotīāṅ khādhiāṅ per tāṅwī bhukhā rihā*, although he ate five breads yet he remained hungry.

ਜੇਕਰ ਤੂੰ ਮੇਰੇ ਨਾਲ ਜਾਵੇਂਗਾ ਤਾਂ ਕੁਝ ਖਟੇਂਗਾ। *jekar tūṅ mere nāl jāweṅgā tān kujh khaten gā*, If you go with me you will earn something.

THE VERB.

The conjugation of the Verb in *Panjābī* is very regular.

All the Verbs, with the exception of the Defective ਹਾਂ *hāṅ* (am) and the auxiliary ਹੋਣਾ *hoṅā*(to be), are divided into two classes Active and Neuter. An Active Verb is one which has an object, Ex. :—ਮੈਂ ਘੋੜੇ ਨੂੰ ਮਾਰਿਆ = *maiṅ ghoṛe nūṅ māriā*, I struck the horse.

A Neuter Verb has no object, Ex. :—ਮੈਂ ਕੁਰਸੀ ਉੱਤੇ ਬੈਠਾ = *maiṅ kursī utte baiṭhā*, I sat on a chair.

The Moods are five in number, *i.e.*, Infinitive, Indicative, Imperative, Subjunctive, and Potential.

The Infinitive always ends in ਨਾ (*nā* or ਣਾ (*ṇā*). To obtain the root cut off the ਨਾ *nā* or ਣਾ *ṇā* and if the Verb ends in ਉਣਾ (*uṇā*) we cut off the ਉ (*u*) as well. This also gives us the 2nd pers, sing, of the Imperative.

Examples:—ਹੋ (*ho*) is the root and 2nd pers, sing, imper, of ਹੋਣਾ *hoṇā*.

ਆ (ā) is the root and 2nd pers, sing, imper, of ਆਉਣਾ āunā

The Present Participle is formed in three different ways ;

1st.—If the root ends in a consonant add ਦਾ (dā) to it.

Ex. :—ਘਲਣਾ ghalnā = to send, ਘਲ ghal = send, ਘਲਦਾ ghaldā = sending

2nd.—If the Verb ends in ਉਣਾ (uṇā), cut off ਣਾ (ṅā) and add ਂਦਾ (ṅdā).

Ex. :—ਆਉਣਾ āunā = to come, ਆ ā = come ਆਉਂਦਾ āuṅdā = coming.

3rd.—If the root ends in a vowel add ਂਦਾ (ṅdā) to it.

Ex. :—ਜਾਣਾ jānā = to go, ਜਾ jā = go. ਜਾਂਦਾ jāṅdā = going.

The Past Participle is formed by adding ਿਆ (iā) to the root.

Ex. :—ਘਲਣਾ ghalnā = to send, ਘਲ ghal = send, ਘਲਿਆ ghaliā = sent. To this rule however there are the following exceptions :—

Infinitive.			Past Participle.		
ਸੌਣਾ	saunā	to sleep.	ਸੁੱਤਾ	suttā	slept.
ਕਰਨਾ	karṇā	to do,	ਕੀਤਾ	kītā	did.
ਲੈਣਾਂ	lainā	to take.	ਲੀਤਾ	lītā	took.
ਦੇਣਾ	denā	to give.	ਦਿੱਤਾ	dittā	gave.
ਪੀਣਾ	pīnā	to drink.	ਪੀਤਾ	pītā	drank.
ਸੀਉਣਾ	sīunā	to sew.	ਸੀਤਾ	sītā	sewed.
ਨ੍ਹਾਉਣਾ	nahāunā	to bathe.	ਨ੍ਹਾਤਾਂ	nahātā	bathed.
ਖਲੋਣਾ	khalonā	to stand.	ਖਲੋਤਾ	khalotā	stood.
ਧੋਣਾ	dhonā	to wash.	ਧੋਤਾ	dhotā	washed.
ਢੈਣਾ	ḍhainā	to fall.	ਢੱਠਾ	ḍhaṭhā	fell.
ਬੈਠਣਾ	baiṭhnā	to sit.	ਬੈਠਾ	baiṭhā	sat.
ਪੀਹਣਾ	pīhnā	to grind.	ਪੀਠਾ	pīṭhā	ground.

Infinitive.			Past Participle.		
ਕੈਹਣਾ	*kahnā*	to say.	ਕਿਹਾ	*kihā*	said.
ਖਾਣਾ	*khānā*	to eat.	ਖਾਧਾ	*khādhā*	ate.
ਜਾਣਾ	*jānā*	to go.	ਗਿਆ	*giā*	went.
ਮਰਨਾ	*marṇā*	to die	ਮੋਇਆ	*moiā*	died.
ਪੈਣਾ	*painā*	to fall.	ਪਿਆ	*piā*	fell.
ਗਾਉਣਾ	*gāunā*	to sing.	ਗਾਵਿਆ	*gāwiā*	sung.

The following Verbs take the regular past participle as well as the irregular :—

Infinitive.			Past Participle. (Irregular).		
ਜਾਣਨਾ	*jāṇṇā*	to know.	ਜਾਤਾ	*jātā*	knew.
ਪਛਾਣਨਾ	*pachhāṇṇā*	to recognise.	ਪਛਾਤਾ	*pachhātā*	recognised.
ਵੇਖਣਾਂ	*wekhnā*	to see.	ਡਿੱਠਾ	*ḍiṭhṭhā*	saw.
ਬੰਨ੍ਹਣਾਂ	*baṅṇhhnā*	to bind.	ਬੱਧਾ	*badhdhā*	bound.
ਡਿੱਗਣਾਂ	*ḍiggnā*	to fall,	ਡਿੱਗਾ	*ḍiggā*	fell.
ਰਿਨ੍ਹਣਾਂ	*rīṇahnā*	to stew.	ਰਿੱਧਾ	*ridhdhā*	stewed.
ਟੁੱਟਣਾਂ	*ṭuṭnā*	to be broken	ਟੁੱਟਾ	*ṭuṭā*	broken.
ਗੁੱਨ੍ਹਣਾਂ	*guṇahnā*	to knead.	ਗੁੱਧਾ	*gudhdhā*	kneaded.
ਖੁਲਨਾਂ	*khulnā*	to be opened.	ਖੁੱਲਾ	*khulā*	open.
ਭਜਨਾਂ	*bhajnā*	to run.	ਭੱਨਾ	*bhannā*	ran.
ਰੁਝਨਾਂ	*rujhnā*	to be engaged	ਰੁੱਧਾ	*rudhā*	engaged.

Note.—The different meanings of the Verb 'to fall,' as given above ;

ਢੈਣਾ *dhainā*
ਡਿੱਗਣਾ, *dignā* } Means to fall.

ਪੈਣਾ *painā*, Means literally, "to lay down," and is used compound with the above ;

Example.—ਓਹ ਮੁੰਡਾ ਆਪਨੇ ਘੋੜੇ ਤੋਂ ਡਿਗ ਪਿਆ = *oh muṇḍā āpne ghoṛe toṅ ḍig piā*, That boy fell off his horse.

The Future Tense is formed in two different ways. If the root ends in a vowel we add to it ਵਾਂਗਾ (*wāṅgā*), Ex. ਜਾਣਾਂ = *jānā*, to go, ਜਾ = *jā*, go, ਜਾਵਾਂਗਾ = *jāwaāṅgā*, will go.

1.—If the root ends in a consonant we add to it ਆਂਗਾ (*āṅgā*), Ex. ਕਰਨਾਂ = *karnā*, to do, ਕਰ = *kar*, do, ਕਰਾਂਗਾ = *karāṅgā*, will do.

2.—(*a*) The Verb ਲੈਣਾ *lainā*, slightly differs from the above for the *ai* is omitted, and a short *a* added, before ਵਾਂਗਾ. *wāṅgā* Ex. ਲਵਾਂਗਾ *lawāṅgā* — will take.

CONJUGATION.

As the Verbs ਹਾਂ *hāṅ* and ਹੋਣਾ *hoṇā* are used extensively in the conjugation of other verbs, and follow none of the above rules we will conjugate them first.

ਹਾਂ = *hāṅ*, am.

PRESENT.

Singular.			Plural.		
1st.—ਮੈਂ ਹਾਂ	*main hāṅ.*	I am, &c.	ਅਸੀਂ ਹਾਂ	*asīṅ hāṇ.*	We are, &c.
2nd.—ਤੂੰ ਹੈਂ	*tūṅ haiṅ.*		ਤੁਸੀਂ ਹੋ	*tusīṅ ho.*	
3rd.—ਓਹ ਹੈ	*oh hai.*		ਓਹ ਹਨ	*oh haṇ.*	

PAST.

		M. F.			M. F.	
1st.—ਮੈਂ	*main.*	ਸਾ, *sā* ਸੀ *sī*, I was &c.	ਅਸੀਂ	*asīṅ.*	ਸੇ, *se* ਸੀਆਂ *siāṅ.*	We were &c.
2nd.—ਤੂੰ	*tū.*		ਤੁਸੀਂ	*tusīṅ.*	ਸਨ *san* ਸੀਆਂ *siāṅ.*	
3rd.—ਓਹ	*oh.*		ਓੱਹ	*oh.*		

EXERCISES.

We are brothers. He was a good boy yesterday. Thou art wrong. They were not at home. I am your father. It is very cold. We were right. He is asleep. You were in his house. They are very bad girls. She is here. I was not blind. You are a tall girl. We were that man's daughters. She was a little lazy. I was his mother.

Note.—ਸੀ *sī* is most commonly used for Masc, Fem. Sing, or Plural, on account of the difficulty in remembering the genders.

ਹੋਣਾ = *hoṇā*, to be or to exist.

Root. ਹੋ, *ho* = exist.

Present Participle.	ਹੁੰਦਾ *hundā* — existing	Conjunctive. ਹੋਕੇ *hoke* = having been.
Past do.	ਹੋਇਆ *hoiā* — existed	Substantive ਹੋਣਵਾਲਾ = *honwālā*, one who is.

INDICATIVE MOOD.

Aorist Tense.

1st.—ਹੋਵਾਂ *howāṅ*	M. F. I may become, &c	ਹੋਈਏ *hoīe*	M.F. We may become, &c.
2nd.—ਹੋਵੇਂ *howeṅ*		ਹੋਵੋ *howo*	
3rd.—ਹੋਵੇ *howe*		ਹੋਣ *hoṇ*	

Present Tense.

Singular.	M.	F.	Plural.	M.	F.
1st.—ਮੈਂ *maiṅ*	ਹੁੰਦਾ, *huṅdā*	ਦੀ. *dī*,	ਅਸੀਂ *asīṅ*	ਹੁੰਦੇ, *huṅde*	ਦੀਆਂ. *dīāṅ*,
2nd.—ਤੂੰ *tūṅ*	I exist, &c.		ਤੁਸੀਂ *tusīṅ*		We exist, &c.
3rd.—ਓਹ *oh*			ਓਹ *oh*		

Definite. Present.

	M.	F.		M.	F.	
1st.—	ਹੁੰਦਾ, *huṅdā*	ਦੀ *dī*	ਹਾਂ *hāṅ*	ਹੁੰਦੇ *huṅde*	ਦੀਆਂ *dīāṅ*	ਹਾਂ *hāṅ*
2nd.—			ਹੈਂ *haiṅ*			ਹੋ *ho*
3rd.—			ਹੈ *hai*			ਹਨ *haṇ*
	I am existing, &c,			We are existing &c,		

Imperfect.

	M.	F.		M.	F.	
1st.— 2nd.— 3rd.—	ਹੁੰਦਾ, *huṅdā*	ਦੀ *dī*	ਸੀ. *sī*, I was existing, &c.	ਹੁੰਦੇ, *huṅde*	ਦੀਆਂ *dīāṅ*	ਸੀ. *sī*, We were existing, &c.

Past.

Singular. Plural.

	M.	F.	M.	F.	
1st.— 2nd — 3rd.—	ਹੋਇਆ, *hoiā*	ਹੋਈ *hoī* I became &c.	ਹੋਏ *hoe*	ਹੋਈਆਂ *hoīāṅ*	We b. came, &c.

Perfect.

	M.	F.		M.	F		
1st — 2nd.— 3rd.—	ਹੋਇਆ, *hoiā*	ਈ *ī*	ਹਾਂ *hāṅ* / ਹੈਂ *haiṅ* / ਹੈ *hai* I have become &c.	ਹੋਏ, *hoe*	ਈਆਂ. *īāṅ*	ਹਾਂ *hāṅ* / ਹੋ *ho* / ਹਨ *han*	We are becoming, &c.

Pluperfect.

	M.	F.		M.	F.		
1st.— 2nd.— 3rd.—	ਹੋਇਆ, *hoiā*	ਈ *ī*	ਸੀ *sī* I had become &c.	ਹੋਏ, *hoe*	ਈਆਂ *īāṅ*	ਸੀ. *sī*,	We were become, &c.

Future.

	M.	F.		M.	F.
1st.—ਹੋਵਾਂ *howāṅ* 2nd.—ਹੋਵੇਂ *howeṅ* 3rd.—ਹੋਵੇ *howe*	ਗਾ, *gā*	ਗੀ *gī* I shall be, &c.	ਹੋਵਾਂ *howāṅ* / ਹੋਵੋ *howo* / ਹੋਣ *hon*	ਗੇ, *ge*	ਗੀਆਂ *gīāṅ* We shall be, &c.

Future Probable.

Singular.

	M.	F.		M.	F.	
1st,— 2nd.— 3rd.—	ਹੁੰਦਾ, *huṅdā*	ਦੀ *dī*	ਹੋਵਾਂ *howāṅ* / ਹੋਵੇਂ *howeṅ* / ਹੋਵੇ *howe*	ਗਾ, *gā*	ਗੀ. *gī*	I may be &c.

Future Probable.

Plural.

M.		F.				M.	F.	
ਹੁੰਦੇ	*hunde*	ਦੀਆਂ	*diāṅ*	ਹੋਵਾਂ *howāṅ* / ਹੋਵੋ *howo* / ਹੋਣ *hon*		ਗੇ, *ge*	ਗੀਆਂ *giāṅ*,	We may be, &c.

Future Perfect.

Singular.

	M.		F.			M.	F.	
1st.— 2nd.— 3rd.—	ਹੋਇਆ	*hoiā*	ਈ *ī*	ਹੋਵਾਂ *howāṅ* / ਹੋਵੇਂ *howeṅ* / ਹੋਵੇ *howe*		ਗਾ, *gā*	ਗੀ *gī*	I may have become &c.

Plural.

	M.		F.			M.	F.	
1st.— 2nd.— 3rd.—	ਹੋਏ,	*hoe*	ਈਆਂ *īāṅ*	ਹੋਵਾਂ *howāṅ* / ਹੋਵੋ *howo* / ਹੋਣ *hon*		ਗੇ, *ge*	ਗੀਆਂ *giāṅ*,	We may have become, &c.

Active Verb.

ਘਲਣਾ *ghalṅā*, to send.

ROOT ਘਲ *ghal*, send.

ACTIVE VERB.

Present Participle	ਘਲਦਾ *ghaldā*, sending	Conjunctive	ਘਲ ਕੇ *ghal ke*, having sent.
Past do.	ਘਲਿਆ *ghaliā*, sent.	Substantive	ਘਲਣ ਵਾਲਾ *ghalanwālā* one who sends.

IMPERATIVE MOOD.

Present.	ਤੂੰ ਘਲ *tūṅ ghal*, send thou.	Remote Future	ਤੂੰ ਘਲੀਂ *tūṅ ghalīṅ* send thou.
	ਤੁਸੀਂ ਘਲੋ *tūsīṅ ghalo*. send ye.		ਤੁਸੀਂ ਘਲਿਓ *tusīṅ ghalio*, send you.

INDICATIVE MOOD.

Aorist Tense

Singular.			Plural.		
1st.—ਘਲਾਂ	*ghalāṅ*	M. F. I may send, &c.	ਘਲੀਏ	*ghalīye*	M.F. We may send, &c.
2nd.—ਘਲੇਂ	*ghaleṅ*		ਘੱਲੋ	*ghalo*	
3rd.—ਘਲੇ	*ghale*		ਘੱਲਣ	*ghalaṅ*	

Present Tense.

		M.	F.			M.	F.
1st.—ਮੈਂ	*maiṅ*	ਘਲਦਾ, *ghaldā.*	ਦੀ *dī.*	ਅਸੀਂ	*asīṅ*	ਘਲਦੇ, *ghalde.*	ਦੀਆਂ *diāṅ.*
2nd.—ਤੂੰ	*tūṅ*		I send, &c.	ਤੁਸੀਂ	*tusīṅ*		We send &c.
3rd.—ਓਹ	*oh*			ਓਹ	*oh*		

Definite Present.

Singular.

	M.	F.			
1st.—	ਘਲਦਾ, *ghaldā,*	ਦੀ *dī.*	ਹਾਂ	*hāṅ*	I am sending, &c.
2nd.—			ਹੈਂ	*haiṅ*	
3rd.—			ਹੈ	*hai*	

Definite Present.

Plural.

1st.—	ਘਲਦੇ, *ghalde,*	ਦੀਆਂ *diāṅ.*	ਹਾਂ	*hāṅ*	We are sending, &c.
2nd.—			ਹੋ	*ho*	
3rd.—			ਹਨ	*han*	

Habitual Present.

Singular.

1st.—	M. ਘਲਦਾ ਹੁੰਦਾ, *ghaldā huṅdā*	ਹਾਂ	*hāṅ*	I am in the habit of sending &c.
2nd.—	F.	ਹੈਂ	*hain*	
3rd.—	ਘਲਦੀ ਹੁੰਦੀ, *ghaldī huṅdī,*	ਹੈ	*hai*	

Habitual Present.

Plural.

M. ਘਲਦੇ ਹੁੰਦੇ *ghalde hunde*	ਹਾਂ *hāṅ*	We are in the habit of sending, &c.
F. ਘਲਦੀਆਂ ਹੁੰਦੀਆਂ *ghaldiāṅ hundiāṅ*	ਹੋ *ho*	
	ਹਨ *han*	

Imperfect,

1st, 2nd, 3rd Singular.—ਘਲਦਾ, *ghaldā*, ਦੀ *dī*, ਸੀ *sī*. I was sending, &c.

1st 2nd 3rd Plural.—ਘਲਦੇ, *ghalde*, ਦੀਆਂ *diāṅ*, ਸੀ *sī*. We were sending, &c.

Imperfect Habitual.

1st, 2nd, 3rd —As in habitual present, but use, ਸੀ *sī* for ਹਾਂ *hāṅ* and its inflected forms.

ਘਲਣਾ	*ghalnā*	to send.	ਸਹਾਇਤਾ ਦੇਣੀ	*sahāitā denī*	to aid.
ਚੁਮਣਾ	*chumnā*	to kiss	ਬੀਜਣਾ	*bījnā*	to sow.
ਦੇਣਾ	*deṇā*	to give.	ਮਿਲਣਾ	*milnā*	to meet.
ਗਾਲ ਕਢਣਾ	*gāl kaḍhnā*	to abuse.	ਜੋੜਨਾ	*joṛnā*	to join.

Translate :—

Kiss your sister. We always aid the poor. I always meet him. The girls are sending food. You were giving me clothes. He was abusing my father. He kisses his aunt. She sends money to them. We are sending these boots. She always abuses me. The women sow the corn. Meet me to-morrow. Send this man. She always gives me food. He is joining a broken table.

Past.

Singular.

1st.—	ਮੈਂ ਘਲਿਆ	*maiṅ ghaliā,*	M. & F. I sent, &c.
2nd.—	ਤੂੰ ਘਲਿਆ	*tūṅ ghaliā*	
3rd.—	ਓਹ ਨੇ ਘਲਿਆ	*oh ne ghaliā*	

Past.

Plural.

1st.—	ਅਸੀਂ ਘਲਿਆ	*asīṅ ghaliā*	M & F. We sent, &c.
2nd —	ਤੁਸੀਂ ਘਲਿਆ	*tusīṅ ghaliā*	
3rd.—	ਓਹਨਾਂ ਨੇ ਘਲਿਆ	*oh nāṅ ne ghaliā*	

Perfect.

Singular.

1st.—ਮੈਂ ਘਲਿਆ ਹੈ	*maiṅ ghaliā hai*	M. & F.	I have sent, &c.
2nd.—ਤੂੰ ਘਲਿਆ ਹੈ	*tūṅ ghaliā hai*		
3rd.—ਓਹ ਨੇ ਘਲਿਆ ਹੈ	*ohne ghaliā hai*		

Perfect.

Plural.

1st.—ਅਸੀਂ ਘਲਿਆ ਹੈ	*asīṅ ghaliā hai*	M. & F.	We have sent, &c.
2nd.—ਤੁਸੀਂ ਘਲਿਆ ਹੈ	*tusiṅ ghaliā hai*		
3rd.—ਓਹਨਾਂ ਨੇ ਘਲਿਆ ਹੈ	*ohnāṅ ne ghaliā hai*		

Pluperfect.

Singular.

1st.—ਮੈਂ ਘਲਿਆ ਸੀ	*maiṅ ghaliā sī*	M. & F.	I had sent, &c.
2nd — ਤੂੰ ਘਲਿਆ ਸੀ	*tūṅ ghaliā sī*		
3rd.—ਓਹਨੇ ਘਲਿਆ ਸੀ	*oh ne ghaliā sī*		

Pluperfect.

Plural.

1st.—ਅਸੀਂ ਘਲਿਆ ਸੀ	*asīṅ ghaliā sī*	M. & F.	We had sent, &c.
2nd.—ਤੁਸੀਂ ਘਲਿਆ ਸੀ	*tusīṅ ghaliā sī*		
3rd.—ਓਹਨਾਂ ਨੇ ਘਲਿਆ ਸੀ	*ohnāṅ ne ghāliā sī*		

Note.—(1.) When the Instrumental case is used, the Verb agrees with the object in number and gender, except when the object is governed by the preposition ਨੂੰ *nūṅ* (to). In the latter case the Verb is used in the form of the 3rd person, sing, masc, as given above.

Ex. :—ਓਹ ਨੇ ਚਿੱਠੀ ਪੜ੍ਹੀ, *oh ne chiṭhṭhī paṛhī*, = He read the letter.

ਓਹ ਨੇ ਆਪਣੀ ਭੈਣ ਨੂੰ ਮਾਰਿਆ *oh ne āpnī bhaiṇ nūṅ māriā*, She struck her sister.

2 The following Verbs do not take, the Agentive case :—

ਲਗਣਾ = *lagṇā*, to begin. ਸਕਣਾ *sakṇā* = to be able. ਚੁਕਣਾ *chukṇā* = to have done.

Translate :—

I sent him away. You have given me a bad rupee. Thou hast struck me. They had sown the seed. I have met him in the village. Thou gavest him a pice. He kissed his mother. We abused them badly. They sowed some flowers. We have lost all our money. They have sent us some fruit. You have killed the child. We had made a chair.

Future.

Singular.

			M.	F.	
1st.—ਘਲਾਂ	*ghalāṅ*	}	ਗਾ *gā*.	ਗੀ *gī*.	I shall send, &c.
2nd.—ਘਲੇਂ	*ghāleṅ*				
3rd.—ਘਲੇ	*ghale*				

Future.

Plural.

			M.	F.	
1st.—ਘਲਾਂ	*ghalāṅ*	}	ਗੇ, *ge*.	ਗੀਆਂ *gīāṅ*.	We shall send, &c.
2nd.—ਘਲੋ	*ghalo*				
3rd.—ਘਲਣ	*ghalan*				

Future Probable.

Singular.

	M.	F.			M.	F.	
1st.—	ਘਲਦਾ *ghaldā*,	ਦੀ *dī*,	ਹੋਵਾਂ *howāṅ*	}	ਗਾ *gā*.	ਗੀ *gī*.	I shall be sending, &c.
2nd.—			ਹੋਵੇਂ *howeṅ*				
3rd.—			ਹੋਵੇ *howe*				

Future Probable.

Plural.

	M.	F.			M.	F.	
1st.—	ਘਲਦੇ *ghalde*,	ਦੀਆਂ *dīāṅ*,	ਹੋਵਾਂ *howāṅ*	}	ਗੇ *ge*,	ਗੀਆਂ *gīāṅ*,	We shall be sending, &c.
2nd.—			ਹੋਵੋ *howo*				
3rd.—			ਹੋਣ *hon*				

Future Tense.

Singular.

	M.	F.
1st.—	ਘਲਿਆ ਹੋਵੇਗਾ *ghalīā howegā*, I shall have sent, &c. (plural same as sing :), We shall have sent, &c.	
2nd.—		
3rd.—		

Translate :—

She will give this to me. We shall be sowing the corn. They will have lost their cattle. I will see where he is. They will be stewing some meat. You will have run the race. You will be eating your dinner. They will kiss all of us. You will sit there. They will be sitting on chairs

SUBJUNCTIVE MOOD.

The Subjunctive or Conditional Mood is formed by prefixing ਜੇ *je*, or ਜੇਕਰ *jekar*, meaning 'if,' before the Indicative mood.

Ex. :—ਜੇ ਮੈਂ ਘਲਦਾ *je main ghaldā* = If I had sent.

ਜੇ ਤੁਸੀਂ ਘਲਦੇ *je tusīn ghalde* = If you had sent.

PASSIVE VOICE.

The Passive Verb is used when we wish to denote that the subject of the sentence is the receiver of the action, as, 'I am beaten,' 'She was struck,' 'They will be punished.'

The Verb is formed by the using of one verb, generally ਜਾਣਾ *jāṇā*, to go, with the past participle of another, for example, ਮਾਰਿਆ ਜਾਣਾ *māriā jāṇā*, (to be beaten).

In the declension the Past Participle retains that form throughout whilst the other Verb follows the same rules used in declining the Active Verb.

Ex. :—ਮੈਂ ਮਾਰਿਆ ਗਿਆਹਾਂ *main māriā giā hān*. I am beaten.

ਓਹ ਮਾਰੀ ਜਾਵੇ ਗੀ *oh mārī jāwegī*, She will be beaten.

ਓਹ ਮਾਰੇ ਗਏ ਸੀ *oh māre gae sī* They were beaten.

There is also another form in common use which is declined regularly with the use of the Verb ਹੋਣਾ *honā*, to be. The form consists of the root of the Verb, to which long *ī* (ੀ) is added, followed by the suffiix ਦਾ *dā*.

Ex. :—ਮਾਰੀ ਦਾ *mārī dā* = being beaten. ਸਾੜੀ ਦਾ *sāṛīdā* = being burnt.

COMPOUND VERBS.

Compound Verbs in *Panjābī* are numerous. They are, as a rule, used only in the Past Tense, and are formed by adding one Verb to the root of another. They have no rule and can only be learnt by practice.

The following are the most common :—

ਸਕਣਾ *sakṇā* = to be able. Ex. :—ਮੈ ਕੁਦ ਸਕਣਾ ਹਾਂ *maiṅ kud sakṇā hāṅ*, I can (am able to) jump.

ਚੁੱਕਣਾ *chukṇa* = to be finished. „ ਮੈਂ ਖਾ ਚੁੱਕਾ ਹਾਂ *māiṅ khā chukkā hāṅ* = I have (am) finished eating

ਸੁੱਟਣਾ *sutṇā* = to throw. „ ਮੈ ਓਹਨੂੰ ਮਾਰ ਸੁਟਿਆ *maiṅ oh ṇūṅ mār sutiā* I killed him.

ਪੈਣਾ *paiṇī* = to lie. „ ਓਹ ਡਿਗ ਪਿਆ ਸੀ *oh ḍig piā sī* = He had fallen down.

These four form Compound Verbs with the root of any other Verb but can not be used alone. The meaning of the two former is the same as in English, but that of the two latter must be acquired by practice.

Other Verbs which are often used in the same manner are, ਜਾਣਾ *jāṇā* (to go). ਦੇਣਾ *denā* (to give), ਲੈਣਾ *laiṇā* (to take), ਆਓਣਾ *āunā* (to come), and ਰਖਣਾ *rakhnā* (to put, to keep).

It must be remembered that, in the above, the root, although the principal part of the Verb, remains uninflected.

The word ਪੈਣਾ *pāinā* when used with the Infinitive of another Verb, also gives a sense of compulsion ; for example :—

ਤੈਂ ਨੂੰ ਜਾਣਾ ਪਵੇਗਾ *taiṅ ṇūṅ jāṇā pawegā* = You must go.

ਮੈਂ ਨੂੰ ਓਹ ਕੰਮ ਕਰਨਾ ਪਿਆ *maiṅ ṇūṅ oh kaṅm karṇā piā* = I was obliged to do that work.

Tho use of the Dative case with this Verb must be carefully noted.

Many Verbs, which may be classed as compound, are formed by using a Noun with ਦੇਣਾ *denā* (to give), ਕਰਨਾ *karṇā* (to do), or ਲੈਣਾ *lainā* (to take), for example.

ਫਾਂਸੀ *phāṅsi*, the gallows.	ਫਾਂਸੀ ਦੇਣਾ *phāṅsī denā*, to hang.
ਕੰਮ *kaṅm*, work.	ਕੰਮ ਕਰਨਾ *kaṅm karṇā*, to work.
ਭਾੜਾ *bhāṛā*, hire.	ਭਾੜਾ ਕਰਨਾ *bhāṛā karṇā*, to hire.
ਮੁੱਲ *mull*, price.	ਮੁੱਲ ਲੈਣਾ *mul lainā*, to buy.

In connection with the above, the Verb ਕਰਨਾ *karṇā*, to do, also signifies "to be in the habit of; example, ਮੈਂ ਰੋਜ ਪੜ੍ਹਿਆ ਕਰਦਾ ਹਾਂ *maiṅ roj paṛhiā kardā hāṅ*, = I read every day.

The following rules regarding Verbs must be carefully noted :—

1.—The Verb ਪਿਛਾ ਕਰਨਾ *pichhā karṇā*, (to pursue) always takes the Genitive case.

Ex. :—ਓਹਨੇ ਫੌਜ (ਸੈਨਾ) ਦਾ ਪਿੱਛਾ ਕੀਤਾ *oh ṇe phauj (saiṇā) dā pichhā kītā*, He pursued the army.

2.—The Verb ਮਿਲਨਾ *milṇā*, (to meet) always takes the Dative case.

Ex. :—ਓਹ ਮੈਨੂੰ ਰਸਤੇ ਵਿਚ ਮਿਲਿਆ *oh maiṅ ṇūṅ raste wichh miliā*
He met me on the road.

3.—To denote respect we use the plural form of the Verb,

Ex. :—ਸਾਹਿਬ ਆਏ ਹਨ *sāhib āe haṇ*, The gentleman has come.

4.—There is no Verb 'To have' in *panjābī*. To express the same meaning we use the Verb 'is,' together with the Preposition ਕੋਲ *kol*, (with).

Ex. :—ਮੇਰੇ ਕੋਲ ਹੈ *mere kol hai*, I have. ਉਸਦੇ ਕੋਲ ਸੀ *us de kol sī*
He had, or she had.

It is also expressed by the use of the Dative case, as in the following example.
ਤੈਨੂੰ ਕੁਛ ਪੀੜ ਹੈ *taiṅ ṇūṅ kuchh pīṛ hai*, Have you any pain ?

It is also expressed by the use of the genitive case. ਤੇਰਾ ਕੋਈ ਪੁਤਰ ਹੈ *terā koī putar hai*, Have you a (any) son.

5.—Sometimes the Infinitive is used to give the same idea as the Present Tense.

Ex. :—ਮੈਂ ਉੱਥੇ ਜਾ ਸਕਨਾ ਹਾਂ *maiṅ uththe jā saknā hāṅ*, Can I go there ?

6.—When the Infinitive is preceded by a preposition it is not inflected, but the final ā is omitted.

Ex. :—ਖਾਨ ਲਈ *khān laī*, for eating. ਲਿਖਣ ਲਈ *likhan laī*, for writing.

7.—The Verb ਲਗਨਾ *lagnā*, has two meanings *viz.*, 'relationship,' and 'cost'

Ex. :—Punjábi Bát Chít, page, 34 last line :—ਜੀਜਾ ਏਹ ਦੋਨੋਂ ਤੇਰੇ ਕੀ ਲਗਦੇ ਹਨ *jijā eh donoṅ tere kī lagde haṇ*, Brother-in-law what relation are both these to you ?

ਇਸ ਤੇ ਤੇਰਾ ਕੀ ਲਗਾ *is te terā kī lagā*, what did it cost you ?

8.—If an Infinitive, with the final (ਾ) ā omitted, be used with the Verb ਦੇਣਾ *deṇā*, to give it gives a sense of permission.

Ex. :— ਓਹ ਨੂੰ ਸੌਣਦੇ *oh ṇūṅ saun de*, let him sleep. ਓਹ ਨੂੰ ਆਉਣ ਦੇ *oh ṇūṅ āun de*, let him come.

9.—Similarly, if used with the Verbs ਲੱਗਨਾ *lagnā*, or ਡਹਿਨਾ *dehinā*, it conveys the idea of a 'beginning,' for example :—

ਓਹ ਕੰਮ ਕਰਨ ਲੱਗੇ *oh kaṅm karan lage*, they began to work.

ਓਹ ਲੜਨ ਡਹੇ *oh laṛaṇ ḍahe*, they began to fight.

10.—By using the particile, ਹੀ *hī* with the present participle we obtain the meaning "immediately" "at the instant of" as :—

ਓਹ ਸੁਣਦਾ ਹੀ ਮਰ ਗਿਆ *oh sundā hī margiā*, immediately on hearing it he died.

ਓਹ ਅੰਦਰ ਵੜਦੀ ਹੀ ਡਿੱਗ ਪਈ *oh aṅdar waṛdī hī ḍig paī*, immediately on entering she fell.

11.—The use of the Conjunctive particle ਕਿ *ki* (having) must be often practised, as it is extremely useful in writing long sentences.

12.—In Panjábi all " indirect " statements must be translated " direct."

Ex. :—' He said he would come ' must be translated ਓਹ ਨੇ ਆਖਿਆ ਕਿ ਮੈਂ ਆਵਾਂਗਾ. *oh ne ākhiā ki maiṅ āwāṅgā.*

13.—The Verb ਚਲਿਆ ਜਾਣਾ *chaliā jāṇā*, when used in one of the ' Imperfect tenses means ' to go ' ; when used in any of the other tenses it means ' to go away,'

Numerals.

1	੧ ਇੱਕ	*ikk.*	17	੧੭ ਸਤਾਰਾਂ	*satārāṅ.*
2	੨ ਦੋ	*do.*	18	੧੮ ਅਠਾਰਾਂ	*aṭhārāṅ.*
3	੩ ਤਿੱਨ	*tin.*	19	੧੯ ਉੱਨੀਂ	*unnīṅ.*
4	੪ ਚਾਰ	*chār.*	20	੨੦ ਵੀਹ	*wīh.*
5	੫ ਪੰਜ	*panj.*	21	੨੧ ਇੱਕੀ	*ikkī.*
6	੬ ਛੇ	*chhe.*	22	੨੨ ਬਾਈ	*bāī.*
7	੭ ਸੱਤ	*satt.*	23	੨੩ ਤੇਈ	*teī.*
8	੮ ਅੱਠ	*aṭhṭh.*	24	੨੪ ਚੱਵੀ	*chavvī.*
9	੯ ਨੌਂ	*nauṅ.*	25	੨੫ ਪੰਜੀ	*panjī.*
10	੧੦ ਦਸ	*das.*	26	੨੬ ਛੱਬੀ	*chhabbī*
11	੧੧ ਯਾਰਾਂ	*yārāṅ.*	27	੨੭ ਸਤਾਈ.	*stāī.*
12	੧੨ ਬਾਰਾਂ	*bārāṅ.*	28	੨੮ ਅੱਠਾਈ	*aṭhṭhāī.*
13	੧੩ ਤੇਰਾਂ	*terāṅ.*	29	੨੯ ਉਨੱਤੀ	*unattī.*
14	੧੪ ਚੌਦਾਂ	*chaudāṅ.*	30	੩੦ ਤੀਹ	*īh.*
15	੧੫ ਪੰਦਰਾਂ	*paṅdrāṅ.*	31	੩੧ ਕੱਤੀ	*kattī.*
10	੧੬ ਸੋਲਾਂ	*solāṅ.*	32	੩੨ ਬੱਤੀ	*battī.*

NUMERALS—*concluded.*

33	੩੩	ਤੇਤੀ	*tetī.*
34	੩੪	ਚੌਂਤੀ	*chauṅtī.*
35	੩੫	ਪੈਂਤੀ	*paiṅtī.*
36	੩੬	ਛੱਤੀ	*chhattī.*
37	੩੭	ਸੈਂਤੀ	*saiṇtī.*
38	੩੮	ਅਠੱਤੀ	*aṭhattī.*
39	੩੯	ਉਨਤਾਲੀ	*uṇtālī.*
40	੪੦	ਚਾਲੀ	*chālī.*
41		ਇਕਤਾਲੀ, ਕਤਾਲੀ	*iktālī, katālī.*
42	੪੨	ਬਤਾਲੀ	*batālī.*
43	੪੩	ਤਰਤਾਲੀ	*tartālī.*
44	੪੪	ਚੁਤਾਲੀ	*chutālī,*
45	੪੫	ਪੰਤਾਲੀ	*paṅtālī.*
46	੪੬	ਛਤਾਲੀ	*chhatālī.*
47	੪੭	ਸੰਤਾਲੀ	*saṅtālī*
48	੪੮	ਅਠਤਾਲੀ	*aṭhtālī.*
49	੪੯	ਉਣਿੰਜਾ	*uniṅjā.*
50	੫੦	ਪੰਜਾਹ	*paṅjāh.*
51	੫੧	ਇਕਵਿੰਜਾ, ਕਵਿੰਜਾ	*ikwiṅjā, kawiṅjā.*
52	੫੨	ਬਵਿੰਜਾ	*bawiṅjā.*
53	੫੩	ਤਰਵਿੰਜਾ	*tarwiṅjā.*
54	੫੪	ਚੁਰਿੰਜਾ	*churiṅjā.*
55	੫੫	ਪਚਵਿੰਜਾ	*pachwiṅjā.*
56	੫੬	ਛਪਿੰਜਾ	*chhapiṅjā.*
57	੫੭	ਸਤਵਿੰਜਾ	*satwiṅjā.*
58	੫੮	ਅਠਵਿੰਜਾ	*aṭhwiṅjā.*
59	੫੯	ਉਨਾਹਠ	*unāhaṭh.*
60	੬੦	ਸੱਠ	*saṭh.*
61	੬੧	ਕਾਠ	*ɩkāṭh.*
62	੬੨	ਬਾਹਠ	*bāhṭh.*
63	੬੩	ਤਰੇਹਠ	*trehṭh.*
64	੬੪	ਚੌਂਹਠ	*chauṅhṭh.*
65	੬੫	ਪੈਂਹਠ	*paiṅhṭh.*
66	੬੬	ਛਿਆਹਠ	*chhiāhṭh.*
67	੬੭	ਸਤਾਹਠ	*satāhṭh.*
68	੬੮	ਅਠਾਹਠ	*aṭhāhṭh.*
69	੬੯	ਉਨਹਤੱਰ	*unahttar.*
70	੭੦	ਸਤੱਰ	*sattar.*
71	੭੧	ਕਹੱਤਰ	*ɩkahattar.*
72	੭੨	ਬਹੱਤਰ	*bahattar.*
73	੭੩	ਤਿਹੱਤਰ	*tihattar.*
74	੭੪	ਚੁਹੱਤਰ	*chuhattar.*
75	੭੫	ਪੰਜਹੱਤਰ	*paṅjhattr.*
76	੭੬	ਛਿਹੱਤਰ	*chhihattr.*
77	੭੭	ਸੰਜਹਤਰ	*saṅjhattar.*
78	੭੮	ਅਠਹਤਰ	*aṭhhattar.*
79	੭੯	ਉਨਾਸੀ	*unāsī.*
80	੮੦	ਅੱਸੀ	*assī.*
81	੮੧	ਇਕਾਸੀ	*ikāsī.*
82	੮੨	ਬਿਆਸੀ	*biāsī.*
83	੮੩	ਤਿਰਾਸੀ	*tirāsī.*

NUMERALS—*concluded.*

84	੮੪ ਚੁਰਾਸੀ	*churāsī.*	94	੯੪ ਚੁਰਾਨਵੇਂ	*churānweṅ.*
85	੮੫ ਪਚਾਸੀ	*pachāsī.*	95	੯੫ ਪਚਾਨਵੇਂ	*pachānweṅ.*
86	੮੬ ਛਿਆਸੀ	*chhiāsī.*	96	੯੬ ਛਿਆਨਵੇਂ	*chhiāṅweṅ.*
87	੮੭ ਸਤਾਸੀ	*satāsī.*	97	੯੭ ਸਤਾਨਵੇਂ	*satānweṅ.*
88	੮੮ ਅਠਾਸੀ	*aṭhāsī.*	98	੯੮ ਅਠਾਨਵੇਂ	*āthānweṅ.*
89	੮੯ ਉਨਾਨਵੇਂ	*unānweṅ.*	99	੯੯ ਨੜਿਨਵੇਂ	*naṛinweṅ.*
90	੯੦ ਨਬੇ	*nabbe.*	100	੧੦੦ ਸੌ	*sau.*
91	੯੧ ਇਕਾਨਵੇਂ, ਕਾਨਵੇਂ	*ikānweṅ.* *kānweṅ.*	101	੧੦੧ ਇਕ ਸੌ ਇਕ, ਇਕੋਤਰ ਸੌ	*iksau ik* or *ikotar sau.*
92	੯੨ ਬਾਨਵੇ	*bānweṅ.*	102	੧੦੨ ਇਕ ਸੌ ਦੋ	*iksau do.*
93	੯੩ ਤਿਰਾਨਵੇਂ	*tirānweṅ.*	103	੧੦੩ ਇਕ ਸੌ ਤਿਨ	*iksau tin.*

and the rest are regular.

Note.—ਦੋ *do,* (two) and ਦੋਵੇਂ *doweṅ* (both) are nominative. Their inflected forms are ਦੋਹਾਂ *dohaṅ.*

Ex. :—ਦੋਵੇਂ ਮੁੰਡੇ ਦੌੜ ਗਏ *doweṅ muṅḍe douṛ gae,* both the boys ran away.

Ex. :—ਦੋਹਾਂ ਮੁੰਡਿਆਂ ਨੇ ਮੈਂਨੂੰ ਮਾਰਿਆ *dohāṅ muṅḍiāṅ ne maiṅ nūṅ māriā,* Both the boys struck me.

Ordinals.

ਪਹਿਲਾ	*pahilā.*	1st.	ਛੀਵਾਂ	*chhīwāṅ.*	6th.
ਦੂਜਾ	*dūjā.*	2nd.	ਸਤਵਾਂ	*satwāṅ.*	7th.
ਤੀਜਾ	*tījā.*	3rd.	ਅਠਵਾਂ	*aṭhwāṅ.*	8th.
ਚੌਥਾ	*chauthā.*	4th	ਨੌਂਵਾਂ	*nauṅwāṅ*	9th.
ਪੰਜਵਾਂ	*paṅjwāṅ*	5th.	ਦਸਵਾਂ	*daswāṅ.*	10th.

The remaining Punjábí Ordinals are formed by adding ਵਾਂ *wāṅ,* to the numerals, such as ਵੀਹਵਾਂ *wīhwāṅ* = 20th ਤੀਹਵਾਂ *tīhwāṅ* = 30th, &c. &c.,

The particle ਕੁ *ku,* is also added to weights, measures and numerals and gives the sense of " about " as ਸੇਰ ਕੁ *serku* = about a seer, ਸੌਕੁ ਜਵਾਨ *sau ku jawāṇ* = about a hundred men, ਮਣਕੁ ਕਣਕ *manku kanak* = about a maund of wheat.

USEFUL TERMS.

Relations.

Masculine.	Feminine.
Widower, ਰੰਡਾ *randā.*	Widow ਰੰਡੀ *randī.*
Husband ਗਭਰੂ *gabhrū.*	Wife ਵਹੁਟੀ *wahuṭī.*
Husband's G; father ਦਦਿਔਰਾ *dadiaurā.*	Wife's G. mother ਨਨੇਹਸ *naṇehas.*
„ father ਸੌਰਾ *saurā.*	„ mother ਸੱਸ *sass.*
„ brother (elder) ਜੇਠ *jeṭh.*	„ sister ਸਾਲ਼ੀ *sālī.*
„ „ (younger) ਦੇਵਰ *dewar.*	
uncle ਪਤਿਹੁਰਾ *patihura.*	Wife's aunt ਪਤਰਸ *patras.*
Wife's G. father ਦਦਿਔਰਾ *dadiaurā.*	Husband's G. mother ਦਦੇਹਸ *dadehas.*
„ father ਸੌਰਾ *saurā.*	„ mother ਸੱਸ *sass.*
„ brother ਸਾਲਾ *sālā.*	„ sister ਨਨਾਣ *naṇān.*
„ uncle ਪਤਿਹੁਰਾ *patihurā.*	„ aunt ਪਤਰਸ *patras.*
Father ਪਿਓ, *pio.* ਬਾਪੂ, *bāpū.* ਭਾਈਆ, *bhāīā.* ਲਾਲਾ *lālā.*	Mother ਮਾਂ *māṅ.*
Father's father ਦਾਦਾ, *dāda.* ਬਾਬਾ *bābā.*	Mother's mother ਨਾਨੀ *nāṇī.*
brother (elder) ਤਾਯਾ *tāyā.*	„ sister ਮਾਸੀ *māsī.*
„ „ (younger) ਚਾਚਾ *chāchā.*	
Mother's father ਨਾਨਾ *nāṇā.*	Father's mother ਦਾਦੀ *dādī.*
„ brother ਮਾਮਾ *māmā.*	„ sister ਭੂਆ *bhūā.*
Son ਪੁਤ੍ਰ *putr.*	Daughter ਧੀ *dhī.*
Son's son ਪੋਤਾ, *potā* ਪੋਤ੍ਰਾ *potrā.*	Daughter's daughter ਦੋਹਤ੍ਰੀ, *dohtri.* ਦੋਹਤੀ *dohtī*

RELATIONS.

Masculine.

Daughter's son ਦੋਹਤ੍ਰਾ, ਦੋਹਤਾ *dohtrā.* *dohtā*

" husband ਜਵਾਈ *jawāī*

Brother ਤਰਾ *bharā.*

Brother's son ਭਤੀਜਾ *bhatījā.*

Sister's " ਭਣੇਵਾਂ *bhanewāṅ.*

" husband ਭਣਵਈਆ *bhanwāīā.*

Step father ਮਤ੍ਰੇਆ ਪਿਉ *matreā pio.*

Maternal aunt's husband ਮਾਸੜ *māsaṛ.*

Paternal " " ਫੁਫੜ *phuphaṛ.*

Brother-in-law (wife's brother) ਸਾਲਾ *sālā.*

Generation ਪੀੜ੍ਹੀ *pīṛī,*

Wife's family ਸੌਰੇ *saure.*

Step relations ਮਤ੍ਰੇਆ *matreā,* (prefix).

Ex. :—ਮਤ੍ਰੇਆ ਭਰਾ step brother. etc.

Feminine.

Son's daughters ਪੋਤ੍ਰੀ, *potrī* ਪੋਤੀ *potī.*

" wife ਨੂੰਹ *nūṅh.*

Sister ਭੈਣ *bhaiṅ.*

Sister's daughter ਭਣੇਵੀਂ *bhaṅewīṅ.*

Brother's " ਭਤੀਜੀ *bhatījī.*

" wife ਭਰਜਾਈ *bharjāī* ਭਾਬੀ *bhābhī.*

Step mother ਮਤ੍ਰੇਈ ਮਾਂ *matreī māṅ.*

Maternal uncle's wife ਮਾਮੀਂ *māmī.*

Paternal " " ਚਾਚੀ *chāchī.*

Sister-in-law (wife sister) ਸਾਲੀ *sālī.*

Husband's brother's wife ਦਰਾਣੀ *drāṇī.*

" e. " " ਜਠਾਣੀ *jaṭhāṇī.*

Parents of betrothed ਕੁੜਮ *kuṛam.*

Bachelor ਕੁਆਰਾ *kuārā.*

Note :—ਮਹਿੱਟਰ *mahiṭṭar,* gives the meaning of orphan.

Ex. :—Father less, ਪਿਓ ਮਹਿਟਰ *piu mahiṭṭar,* mother less. ਮਾਂ ਮਹਿੱਟਰ *māṅ mahiṭṭar.*

COLOURS.

Ordinary.

ਲਾਲ	*lāl*	red.
ਚਿੱਟਾ	*chiṭṭa*	white.
ਨੀਲਾ	*ṇīlā*	blue.
ਕਾਲਾ	*kālā*	black.
ਪੀਲਾ	*pīlā*	yellow.

Horses.

ਸਬਜ਼ਾ	*sabjā*	grey.
ਗੱਰਾ	*garrā*	roan.
ਮੁਸ਼ਕੀ	*mushkī*	black.
ਕੁਮੈਤ	*kumait*	bay.
ਸੁਰੰਗ	*suraṅg*	chestnut.

COLOURS—*concluded.*

Ordinary.			Horses		
ਹਰਾ	*harā*	green.	ਸਮੰਦ	*samand*	dun.
ਬਦਾਮੀ	*badāmī*	brown.	ਅਬਲਕ	*ablak*	piebald.
ਅਸਮਾਨੀ	*asmānī*	sky blue.	ਗੋਰਾ	*gora*	iron grey. red (cattle).
ਪਿਆਜੀ	*piājī*	pink.	ਬੱਗਾ	*baggā*	white (cattle).
ਭੂਸਲਾ	*bhūslā*	brown.			
ਕਿਰਮਚੀ	*kiramchī*	crimson.			
ਸੰਤਰਾ ਰੰਗ	*santrā rang*,	orange.			

TRADES AND PROFESSIONS.

ਸਰਾਫ	*saraph*	banker.	ਸੁਨਿਆਰਾ	*suṇiārā*	goldsmith.
ਨਾਈ	*ṇāī*	barber.	ਘਸਿਆਰਾ	*ghasiārā*	grass cutter.
ਲੁਹਾਰ	*luhār*	blacksmith.	ਪਸਾਰੀ	*pasārī*	grocer.
ਮਲਾਹ	*malāh*	boatman.	ਸਹੀਸ	*sahīs*	groom.
ਜਿਲਦ ਗਰ	*jildgar*	book-binder.	ਰਾਹ ਮਾਰ	*rāh mār*	highwayman.
ਕਿਤਾਬ ਫਰੋਸ਼	*kitāb pharosh*	book-seller.	ਸਲੋਤਰੀ	*salotrī*	horse doctor.
ਪਥੇਰਾ	*patherā*	brick-maker.	ਭਠਿਆਰਾ	*bhaṭhiārā*	innkeeper.
ਕਸਾਈ	*kasāī*	butcher.	ਜੁਵਾਹਰੀ	*juwāhrī*	jeweller.
ਤ੍ਰਖਾਨ	*tarkhāṇ*	carpenter.	ਮਜੂਰ	*majūr*	labourer.
ਕੋਚਵਾਨ	*kochwāṇ*	coachman.	ਰਾਜ	*rāj*	mason.
ਹਲਵਾਈ	*halwāī*	confectioner.	ਦਾਈ	*dāī*	nurse (for a child).
ਠੇਕੇਦਾਰ	*ṭhekedār*	contractor.	ਗਾਂਧੀ	*gāndhī*	perfumer,
ਰਸੋਈਆ	*rasoīā*	cook.	ਅਕਸੀ ਤਸਵੀਰ ਵਾਲਾ	*aksī taswīr wālā*	photographer.
ਕਸਾਨ	*kasāṇ*	cultivator.	ਪੁਲਸ ਵਾਲਾ	*pulaswālā*	policeman.
ਡਾਕਦਾਰ	*ḍākdār*	doctor.	ਡਾਕ ਵਾਲਾ	*ḍāk wālā*	postman.
ਲਲਾਰੀ	*lalārī*	dyer.			

TRADE AND PROFESSIONS—*concluded*

ਜਿਮੀਂਦਾਰ	*jimīṅdār*	farmer.
ਨਾਲਬੰਦ	*ṇālbaṅd*	farrier.
ਰੌਲ	*raul*	fortune teller.
ਕਸੇਰਾ	*kaserā*	founder (metal.)
ਦਾਸ	*dās*	servant (m).
ਦਾਸੀ	*dāsī*	servant (f).
ਦਰਜੀ	*darjī*	tailor.
ਉਸਤਾਦ	*ustād*	teacher.
ਘੜੀ ਸਾਜ	*ghaṛī sāj*	watchmaker.
ਘੁਮਿਆਰ	*ghumiār*	potter.
ਚੋਰ	*chor*	robber, thief.
ਸ਼ਗਿਰਦ	*shagird*	scholar.
ਮੋਚੀ	*mochī*	shoemaker.
ਧੋਬੀ	*dhobī*	washerman.
ਧੋਬਨ	*dhoban*	washerwoman.
ਝੀਊਰ	*jhīur*	water carrier (Hind :)
ਬਹਿਸ਼ਤੀ	*bhistī*	„ (Moh :)
ਲਕੜਹਾਰਾ	*lakṛ hārā*	wood cutter.

ENGLISH WORDS USED IN PANJABI.

ਅਜੀਟਨ	*ajīṭaṇ*	adjutant.
ਬਾਰਕ	*bārak* (F).	barrack.
ਕਾਫੀ	*kāphī* (F).	coffee.
ਕਰਨੈਲ	*karṇail*	colonel.
ਕਪਤਾਨ	*kaptāṇ*	captain.
ਕਮਾਨ	*kamāṇ*	command.
ਕਮਸਰੇਟ	*kamsareṭ* (F).	commissariat.
ਕਮਿਸਨਰ	*kamisṇar*	commissioner.
ਕੰਪਨੀ	*kaṅpṇī* (F).	company.
ਕਾਗ	*kāg*	cork.
ਕੋਚਵਾਨ	*kochwāṇ*	coachman.
ਕੌਂਸਲ (F).	*kauṅsal*	council,
ਡਾਕਦਾਰ	*ḍākdār*	doctor.
ਫੁਟ	*phuṭ*	foot (12 ins).
ਅਪੀਲ	*apīl* (F).	appeal.
ਜਰਨੈਲ	*jarṇail*	general.
ਕੋਟ ਮਾਸਟਰ	*koṭ māsṭar*,	quarter-master.
ਹਸਪਤਾਲ	*hospatāl*	hospital.
ਲਾਲਟੈਨ (F)	*lālṭaiṇ*	lantern,
ਲਫਟੈਨ	*laphṭaiṇ*	lieutenant.
ਮੇਜਰ	*mejar*	major,
ਮਿਸਕੋਟ (F).	*miskoṭ*	mess.
ਅੜਦਲੀ	*aṛdlī*	orderly.
ਪਰੇਟ (F).	*pareṭ*	parade.
ਜੇਹਲਖਾਨਾ	*jehl-khānā*	jail.
ਰੇਲ (F).	*rel*	rail.
ਰਪਟ (F).	*rapaṭ*	report.
ਸਟੇਸ਼ਨ	*sṭeshaṇ*	station.
ਤੌਲੀਆ	*tauliā*	towel.

ENGLISH WORDS USED IN PANJABI.

ਕਾਂਟੀਨ	*kāṅṭīṇ*	canteen.
ਸਾਰਟੀਫਿਕੇਟ	*sārṭīphikeṭ*	certificate.
ਅਫ਼ਸਰ	*afsar*	officer.
ਮੇਖਜ਼ੀਨ (F).	*mekhjīṇ*	magazine.
ਕੋਟ ਗਾਰਡ	*kot gārḍ*	quarter guard.
ਕਮੇਟੀ	*kameṭī*	committee.
ਡੀਪੂ	*ḍīpū*	depot.
ਸਕਤ੍ਰ	*sakatar*	secretary.
ਟਿਕਸ, ਟਿਕਟ	*ṭikas, ṭikat,*	stamp, ticket.
ਸੰਤਰੀ	*santrī*	sentry.
ਮੀਲ	*mīl*	mile.
ਕਮਾਨੀਅਰ	*kamāniar*	commandar.
ਬਹਿਰਾ	*bahirā*	bearer.
ਤੋਸ	*tos*	toast.
ਪਾਰਸਲ	*pārsal*	parcel.
ਤੁਰਪ	*turap*	troop.
ਰਾਸ਼ਨ	*rāshaṇ*	ration.
ਚੀਪਕੋਰਟ	*chīp korṭ*	chief court.
ਪਿੰਨਸ਼ਨ	*pinshaṇ*	pension.
ਰੈਜੀਡੰਟ	*raijīḍanṭ*	resident.
ਟੋਟਲ	*ṭotal*	total.
ਲੈਨ	*laiṇ*	line.

TIME.

ਪਲ	*pal*	moment.
ਮਿੰਟ	*miṅṭ*	minute.
ਘੈਂਟਾ	*ghaiṅṭā*	hour.
ਘੜੀ	*ghaṛī*	Indian hour (24 mins).
ਪਹਿਰ	*pahir*	watch (3 hrs.)
ਦਿਨ	*diṇ*	day.
ਅਠਵਾਰਾ, ਸਾਤਾ	*aṭhwārā, sātā*	week.
ਮਹੀਨਾ	*mahīṇā*	month.
ਵਰਹਾ	*warhā*	year.
ਤੜਕਾ	*taṛkā*	dawn.
ਸਵੇਰ	*sawer*	morning.
ਦੁਪਹਿਰ	*dupahir,*	mid-day.
ਲੌਢਾ ਵੇਲਾ	*laudāwelā,*	after-noon.
ਸੰਧਿਆ, ਤਰਕਾਲਾਂ	*sandhiā*, *tarkālāṅ*	evening.
ਰਾਤ	*rāt*	night.
ਅੱਧੀ ਰਾਤ	*adhī rāt,*	midnight.
ਅੱਜ	*ajj*	to-day.
ਕਲ	*kal*	yesterday or to-morrow.
ਵੇਲਾ	*welā*	time.
ਅਜ ਰਾਤ	*ajjrāt*	to-night.
ਕਲ ਰਾਤ	*kal rāt*	last night or, tomorrow night.
ਪਰਸੋਂ	*parsoṅ*	day before yesterday.
ਪਿਛਲੇ ਅਠਵਾਰੇ	*pichhle aṭhwāre,*	last week.
ਪਿਛਲੇ ਮਹੀਨੇ	*pichhle mahīne*	last month.
ਪਿਛਲੇ ਵਰਹੇ	*pichhle warhe,*	last year.
ਅਗਲੇ ਅਠਵਾਰੇ	*agle aṭhwāre,*	next week.
ਅਗਲੇ ਮਹੀਨੇ	*agle mahīne,*	next month.
ਅਗਲੇ ਵਰਹੇ	*agle warhe,*	next year

Table of Weights.

ਅੱਧੀ ਛਟਾਂਕ *addhī chhatāṅk*, one ounce

ਛਟਾਂਕ *chhatāṅk*, two ounces.

ਅਧ ਪਾ *adh pā*, 8th of a seer.

ਪੌਣਾ ਪਾ *pauṅā pā*, 3 chhittanks.

ਪਾ *pā*, 4th of a seer.

ਸਵਾ ਪਾ *sawā pā*, 5 chhittanks.

ਡੂਢ ਪਾ *ḍūḍh pā*, 6 chhittanks.

ਅਧ ਸੇਰ *adh ser*, 8 chhittanks or half seer.

ਤਿਨ ਪਾ *tin pā*, 12 chhittanks or ¾ of a [seer.

ਸੇਰ *ser*, 16 chhittanks.

ਸਵਾ ਸੇਰ *sawā ser*, one seer and a quarter.

ਡੂਢ ਸੇਰ *ḍūḍh ser*, one seer and a half.

ਪੌਣੇ ਦੋਸੇਰ *paune do ser*, one seer and [three quarters.

ਦੋ ਸੇਰ *do ser*, two seers or nearly 4 lbs.

ਸਵਾ ਦੋ ਸੇਰ *sawā do ser*, two seers and [a quarter.

ਢਾਈ ਸੇਰ *ḍhāī ser*, two and a half seers.

ਪੌਣੇ ਤਿੰਨ ਸੇਰ *paune tin ser*, two seers and [three quarters.

ਤਿੰਨ ਸੇਰ *tin ser*, three seers.

ਸਵਾ ਤਿਨ ਸੇਰ *sawā tin ser*, three seers and a quarter.

ਸਾਢੇ ਤਿਨ ਸੇਰ *sāḍhe tin ser*, three seer and a half.

ਪੌਣੇ ਚਾਰ ਸੇਰ *paune chār ser*, three seers and three quarters.

ਚਾਰ ਸੇਰ *chār ser*, four seers.

ਪੰਜ ਸੇਰ *panj ser*, or ਵੱਟੀ *waṭṭī*, five seers.

ਧੜੀ *dhaṛī*, ten seers.

ਧੌਣ *dhaun*, twenty seers.

ਮਣ *man*, 40 seers.

ਮਾਣੀ *mānī*, 12 maunds.

Days of the Week.

ਐਤਵਾਰ *aitwār*, Sunday.

ਸੋਮਵਾਰ *somwār*, Monday.

ਮੰਗਲਵਾਰ *maṅgalwār*, Tuesday.

ਬੁਧਵਾਰ *budhwār*, Wednesday.

ਵੀਰਵਾਰ *vīrwār*, Thursday.

ਸ਼ੁਕਰਵਾਰ *shukarwār*, Friday.

ਛਨਿਛਰਵਾਰ *chhaṇichhar wār*, Saturday.

The Months.

ਮਾਘ *māgh*, January.

ਫੱਗਣ *phaggan*, February.

ਚੇਤ *chet*, March.

ਵਿਸਾਖ *wisākh*, April.

ਜੇਠ *jeṭh*, May.

ਹਾੜ *hāṛ*, June.

ਸਾਵਣ *sāwan*, July.

ਭਾਦਰੋਂ *bhādroṅ*, August.

ਅੱਸੂ *assū*, September.

ਕੱਤਕ *kattak*, October.

ਮੱਘਰ *maghghar*, November.

ਪੋਹ *poh*, December.

* Every Punjabi month begins from about the middle of English month of the same names.

The Seasons.

ਸਿਆਲ *siāl* or ਸਰਦੀ *sardī*, the cold weather.

ਬਹਾਰ *bahār* ਬਸੰਤ ਰੁਤ *basant rut*, the spring.

ਗਰਮੀ *garmī* or ਹੁਨਾਲ *hunāl*, the hot weather.

ਬਰਸਾਤ *barsāt* or ਚੁਮਾਸਾ *chumāsā*, the rainy weather.

The principal points of the Compass.

North ਉਤ੍ਰ *uttar* or ਪਹਾੜ *pahāṛ*.

East ਪੂਰਬ *pūrab* or ਚੜ੍ਹਦਾ *chaṛhdā*.

South ਦੱਖਣ *dakhkhan*.

West ਪੱਛਮ *pachcham* or ਲੈਂਹਦਾ *lainhdā*.

Military Words.

Accoutrements { ਕੀਲ ਕਾਂਟਾ, *kīl kāṅṭā*. ਜੰਗੀ ਅਸਬਾਬ *jangī asbāb*.

Admonish (to) ਡਾਂਟਣਾ *dāṅṭnā*.

Advance (to) ਅੱਗੇ ਵਧਣਾ *agge wadhnā*.

Aim (to) ਨਿਸ਼ਾਨਾ ਬਨ੍ਹਣਾ *nishānā banhnā*.

Ammunition ਗੋਲੀਸਿੱਕਾ *golī sikkā*.

Arms ਹਥਿਆਰ *hathiār*.

Army (f) ਸੈਨਾ, *sainā* ਫੌਜ *phauj*.

Arrears of pay (f) ਪਿਛਲੀ ਤਲਬ *pichhlī talab*.

Arrow ਤੀਰ *tīr*.

Artillery ਤੋਪਖਾਨਾ *topkhānā*.

Attestation paper { ਸ਼ਪਾਹੀ ਦੇ ਕਰਾਰ ਨਾਮੇ ਦਾ ਕਾਗਤ *shapāhī de karār nāme dā kāgat*.

Axe ਕੁਹਾੜਾ *kuhāṛā*.

Bail (f) ਜਮਾਨਤ *jamānat*.

Baggage ਨਿੱਕ ਸੁੱਕ, ਅਸਬਾਬ *nikk sukk, asbāb*.

Battle (f) ਲੜਾਈ *laṛāī*.

Ball (cannon) ਗੋਲਾ *golā*.

Bayonet (f) ਸੰਗੀਨ *sangīn*.

Belt (f) ਪੇਟੀ *peṭī*.

Blow up (to) ਉਡਾ ਦੇਣਾ *uḍā denā*.

Bow ਕਮਾਨ *kamān*.

Burnish ਚਿਲਕਾਉਣਾ *chilkāunā*.

Bullet (f) ਗੋਲੀ *golī*.

Camp ਕੰਪੂ *kanpū*.

Camp (rest) ਪੜਾ *paṛā*.

Camp (of exercise) ਜਲਸਾ *jalsā*.

Cantonment (f) ਛੌਣੀ *chhaunī*.

Cannon (f) ਤੋਪ *top*.

Cartridge ਕਾਰਤੂਸ *kārtūs*.

MILITARY WORDS—continued.

Cavalry ਰਸਾਲਾ *rasālā.*

Cell ਕਾਂਜ਼ੀ ਹੌਦ *kānjī haud.*

Charge, or crime ਦੋਸ਼, *dosh* ਜੁਰਮ *juram.*

Clasp (f) ਕੜੀ *kaṛī.*

Cleaning rags (f) ਲੀਰ, *līr* ਟੱਲੀ *ṭallī.*

Compensation (for dearness of provisions) (f) { ਮੈਂਘਾਈ, *mainghāī.* ਖਰਾਕੀ *khurākī.* }

Compensation, (for any thing else) } ਭੱਤਾ *bhattā.*

Corporal ਨੈਕ *naik.*

Coward ਡਰਪੋਕ *darpok.*

Decision ਫੈਸਲਾ *phaislā*

Dagger (f) ਕਟਾਰ *kaṭār.*

Defence ਬਚਾ *bachā.*

Defeat (f) ਹਾਰ *hār* ਸ਼ਕਸਤ *shakast.*

Deserter ਭਗੌੜਾ *bhagauṛā.*

Detachment ਦਸਤਾ *dastā.*

Discharge (man) ਨਾਂ ਕਟਣਾ *nā kaṭṇā.*

Discharge (gun) ਚਲਾਓਣਾ *chalaunā.*

Ditch (f) ਖਾਈ *khāī.*

Enemy ਵੈਰੀ *wairī.*

Enlist (to) ਭਰਤੀ ਕਰਨਾ *bhartī karnā.*

Evidence (f) ਉਗਾਹੀ *ugāhī.*

Fire (gun) ਚਲਾਉਣਾ *chalāunā.*

Flag ਝੰਡਾ *jhaṇḍā,* ਨਸ਼ਾਨ *nashāṇ.*

Flight (f) ਭਾਜੜ *bhājaṛ.*

Foot soldier ਪੈਦਲ *paidal.*

Fort ਕਿਲਾ *kilā.*

Fortification (f) ਕਿਲਾ ਬੰਦੀ *kilā bandī.*

Fringe of turban ਝਾਲਰ *jhālar*

Furlough (f) ਰਜਾ *rajā.*

Garrison (f) ਕਿਲੇਦੀ ਫੌਜ *kile dī phauj.*

Guard ਪੈਹਰਾ *paihrā.*

Guide ਸਰਦਾਰ *sardār.*

Guilty ਦੋਸੀ *doshī.*

Gun (f) ਬੰਦੂਕ *bandūk.* ਬਦੂਕ *badūk.*

Halting place ਮੁਕਾਮ *mukām.*

Halt (to) ਮੁਕਾਮ ਕਰਨਾ *mukām karnā.*

Haversack ਝੋਲਾ *jholā.*

Helmet (f) ਟੋਪੀ *topī.*

Hostage, (f) ਢੱਕ *dhakk.*

Imprisonment, (f) ਕੈਦ *kaid.*

Indian articles of war { ਲਸ਼ਕਰੀ ਆਈਨ } *lashkarī āīṇ.*

Infantry (f) (British) { ਲਾਲ ਕੁੜਤੀ } *lāl kuṛtī*

Infantry (f) (Native) { ਕਾਲੀ ਪਲਟਣ } *kālī palṭan.*

Innocent ਬਦੋਸ *bados.*

Inquiry (f) ਤਕੀਕਾਤ *takīkāt*

Intrenchment ਮੋਰਚਾ *morchā*

Jail ਜੇਲਖਾਨਾ *jel kkāṇā.*

MILITARY WORDS—continued.

Javelin ਨੇਜਾ *nejā.*

Kit ਅਸਬਾਬ *asbāb.*

Knickerbockers ਤੰਬਾ *tanbā.*

Knife (f) ਛੁਰੀ *chhurī.*

Load (to) ਲਦਣਾ *ladnā.*

Loop hole ਮੋਰੀ (*f*) *morī.*

Ladder (f) ਪੌੜੀ *pauṛī.*

Lance ਨੇਜਾ *nejā* ਬਰਛਾ *barchcha.*

Lead ਸਿੱਕਾ *sikkā.*

Magazine (f) ਮੇਖਜੀਨ *mekhjīn.*

March (to) ਕੂਚਕਰਨਾ *kūch karnā.*

Medal (war) ਤਕਮਾ *takmā.*

Measurement ਨਾਪ *nāp.*

Mine (f) ਸੁਰੰਗ *surang.*

Muster (to) ਗਿਣਤੀ ਕਰਨੀ *gintī karṇī*

* Native officer (Lieutenant) } ਜਮਾਦਾਰ *jamādār.*

Native officer (Captain) ਸੂਬੇਦਾਰ *sūbedār.*

Native Officer (Major) ਸੂਬੇਦਾਰ ਮੇਜਰ *sūbedār mejar.*

Native Officer (Adjutant) ਅਜੀਟਨ ਜਮਾਦਾਰ *ajīṭan jamādār.*

Oath (f) ਸੌਂਹ *saunh.*

Pickaxe (f) ਗੈਂਤੀ *gentī.*

Pistol ਪਿਸਤੌਲ, *pistaul* ਤਮਾਂਚਾ *tamānchā.*

Powder ਦਾਰੂ *dārū.*

Prisoner ਕੈਦੀ *kaidī.*

Punishment (f). ਸਜਾ *sajā.*

Parade (f). ਪਰੇਟ, *pareṭ* ਕਵੈਦ *kawaid*

Pay (f) ਤਲਬ *talab.*

Pay Master ਬਖ਼ਸ਼ੀ *bakhshī.*

Peace (f) ਸੁਲ੍ਹਾ *sulhā.*

Pension (f) ਪਿਨਸ਼ਨ *pinshan* ਇੰਗਸ *ingas.*

Pouch (f) ਖੀਸੀ *khīsī*

„ large (f) ਖਲੀਤੀ *khalītī.*

Pouch ਤੋਸ਼ਦਾਨ *toshdān.*

Quoit ਚਕਰ *chakkar*

Rampart (f) ਸਫੀਲ, *saphīl* ਫਸੀਲ *phasīl.*

Rank ਹੁੱਦਾ *huddā.*

Range (f) ਚਾਂਦਮਾਰੀ *chānd mārī.*

Ration (f) ਰਸਦ *rasad.*

Rebel ਫਸਾਦੀ *phasādī.*

Recruit ਰੰਗਰੂਟ *rangrūt.*

Regiment (f) ਪਲਟਨ *palṭan.*

Riband ਫੀਤਾ *phītā.*

Sappers and miners (f) } ਸਫਰਮੈਨਾ *sapharmainā.*

Sash ਜਾਲ *jāl*

---

* In the Native Cavalry there are four grades ਜਮਾਦਾਰ, *jamādār.* ਰਸਾਈਦਾਰ, *rasāīdār.* ਰਸਾਲਦਾਰ, *rasāldār.* ਰਸਾਲਦਾਰ ਮੇਜਰ, *rasāldār mejar.* The Adjutant is called ਵਰਦੀ ਮੇਜਰ = *wardī mejar.*

MILITARY WORDS—continued.

Scabbard (f) ਮਿਆਨ *miāṇ.*

Sergeant (Infantry) ਹੌਲਦਾਰ *hauldār.*

Sergeant (Cavalry) ਦਫੇਦਾਰ *daphedār.*

Sentence ਹੁਕਮ, *hukam* ਫਤਵਾ *phatwā.*

Shield (f) ਢਾਲ *ḍhāl.*

Soldier ਸਪਾਹੀ *sapāhī.*

Spear (f) ਬਰਛੀ *barchhī.*

Sword (f) ਤਲਵਾਰ *talwār.*

Target practice (f) ਚਾਂਦ ਮਾਰੀ *chāndmārī.*

Tent ਤੰਬੂ *tanbū.*

Transport (f) ਭਾਰਬਰਦਾਰੀ *bhār bardārī.*

Troop ਤੁਰਪ *turap.*

Turban { large ਸਾਫਾ *sāfā.*
small (f) ਪੱਗ *pagg.*

Uniform (f) ਬਰਦੀ *bardī.*

Valley (f) ਘਾਟੀ *ghāṭī.*

Victory (f) ਫਤੇ, ਜੈ *phate, jai.*

War (f) ਲੜਾਈ *laṛāī.*

Wallet (f) ਖੁਰਜੀਨ *khurjīṇ.*

Warn (to) ਜਤਾਉਣਾਂ *jatāuṇā.*

Water-bottle ਲੋਟਾ *loṭā.*

Warrior ਸੂਰਮਾ *sūrmā.*

Witness ਉਗਾਹ *ugāh.*

Civil Engineering Words.

Account ਲੇਖਾ *lekhā.*

Account book (f) ਹਿਸਾਬ ਦੀ ਕਿਤਾਬ *hisāb dī kitāb.*

Adjust (to) ਠੀਕ ਕਰਨਾ *ṭhīk karnā.*

Advance of money } (f) ਅਗੇਤ੍ਰੀ ਤਲਬ *agetrī talab.*

Agreement ਕਰਾਰ *karār.*

Arch ਮਹਰਾਬ *mahrāb.*

Axe (f) ਕੁਹਾੜੀ *kuhāṛī.*

Badge (f) ਚਪੜਾਸ *chapṛās.*

Bamboo ਵਾਂਸ *wāṅs.*

Bamboo framed work on which tiles or thatch are laid. } ਠਾਠ *ṭhāṭh.*

Bank (of river) ਕੰਢਾ *kanḍhā.*

Bar (a door bolt) (f) ਬਿਲੀ *billī.*

Barrel ਪੀਪਾ *pīpā.*

Basket (small) (f) ਟੋਕਰੀ *ṭokrī.*

Basket (large) ਟੋਕਰਾ *ṭokrā.*

CIVIL ENGINEERING WORDS—continued.

Beam (f) ਕੜੀ *kaṛī.*

Bellows, (small) (f) ਧੌਂਕਨੀ *dhaunkṇī.*

Blacksmith ਲੁਹਾਰ *luhār.*

Bolt (f) ਚਿਟਕਣੀ *chiṭkanī.*

Brick (f) ਇਟ *iṭṭ.*

Brick-bat ਰੋੜਾ *roṛā.*

Brick dust (f) ਸੁਰਖੀ *surkhī.*

„ (sun dried) (f) ਕੱਚੀ ਇੱਟ *kachchī iṭṭ*

„ (half burnt) (f) ਪਿੱਲੀ ਇੱਟ *pillī iṭṭ.*

„ (well burnt) (f) ਪੱਕੀ ਇੱਟ *pakkī iṭṭ.*

Brick kiln ਆਵਾ *āwā*

Bridge ਪੁਲ *pul.*

Build (to) ਉਸਾਰਨਾ *usārnā* ਬਨਾਉਣਾ *banāuṇā.*

Building (f) ਹਵੇਲੀ, *hawelī* (m) ਮਕਾਨ *makān.*

Bungalow ਬੰਗਲਾ *banglā.*

Canal ਨਹਿਰ (F) *nahir.*

Carpenter ਤ੍ਰਖਾਣ *tarkhān.*

Ceiling ਛਤ ਬੰਦੀ *chhat bandī.*

Cement ਮਸਾਲਾ *masālā.*

Chain ਜੰਜੀਰ *janjīr.*

Door ਬੂਹਾ *būhā.*

Door (frame) (f) ਚੁਕਾਠ *chukāṭh.*

Earth-work ਮਿੱਟੀ ਦਾ ਕੰਮ *miṭṭī dā kanm.*

Excavation (f) ਖੁਦਾਈ *khudāī.*

Foundation (f) ਨੀਂਹ *nīnh.*

Glue (f) ਸੁਰੇਸ਼ *suresh.*

Height (f) ਉਚਾਈ *uchāī.*

Hinge ਕਬਜਾ *kabjā*

Instrument ਹਥਿਆਰ *hathiār.*

Iron ਲੋਹਾ *lohā.*

Labourer ਮਜੂਰ *majūr.*

Ladder (f) ਪੌੜੀ *pauṛī.*

Level ਬਰਾਬਰ *brābar.*

Lime ਚੂਨਾ *chūnā.*

„ (quick) ਕੱਚਾ ਚੂਨਾ *kachchā chūnā.*

„ (slackened) ਬੁਝਿਆ ਹੋਇਆ ਚੂਨ *bujhiā hoiā chūnā.*

Mallet (f) ਮੁੰਗਲੀ *munglī.*

Mat (f) ਸਫ, *saph* ਫੂੜੀ *phūṛī.*

Measure (to) ਨਾਪਣਾ, *nāpṇā.* ਮਿਣਨਾ *minṇā.*

Mark ਨਿਸ਼ਾਨ *nishān.*

Plan ਨਕਸ਼ਾ *nakshā.*

Plank ਤਖਤਾ *takhtā.*

Plinth (f) ਕੁਰਸੀ *kursī.*

Pocket book ਖੀਸੇ ਦੀ ਕਤਾਬ *khīse dī katāb.*

Rafter (f) ਕੜੀ *kaṛī.*

Rammer ਦੁਰਮਟ *durmat.*

Reservoir ਹੌਜ *hauj.*

CIVIL ENGINEERING WORDS—concluded.

Roof (f) ਛੱਤ *chhatt.*

„ truss (f) ਕੈਂਚੀ *kainchī.*

Room ਕਮਰਾ, *kamrā* (f) ਕੋਠੜੀ *kothṛī.*

Root up (to) ਉਖਾੜਨਾ *ukhāṛnā*

Rope ਰੱਸਾ, *rassā* (f) ਰੱਸੀ *rassī.*

Sand (f) ਰੇਤ *ret.*

Sand-paper ਰੇਗਮਾਲ *regmāl.*

Saw (f) ਆਰੀ *ārī.*

Screw ਪੇਚ *pech.*

Scaffold (f) ਮਚਾਨ *machān*

Sketch ਨਕਸ਼ਾ *nakshā,*

Spear (f) ਬਰਛੀ *barchhī.*

Spike (f) ਮੇਖ *mekh.*

Tape ਫੀਤਾ *phītā.*

Tile ਖਪਰਾ *khaprā.*

Wall (f) ਕੰਧ *kandh.*

White-wash (f) ਕਲੀ *kalī.*

Window (f) ਖਿੜਕੀ *khiṛkī.*

Medical.

PARTS OF BODY.

Ankle ਗਿੱਟਾ *giṭṭā.*

Arm (f) ਬਾਂਹ *banh.*

Armpit (f) ਕੱਛ *kachhchh.*

Arm (upper) ਡੌਲਾ *daulā.*

Back (f) ਪਿਠ *piṭh.*

Back bone (f) ਕਮਰੋੜ *kamroṛ.*

Beard (f) ਦਾੜ੍ਹੀ *dāṛhī.*

Belly ਢਿਡ *ḍhiḍ.*

Blood ਲਹੂ *lahū.*

Bone (f) ਹੱਡੀ *haḍḍī.*

Brain ਮਗਜ *magaj.*

Calf (f) ਪਿੱਲੀ *pillī.*

Cheek (f) ਗੱਲ੍ਹ *gallah.*

Chest (f) ਛਾਤੀ *chhātī.*

Chin (f) ਠੋਡੀ *ṭhoḍī.*

Ear ਕਨ *kan.*

Elbow (f) ਅੜਕ *aṛak.*

Eye (f) ਅੱਖ *akkh.*

Eyeball ਡੇਲਾ *ḍelā.*

Eye brows (f) ਭਵਾਂ *bhawān.*

Eye lashes (f) ਝਿਮਣੀਆਂ *jhimnīān.*

Face ਮੂੰਹ, *mūnh* ਚੇਹਰਾ *chehrā.*

MEDICAL—continued.

Finger (f) ਉਂਗਲੀ *uṅglī*

do. (little) (f) ਚੀਚੀ *chīchī*.

Flesh ਮਾਸ *mās*.

Foot ਪੈਰ *pair*.

Forehead ਮੱਥਾ *maththā*.

Grinder (molar) (f) ਦਾੜ੍ਹ *dāṛh*.

Gum ਮਸੂੜ੍ਹਾ *masūṛhā*.

Hand ਹੱਥ *haththa*.

Hair ਵਾਲ *wāl*.

Head ਸਿਰ *sir*.

Heart ਦਿਲ *dil*.

Heel (f) ਅੱਡੀ *aḍḍī*.

Hip ਕੂਲਾ *kūlā*.

Joint ਜੋੜ *joṛ*.

Kidney ਗੁਰਦਾ *gurdā*.

Knee ਗੋਡਾ *goḍā*.

Leg (f) ਲੱਤ *latt*.

Lip ਹੋਠ *hoṭh*.

Liver ਕਲੇਜਾ *kalejā*.

Loin (m) ਲੱਕ, *lakk* (f) ਕਮਰ *kamar*.

Lung ਫੇਫੜਾ *phephṛā*.

Mouth ਮੂੰਹ *mūṅh*.

Moustaches (f) ਮੁੱਛਾਂ *muchhāṅ*.

Nail ਨੌਂਹ *naunh*.

Navel (f) ਧੁੱਨੀ *dhunnī*.

Neck (f) ਗਿੱਚੀ *gichchī* ਧੌਣ *dhauṇ*.

Nose ਨੱਕ *ṇakk*.

Nostril (f) ਨਾਸ *nas*.

Palm (f) ਹਥ ਦੀ ਤਲੀ *hath dī talī*.

Pulse (f) ਨਾੜੀ, *nāṛī* ਨਬਜ *nabaj*.

Rib (f) ਪਸਲੀ *paslī*.

Shoulder ਮੋਹਢਾ *mohḍhā*.

Side (f) ਵੱਖੀ *wakhkhī*.

Skull (f) ਖੋਪਰੀ *khoprī*.

Sole (f) ਪੈਰਦੀ ਤਲੀ *pair dī talī*.

Stomach ਮੇਹਦਾ *mehdā*.

Teeth ਦੰਦ *dand*.

Tendon (f) ਨਾੜ *nāṛ*.

Thigh ਪੱਟ *paṭṭ*.

Throat ਗਲਾ *galā* ਸੰਘ *saṅgh*.

Thumb ਅੰਗੂਠਾ *aṅgūṭhā*.

Toe (f) ਪੈਰ ਦੀ ਉਂਗਲੀ *pair dī uṅglī*.

Tongue. (f) ਜੀਭ *jībh*.

Wrist (f) ਬੀਣੀ *bīṇī*.

Medicines.

Acacia Gum (f) ਕਿੱਕਰ ਦੀ ਗੂੰਦ *kikkar dī gūṅd.*

Aconite ਮਿੱਠਾ ਤੇਲੀਆ *miṭṭhā telīā.*

Aloes ਮੁਸੱਬਰ *musabbar.*

Assafœtida (f) ਹਿੰਗ *hiṅg.*

Alum (f) ਫਟਕੜੀ *phaṭkaṛī.*

Ammonia Chloride ਨਸਾਦਰ *ṇasādar.*

Antimony ਸੁਰਮਾ *surmā.*

Areca nut (f) ਸੁਪਾਰੀ *supārī.*

Arsenic Alba ਚਿੱਟਾ ਸੰਖੀਆ *chiṭṭā saṅkhīā.*

Benzoin. ਲੋਬਾਨ *lobāṇ.*

Bitter apple. ਤੁੰਮਾ *tummā.*

Borax. ਸੁਹਾਗਾ *suhāgā.*

Calomel. ਰਸ ਕਪੂਰ *ras kapūr.*

Camphor ਮੁਸ਼ਕ ਕਪੂਰ *mushak kapūr.*

Cannabis Indica ਗਾਂਜਾ *gāṅjā.*

Cardamum (f) ਲਾਚੀ *lāchī.*

Clov's ਲੌਂਗ *lauṅg.*

Catacheu ਕੱਥਾ *kaththā.*

Chalk (f) ਪਾਂਡੋ *pāṅḍo.*

Coriander (f) ਧਣੀਆਂ *dhaṇīāṅ.*

Cucumber. ਖੀਰਾ *khīrā.*

Croton seed ਜਮਾਲ ਗੋਟਾ *jamāl goṭā.*

Datura ਧਤੂਰਾ *dhatūrā.*

Fig (f) ਹਜੀਰ *hajīr.*

Fennel Fruit ਸੋਏ *soe.*

Honey (f) ਸ਼ਹਿਦ *shahid.*

Lemon ਨਿੰਬੂ *ṇiṅbū.*

Lime ਚੂਨਾ *chūṇā.*

Lime juice ਨਿੰਬੂ ਦਾ ਅਰਕ *ṇiṅbū dā arak.*

Linseed (f) ਅਲਸੀ *alsī.*

Mace (f) ਜਲਵਤ੍ਰੀ *jalwatrī.*

Mori or Melboury } ਤੂਤ ਬਦਾਨਾ *tūt badāṇā.*

Mustard (f) ਰਾਈ *rāī.*

Musk (f) ਕਸਤੂਰੀ *kastūrī.*

Nux vomica ਕੁਚਲਾ *kuchlā.*

Nutmeg ਜੈਫਲ *jaiphal.*

Poppy head ਪੋਸਤ *post.*

Prune ਆਲੂਬੁਖਾਰਾ *ālū bukhārā.*

Sarsaparilla ਉਸ਼ਬਾ *ushbā.*

Sulphur (f) ਗੰਧਕ *gaṅdhak.*

Tamarind ਇੰਬਲੀ *iṅblī.*

Turpentine ਤਾਰਪੀਨ *tārpīṇ.*

Vinegar. ਸਿਰਕਾ *sirkā.*

Wax (f) ਮੋਮ *mom.*

Yolk of Egg (f) ਆਂਡੇ ਦੀ ਜ਼ਰਦੀ *āṅḍe dī jardī.*)

Diseases.

Abortion ਕੱਚਾ ਨਿਕਲਜਾਨਾ *kachchā ṇikul jāṇā.*

Abscess ਫੋੜਾ *phoṛā.*

Acne ਥਿੱਮ *thimm.*

Ache (f) ਪੀੜ *pīṛ.*

Ague ਕਾਂਬੇ ਦਾ ਤਪ *kāṅbe dā tap.*

Ascites ਜਲੌਂਧਰ *jalaudhar.*

Blind ਅੰਨ੍ਹਾ *aṇṇhā.*

Bald ਗੰਜਾ *gaṅjā.*

Bubo (f) ਵੱਧ *wadhdh.*

Cataract ਮੋਤੀਆ ਬਿੰਦ *motīā biṅd.*

Catarrh ਜੁਖਾਮ *jukhām.*

Cut ਚੀਰ *chīr.*

Consumption ਤਪ ਦਿੱਕ *tap dikk.*

Cough (f) ਖੰਘ *khaṅgh.*

Cholera ਹੈਜਾ *haijā.*

Coma (f) ਬਿਹੋਸ਼ੀ *bihoshī.*

Deaf ਬੋਲਾ *bolā.*

Dumb ਗੂੰਗਾ *guṅgā.*

Diarrhœa. ਦਸਤ *dast.*

Dysentery ਪੇਚਸ਼, *pechash* ਮਰੋੜ *maroṛ*

Dyspepsia (f) ਬਦ ਹਜਮੀ *bad hajmī.*

Fever ਤਪ *tap.*

Fever (enteric) ਬਰੱਬਰ ਦਾ ਤਪ *barabbar dā tap.*

Gout ਗੰਠੀਆ *gaṅṭhīā.*

Gonorrhœa ਸੁਜਾਖ *sujākh.*

Headache (f) ਸਿਰਪੀੜ *sir pīṛ*

Heart disease (f) ਦਿਲ ਦੀ ਬਮਾਰੀ *dil dī bamārī.*

Hemiplegia ਅਧਰੰਗ *adhraṅg.*

Itch (f) ਖੁਰਕ *khurk.*

Leprosy ਕੋਹੜ *kohṛ.*

Lumbago (f) ਕਮਰ ਦੀ ਪੀੜ *kamr dī pīṛ.*

Lame ਲੰਙਾ *laṅṅgā.*

Liver complaint (f) ਕਲੇਜੇ ਦੀ ਪੀੜ *kaleje dī pīṛ.*

Onychia ਚੰਦਰਾ *chaṅdrā.*

Piles (f) ਬਵਾਸੀਰ *bawāsīr.*

Prickly heat (f) ਪਿੱਤ *pitt.*

Pimple (f) ਫਿੰਮਣੀ *phiṅmnī.*

Rheumatism ਵਾਈ *wāī.*

Small-pox (f) ਮਾਤਾ *mātā.*

Spermatorhœa ਮਣੀ ਝੜਨਾ *manī jhaṛṇā*

Spermatote (sting) ਡੰਗ *ḍaṅg*

Swelling (f) ਸੋਜ *soj.*

Wound ਜਖਮ, *jakham* ਘਾਓ *ghāo.*

Worm ਕੀੜਾ *kīṛā.*

Judicial Words.

Adjure, (to) ਸੌਂਹ ਦੇਣੀ *saunh denī.*

Agreement (f) ਲਿਖਤ *likhat.*

Allowance ਭੱਤਾ *bhattā.*

Altercation ਝਗੜਾ *jhagṛā.*

Assault (f) ਮਾਰਕੁੱਟ *mār kuṭṭ.*

Borrow (to) ਹੁਦਾਰ ਲੈਣਾ *hudār laiṇā.*

Bribe (f) ਵੱਢੀ *waḍhḍhī.*

Charge ਦੋਸ਼ *dosh.*

Claim ਦਾਵਾ *dāwā.*

Complaint (f) ਫਰਿਆਦ, *phriād.* ਨਾਲਸ਼ *ṇālash.*

Court (f) ਕਚਹਰੀ *kachahrī.*

Criminal (f) ਫੌਜਦਾਰੀ *phaujdārī.*

Defence ਬਚਾ *bachā.*

Defendant ਮੁਦੈਲਾ *mudailā.*

Evidence (f) ਉਗਾਹੀ *ugāhī.*

Pleader ਵਕੀਲ *wakīl.*

Plunder (f) ਲੁੱਟ *luṭṭ.*

Prosecute (to) ਪਕੜ ਲੈਣਾ *pakaṛ laiṇā.*

Rigorous Imprisonment ਸਖਤ ਕੈਦ *sakhat kaid.*

Fetters (f) ਬੇੜੀਆਂ *beṛīāṅ.*

Fine ਜਰਮਾਨਾ, *jarmāṇā* ਡੱਨ *ḍaṇṇ.*

Forgery (f) ਜਾਲਸਾਜੀ *jālsājī.*

Gambling ਜੂਆ *jūā.*

Handcuffs (f) ਹਥਕੜੀਆਂ *hathkaṛīāṅ.*

Inquire into (to) ਵਿਚਾਰਕਰਨਾ *wichār karṇā.*

Jury (f) ਪਚੈਤ *pachait.*

Justice ਨਿਆਂ *ṇiāṅ.*

Law ਕਨੂਨ *kaṇūṇ.*

Law suit ਮੁਕਦਮਾ *mukadmā.*

Mortgage (to) ਗਹਣੇ ਧਰਨਾ *gahne dharṇā*

Murder (to) ਖੂਨਕਰਨਾ *khūṇ karṇā.*

Oath (f) ਸੌਂਹ *saunh.*

Ornament ਗਹਣਾ *gahṇā.*

Perjury (f) ਝੂਠੀਸੌਂਹ *jhūṭhī saunh.*

Petition ਅਰਜੀ *arjī.*

Robbery ਧਾੜਾ *dhāṛā.*

Thief ਚੋਰ *chor.*

Theft (f) ਚੋਰੀ *chorī.*

Witness ਉਗਾਹ *ugāh.*

Persian wheel.

ਹਰਟ, ਹਲਟ	*hart, halt*	persian wheel.
ਢੋਲ	*ḍhol*	upper. „
ਚੁਹੱਕਲੀ	*chuhakklī*	(f) lower „
ਤਕਲਾ	*taklā*	axis of upper wheel.
ਕਾਂਢਣ	*kāṅjan*	crossbeam.
ਕੁੱਤਾ	*kuttā*	stop-cock.
ਪੰਜਾਲੀ	*paṅjālī*	(f) yoke.
ਬੈੜ	*baiṛ*	water wheel.
ਮਾਲ੍ਹ	*mālh*	(f) rope.
ਟਿੰਡ	*ṭiṅḍ*	(f) earthen water pot.
ਨਸਾਰ	*ṇasār*	(f) wooden trough.
ਗਾਹਦੀ	*gāhdī*	(f) driving seat.
ਆਡ	*āḍ*	(f) water channel.
ਪੁਰਾਣੀ	*purāṇī*	(f) driving whip.

Plough.

ਹੱਲ	*hall*	plough.
ਫਾਲਾ	*phālā*	colter of a plough.
ਪੰਜਾਲੀ	*paṅjālī*	(f) yoke.
ਕੁੜ	*kuṛ*	body of plough.
ਸੁਹਾਗਾ	*suhāgā*	leveller.
ਹੱਥਾ	*haththā*	(m) handle.
ਹੱਥੀ	*haththī*	(f) handle.

Land.

ਚਾਹੀ	*chāhī*	(f) land watered by well.
ਨਹਿਰੀ	*ṇahirī*	(f) land watred by canal.
ਬਰਾਨੀ ਮਾਰੂ	*barāṇī māru*	(f) depending upon rain.
ਬੇਟ	*beṭ*	low land near the river.
ਟਿੱਬਾ	*ṭibbā*	high land.
ਬੰਜਰ	*banjar*	barren or waste land.
ਰੋਹੀ	*rohī*	(f) sandy land.
ਨੁਆਣ	*ṇuāṇ*	low land.
ਰੜਾ	*raṛā*	level ground.
ਰੱਖ	*rakhkh*	(f) land reserved by Government
ਬੀੜ	*bīṛ*	(f) meadow.

Agriculture.

ਹਾਲੀ	*hālī*	ploughman.
ਪੈਲੀ	*pailī*	(f) a field.
ਕਿਯਾਰਾ	*kiyārā*	a part of a field.
ਪੱਠੇ	*paṭhṭhe*	fodder.
ਮੂਸਲ	*mūsal*	a stack of wheat chaff.
ਗਾਹੁਣਾ	*gāhuṇā*	to thresh.
ਤੂੜੀ	*tūṛī*	(f) chaff.
ਪਿੜ	*piṛ*	a place where grain [is stacked up or threshing floor.
ਗਾਹੀ	*gāhī*	(f) threshing.
ਖੇਤ	*khet*	field.
ਬਿਆਈ	*biāī*	(f) sowing.
ਬੀਜਣਾ	*bījṇā*	to sow.
ਵਾਹੀ	*wāhī*	(f) The profession of cultivator, or ploughing land.
ਵਹਾਈ	*wahāī*	(f) ploughing.
ਵਾਢੀ	*wāḍhī*	(f) cutting.
ਬੀ	*bī*	seed.
ਹੋਲਾਂ	*holāṅ*	(f) roasted gram.
ਡੱਡੇ	*ḍaḍḍe*	gram (with husk).
ਖੂਹ	*khūh*	well.
ਹਲਟ	*halṭ*	persian wheel..
ਗੱਨਾ	*gaṇṇā*	sugar cane.
ਟੀਂਡਾ	*ṭīṅḍā*	cotton bud.
ਸਿੱਟਾ	*siṭṭā*	ear of wheat, &c.
ਛੱਲੀ	*chhallī*	(f) ear of Indian-corn.
ਵੱਟ	*waṭṭ*	(f) boundary of field.
ਮਣਾ	*maṇā*	a place of observation.
ਭਰੀ	*bharī*	(f) a load of grass, &c.
ਪੂਲਾ	*pūlā*	small load of grass &c.
ਫਸਲ	*ph asal*	(f) crop.
ਪੱਕਣਾ	*pakkṇā*	to ripen.
ਵਢਣਾ	*waḍhṇā*	to reap.
ਗੁਡਿਹਾਲ	*guḍihāl*	a place where [sugar is made.
ਵੇਲਣਾ	*welṇā*	sugar mill.
ਖੋਰੀ	*khorī*	(f) dry leaves of sugar cane.
ਚੜਸ	*charas*	} leathern bucket for irrigation.
ਚੜਸਾ	*charsā*	
ਸਿੰਜਣਾ	*sinjṇā*	to water,
ਖਾਤ	*khāt*	(f) manure.
ਜੋਗ	*jog*	(f) pair of bullocks.
ਭਿਆਲੀ	*bhiālī*	(f) partnership.
ਰੇਹ *reh* / ਖਾਤ *khāt* } ਪਾਉਣਾ	*pāuṇā*,	to manure.
ਮਾਲ੍ਹ	*māl̤h*	(f) rope of persian wheal
ਟਿੰਡ	*ṭiṅḍ*	(f) earthen pot „ „

AGRICULTURE—*concluded.*

ਹਿੱਸਾ	*hissā*	part.
ਬਿਗਾਹ	*bigāh*	120 feet square.
ਵਾਰੀ	*wārī*	(f) turn.
ਜੋਣਾ	*joṇā*	to yoke.
ਸੇਪੀ	*sepī*	a kind of servant who does not get monthly wages but gets so much on cutting the crops and so much on births, marriages, &c.
ਕਿਆਰਾ	*kiārā*	part of a field.
ਕਿਆਰਾ ਮੋੜਨਾ	*kiārā muṛṇā*	to conduct water from one part of a field to another.
ਫਲਾ	*phalā*	a square wooden frame slightly loaded.
ਮੇਹੜ	*mehaṛ*	the oxen of a threshing floor; the rope by which the line of oxen treading out the corn are tied.
ਸੈਂਡ	*saiṅḍ*	a mixture of wheat and chaff, &c.
ਖਲਵਾੜਾ	*khalwāṛā*	a stock of grains.
ਮੂਸਲ	*mūsal*	stack of chaff.
ਨਾੜ	*nāṛ*	(f) wheat straw.
ਬੋਕਾ	*bokā*	leathern bucket.

Cookery.

ਦੇਚਕਾ	*dechkā*	a brass cooking vessel.
ਤਵਾ	*tawā*	an iron pan for cooking bread.
ਕੜਾਹੀ	*kaṛāhī*	(f) a frying pan.
ਕੜਛੀ	*kaṛchhī*	(f) cooking spoon.
ਭਾਂਡੇ	*bhāṅḍe*	cooking pots.
ਥਾਲੀ	*thālī*	(f) a small brass or metal dish.
ਛੰਨਾ	*chhannā*	a metal drinking cup.
ਢੱਕਣ	*ḍhakkan*	(f) a cover.
ਕੌਲ	*kaul*	a small metal drinking cup.
ਭਬਕਾ	*bhabkā*	a small metal drinking glass.
ਤਾਸੀ	*tāsī*	(f) small metal dish.
ਦੇਚਕੀ	*dechkī*	(f) a small brass cooking vessel.
ਗਾਗਰ	*gāgar*	(f) a large brass pitcher.
ਗਲਾਸ	*galās*	(f) tumbler.
ਘੜਾ	*ghaṛā*	an earthen-pitcher.
ਚੁਲ੍ਹਾ	*chulhā*	fire-place.
ਲੋਹ	*loh*	(f) a large pan used for cooking bread.
ਥਾਲੀ	*thālī*	(f) a metal plate.
ਚੁਮਟਾ	*chumṭā*	(m) tongs.

Punjabi Instruments.

ਚਰਖਾ	*charkhā*	spinning wheel.	ਦੌਰੀ	*dauri*	f) a small earthen
ਵੇਲਣਾ	*welnā*	sugar mill.	ਕੂੰਡੀ	*kūṅḍī*	[or stone mortar.
ਉਖਲੀ	*ukhlī*	(f) mortar.	ਘੋਟਣਾ	*ghoṭnā*	a small wooden
ਚੱਕੀ	*chakkī*	(f) a corn mill.	ਡੰਡਾ	*ḍaṅḍā*	pestle.
ਬੁਹਾਰੀ ਬੌਕਰ	*buhārī baukar*	(f) a brush.	ਚਾਟੀ	*chāṭī*	(f) a large earthern [vessel.
ਛੱਜ	*chhajj*	a winnowing instrument.	ਮਧਾਣੀ	*madhāṇī*	(f) churning staff.
			ਤਕੜੀ	*takṛī*	(f) scale.

Some Important words referring to milk.

ਦੁਧ	*dudh*	milk.	ਮੱਖਣ,	*makhkhan*	butter.
ਦੁਧ ਕਾੜ੍ਹਨਾ	*dudh kāṛhṇā,*	to boil milk.	ਮਖਣੀ	*makhnī*	butter.
ਧਾਰ ਕਢਣਾ	*dhār kaḍhnā*	to milk.	ਅਧਰਿੜਕਿਆ	*adhriṛkiā*	half churned.
ਦਹੀਂ	*dahīṅ*	(f) curd.	ਪਨੀਰ	*panīr*	cheese.
ਦਹੀਂ ਜਮਾਉਣਾਂ	*dahīṅ jamāunā*	to curd.	ਮਲਾਈ	*malāī*	(f) cream.
ਦਹੀਂ ਰਿੜਕਣਾ	*dahiṅ riṛknā,*	to churn.	ਮਧਾਣੀ	*madhāṇī*	(f) a churn.
ਲੱਸੀ, ਛਾਹ	*lassī chhāh*	(f) butter milk.	ਰਿੜਕਨਾ	*riṛknā*	to churn.

Winter Crops.

ਹਾੜ੍ਹੀ	*hāṛī*	(f) winter crops.	ਬੇਰੜਾ	*berṛā*	gram and wheat mixed
ਛੋਲੇ	*chhole*	gram.	ਸੇਂਜੀ	*senjī*	(f) kind of grass.
ਕਾਬਲੀ ਛੋਲੇ	*kāblī chhole*	white gram.	ਖਰਬੂਜਾ	*kharbūjā*	melon.
ਕਣਕ	*kanak*	(f) wheat.	ਹਦਵਾਣਾ	*hadwāṇā,*	water melon.
ਜੌਂ	*jauṅ*	barley.	ਗੰਡਾ,	*gaṅḍā.*	onion.
ਸਰੋਂ	*saroṅ*	(f) oil seed.	ਰੁੱਪਾ	*ruppā.*	onion.
			ਬਤਾਊਂ	*batāūṅ*	brinjals.

* *Note* :—There are two Crops in the Punjab, one is ਹਾੜ੍ਹੀ *hāṛī,* being cut about the month of ਹਾੜ *hāṛ,* and the second is ਸੌਣੀ *saunī,* sown in the month of ਸੌਣ.

Summer Crops.

ਸੌਣੀ	*saunī*	(f) summer crops
ਜੁਆਰ	*juār*	(f) Indian-corn.
ਚਰੀ	*charī*	(f) millet.
ਮੋਠ	*moṭh*	a kind of dal.
ਮਾਂਹ	*māṅh*	a kind of dal.
ਕਪਾਹ	*kapāh*	(f) cotton.
ਕਮਾਦ	*kamād*	sugar cane (field)
ਗੱਨਾ	*gaṇṇā*	sugar cane.
ਮੂਲੀ	*mūlī*	(f) radish.
ਗਾਜਰ	*gājar*	(f) carrot.
ਗੋਂਗਲੂ	*goṅglū*	turnip.
ਬਾਜਰਾ	*bājrā*	a kind of grain
ਝੋਨਾ	*jhoṇā*	paddy.

Cattle.

ਵੱਗ	*wagg*	a herd of cattle.
ਇੱਜੜ	*ijjaṛ*	a flock of goats and sheep.
ਡੰਗਰ	*ḍaṅgar*	cattle.
ਢੱਗਾ	*ḍhaggā*	bullock.
ਪਸੂ	*pasū*	beast.
ਝੋਟਾ, *jhoṭā*. ਮਹਿਆਂ	*mahiāṅ*	male buffalo.
ਵਛਾ	*wachhā*	a young calf.
ਗਾਂ, *gāṅ*. ਗਊ	*gaū*	(f) cow.
ਲਵੇਰੀ	*lawerī*	(f) milch cow.
ਭੇਡ	*bheḍ*	(f) sheep.
ਲੇਲਾ	*lelā*	lamb.
ਪਠੋਰਾ	*paṭhorā*	a kid.
ਮਹੀਂ, *mahīṅ*. ਮੰਝ	*manjh*,	(f) female buffalo.
ਕੱਟਾ	*kaṭṭā*	a young buffalo.
ਕੱਟੀ, *kaṭṭī*. ਝੋਟੀ	*jhoṭī*,	(f) female do.
ਬੌਲਦ, *bauld* ਬਲਦ	*bald*,	an ox.
ਸਾਨ੍ਹ	*sāṇh*,	bull kept for breeding.
ਜਾਲੀ	*jālī*	a shepherd.
ਵਾਗੀ	*wāgī*	a cowherd.
ਊਠ	*ūṭh*	camel.
ਡਾਚੀ	*ḍāchī*	female camel.
ਖੁਰਲੀ	*khurlī*	manger.
ਖੋਤਾ	*khotā*	an ass.

PART II

LESSON I.

NOUNS.

Masculine.			Feminine.		
ਮਨੁਖ	*manukh*	man.	ਤੀਮੀ	*tīmī*	woman.
ਪਿਓ	*pio*	father.	ਮਾਂ	*māṅ*	mother.
ਭਰਾ	*bharā*	brother.	ਭੈਣ	*bhain*	sister.
ਗਭਰੂ	*gabhrū*	husband.	ਵਹੁਟੀ	*wahuṭī*	wife.
ਚਾਚਾ	*chāchā*.	uncle.	ਚਾਚੀ	*chāchī*	aunt.
ਮੁੰਡਾ	*muṅḍā*	boy.	ਕੁੜੀ	*kuṛī*	girl.
ਪੁਤ੍ਰ	*puttr*	son.	ਧੀ	*dhī*	daughter.
ਭਤੀਜਾ	*bhatījā*	nephew.	ਭਤੀਜੀ	*bhatījī*	niece.

ADJECTIVES.

ਸੋਹਣਾ	*sohṇā*	handsome.	ਕੋਝਾ	*kojhā*	ugly.
ਉੱਚਾ	*uchchā*	high.	ਨੀਵਾਂ	*nīwāṅ*	low.
ਕਾਣਾ	*kāṇā*	one-eyed.	ਅੰਨ੍ਹਾਂ	*annhāṅ*	blind.
ਤੰਗ	*taṅg*	tight.	ਢਿੱਲਾ	*ḍhillā*	loose.

VERBS.

ਆਉਣਾ	*āuṇā*	to come.	ਜਾਣਾ	*jāṇā*	to go.
ਬੈਠਣਾ	*baiṭhṇā*	to sit.	ਖੜਾ ਹੋਣਾ	*khaṛā hoṇā*,	to stand.
ਪੜ੍ਹਨਾ	*paṛhṇā*	to read.	ਲਿਖਣਾ	*likhṇā*	to write.
ਲੈਣਾ	*laiṇā*	to take.	ਦੇਣਾ	*deṇā*	to give.

Examples.

ਮਨੁੱਖ ਆਉਂਦਾ ਹੈ — *manukh āuṅdā hai*, The man comes.

ਮੁੰਡਾ ਪੜ੍ਹਦਾ ਸੀ — *muṅḍā paṛhdā sī*, The boy was reading.

ਓਹ ਕੁੜੀ ਸੋਹਣੀ ਹੈ — *oh kuṛī sohṇī hai,* That girl is handsome.

ਮੇਰਾ ਪਿਉ ਅੰਨ੍ਹਾਂ ਮਨੁਖ ਸੀ — *merā pio aṇṇhāṅ manukh sī,* My father was a blind man.

ਉਸਦਾ ਗਭਰੂ ਲਿਖਦਾ ਸੀ — *usdā gabhrū likhdā sī,* Her husband was writing.

ਮੇਰੀ ਵਹੁਟੀ ਨਿਆਣੀ ਤੀਮੀ ਹੈ — *merī wahuṭī ṇiānī tīmī hai,* My wife is an ignorant woman.

ਉਸਦੀ ਧੀ ਦੌੜਦੀ ਹੈ — *usdī dhī dauṛdī hai,* His daughter is running.

ਤੁਹਾਡਾ ਚਾਚਾ ਸਿਆਨਾ ਮਨੁੱਖ ਹੈ — *tuhāḍā chāchā siānā munukh hai,* Your uncle is a wise man.

Translate into Punjābī.

That boy is my son. She is my sister's daughter. That woman is very ugly. His uncle will come to-morrow. That girl was handsome. He is reading my book His niece will sit here. My mother is one- eyed.

Note.—For English words not given, please see English Punjábi Vocabulary, new edition and for Punjábi words see the Vocabulary at the end.

Translate into English.

ਉਸਦਾ ਪੁਤ੍ਰ ਲਾਹੌਰ ਨੂੰ ਗਿਆ ਹੈ। ਓਹ ਮੁੰਡਾ ਜੁਆਨ ਹੈ। ਮੇਰਾ ਪਿਓ ਕੱਲ ਦਿੱਲੀ ਨੂੰ ਜਾਵੇਗਾ। ਸਾਡਾ ਚਾਚਾ ਕਲ ਲਾਹੌਰੋਂ ਆਵੇਗਾ। ਜਦ ਮੈਂ ਉਥੇ ਗਿਆ ਤੀਮੀ ਲਿਖਦੀ ਸੀ। ਤੇਰੀ ਚਾਚੀ ਸਿਆਨੀ ਤੀਮੀ ਹੈ। ਮੇਰਾ ਭਤੀਜਾ ਪੋਥੀ ਦੇਂਦਾ ਹੈ॥ ਉਸਦਾ ਪਿਉ ਬੁਢਾ ਮਨੁੱਖ ਹੈ॥

LESSON II.

NOUNS.

Masculine			Feminine		
ਘੋੜਾ	*ghoṛā*	a horse.	ਘੋੜੀ	*ghoṛī*	a mare.
ਖਚਰਾ	*khachrā*	a mule.	ਖੱਚਰ	*khachchar*	a mule. (fem.)

ਬੈਲ	*bail*	an ox.	ਗਊ	*gaū*	cow.
ਕੁੱਤਾ	*kuttā*	a dog.	ਕੁੱਤੀ	*kuttī*	bitch.
ਟੱਟੂ	*ṭaṭṭū*	a pony.	ਬਕਰੀ	*bakrī*	she goat.
ਹਾਥੀ	*hāthī*	an elephant.	ਬਿੱਲੀ	*billī*	cat.
ਊਠ	*ūṭh*	a camel.	ਸਾਂਢਨੀ	*sāṅḍhnī*	dromedary.
ਖੋਤਾ	*khotā*	donkey.	ਭੇਡ	*bheḍ*	sheep.

ADJECTIVES.

ਸਿੱਧਾ	*sidhdhā*	straight.	ਵਿੰਗਾ	*wiṅgā*	crooked.
ਗੁੰਗਾ	*guṅgā*	dumb.	ਬੋਲਾ	*bolā*	deaf.
ਚੁਸਤ	*chust*	active.	ਜਿੱਲ੍ਹਾ	*jillhā*	slow.
ਲੰਮਾ	*lanmā*	long.	ਮਧਰਾ	*madhrā*	short.

VERBS.

ਸੌਣਾ	*saunā*	to sleep.	ਜਾਗਣਾ	*jāgṇā*	to be awake.
ਮਰਨਾ	*marṇā*	to die.	ਜੀਉਣਾ	*jīuṇā*	to live.
ਖਾਣਾ	*khāṇā*	to eat.	ਪੀਣਾ	*pīṇā*	to drink.
ਲੇਟਣਾ	*leṭnā*	to lie down,	ਉਠਣਾ	*uṭhṇā*	to get up.

Examples.

ਮੇਰਾ ਘੋੜਾ ਚੰਗਾ ਹੈ	*merā ghoṛā chaṅgā hai,*	My horse is a good one.
ਓਹ ਕੁੱਤਾ ਭੌਂਕਦਾ ਹੈ	*oh kuttā bhauṅkdā hai,*	That dog is barking.
ਵੱਛਾ ਲੇਟੇਗਾ	*wachchā leṭegā*	The calf will lie down.
ਸਾਰੀਆਂ ਭੇਡਾਂ ਕਾਲੀਆਂ ਹਨ ।	*sāriāṅ bheḍāṅ kālīāṅ haṇ,*	All the sheep are black
ਉਸਦਾ ਬੈਲ ਮਾਂਦਾ ਹੈ ।	*usdā bail māṅdā hai,*	His ox is sick.
ਤੁਹਾਡੀ ਖੱਚਰ ਬਹੁਤ ਮੱਠੀ ਹੈ	*tuhāḍī khachchar bahut maṭhṭhī hai,*	Your mule is very slow.

ਮੇਰੀ ਗਊ ਛੇਤੀ ਆਵੇਗੀ ।	*merī gaū chhetī āwegī,*	My cow will come soon.
ਸਾਂਢਨੀ ਵੱਡੀ ਤੇਜ ਦੌੜਦੀ ਹੈ ॥	*sāṅḍhnī waḍḍī tej dauṛdī hai,*	The dromedary runs very fast.

Translate into Punjābī.

That boy is striking the goat. Is that mule blind? The elephant is a large animal. That girl is very active. Her husband was young and she was old. That old man is deaf and dumb. The pony is drinking water. That bitch is blind.

Translate into English

ਮੇਰਾ ਘੋੜਾ ਚਲਾਕ ਹੈ। ਤੁਸਾਡੀ ਖੱਚਰ ਮੱਠੀ ਹੈ। ਸਾਡੇ ਤਿਨ ਬੈਲ ਮਰ ਗਏ, ਓਹ ਬੁਢਾ ਬੈਲ ਜੀਉਂਦਾ ਹੈ। ਕੱਲ ਤਿਨ ਭੇਡਾਂ ਆਉਣ ਗੀਆਂ। ਇਹ ਬਕਰੀ ਕਾਣੀ ਹੈ ਕਿ ਅਨ੍ਹੀ। ਖੋਤਾ ਲੇਟਦਾ ਹੈ। ਓਹ ਕੁੜੀ ਕੋਝੀ ਹੈ।

LESSON III.

NOUNS.

Masculine.			Feminine.		
ਦੀਵਾ	*dīwā*	lamp.	ਵੱਟੀ	*waṭṭī*	wick.
ਕਾਗਤ	*kāgat*	paper.	ਲਿਖਣ	*likhan*	pen.
ਲਫਾਫਾ	*laphāphā*	envelope.	ਪੋਥੀ	*pothī*	book.
ਸ਼ਾਹੀ ਚੂਸ	*shāhī chūs*	blotting paper.	ਮੇਜ	*mej*	table.
ਕਾਚੂ	*kāchū*	knife.	ਸ਼ਾਈ	*shāī*	ink.
ਕਲਮਦਾਨ	*kalamdān*	pen box.	ਦੁਆਤ	*duāt*	inkstand.
ਸੰਦੂਕ	*sandūk*	box.	ਮੋਹਰ	*mohar*	seal.
ਜੰਦਰਾ	*jandrā*	lock.	ਕੁੰਜੀ	*kunjī*	key.

ADJECTIVES.

ਚੰਗਾ	*changā*	good	ਮੰਦਾ, ਬੁਰਾ	*mandā, burā*	bad.
ਵੱਡਾ	*waḍḍā*	big.	ਛੋਟਾ	*chhoṭā*	little.
ਔਖਾ	*aukhā*	difficult.	ਸੌਖਾ	*saukhā*	easy.
ਸਾਫ	*sāph*	clean.	ਮੈਲਾ	*mailā*	dirty.

VERBS.

ਬਨ੍ਹਨਾ	*banhnā*	to fasten.	ਢਿੱਲਾ ਕਰਨਾ	*dhillā karnā*,	to loose.
ਲਭਨਾ	*labhnā*	to find.	ਗੁਆਉਨਾ	*guāuṇā*	to lose.
ਉੱਚਾ ਕਰਨਾ	*uchchā karnā*	to raise.	ਨੀਵਾਂ ਕਰਨਾ	*nīwān karnā*	to lower.
ਸੋਚਨਾ	*sochnā*	to think.	ਵੇਖਨਾ	*wekhnā*.	to see.

Examples.

ਤੂੰ ਥੋੜਾ ਜਿਹਾ ਸ਼ਾਹੀ ਚੂਸ ਦਾ ਟੁਕੜਾ ਲਿਆਵੇਂਗਾ *tūṅ thoṛā jihā shāhī chūs dā ṭukṛā liyāwengā*, Will you bring a piece of blotting paper ?

ਜੰਦਰਾ ਮਾਰਕੇ ਕੁੰਜੀ ਮੈਨੂੰ ਦੇਹ *jandrā mār ke kunjī mainūṅ deh*, Lock it up and give me the key.

ਦੁਵਾਤ ਵਿਚ ਕੁਝ ਸ਼ਾਹੀ ਪਾ *duwāt wich kujhjh shāhī pā* Put some ink in the inkstand.

ਮੈਂ ਕਾਚੂ ਨਾਲ ਲਿਖਣ ਘੜੀ *main kāchū nāl likhan ghaṛī*, I sharpened the pen with a pe nknife.

ਓਹ ਵੱਡਾ ਚੰਗਾ ਕੁੱਤਾ ਹੈ *oh waḍḍā changā kuttā hai*, That is a very good dog.

ਮੇਰੀ ਮੋਹਰ ਕਿੱਥੇ ਹੈ *merī mohar kiththe hai*, Where is my seal ?

Translate into Punjābī.

Where is the key of that box ? Where is that big lock ? My son wants a seal. Give him one book. Is that inkstand clean ? The wick of that lamp is very bad. Lower the box on the table. It is easy to raise the lid of that box.

Translate into English

ਇਸ ਦੀਵੇ ਦਾ ਚਾਨਨਾ ਚੰਗਾ ਹੈ। ਉਹ ਪੋਥੀ ਪਹਿਲੀ ਨਾਲੋਂ ਔਖੀ ਹੈ। ਮੇਰੀ ਲਿਖਣ ਟੁੱਟ ਗਈ ਹੈ। ਮੈਂ ਸਾਰੇ ਕਾਗਤ ਮੇਜ਼ ਤੇ ਰਖ ਦੇਵਾਂਗਾ। ਤੇਰਾ ਪੁਤ੍ਰ ਕੇੜ੍ਹੀ ਪੋਥੀ ਪੜ੍ਹਦਾ ਹੈ। ਕਪੜੇ ਸੰਦੂਕ ਵਿਚ ਪਾਕੇ ਜੰਦਰਾ ਮਾਰ ਦੇ। ਕੁੰਜੀ ਖਰਾਬ ਹੋ ਗਈ ਹੈ। ਮੇਰਾ ਜੁਆਈ ਅੰਦਰ ਸੁਤਾ ਪਿਆ ਹੈ।

LESSON IV.

NOUNS.

Masculine.

ਸਪਾਹੀ	*sapāhī*	soldier.
ਰਸਾਲਾ	*rasālā*	cavalry.
ਨੇਜਾ	*nejā*	lance.
ਤੋਪਖਾਨਾ	*topkhānā*	artillery.
ਹਥਿਆਰ	*hathiār*	weapon.
ਭੂਰਾ	*bhūrā*	blanket.
ਤੋਬਰਾ	*tobrā*	nosebag.
ਕਿਲਾ	*kilā*	fort.

Feminine.

ਤੋਪ	*top*	cannon.
ਕਾਠੀ	*kāṭhī*	sa ddle.
ਸੰਗੀਨ	*saṅgīn*	bayonet.
ਕਾਲੀ ਪਲਟਨ	*kālī palṭaṇ*	Native Infantry.
ਲਾਲ ਕੁੜਤੀ	*lāl kuṛtī*	British Infantry.
ਲਗਾਮ	*lagām*	bridle.
ਬਦੂਕ	*badūk*	gun.
ਤਲਵਾਰ	*talwār*	sword.

ADJECTIVES.

ਚਮਕਦਾ	*chamkadā*	bright.
ਖਾਲੀ	*khālī*	empty.
ਨਵਾਂ	*nawāṅ*	new.
ਜੋਰ ਨਾਲ	*jor nāl*	firmly.
ਜੰਗਾਲੀ	*jaṅgālī*	rusty.
ਭਰਿਆ ਹੋਇਆ	*bhariā hoiā*	full.
ਪੁਰਾਨਾ	*purānā*	old.
ਢਿੱਲਾ ਢਿੱਲਾ	*ḍhillā ḍhillā*,	loosely.

VERBS.

ਭਰਨਾ	*bharṇā*	to load (gun.)
ਫੜਨਾ	*pharṇā*	to hold.
ਰਖਨਾ	*rakhṇā*	to put.
ਖਿੱਚਨਾਂ	*khichchṇā*	to draw.
ਚਲਾਉਨਾ	*chalāuṇā*	to fire.
ਪਹੁੰਚਨਾ	*pahuṅchṇā*	to arrive.
ਕਮਾਨ ਕਰਨਾ	*kamāṇ karṇā*,	to command.
ਖੁਆਉਨਾ	*khuāunā*	to feed.

Examples.

ਇਹ ਨਵਾਂ ਭੂਰਾ ਕਾਠੀ ਦੇ ਲਈ ਲੈ ॥ *ih nawāṅ bhūrā kāṭhī de laī lai,* Here is a new blanket for the saddle.

ਓਹ ਤਲਵਾਰ ਪੁਰਾਨਾ ਹਥਿਆਰ ਹੈ *oh talwār purāṇā hathiār hai,* That sword is an old weapon.

ਤੋਪ ਕਦ ਕਿਲੇ ਤੇ ਪਹੁੰਚੇਗੀ। *top kad kile te pahuṅchegī,* When will the cannon arrive at the fort ?

ਲਾਲ ਕੁੜਤੀ ਅਜ ਆਈ ਹੈ। *lāl kuṛtī aj āī hai,* The British Infantry arrived to-day.

ਆਪਨਾ ਬਦੂਕ ਭਰਕੇ ਚਲਾ *āpṇī bădūk bhar ke chalā,* Load your gun and fire it.

ਪੁਰਾਨਾ ਤੋਬਰਾ ਖਾਲੀ ਜਾਂ ਭਰਿਆ ਹੋਇਆ ਹੈ। *purānā tobrā khālī jāṅ bhariā hoiā hai* Is the old nosebag empty or full ?

ਸਪਾਹੀਆਂ ਨੇ ਆਪਨੇ ਨੇਜੇ ਘੁਟਕੇ ਫੜੇ ॥ *sapāhīāṅ ne āpṇe neje ghuṭke phaṛe,* The men held their lances firmly.

Translate into Punjābī.

Who commands the native infantry regiment in Umballa ? Where are the artillery barracks ? They will fir e a cannon to-day. The,infanrty have guns, and the cavalry lances. Draw sword. That soldier's sword is very rusty. Put the saddle and bridle on a blanket. When will the artillory arrive at the fort.

Translate into Englih.

ਇਹ ਜੰਗਾਲੀ ਬਦੂਕ ਕਿਸਦੀ ਹੈ। ਉਸ ਤੋਬਰੇ ਵਿਚ ਕਿਨਾ ਦਾਨਾ ਸੀ । ਤੋਪਖਾਨਾ ਕਦ ਤਕ ਕਿਲੇ ਵਿਚ ਰਹੇਗਾ। ਪੁਰਾਨਾ ਭੂਰਾ ਤੂੰ ਲੈ ਤੇ ਨਵਾਂ ਮੈਨੂੰ ਦੇਹ। ਰਸਾਲੇ ਵਾਲੇ ਹੁਣ ਕਿੱਥੇ ਹਨ। ਮੇਰੀ ਸੰਗੀਨ ਅਜ ਮੈਲੀ ਹੈ ਇਸ ਕਰਕੇ ਮੈਂ ਸਾਫ ਕਰਕੇ ਲਾਵਾਂਗਾ। ਟੱਟੂ ਨੂੰ ਦਾਨਾ ਖੁਆਕੇ ਖੱਚਰ ਨੂੰ ਲਿਆ। ਸਾਡੀ ਘੋੜੀ ਵੱਡੀ ਲਮੀ ਹੈ।

LESSON V.

NOUNS.

Masculine.			Feminine.		
ਦਫਤਰ	*daphtar*	office.	ਨੌਕਰੀ	*naukrī*	duty.
ਦਰਾਬੀ	*darābī*	driver.	ਕੰਪਨੀ	*kaṅpaṇī*	company.
ਨੁਕਤਾ	*nuktā*	head collar.	ਲੈਨ	*laiṇ*	line,
ਗੁਦਾਮ	*gudām*	godown.	ਫੌਜ	*phauj*	army.

Masculine.			Feminine		
ਦਾਣਾ	*dāṇā*	gram.	ਲੜਾਈ	*laṛāī*	battle.
ਅਫਸਰ	*aphsar*	officer.	ਸੰਗੀਨ	*sangīṇ*	bayonet.
ਅਸਤਬਲ	*astabal*	stable.	ਹਾਰ	*hār*	defeat.
ਘੈਂਟਾ	*ghaiṇṭā*	hour.	ਜਿੱਤ	*jitt*	victory.

ADJECTIVES.

ਸ਼ਰਾਬੀ	*sharābī*	drunk.	ਸੁੱਤਾ ਹੋਇਆ	*sutā hoiā*	asleep
ਸੁਰੰਗ	*surang*	chestnut (horse)	ਸਭ ਤੇ ਚੰਗਾ	*sabh te changā*	best.
ਹਰਇੱਕ	*har ikk*	each.	ਤਾਜਾ	*tājā*	fresh.
ਸਚ ਮੁਚ	*sach much*	surely	ਭੁੱਜਾ ਹੋਇਆ	*bhujjā hoiā*	parched.

VERBS.

ਦੋਸ਼ ਲਗਣਾ	*dosh lagṇā*,	to be charged.	ਮੁਲ ਭਰਨਾ	*mul bharṇā*	to pay for.
ਲੈਣਾ	*laiṇā*	to take.	ਮਾਲਸ਼ ਕਰਨਾ	*mālish karṇā*,	to groom.
ਲਭਨਾ	*labhṇā*	to be found.	ਵੇਖਨਾ	*wekhṇā*	to inspect.
ਬਾਹਰ ਨਿਕਲਨਾ	*bāhar ṇikalṇā*,	to get out	ਕਵੈਦ ਕਰਨਾ	*kawaid karṇā*.	to parade.

Examples.

ਉਸ ਤਬੇਲੇ ਵਿੱਚ ਕਿੱਨੇ ਘੋੜੇ ਹਨ *us tabele wichch kiṇṇe ghoṛe haṇ*, How many horses are there in that stable ?

ਕਲ ਉਹ ਨੌਕਰੀ ਤੇ ਸ਼ਰਾਬੀ ਸੀ *kal oh ṇaukrī te sharābī sī*, Yesterday he was drunk whilst on duty.

ਹਰ ਇਕ ਘੋੜੇ ਨੂੰ ਨੁਕਤਾ ਲਾ *har ik ghoṛe ṇūṅ ṇuktā lā*, Put a head collar on each horse.

ਓਹ ਘੋੜੀਆਂ ਲੈਨ ਵਿੱਚ ਰੋਜ ਪੰਜ ਘੈਂਟੇ ਮਾਲਸ ਕੀਤੀਆਂ ਜਾਂਦੀਆਂ ਹਨ ।
oh ghoṛīāṅ laiṇ wichch roj pañj ghaiṇṭe mālish kītīāṅ jāṅdīāṅ haṇ. Those mares are groomed for five hours every day in the lines.

ਜੌਂ ਭੁਜੇ ਹੋਏ ਛੋਲਿਆਂ ਨਾਲ ਲਭੇ ਸੀ *jauṅ bhuje hoe chholiāṅ ṇāl labhe sī*, The barley was found with the parched gram.

ਕਲ ਅੱਠ ਵਜੇ ਅਫਸਰ ਸੁਰੰਗ ਘੋੜੇ ਵੇਖੇਗਾ

kal athth waje aphsar surang ghore wekhe gā, The officer will inspet the chestnut horses to-morrow at 8 o'clock.

Translate into Punjābi

Bring that man before the officer to-morrow. Sir this sentry was found asleep. The driver has not cleaned that head collar. Were you in the battle last year? Each man and officer in the army paraded for inspection. You must groom the horses in the lines and not in the stable. Have you found his bayonet yet? It was not a defeat but a victory.

Translate into English

ਉਸ ਘੋੜੀ ਦਾ ਨੁਕਤਾ ਟੁਟ ਗਿਆ ਹੈ। ਤੂ ਆਪਨੇ ਘੋੜੇ ਨੂੰ ਕਿੰਨਾ ਦਾਨਾ ਦੇਂਦਾ ਹੈਂ। ਉਸਨੇ ਮੇਰੀ ਚਿੱਠੀ ਪੜ੍ਹੀ ਸੀ। ਉਸ ਤੀਮੀ ਨੇ ਇਕ ਸੇਰ ਜੌਂ ਮੈਨੂੰ ਦਿਤੇ ਸੀ। ਫੂਲਾ ਸਿੰਘ ਨੂੰ ਨੌਕਰੀ ਤੇ ਗੈਰ ਹਾਜ਼ਰ ਹੋਣ ਦਾ ਦੋਸ਼ ਲਗਾ। ਇਸ ਰਸਾਲੇ ਵਿੱਚ ਕਿੰਨੇ ਵਜੇ ਮਾਲਸ਼ ਹੁੰਦੀ ਹੈ। ਉਸ ਘੋੜੀ ਨੂੰ ਪਾਨੀ ਪਲਾਉਣ ਦੇ ਲਈ ਬਾਹਰ ਕੱਢ।

LESSON VI.

NOUNS

Masculine.			Feminine.		
ਮੂੜ੍ਹਾ	*mūṛhā*	stool.	ਕੁਰਸੀ	*kursī*	chair.
ਪ੍ਰਸਾਦ *	*parsād*	dinner,	ਚਾ	*chā*	tea.
ਪਨੀਰ	*panīr*	cheese.	ਕਾਲੀ ਮਿਰਚ	*kālī mirch*	pepper.
ਮੱਖਨ	*makhkhaṇ*	butter.	ਰਾਈ	*rāī*	mustard.
ਪਿਆਲਾ	*piālā*	cup.	ਰਕਾਬੀ	*rakābī*	plate.
ਚਮਚਾ	*chamchā*	spoon.	ਪਿਰਚ	*pirch*	saucer.
ਲੂਣ	*lūṇ*	salt.	ਭਾਜੀ	*bhājī*	vegetable.
ਫਲ	*phal*	fruit.	ਗੋਭੀ	*gobhī*	cabbage.
ਫੁਲ	*phul*	flower.	ਖੰਡ	*khaṇḍ*	sugar.
ਚੌਲ	*chaul*	rice.	ਦਾਲ	*dāl*	dhal.

* Particular name used by Sikhs. Commonly ਰੋਟੀ, *roṭī* ਰਸੋਈ *rasoī.*

ADJECTIVES.

ਕੌੜਾ	*kauṛā*	bitter,	ਮਿੱਠਾ	*miṭhā*	sweet.
ਮੋਟਾ	*moṭā*	thick.	ਪਤਲਾ	*patlā*	thin.
ਸਾਰਾ	*sārā*	whole.	ਟੁੱਟਾ ਹੋਇਆ	*ṭuṭā hoiā*	broken.
ਤਾਜਾ	*tājā*	fresh.	ਬਿਹਾ	*bihā*	stale.
ਤੱਤਾ	*tattā*	hot.	ਠੰਡਾ	*ṭhaṅḍā*	cold.
ਤੇਜ	*tej*	sharp.	ਖੁੰਡਾ	*khuṅḍā*	blunt.
ਚੌਰਸ	*chauras*	square.	ਗੋਲ	*gol*	round.
ਸੁੱਕਾ	*sukkā*	dry.	ਗਿੱਲਾ	*gillā*	wet.

VERBS.

ਉਬਾਲਨਾ	*ubālṇā*	to boil.	ਪਕਾਉਨਾ	*pakāuṇā*	to cook.
ਤਲਨਾ	*talṇā*	to fry.	ਕਬਾਬ ਕਰਨਾ	*kabāb karṇā*	to roast.
ਭਰਨਾ	*bharṇā*	to fill.	ਖਾਲੀ ਕਰਨਾ	*khālī karṇā*	to empty.
ਪਾਉਨਾ	*pāuṇā*	to put on.	ਲਾਹਨਾ	*lāhṇā*	to take off.
ਚਖਨਾ	*chakhṇā*	to taste.	ਤੋੜਨਾ	*toṛṇā*	to break.
ਉਗਨਾ	*ugṇā*	to grow.	ਸੁੰਘਨਾ	*suṅghṇā*	to smell.

Examples.

ਕੁਰਸੀ ਮੇਜ਼ ਦੇ ਕੋਲ ਰੱਖ *kursī mej de kol rakh*, Put the chair near the table.

ਚਾ ਨਾਲ ਖੰਡ ਰਲਾ *chā nāl khaṅḍ ralā*, Mix sugar with the tea.

ਕਲ ਮਾਲੀ ਫੁਲ ਲਿਆਇਆ ਸੀ ਕਿ ਨਹੀਂ *kal mālī phul liāiā si kī nahīṅ* Did tbe gardner bring the flowers yesterday or not ?

ਜੇ ਮੇਰਾ ਪ੍ਰਸ਼ਾਦ ਤਿਆਰ ਹੈ ਤਾਂ ਲੈ ਆ *je merā parshād tiār hai tāṅ lai ā*, If my dinner is ready bring it.

ਇਹ ਫਲ ਤਾਜਾ ਹੈ ਜਾਂ ਬਿਹਾ *ih phal tājā hai jāṅ bihā*, Is this fruit fresh or stale.

ਓਹ ਕੁੜੀ ਚਮਚੇ ਨਾਲ ਚੌਲ ਖਾਂਦੀ ਸੀ *oh kuṛī chamçhe nāl chaul khāṅdī sī,*
That girl was eating rice with a spoon.

ਸਾਡੇ ਆਦਮੀ ਚੌਲ ਤੇ ਦਾਲ ਖਾਂਦੇ ਹਨ *sāḍe ādmī chaul te dāl khāṅde han,*
Our people enjoy rice and dhal.

Translate into Punjābī.

Fill that round cup with dry salt. Taste these vegetables they are very bitter Place the cup and saucer on the stool and the wet plate on the table. Have you boiled the cabbage ? Is it hot or cold ? Can you eat a whole cheese ? The mustard is too thick, and the butter too thin. There is no pepper on the table. Some fruit is very sweet that grows upon trees.

Translate into English.

ਪ੍ਰਸਾਦ ਜਮੀਨ ਤੇ ਨਾ ਰਖਕੇ ਖਾ। ਕਾਲੀਆਂ ਮਿਰਚਾਂ ਨਾਲ ਭਾਜੀ ਦਾ ਸੁਆਦ ਚੰਗਾ ਬਨ ਜਾਂਦਾ ਹੈ। ਇਸ ਦੁਧ ਵਿਚ ਮਿੱਠਾ ਘੱਟ ਹੈ ਹੋਰ ਖੰਡ ਪਾ ਦੇ। ਇਕ ਚਿਠੀ ਇਸ ਸਪਾਹੀ ਦੀ ਬਾਬਤ ਲਿਖਕੇ ਅਜੀਟਨ ਸਾਹਿਬ ਨੂੰ ਘਲ। ਬਾਹਲੇ ਮਨੁਖ ਪਿੰਡਦੇ ਫਲ ਫੁਲ ਵੇਚਕੇ ਗੁਜਾਰਾ ਕਰਦੇ ਹਨ। ਓਹ ਬੈਲ ਜੋ ਤੂੰ ਕਲ ਲਿਆ ਸੀ ਵੱਡਾ ਸੋਹਣਾ ਸੀ ਮੇਰੀ ਗਊ ਹੁਨ ਅਠ ਸੇਰ ਪੱਕਾ ਦੁਧ ਦੇਂਦੀ ਹੈ। ਜਦ ਮੈਂ ਉਥੇ ਗਿਆ ਤਾਂ ਗਭਰੂ ਵਹੁਟੀ ਆਪਸ ਵਿਚ ਗੱਲਾਂ ਕਰਦੇ ਸੀ॥

LESSON VII.

NOUNS.

Masculine.			Feminine.		
ਛੋਲੇ	*chhole*	gram.	ਜਮੀਨ	*jamiṇ*	land.
ਝੋਨਾ	*jhoṇā*	rice (with husk).	ਕਣਕ	*kanak*	wheat.
ਖੇਤ	*khet*	field.	ਛਾਂ	*chhāṅ*	shade.
ਹਲ	*hal*	plough.	ਫਸਲ	*phasal*	crops.
ਰਾਹ	*rāh*	road.	ਕਪਾਹ	*kapāh*	cotton (raw)

Masculine.			Feminine.		
ਘਾਹ	*ghāh*	grass.	ਮਕਈ	*mukai*	maize.
ਜੌਂ	*jauṅ*	barley.	ਸਰੋਂ	*saroṅ*	oil seed.
ਬਿਰਛ	*birachh*	tree.	ਜਵਾਰ	*jawār*	indian corn.
ਫਲ	*phal*	fruit.	ਰੂੰ	*rūṅ*	cotton.
ਫੁਲ	*phul*	flower.	ਝੋਨੇ ਦੀ ਪਨੀਰੀ	*jhone dī paṇīrī,*	rice plant.

VERBS.

ਵਾਹੁਣਾ	*wāhuṇā*	to cultivate.	ਲਾਉਣਾ	*lāunā*	to plant.
ਬੀਜਣਾ	*bījṅā*	to sow.	ਨਾਸ ਕਰਨਾ	*nās karṇā*	to destroy.
ਵਢਣਾ	*waḍhnā*	to reap.	ਝੜ ਪੈਣਾ	*jhaṛ paiṇā*	to fall.
ਸੁਹਾਗਾ ਫੇਰਨਾ	*suhāgā pherṇā*	to harrow.	ਪੁੰਗਰਨਾ	*puṅgarṇā*	to sprout.
ਮਾਰਿਆ ਜਾਨਾਂ	*māriā jāṇā,*	to blight.	ਕਮਲਾ ਜਾਣਾ	*kamlā jāṅā*	to wither.

Examples.

ਹੁਣ ਛੋਲੇ ਸਸਤੇ ਹੁੰਦੇ ਜਾਂਦੇ ਹਨ *hun chhole saste hunde jāṅde haṇ,* Now the gra is getting cheap.

ਐਤਕੀ ਫਸਲਾਂ ਵੱਡੀਆਂ ਚੰਗੀਆਂ ਹਨ *aitakī phaslāṅ waḍḍiāṅ chaṅgiāṅ haṇ,* This time the crops are very good.

ਕਣਕ ਅਗਲੇ ਮਹੀਨੇ ਪੱਕ ਜਾਵੇ ਗੀ। *kanak agle mahīne pakk jāwegī,* The wheat will be ripe next month.

ਮੈਂ ਆਪਣੇ ਖੇਤ ਵਿੱਚ ਜੌਂ ਬੀਜੇ ਹਨ। *maiṅ āpne khet wichch jauṅ bīje haṇ,* I hav sown barley in my field.

ਕਲ ਮੈਂ ਤੇਰੇ ਲਈ ਕੋਈ ਨਵਾਂ ਫਲ ਲਿਆਵਾਂ ਗਾ *kal maiṅ tere laī koī nawā phal liāwāṅgā,* To-morrow, I will bring some new fruit for you.

ਘੋੜਿਆਂ ਨੂੰ ਜਵਾਰ ਖੁਆਉਣੀ ਚਾਹੀਏ *ghoṛiāṅ nūṅ jawār khuāunī chāhīe,* The horses ought to get a feed of Indian corn.

ਤੂੰ ਆਪਣੀ ਜਮੀਨ ਵਿਚ ਕੀ ਬੀਜੇਂਗਾ *tūṅ āpṇī jamīn wich kī bījeṅgā,* What will you sow on your land ?

ਕਿੰਨੇ ਸੇਰ ਰੂੰ ਸੀ ? *kinne ser rūṅ sī ?* How many seers of cotton were there ;

Translate into Punjābī.

The farmer's plough is broken. When will the wheat be ripe ? Plant some flowers the shade of that high tree. The road runs through the fields. That is a field of rice. When the barley is ripe it will be reaped The rice plant must be sown in water. The maize was blighted last year by the rain. The flowers on that plant are sprouting. All the leaves fall from the trees in winter. To cultivate your land you must harrow it and destroy the weeds. The sun withered all the fruit trees.

Translate into English.

ਕਦ ਤੁਸੀ ਇਸ ਖੇਤ ਨੂੰ ਵਾਹਿਆ ਸੀ ? ਅਜ ਪੰਦਰਾਂ ਦਿਨ ਹੋਏ ਹਨ। ਤੂੰ ਉਸ ਬ੍ਰਿਛ ਦੀ ਛਾਂ ਹੇਠ ਬੈਠ ਮੈਂ ਤੈਨੂੰ ਇਕ ਫਲ ਖਾਨ ਦੇ ਲਈ ਦੇਵਾਂਗਾ। ਇਹ ਰਾਹ ਕਿਧਰ ਨੂੰ ਜਾਂਦਾ ਹੈ ? ਦੀਵੇ ਵਿਚ ਤੇਲ ਪਾਕੇ ਰਖ। ਸਰੋਂ ਕਦ ਬੀਜੀ ਜਾਂਦੀ ਹੈ। ਮੈਂ ਆਪਣੇ ਘੋੜੇ ਨੂੰ ਕਲ ਮਕਈ ਦਿੱਤੀ। ਕਲ ਅਸੀਂ ਦੁਧ ਚੌਲ ਖਾਵਾਂਗੇ। ਇਸ ਬੈਲ ਨੂੰ ਥੋੜਾ ਹੋਰ ਘਾਹ ਪਾ। ਜੁਵਾਰ ਦੀ ਰੋਟੀ ਵਡੀ ਚੰਗੀ ਬਣਦੀ ਹੈ।

LESSON VIII.

NOUNS.

Masculine.			Feminine.		
ਰਾਜਾ	*rājā*	king.	ਰਾਣੀ	*rāṇī*	queen.
ਵਜੀਰ	*wajīr*	minister.	ਕਚਹਿਰੀ	*kachahrī*	court.
ਕੈਦੀ	*kaidī*	prisoner.	ਸਰਕਾਰ	*sarkār*	government.
ਹਥਿਆਰ	*hathiār*	arms.	ਕਵੈਦ	*kawaid*	parade.
ਤੀਰ	*tīr*	arrow.	ਕਮਾਨ	*kamān*	bow.
ਗੋਲਮਦਾਜ	*golamdāj*	gunner.	ਪਲਟਨ	*palṭan*	regiment.

Masculine.		
ਮੋਰਚਾ	*morchā*	battery.
ਤੰਬੂ	*tanbū*	tent.
ਝੰਡਾ	*jhanḍā*	flag.
ਨੌਕਰ	*ṇaukar*	servant
ਤਕਮਾ	*takmā*	medal.

Feminine.		
ਢਾਲ	*ḍhāl*	shield.
ਨਾਲੀ	*ṇālī*	barrel.
ਬਰਛੀ	*barchhī*	spear.
ਗੋਲੀ	*golī*	bullet.
ਗਦਰ, ਫਸਾਦ	*gardar, phasād,*	mutiny.

VERBS.

ਭੱਜ ਜਾਨਾ	*bhajj jāṇā*	to escape.
ਮਿਲਨਾ	*milṇā*	to get.
ਇਨਾਮ ਦੇਣਾ	*ṇām denā,*	to reward.
ਚੜ੍ਹਾਉਨਾ	*charhāuṇā*	to hoist.
ਮਾਰਿਆ ਜਾਨਾ	*māriā jāṇā*	to be killed.
ਵਰਤਿਆ ਜਾਨਾ	*wartiā jāṇā,*	to be used.
ਆਖਣਾ	*ākhnā*	to tell,
ਚੱਕ ਵਢਣਾ	*chakk waḍhnā,*	to bite.

Examples.

ਰਾਜਾ ਸ਼ਕਾਰ ਨੂੰ ਗਿਆ ਹੈ *rājā shakār nūṅ giā hai,* The king has gone hunting.

ਰਾਨੀ ਕਦੋਂ ਆਵੇਗੀ *rānī kadoṅ āwegī ?* When will the queen come ?

ਕੈਦੀ ਕੈਦ ਖਾਨੇ ਵਿਚੋਂ ਭੱਜ ਗਿਆ ਹੈ *kaidī kaid khāne wichoṅ bhaj giā hai,* The prisoner has escaped from the jail.

ਤੀਰ ਕਮਾਨ ਪੁਰਾਨੇ ਹਥਿਆਰ ਹਨ *tīr kamāṇ purāṇe haththiār han,* Bows and arrows are old weapons.

ਝੰਡਾ ਵੱਡੇ ਤੰਬੂ ਤੇ ਚੜ੍ਹਾ *jhanḍā waḍḍe tanbū te cha~hā,* Hoist the flag above the large tent.

ਗੋਲਮਦਾਜ ਨੂੰ ਹੁਕਮ ਮੋੜਨ ਦੇ ਕਰਕੇ ਦੋਸ਼ ਲਗਾ *golamdāj nūṅ hukam moṛaṇ de karke dosh laggā,* The gunner was charged witn mutiny.

Translats into Panjābī.

How many of the enemy's soldiers were killed in that battle ? Now-a-days guns and cannons are used in war. At the time for parade fifty men were absent. The regiments were victorious in Africa. Will the government reward them? Yes they will get a medal and a clasp for each victory. Tell my servant to take the bullet out of the barrel. The minister owned a very old shield and spear.

Translate into English.

ਵਜੀਰ ਰਾਜਿਆਂ ਦੀ ਅਕਲ ਹੁੰਦੇ ਹਨ। ਕੈਦੀ ਨੇ ਦਰੋਗੇ ਦੇ ਹੱਥ ਉਤੇ ਚੱਕ ਵਢ ਖਾਧਾ। ਪੰਦਰਾਂ ਮਨੁਖ ਇਕ ਤੰਬੂ ਵਿਚ ਸੁੱਤੇ ਪਏ ਸੀ। ਜਦ ਝੰਡਾ ਹਿਲੇ ਤੁਸੀ ਉੱਸੇ ਵੇਲੇ ਸਾਡੇ ਕੋਲ ਆਜਾਓ । ਮੇਰਾ ਨੌਕਰ ਸਾਰਾ ਕੰਮ ਆਪਨੀ ਖੁਸ਼ੀ ਨਾਲ ਕਰਦਾ ਹੈ ਕਰਮ ਸਿੰਘ ਦੇ ਦੋਵੇਂ ਤਕਮੇ ਗੁਆਚ ਗਏ ਹਨ। ਅਗੇ ਢਾਲ ਤਲਵਾਰ ਨਾਲ ਲੜਾਈ ਹੁੰਦੀ ਸੀ। ਪਰਸੋਂ ਛੁਟੀ ਕਰਕੇ ਕਚਹਰੀ ਬੰਦ ਰਹੇਗੀ।

LESSON IX.

NOUNS.

Masculine.			Feminine.		
ਸਿਆਲ	*siāl*	cold weather.	ਰੁਤ	*rut*	weather, season.
ਹੁਨਾਲ	*huṇāl*	hot weather.	ਬਰਸਾਤ	*barsāt*	rainy weather.
ਮੀਂਹ	*mīṅh*	rain.	ਬਿਜਲੀ	*bijlī*	lightning.
ਬੱਦਲ	*baddal*	cloud.	ਲੋ	*lo*	hot wind.
ਸੂਰਜ	*sūraj*	sun.	ਓਸ	*os*	dew.
ਚੰਦਰਮਾਂ	*chandarmāṅ*	moon.	ਠੰਡ	*ṭhaṇḍ*	cold.
ਤਾਰਾ	*tārā*	star.	ਗਰਮੀ	*garmī*	heat.
ਅਕਾਸ	*akās*	sky.	ਹਨੇਰੀ	*haṇerī*	dust storm.
ਕੋਰਾ	*korā*	snow.	ਵਾ	*wā*	air.
ਗੜੇ	*gaṛe*	hail.	ਧੁੰਦ	*dhuṇd*	fog, mist.

VERBS.

ਪੈਣਾ *paiṇā* ਡਿਗਣਾ *ḍignā*	to fall.	ਚੁੰਗਾ ਜਾਣਨਾ	*chungā jāṇṇā*, tc
ਲਿਸ਼ਕਣਾ *lishaknā*	to flash.	ਦਿਸਣੋਂ ਰਹਿਣਾ	*disnoṅ rahr* to disap

ਵੇਖਣਾ	*wekhnā*	to see.	ਸਕਣਾ	*sakṇā*	to be able.
ਦਿਸਣਾ	*disnā*	to be seen.	ਰਹਿਣਾ	*rahṇā*	to continue.
ਠਹਿਰਨਾ	*ṭhahrṇā*	to stay.	ਖਰਾਬ ਕਰਨਾ	*kharāb karṇā*,	to spoil.
ਕਰਨਾ	*karṇā*	to cause.	ਢਕਣਾ	*dhaknā*	to cover.

Note :—Actions of the elements such as 'rain falling', 'sun shining', lightning 'flashing 'is cold,' 'is hot,' are usually expressed by the Verb ਪੈਣਾ to fall.

Examples.

ਪਿਛਲੇ ਸਿਆਲਵਿਚ ਵੱਡਾ ਭਾਰਾ ਮੀਂਹ ਪਿਆ *pichhle siāl wich waḍḍā bhārā mīṅh iā*, Last winter very heavy rain fell.

ਬਿਜਲੀ ਲਿਸ਼ਕਦੀ ਸੀ *bijlī lishkdī sī*, The lightning was flashing.

ਹੁਨਾਲ ਵਿਚ ਮੈਂ ਘਰ ਰਹਿੰਦਾ ਹਾਂ *huṇāl wich main ghar rahiṅdā hāṅ*, In the hot weather I stay in the house.

ਕਦੀ ਅੰਬਾਲੇ ਵਿੱਚ ਕੋਰਾ ਪੈਂਦਾ ਹੈ *kadi ambāle wichch korā paiṅdā hai*, Does snow ever fall in Umballa ?

ਨਹੀਂ ਪਰ ਸਿਆਲ ਵਿੱਚ ਅਸੀ ਪਹਾੜਾਂ ਉੱਤੇ ਵੇਖ ਸਕਦੇ ਹਾਂ *nahīṅ par siāl wichch asīṅ pahāṛāṅ utte wekh sakde hāṅ*, No, but we can see it on the hills in the cold weather.

ਧੁੰਦ ਸ਼ਾਇਦ ਕਈ ਦਿਨਾਂ ਤੀਕ ਰਹੇ *dhuṅdh shāid kaī dinȧṅ tīk rahe*, The fog may continue for many days.

Translate into Punjābī.

Last night no clouds were seen. The rainy weather causes much damage to the crops. If the weather is fine, the dew soon disappears. We could see each other when the lightning flashed. The sun's light is much bright than that of the moon. Do you prefer the cold or the heat ? Does more rain fall in Umballa or in Delhi ?

Translate into English.

ਅਜ ਅਕਾਸ ਬਿਲਕੁਲ ਨਿਰਮਲ ਹੈ। ਰਾਤ ਵੇਲੇ ਸਾਨੂੰ ਨਿਰਾ ਚੰਦਰਮਾਂ ਤੇ ਤਾਰੇ ਦਿਸਦੇ ਹਨ। ਹਨੇਰੀ ਤੋਂ ਪਿਛੇ ਵਾ ਠੰਢੀ ਵਗਦੀ ਹੈ। ਸਿਆਲ ਵਿਚ ਤੱਤੀ ਵਾ ਚੰਗੀ ਲਗਦੀ ਹੈ। ਮੀਂਹ ਪੈਣ ਨਾਲ ਸਾਰੇ ਬਿਰਛ ਭਿਗ ਪਏ। ਕਲ ਰਾਤ ਬਿਜਲੀ ਪੈਣ ਨਾਲ ਇਕ ਮਨੁੱਖ ਤੇ ਦੋ ਬਲਦ ਮਾਰੇ ਗਏ। ਗਰਮੀ ਵਿਚ ਲੋਕ ਠੰਢੀ ਵਾ ਚਾਹੁੰਦੇ ਹਨ। ਬਰਸਾਤ ਵਿਚ ਡੰਗਰ ਪਸ਼ੂ ਵਡੇ ਰਾਜੀ ਹੋਕੇ ਨ੍ਹਾਉਂਦੇ ਤੇ ਘਾ ਚੁਗਦੇ ਹਨ।

LESSON X.

NOUNS.

Masculine.			Feminine.		
ਕਾਰਤੂਸ	*kārtūs*	cartridge.	ਝਾੜੀ	*jhāṛī*	bush.
ਸ਼ਕਾਰ	*shakār*	game.	ਬਤਕ	*batak*	duck.
ਸਹਿਆ	*sahiā*	hare.	ਮੱਛੀ	*machhī*	fish.
ਗਿਦੜ	*giddaṛ*	jackal.	ਝੀਲ	*jhīl*	lake.
ਬਰਛਾ	*barchhā*	spear.	ਮੁਰਗਾਬੀ	*murgābī*	water-fowl.
ਸ਼ੇਰ	*sher*	lion.	ਕੁਕੜੀ	*kukṛī*	hen
ਤਿਤਰ	*titar*	partridge.	ਬੁਲਬੁਲ	*bulbul*	nightingale.
ਸੂਰ	*sūr*	pig.	ਚਿੜੀ	*chiṛī*	sparrow.
ਦਾਰੂ	*dārū*	powder.	ਘੁੱਗੀ	*ghuggī*	dove.
ਬਟੇਰਾ	*baṭerā*	quail.	ਇੱਲ	*ill.*	kite.
ਸਰਕੜਾ	*sarkaṛā*	reeds.	ਲੂਮੜੀ	*lūmṛī*	fox.
ਛੱਰ੍ਹਾ	*chharrā*	shot.	ਸ਼ੇਰਨੀ	*shernī*	lioness.
ਚਾਹਾ	*chāhā*	snipe.	ਹਰਨੀ	*harṇī*	doe.

VERBS.

ਉਡਨਾ	*uḍṇā*	to fly.	ਮਾਰਨਾ	*mārṇā*	to beat.
ਕੱਠਾ ਕਰਨਾ	*kaṭhṭhā karṇā,*	to collect.	ਖੋਜ ਲਾਉਣਾ	*khoj lāuṇā*	to track.
ਮਾਰ ਸੁਟਨਾ	*mār suṭṇā*	to kill.	ਮੋੜਨਾ	*moṛṇā*	to turn.
ਬਰਛਾ ਮਾਰਨਾ	*barchhā mārṇā,*	to spear.	ਸਵਾਰੀ ਕਰਨਾ	*sawārī karṇā,*	to ride.
ਲੁਕਾਉਣਾ	*lukāuṇā*	to hide.	ਵਿਨ੍ਹਣਾ	*wiṇhṇā.*	to pierce.

Examples.

ਅਸਾਂ ਬਰਛੇ ਨਾਲ ਦੋ ਸੂਰ ਮਾਰੇ *asāṅ barchhe nāl do sūr māre*, We killed two pigs with a spear.

ਬਟੇਰੇ ਅਕਸਰ ਕਣਕ ਵਿਚ ਮਿਲਦੇ ਹਨ *baṭere aksar kanak wich milde han*, Quails are generally found in the wheat.

ਤਿੱਤਰ ਚਿੜੀ ਨਾਲੋਂ ਵਡਾ ਪੰਛੀ ਹੈ । *titar chiṛī nāloṅ waḍḍā pañchhī hai*, The partridge is a larger bird than the sparrow.

ਉਸਦਾ ਬਰਛਾ ਟੁਟ ਗਿਆ ਨਹੀਂ ਤਾਂ ਓਹ ਚੀਤੇ ਨੂੰ ਮਾਰ ਸੁਟਦਾ *usdā barchhā ṭuṭ giā nahīṅ tāṅ oh chīte nūṅ mār suṭdā*, He broke his spear or he would have killed the tiger.

ਮੈਂ ਪਹਿਲੇ ਵਾਰ ਨਾਲ ਸੂਰ ਨੂੰ ਵਿੱਨ੍ਹ ਦਿਤਾ *maiṅ pahle wār nāl sūr nūṅ winnh dittā*, I pierced a pig with the first blow.

Translate into Punjābī.

The day before yesterday we went shooting. Is there a cartridge in your gun? No it is loaded with powder and shot. When they collect the game they will find amongst it a kite, seven doves a nightingale and two snipe, When tracking a deer I turned a fox and rode after it for a mile or more. Hares and jackals are the only game found near Umballa.

Translate into English.

ਉਸ ਨੇ ਪਿਛੋਂ ਦੀ ਗਿਦੜ ਨੂੰ ਬਰਛਾ ਮਾਰਿਆ । ਕਦੀ ਤੁਸੀ ਤਲਵਾਰ ਨਾਲ ਵੀ ਸ਼ਕਾਰ ਮਾਰਿਆ ਹੈ । ਇਨ੍ਹਾਂ ਸਰਕੜਿਆਂ ਵਿਚ ਲੁਕ ਰਹੁ ਜਦ ਤੀਕ ਕੁਲੀ ਝਾੜੀਆਂ ਨੂੰ ਝਾੜਨ । ਉਸ ਝੀਲ ਵਿਚ ਬਥੇਰੀਆਂ ਮਛੀਆਂ ਹਨ । ਕੀ ਉਸ ਵਿਚ ਮੁਰਗਾਬੀਆਂ ਬੀ ਹਨ? ਹਿੰਦੁਸਤਾਨ ਵਿਚ ਸ਼ੇਰ ਤਾਂ ਘਟ ਹਨ ਪਰ ਚੀਤੇ ਬਥੇਰੇ ਹਨ । ਪੜਾ ਤੇ ਬਹੁਤ ਸਾਰੀਆਂ ਬਤਕਾਂ ਉਡੀਆਂ ।

LESSON XI.

NOUNS.

Masculine.			Feminine.		
ਲੇਖਾ	*lekhā*	account.	ਵਹੀ	*wahī*	ledger

Masculine.			Feminine.		
ਰੋਜਨਾਮਚਾ	*roj nāmchā,*	day book.	ਰੋਕੜ	*rokaṛ*	cash book.
ਚਪੜਾਸੀ	*chapṛāsī*	peon.	ਲਿਖਤ ਪੜ੍ਹਤ	*likhat paṛht,*	correspondence
ਰੂਲ	*rūl*	ruler.	ਚਿੱਠੀ	*chiṭhṭhī*	letter.
ਫੀਤਾ	*phītā*	tape.	ਪਿਨਸਲ	*pinsal*	pencil.
ਬਪਾਰੀ	*bapārī*	merchant.	ਲਾਖ	*lākh*	sealing-wax
ਅਸਲ	*asal*	capital (money.)	ਸਹੀ	*sahī*	signature.
ਰਬੜ	*rabaṛ*	rubber.	ਪੱਤ੍ਰੀ	*patrī*	almanac.
ਬਾਬੂ	*bābū*	clerk	ਤਰੀਕ	*tarīk*	date.
ਵਡਾ ਬਾਬੂ	*waḍḍā bābū,*	head clerk.	ਗੋਂਦ	*gond*	gum.

VERBS.

ਨਕਲ ਕਰਨਾ	*nakal karṇā*	to copy.	ਬੁਝਾਉਣਾ / ਮਿਟਾਉਣਾ	*bujhāuṇā* / *miṭāuṇā*	to erase.
ਵਰਤਨਾ	*wartṇā*	to use.	ਵੇਖਣਾ	*wekhṇā*	to look.
ਘਲਣਾ	*ghalṇā*	to send.	ਤੇਜ ਕਰਨਾ	*tej karṇā*	to sharpen
ਮੁਲ ਲੈਣਾ	*mul laiṇā*	to buy.	ਲਿਆਉਣਾ	*liāuṇā*	to bring.
ਮਿਲਾਉਣਾ	*milāuṇā*	to compare.	ਕਰਨਾ	*karṇā*	to do.
ਸਹੀ ਪਾਉਣਾ	*sahī pāuṇā*	to sign.	ਮੋਹਰ ਲਾਉਣਾ	*mohar lāuṇā*	to seal.

Examples.

ਪੱਤ੍ਰੀ ਵਿਚ ਵੇਖਕੇ ਦਸ ਜੋ ਅਜ ਕੀ ਤਰੀਕ ਹੈ *patrī wich wekh ke das jo aj kī tarīk hai*
Look in the almanac and tell me what the date is.

ਹਜ਼ੂਰ, ਅਜ ਬੁਧਵਾਰ ੨੭ ਮਾਰਚ ਸੰਨ ੧੯੦੧ ਹੈ *hajūr aj budhwār 27 March san 1901 hai.* Sir, it is Wednesday the 27th of March 1901.

ਵਡੇ ਬਾਬੂ ਨੂੰ ਆਖ ਇਸ ਕਾਗਤ ਤੇ ਸਹੀ ਪਾਕੇ ਲਫਾਫੇ ਤੇ ਮੋਹਰ ਲਾਦੇ *waḍḍe bābū nūṅ ākh is kāgat te sahī pāke laphāphe te mohar lā de* Tell the head clerk to sign this paper and seal up the envelope

ਉਸ ਬਾਬੂ ਨੇ ਸਾਰਾ ਫੀਤਾ ਗੁਆ ਦਿਤਾ ਹੈ । *us bāhū ne sārā phītā guā dittā hai,* That clerk has lost all the tape.

ਅਜੇ ਚਪੜਾਸੀ ਲਿਖਤ ਪੜ੍ਹਤ ਦੇ ਕਾਗਤ ਲਿਆਇਆ ਹੈ ਕਿ ਨਹੀਂ । *aje chaprāsī, likhat paṛhat de kāgat liāiā hai ki nahīn,* Has the peon brought back the correspondence yet?

ਨਹੀ ਸਾਹਿਬ ਉਸਨੇ ਓਹੁ ਬਜ਼ਾਰ ਵਿੱਚ ਗਵਾਈ ਸੀ *nahīṅ sāhib usne oh bajār wich gawāī sī,* No Sir, he lost it in the bazar.

Translate into Punjābī.

Copy my account in this book. Give the peon eight annas to buy a new ruler. Pay the man his wages and discharge him because he cannot do his work properly. Do not erase the pencil marks in the cash book. How many clerks are there in your office? There are six clerks and two head clerks. Has the merchant sent back the correspondence yet? No, he has not signed it yet?

Translate into English.

ਚਪੜਾਸੀ ਨੂੰ ਆਖ ਜੋ ਇਹ ਤਿੰਨ ਪਿਨਸਲਾਂ ਘੜਦੇ । ਵਡਾ ਬਾਬੂ ਰਬੜ ਵਰਤਦਾ ਹੈ । ਇਹ ਚਿਠੀ ਸੁਦਾਗਰ ਵੱਲ ਭੇਜ ਕੇ ਸਹੀ ਪੁਆ । ਇਹ ਸਾਰੇ ਕਾਗਤ ਕਿੱਨੇ ਚਿਰ ਵਿਚ ਨਕਲ ਹੋ ਸਕਨਗੇ । ਤੂੰ ਇਹ ਕਾਗਤ ਸ਼ਾਹੀ ਆਦਕ ਚੀਜ਼ਾਂ ਮੁਲ ਲੈਕੇ ਖਰਚ ਕਰਦਾ ਹੈਂ । ਜੇਕਰ ਮੇਰੀ ਛੁਰੀ ਤੇਜ ਨਾ ਹੁੰਦੀ ਤਾਂ ਹਰਨ ਦਾ ਮਾਸ ਨਾ ਵਢ ਸਕਦੀ । ਮੋਹਰ ਲਾਕੇ ਇਹ ਸਾਰੀਆਂ ਚਿਠੀਆਂ ਰਜਿਸਟਰੀ ਕਰਵਾ । ਇਹ ਅੱਖਰ ਕਿਸਨੇ ਬਣਾਏ ਹਨ ?

LESSON XII.

NOUNS.

	Masculine.			Feminine.	
ਘਰ	*ghar*	house.	ਛਤ	*chhat*	roof.
ਪਿੰਡ	*piṅḍ*	village.	ਝੁਗੀ	*jhugī*	hut.
ਨੱਗਰ	*naggar*	town	ਹੱਟੀ	*haṭṭī*	shop.

Masculine.			Feminine.		
ਸ਼ਹਿਰ	*shahir*	city.	ਗਲੀ	*galī*	street.
ਥਾਣਾ	*thāṇā*	police station.	ਚੌਂਕੀ	*chauṅkī*,	police station (branch)
ਥਾਣੇਦਾਰ	*thāṇe dār*	deputy inspector (police).	ਹਵਾਲਾਟ	*hawālāṭ*	cell.
ਮੋੜ	*moṛ*	corner.	ਬਾਰੀ	*bārī*	window.
ਬੂਹਾ	*būhā*	door.	ਕੰਧ	*kaṅdh*	wall.
ਅਸਬਾਬ	*asbāb*	furniture.	ਪੌੜੀ	*pauṛī*	stairs.
ਖੂਹ	*khūh*	well.	ਕੜੀ	*kaṛī*	beam.
ਛੱਪਰ	*chhappar*	thatch.	ਕੋਠੜੀ	*koṭhṛī*	room.
ਚੋਰ	*chor.*	thief	ਲਾਲਟੈਨ	*lālṭaiṇ*	lantern.

VERBS.

ਝੁਗੀ ਪਾਉਣਾ	*jhuggī pāuṇā*,	to build (a hut).	ਭਜ ਜਾਣਾ	*bhaj jāṇā*	to runaway.
ਰਾਖੀ ਕਰਨਾ	*rākhī karṇā*	to look after.	ਪੁਜਣਾ	*pujṇā*	to reach.
ਜੰਦਰਾ ਭੰਨਣਾ	*jaṅdrā bhaṇṇā*	to break into.	ਖੋਲਣਾ	*kholṇā*	to open.
ਤਲਾਸ਼ੀ ਲੈਣਾ	*talāshī lainā*	to search (person.)	ਅੱਗ ਲਾਉਣਾ	*agg lāuṇā*	to set fire to.
ਫਾਸੀ ਦੇਣੀ	*phāsī deṇī*	to hang (person).	ਬਲਣਾ	*balṇā*	to be lit.
ਟੁਟ ਜਾਣਾ	*tuṭ jāṇā*	to be broken.	ਢਾਇਆ ਜਾਣਾ	*ḍhāiā jāṇā*	to be pulled down.

Examples.

ਚੌਂਕੀ ਤੇ ਸਦਾ ਤਿੱਨ ਆਦਮੀਆਂ ਦੀ ਨੌਕਰੀ ਹੁੰਦੀ ਹੈ *chauṅkī te sadā tin ādmīāṅ dī naukrī huṅdī hai,* Three men are always on duty at the sub-station.

ਦਿਨ ਡੁੱਬੇ ਸੜਕ ਦੇ ਕਨਾਰੇ ਕਨਾਰੇ ਲਾਲਟੈਨਾਂ ਬਾਲੀਆਂ ਜਾਂਦੀਆਂ ਹਨ *din ḍubbe saṛak de kaṇāre kaṇāre lālṭaināṅ bālīāṅ jāṅdīāṅ haṇ,* The lanterns along the road-side are lit at sunset.

ਤੇਰਾਂ ਚੋਰ ਘਰ ਦਾ ਜੰਦਰਾ ਭੰਨਕੇ ਭਜ ਗਏ । *terāṅ chor ghar dā jaṅdrā bhaṇke bhaj gae,* Thirteen thieves, having broken into the house, ran away.

ਇਸ ਪਿੰਡ ਦੇ ਲੋਕ ਕੀ ਬੀ ਬੀਜਦੇ ਹਨ । *is piṇḍ de lok kī bī bījde han,* What seed do the people of this village sow ?

ਉਸ ਚੋਰ ਨੂੰ ਜਿਸ ਨੇ ਘਰ ਨੂੰ ਅਗ ਲਾਈ ਫਾਂਸੀ ਦੇਹ । *us chor nūṅ jis ne ghar nūṅ agg lāī phāṅsī deh,* Hang the thief who set fire to the house.

ਕਿਸਵੇਲੇ ਓਹ ਆਪਨੀ ਹੱਟੀ ਖੋਲਦਾ ਹੈ । *kis wele uh āpṇī haṭṭī kholdā hai,* At what time does he open his shop ?

Translate into Punjābī.

When the crops are ripe the farmers build a hut near to look after them. They tried to get the furniture through the door into the house. The large iron beam at the corner of the roof fell into the street. The town of Umballa is much larger than the village of kálká The police station stands at the corner of the second street on the left. There are no windows into the walls of the cells.

Translate into English.

ਕਲ ਸਾਡੇ ਪਿੰਡ ਵਿਚ ਥਾਨੇਦਾਰ ਆਇਆ ਸੀ । ਇਕ ਜੱਟ ਦਾ ਅਸਬਾਬ ਚੋਰੀ ਹੋ-ਗਿਆ ਸੀ। ਚੋਰਾਂ ਦਾ ਕੁਝ ਪਤਾ ਨਹੀਂ ਲਗਾ। ਮੀਂਹ ਪੈਣ ਨਾਲ ਸਾਡੀ ਛੱਤ ਚੋ ਪਈ। ਪੰਜ ਛੀ ਬਦਮਾਸ਼ ਹਵਾਲਾਟ ਵਿਚ ਹਨ। ਮੇਰੀ ਅੰਦਰਲੀ ਕੰਧ ਪਾਟ ਗਈ ਹੈ ਤੇ ਘਰ ਢੈਣ ਦਾ ਡਰ ਹੈ। ਇਸ ਬੂਹੇ ਦੀ ਲਕੜ ਕੀੜੇ ਨੇ ਖਾ ਲੀਤੀ ਹੈ।

LESSON XIII.

NOUNS.

Masculine.			Feminine.		
ਸਾਫਾ	*sāphā*	large turban.	ਕਮੀਜ	*kamīj*	shirt.
ਤਾਜ	*tāj*	crown.	ਮਾਲਾ	*mālā*	necklace.
ਰੁਮਾਲ	*rumāl*	handkerchief.	ਫਤੂਹੀ	*phatūhī*	waistcoat.
ਕੋਟ	*koṭ*	coat.	ਜੁਰਾਬਾਂ	*jurābāṅ*	stockings.
ਪਜਾਮਾ	*pajāmā*	trousers.	ਜੁੱਤੀ	*juttī*	shoes.
ਦਸਤਾਨੇ	*dastāne*	gloves.	ਧੋਤੀ	*dhotī*	loin cloth.

Masculine.			Feminine		
ਬੂਟ	*būṭ*	boot.	ਬਰਾਂਡੀ	*barāṅḍī*	great coat.
ਕਪੜੇ	*kapṛe*	clothes.	ਮੁੰਦਰੀ	*muṅdarī*	ring.
ਬਕਸੂਆ	*baksūā*	buckle.	ਟੋਪੀ	*ṭopī*	hat, cap.
ਛੱਲਾ	*chhallā*	ring (plain).	ਸੁਥਨ	*suthaṇ*	trousers.
ਸਰਹਾਨਾਂ	*surhāṇā*	pillow.	ਨਥ	*ṇath*	nose ring.
ਗਲਾ ਬੰਦ	*gulāband*	neck tie.	ਚੱਦਰ	*chaddar*	sheet.
			ਚੂੜੀਆਂ	*chūṛīāṅ*	bracelets.

VERBS.

ਢਕਨਾ	*ḍhakṇā*	to cover.	ਪਹਿਨਨਾ	*pahinaṇā*	to wear.
ਬਣਨਾਂ	*bunṇāṇ*	to be made	ਕੰਮ ਕਰਨਾ	*kaṅm karṇā*	to work.
ਪਸਿੰਦਕਰਨਾ	*pasiṅd karṇā*	to like.	ਮੁਲਲੈਣਾ	*mul laiṇā*	to buy.
ਗੁਆਉਣਾ	*guāuṇā*	to lose.	ਦਿਸਣਾ	*disṇā*	to look (appear.)

Examples.

ਉਸਦਾ ਸਾਫਾ ਸਿਧਾ ਨਹੀ *usdā sāphā sidhā nahīṅ.* His turban is not straight.

ਤੁਹਾਨੂੰ ਬਰਸਾਤ ਵਿਚ ਬਰਾਂਡੀ ਪਹਿਨਨੀ ਚਾਹੀਦੀ ਹੈ *tuhāṇūṅ barsāt wich barāṅḍī pahinṇī chhāhidī hai,* You must wear your greatcoat in the rainy weather.

ਤੁਹਾਡੇ ਭਰਾ ਦਾ ਘੁਟੱਨਾ ਕਿਸ ਚੀਜ ਦਾ ਬਨਿਆ ਹੋਇਆ ਸੀ। *tuhāḍe bharā dā ghuṭaṇṇā kis chīj dā baṅīā hoiā sī,* Of what material were your brother' trousers made ?

ਜਦ ਦੇਸੀ ਮਨੁਖ ਕੰਮ ਕਰਦੇ ਹਨ ਧੋਤੀ ਤੋਂ ਬਿਨਾ ਹੋਰ ਕੋਈ ਕਪੜਾ ਨਹੀਂ ਪਾਉਂਦੇ *jad desī maṇukh kaṅm karde haṇ dhotī toṅ biṇāṅ hor koī kapṛā nahīṅ pāoṅde,* When natives work they wear nothing else but a loin cloth.

ਉਸਦੀ ਟੋਪੀ ਤੇ ਕਪੜੇ ਹੜ ਵਿਚ ਰੁੜ ਗਏ *us dī ṭopī te kapṛe haṛ wich ruṛh gae,* He lost his cap and clothes in the flood.

ਉਸਦੇ ਬੂਟ ਅੰਦਰ ਜਰਾਬਾਂ ਪਈਆਂ ਹੈਸਨ *us de būt andar jurābāṅ paīāṅ hai san,*

His stockings were down over his boots.

Translate into Punjābī.

The king's crown is made of gold and is covered with precious stones. That woman's coat is too tight, and her trousers are too long. Some soldiers wear boots and others do not. I bought a beautiful gold ring and a valuable necklace last month. My father's coat and waistcoat are made of fine blue cloth. Woollen gloves are better than cotton ones for the winter.

Translate into English.

ਦੇਸੀ ਤ੍ਰੀਮੀਆਂ ਨਕ ਵਿਚ ਨਥ ਤੇ ਹਥਾਂ ਵਿਚ ਚੂੜੀਆਂ ਪਸਿੰਦ ਕਰਦੀਆਂ ਹਨ । ਤੁਹਾਨੂੰ ਰੇਸ਼ਮੀ ਰੁਮਾਲ ਤੇ ਗਰਮ ਕਮੀਜ ਚੰਗੀ ਲਗਦੀ ਹੈ । ਧੁਪ ਵਿਚ ਸਾਹਿਬ ਲੋਕਾਂ ਦੀ ਟੋਪੀ ਵਡੀ ਚੰਗੀ ਮਲੂਮ ਹੁੰਦੀ ਹੈ । ਅਜ ਅਸੀ ਨਵੇਂ ਕਪੜੇ ਵਟਾਵਾਂ ਗੇ । ਮੈਂ ਨੂੰ ਇਕ ਸਰਹਾਨਾ ਤੇ ਚਦਰ ਬਿਸਤਰੇ ਲਈ ਬਥੇਰੀ ਹੈ । ਅਜ ਕਲ ਠੰਢ ਬਹੁਤ ਨਹੀਂ ਇਸ ਕਰਕੇ ਰਜਾਈ ਦੀ ਲੋੜ ਨਹੀਂ ।

LESSON XIV.

NOUNS.

Masculine.			Feminine.		
ਬਾਗ	*bāg*	garden.	ਬਗੀਚੀ	*bagīchī*	small garden.
ਜੰਗਲ	*jangal*	forest.	ਗੱਡੀ	*gaḍḍī*	cart.
ਹੱਲ	*hall*	plough.	ਖਰਲੀ	*khurlī*	manger.
ਪਿੰਜ	*pinj*	wheel.	ਵਾੜ	*wāṛ*	hedge
ਬੰਬ	*banb*	shafts.	ਕਹੀ	*kahī*	spade.
ਟਪ	*ṭap*	hood (cover).	ਛਾਨਨੀ	*chhāṇaṇī*	sieve.
ਕਖ	*kakh*	fodder (fields &c).	ਆਡ	*āḍ*	water-trough.
ਕੁਦਾਲ	*kudāl*	pickaxe.	ਕਿਆਰੀ	*kiārī*	garden bed.
ਜੰਦਰਾ	*jandrā*	pitchfork.	ਆਰੀ	*ārī*	saw.
ਕੁਹਾੜਾ	*kuhāṛā*	axe.			

VERBS.

ਲੋੜ ਪੈਨੀ	*lor paini*	to need.	ਛਨਨਾ	*chhannā*	to sift.
ਪਾੜਨਾ	*pārnā*	to tear.	ਵਢ ਦੇਣਾ	*wadh denā*	to cut down.
ਪੁਟਨਾ	*putnā*	to dig.	ਕਟ ਸੁਟਨਾ	*kat sutnā*	to cut down.
ਪੀਨਾ	*pīnā*	to drink.	ਸਵਾਰਨਾ	*sawārnā*	to trim.
ਵਗਨਾ	*wagnā*	to flow.	ਛਾਂਟਨਾ	*chhāntnā*	to trim.

Translate into Punjābī.

My garden is full of flowers, but his is full of weeds. You will need many axes to cut down that forest. Corn is put in the manger for the horse to eat. My father has a small garden in the village. The pony broke the shafts of the cart. You cannot trim the hedge with a saw for the bushes are too small. Take the horse out of the carriage and lead him to the water-trough to drink. The water from the well runs through the aqueduct and flows over the garden-beds. Put the corn in a sieve, sift it and the dust will fall out. The soldier broke the wheel of the cart and tore the hood to pieces. That plough is a good one, but the ploughshare is broken. A pickaxe is better than a spade for digging in hard ground

Translate into English.

ਮੈ ਨੂੰ ਉਸ ਜੰਗਲ ਵਿਚ ਇਕ ਬੁੱਢਾ ਤੇ ਬੁੱਢੀ ਮਿਲੇ। ਬੁੱਢਾ ਅੱਨ੍ਹਾਂ ਸੀ ਤੇ ਉਸਦੀ ਵਹੁਟੀ ਲੰਙੀ। ਉਸ ਵੇਲੇ ਮੇਰੀ ਟਮ ਟਮ ਦਾ ਬੰਬ ਟੁਟ ਗਿਆ ਸੀ ਇਸ ਕਰਕੇ ਮੈਂ ਉਥੇ ਖੜੋ ਕੇ ਉਨ੍ਹਾਂ ਦਾ ਹਾਲ ਚਾਲ ਪੁਛਨ ਲਗਾ। ਮੈਂ ਉਨ੍ਹਾ ਨੂੰ ਕੁਝ ਰੋਟੀ ਤੇ ਮਾਸ ਜੋ ਮੇਰੇ ਕੋਲ ਸੀ ਦਿੱਤਾ। ਇਕ ਜਟ ਦੇ ਮੁੰਡੇ ਨੇ ਗੁਸੇ ਵਿਚ ਆਕੇ ਆਪਣੇ ਬਕਰੇ ਨੂੰ ਕੁਹਾੜੇ ਨਾਲ ਵਢ ਸੁਟਿਆ। ਤੇਰੇ ਬਗੀਚੇ ਦੇ ਨੇੜੇ ਕੋਈ ਨਹਿਰ ਜਾਂ ਸੂਆ ਵਗਦਾ ਹੈ।

LESSON XV.

NOUNS.

Masculine.			Feminine.		
ਦਰਯਾ	*dariā*	river.	ਨਦੀ	*nadi*	stream.

Masculine.			Feminine		
ਪਹਾੜ	*pahāṛ*	mountatin.	ਪਹਾੜੀ	*pahāṛī*	hill.
ਮਦਾਨ	*madāṇ*	plain.	ਧਾਰ	*dhār*	current.
ਮਿਲਾਪ	*milāp*	confluence (river.)	ਲਹਰ	*lahar*	wave.
ਕੰਢਾ	*kaṇḍhā*	bank („).	ਬੇੜੀ	*beṛī*	boat.
ਨਿਕਾਸ	*ṇikās*	source („).	ਮਹਰਾਬ	*mahrāb*	arch.
ਥਲ	*thal*	bed („).	ਘਾਟੀ	*ghāṭī*	valley.
ਪੁਲ	*pul*	bridge.	ਚਟਾਨ	*chaṭāṇ*	rock.
ਚੋਆ	*choā*	spring.	ਰੇਤ	*ret*	sand.
ਜਹਾਜ	*jahāj*	ship.	ਝਾੜੀ	*jhāṛī*	bush.
ਘਾਟ	*ghāṭ*	ferry.	ਚੋਟੀ	*choṭī*	summit.
ਤੂਫਾਨ	*tūphāṇ*	storm.	ਵਾ	*wā*	wind.

VERBS.

ਹੜ ਆਉਣਾ	*haṛ āuṇā*	to flood.	ਤੇੜ ਪੈਣਾ	*teṛ paiṇā*	to split.
ਜਲ ਥਲ ਹੋਣਾ	*jal thal hoṇā,*	to overflow.	ਉਸਾਰਣਾ	*usārṇā*	to build.
ਟੁਟ ਜਾਣਾ	*ṭuṭ jāṇā,*	to give way.	ਚੱਪਾ ਲਾਉਣਾ	*chappā lāoṇā*	to row.
ਪਾਰ ਹੋਣਾ	*pār hoṇā*	to cross.	ਪਹੁੰਚਣਾ	*pahuṅchṇā*	to reach.
ਮਿਲਣਾ	*milṇā*	to join.	ਡੁਬਣਾ	*ḍubṇā*	to sink.

Examples.

ਜਦ ਕਈ ਨਦੀਆਂ ਆਪਸ ਵਿਚ ਮਿਲਦੀਆਂ ਹਨ ਤਾਂ ਦਰਿਆ ਬਣਦਾ ਹੈ *jad kaī ṇadīāṅ āpas wich mildīāṅ haṇ tāṅ dariā baṇdā hai,* When several streams join together they form a river.

ਕਲਕਤੇ ਦੇ ਨੇੜੇ ਸਾਰੇ ਦਰਿਆ ਸਮੁੰਦਰ ਵਿੱਚ ਪੈਂਦੇ ਹਨ *kalkatte de neṛe sāre dariā samundar wich painde haṇ,* Near Calcutta all the rivers fall into the sea.

ਲਹਿਰਾਂ ਇਨੀਆਂ ਉੱਚੀਆਂ ਚੜ੍ਹੀਆਂ ਜੋ ਬੇੜੀ ਡੁਬ ਗਈ *laihrāṅ iniāṅ uchīāṅ charhīāṅ jo berī ḍub gaī,* The waves rose so high that the boat sunk.

ਗੰਗਾ ਦਾ ਪੁਲ ਜੋ ਦਿੱਲੀ ਉਪਰ ਹੈ ਉਸਦੀਆਂ ਕਈ ਚੰਗੀਆਂ ਮਹਿਰਾਬਾਂ ਹਨ *gaṅgā dā pul jo dillī uppar hai usdīāṅ kaī chaṅgīāṅ mahrābāṅ haṇ,* The bridge over the Ganges, at Delhi has many fine arches.

Translate into Punjābī.

In summer the bed of the river is quite dry and people come for the sand to put in their gardens. The source of the Indus is amongst the Himalaya mountains in Afghanistan. When the Sutlej overflowed its banks the bridge gave way. The army crossed the plain and reached the shelter of the hills. The Ravee flows through a beautiful valley in the Punjab. Rocks and bushes cover the summit of the hill. He had built the bridge firmly but the strong wind completely destroyed the centre arch. You may row us across the ferry in your boat. We shall find a spring of cold, clear water on the hill-side.

Translate into English.

ਅਜ ਕਲ ਪਹਾੜ ਤੇ ਮਦਾਨ ਵਿਚ ਸਾਰੇ ਮੀਂਹ ਪੈ ਰਿਹਾ ਹੈ । ਪਰਸੋਂ ਰਾਤ ਇੱਨਾ ਜੋਰਦਾ ਮੀਂਹ ਪਿਆ ਜੋ ਘਗਰ ਦਾ ਪੁਲ ਟੁਟ ਗਿਆ। ਇਕ ਬੇੜੀ ਦਰਿਆ ਵਿਚ ਤਰਦੀ ਤਰਦੀ ਡੁਬ ਗਈ। ਮੀਂਹ ਨਾਲ ਇਸ ਅਲਾਕੇ ਵਿਚ ਤਾਂ ਜਲ ਥਲ ਹੋਗਿਆ ਹੈ। ਜਦ ਅਸੀ ਨਦੀ ਦੇ ਪਾਰ ਹੋਏ ਉਸੇ ਵੇਲੇ ਪੁਲ ਟਟ ਗਿਆ। ਬਿਆਸ ਦਰਿਆ ਬਰਸਾਤ ਵਿਚ ਭਰ ਜਾਂਦਾ ਹੈ ਤੇ ਉਸ ਦਾ ਪਾਟ ਕੋਈ ਡੂਢ ਮੀਲ ਦਾ ਹੋ ਜਾਂਦਾ ਹੈ।

TRANSLATION EXERCISES.

No. 1.

A dog was crossing a *bridge*[1] over a small *stream*[2] with a *piece*[3] of *meat*[4] in his mouth. He saw his *shadow*[5] in the water. *Thinking*[6] it was another dog he stopped. *Being greedy*[7] he *snatched*[8] at the shadow and *in doing so*[9] he dropped the piece of meat. It sank to the *bottom*[10] of the stream and *was lost*[11].

1 ਪੁਲ 2 ਨਦੀ 3 ਟੁਕੜਾ 4 ਮਾਸ 5 ਪਰਛਾਵਾਂ 6 ਸੋਚਕੇ conjunctive 7 ਲੋਭ ਕਰਕੇ 8 ਹਥ ਮਾਰਿਆ past tense 9 ਅਜਿਹਾ ਕਰਨ ਵਿਚ 10 ਥਲੇ 11 ਗੁਆਚ ਗਿਆ passive voice.

No. 2.

A *shepherd*[1] had a large *flock*[2] of sheep which *used to graze*[3] on the hillsides a *long way*[4] from his home. *At one time*[5] he had seven hundred *lambs*[6] in *his care*[7]. He would have lost all these *if it had not been for his dog*[8]. One very *dark night*[9] all the lambs *scampered off in different directions*[10], and were soon *out of sight*[11].

1 ਪਾਲੀ 2 ਇਜੜ 3 ਚਾਰਿਆ ਕਰਦਾ ਸੀ 4 ਵਡੀ ਦੂਰ 5 ਇਕ ਵਾਰ 6 ਲੇਲਾ 7 ਓਹਦੀ ਰਖਵਾਲੀ ਵਿਚ 8 ਜੇਕਰ ਓਹਦਾ ਕੁਤਾ ਨਾ ਹੁੰਦਾ note the idiom 9 ਹਨੇਰੀ ਰਾਤ 10 ਏਧਰ ਓਧਰ ਖਿੰਡ ਗਏ 11 ਦਿਸਣੋਂ ਰਹ ਗਏ

No. 3.

The shepherd, *in great trouble*[1], called to his dog, but, to *his surprise*[2] it had left him. He spent the whole night searching amongst the hills *for miles around*[3] At last *day came*[4], and, as he could see *neither dog nor sheep*[5], he started for home. On *his way*[6] there he found all the sheep in a *deep hollow*[7] and his faithful dog watching over them.

1 ਵਡੇ ਔਖ ਵਿਚ 2 ਅਚਰਜ ਹੋਇਆ 3 ਇਰਦ ਗਿਰਦ ਕਈ ਮੀਲਾਂ ਤੀਰ 4 ਦਿਨ ਨਿਕਲ ਆਇਆ 5 ਨਾ ਕੁਤਾ ਨਾਂ ਭੇਡਾਂ 6 ਜਦ ਓਹ ਘਰ ਨੂੰ ਆ ਰਿਹਾ ਸ 7 ਡੂੰਘਾ ਟੋਆ

Note.—The meaning of the words in italic are given below.

No. 4.

One *cold December morning*[1] at the beginning of this *century*[2] an army was crossing the mountains. The soldiers *looked*[3] *thin* and tired from *want of food*[4] *and sleep*; the horses that were *dragging*[5] *the guns stumbled at*[6] *every step.* There was one boy however in that army who marched *merrily*[7] along *as if he had*[8] *not suffered at all.* His name was Arthur Graham, and he was General Macdonalds's own drummer. He had been in many battles but had received no wound, *and nothing*[9] *could make him weary.*

1 ਦਸੰਬਰ ਦੇ ਮਹੀਨੇ ਦੀ ਠੰਡੀ ਸਵੇਰੇ 2 ਸਦੀ (f) 3 ਲਿੱਸੇ ਮਲੂਮ ਹੁੰਦੇ ਸੀ 4 ਭੁਖ ਤੇ ਨੀਂਦ ਦੇ ਮਾਰੇ note the idiom 5 ਤੋਪਾਂ ਘਸੀਟ ਰਹੇ ਸੀ 6 ਪੈਰ ਪੈਰ ਤੇ ਠੋਕਰ ਖਾਂਦੇਸੀ 7 ਖੁਸ਼ੀ ਖੁਸ਼ੀ 8 ਜਿਸ ਤਰਾਂ ਓਹਨੂੰ ਕੋਈ ਔਖ ਨਹੀਂ ਹੋਇਆ ਹੁੰਦਾ 9 ਅਰ ਓਹ ਕਿਸੀ ਚੀਜ ਤੇ ਥਕਦਾ ਨਾ ਸਾ

No. 5.

One day three natives were *going*[1] *along* the *Grand*[2] *Trunk* road from Umballa to Delhi. A large fair was being held at the *latter*[3] *place* and they wished to attend it. One of the men had twenty rupees in his turban, and the other two had *no money*[4] *at all.* They carried with them however some gold and silver ornaments which they hoped to sell at the fair and so obtain money to spend on *whatever*[5] *they wished to buy.* *Whilst passing*[6] *through a wood* they were attacked by *robbers*[7] who took away the *gold and silver*[8] *work.* The man who had the money seeing how unfortunate his companions were, very kindly told them that *all he had*[9] *they might share.*

1 ਤੁਰੇ ਜਾ ਰਹੇ ਸੀ 2 ਬਾਦਸ਼ਾਹੀ ਸੜਕ 3 ਪਿਛਲੀ ਥਾਂ such phrases are used very seldom in Punjābi, 4 ਮੁਲੋਂਹੀ ਕੁਝ ਨਹੀਂਸੀ 5 ਜਿਸ ਚੀਜਦੀ ਮੁਲ ਲੈਣ ਦੀ ਓਹਨਾਂ ਨੂੰ ਚਾਹ ਹੋਵੇ 6 ਜਦ ਓਹ ਇਕ ਜੰਗਲ ਵਿਚ ਦੀ ਲੰਘ ਰਹੇ ਸੇ 7 ਧਾੜਵੀ 8 ਸੋਨੇ ਚਾਂਦੀਦੇ ਗਹਿਣੇ 9 ਜੋ ਮੇਰੇ ਕੋਲ ਹੈ ਓਹ ਵੰਡ ਖਾਓ

No. 6.

We rode for about four miles across the plain and then arrived at a large mosque *sheltered*[1] *in a grove of trees. On the further*[2] *side* of the mosque was a lake in which were large numbers of fish. These fishes were *from six inches to* [3]*two-and-a-half feet long.* Their colour was a [4]*bright red* with three or four [5]*blue stripes* along the back. Several natives were seated on the bank of the lake feeding the fish with bread and [6]*parched barley.* There were only two [7]*priests* in front of the temple. One of these, an old man with a long white beard came up to us and [8]*asked for alms.* As we had no money we promised to give him something [9]*when next we come that way.*

1 ਜੋ ਦਰਖਤਾਂ ਦੇ ਝੁੰਡ ਨਾਲ ਢਕੀ ਹੋਈ ਸੀ 2 ਅਗਲੇ ਪਾਸੇ 3 ਛੇ ਇੰਚ ਤੇ ਢਾਈ ਫੁਟ ਤੀਕ ਲੰਮੀਆਂ ਸੀਆਂ Inch and foot are English words used in Punjabi as shown on the list page, 39 4 ਗੂੜ੍ਹਾ ਲਾਲ 5 ਨੀਲੀਆਂ ਧਾਰੀਆਂ 6 ਭੁਜੇ ਹੋਏ ਜੌਂ 7 Hindus call ਪੁਜਾਰੀ, Muhammadans ਮਜਾਉਰ Christians ਪਾਦਰੀ 8 ਕੁਝ ਭਿਛਿਆ ਮੰਗੀ 9 ਜਦ ਅਸੀ ਫੇਰ ਇਥੇ ਆਵਾਂਗੇ ॥

No. 7.

Our regiment was ordered to advance towards Delhi [1]*to prevent a party of the enemy from escaping.* As we marched through the [2]*thick* jungle our guide disappeared. Not a man in the squadron knew where we were and so we halted for the night about seven miles from the city. As there was [3]*plenty of grass* the [4]*bits* were taken out of the horses mouths. But, not knowing where the enemy were, we [5]*very wisely decided* not to remove the saddles, and only loosened the girths.

1 ਵੈਰੀ ਦੀ ਟੋਲੀ ਨੂੰ ਭਜਣ ਤੇ ਰੋਕਣ ਵਾਸਤੇ 2 ਸਿਘਣਾ 3 ਬਥੇਰਾ ਘਾਹ 4 ਦਹਾਨਾ 5 ਅਸੀ ਵਡੀ ਅਕਲ ਨਾਲ ਏਹ ਸਲਾਹ ਕੀਤੀ

No. 8.

[1]*On our arrival in India* we proceeded [2]*by rail* to Khandáwa. This is a very small village and the people seem to be very poor. It appears that [3]*they depend for their living on the parties of soldiers passing through to the Punjab.* Whilst staying in the [4]*camp* I saw a fine [5]*herd of camels* which had [6]*just* arrived. They had come a distance

of forty six [7]*miles* that day but were not tired at all. There was *one young* [8]one amongst them which the owner said was *only four* [9]*months old*. The men were very much amused at its gambols. *One man ventured* [10]*too near* and *received a nasty* [11]*kick in the stomach*. He was ill for many days and said he should always in the future [12]*hate the sight of a camel.*

1 ਜਦ ਅਸੀ ਹਿੰਦੁਸਤਾਨ ਵਿਚ ਪਹੁੰਚੇ 2 ਰੇਲ ਦੇ ਰਾਹ Rail is an English word used in Punjábi 3 ਉਨ੍ਹਾਂ ਦਾ ਗੁਜਾਰਾ ਉਨ੍ਹਾਂ ਸਪਾਹੀਆਂ ਦੀਆਂ ਟੋਲੀਆਂ ਪੁਰ ਚਲਦਾ ਸਾ ਜੇਹੜੇ ਪੰਜਾਬ ਨੂੰ ਉਸ ਪਿੰਡ ਦੇ ਵਿਚ ਦੀ ਲੰਘ ਕੇ ਜਾਂਦੇ ਸੇ 4 ਕੂੰਚ 5 ਊਠਾਂ ਦਾ ਛੇੜ 6 ਹਨੇ 7 ਮੀਲ 8 ਤੋਤਾ 9 ਨਿਰਾ ਚਾਰ ਮਹੀਨਿਆਂ ਦਾ ਸੀ 10 ਦਲੇਰੀ ਕਰਕੇ ਬਿਲਕੁਲ ਨੇੜੇ ਚਲਾ ਗਿਆ 11 ਢਿਡਵਿਚ ਡਾਢੀ ਲਤ ਖਾਹਦੀ 12 ਊਠ ਦੇ ਨੇੜੇ ਨਹੀਂ ਜਾਵਾਂਗਾ

No. 9

The week before we left the [1]*station* on our march to Kabul there was a *fearful* [2]*rainstorm* Rain and snow fell for three days [3]*without ceasing* and not a soul went out of doors. When we attempt to leave on the Wednesday, we found it impossible to go more than a few yards outside the walls of the village, for the [4]*surrounding country was flooded* ; and in some places the water was up to a man's neck. The inhabitants *were* [5]*bewailing* their losses, *for a great many had* [6]*not lost only their crops but their cattle and would be in a very bad* [7]*way for months.*

1 ਛੌਣੀ (f) 2 ਭਯਾਨਕ ਮੀਂਹ ਝਖੜ 3 ਲਗਾਤਾਰ 4 ਆਸ ਪਾਸ ਦੇ ਪਿੰਡਾਂ ਵਿਚ ਹੜ ਆਇਆ ਹੋਇਆਸੀ। 5 ਰੋਂਦੇ ਸੇ 6 ਕਿਉਂ ਜੋ ਬਥੇਰਿਆਂ ਦੀਆਂ ਨਾ ਨਿਰੀਆਂ ਫਸਲਾਂ ਹੀ ਵਰਾਨ ਹੋਈਆਂ ਸਗਆਂ ਓਨਾਂ ਦੇ ਡੰਗਰ ਵੀ ਜਾਂਦੇ ਰਹੇ 7 ਤੇ ਕਈਆਂ ਮਹੀਨਿਆਂ ਤੀਕ ਉਨ੍ਹਾਂ ਦਾ ਬੁਰਾ ਹਾਲ ਰਿਹਾ।

No. 10.

About two years ago a fire [1]*broke out in the* [2]*quarters* of the Native Infantry [3]*then stationed in Peshāwar*. A native woman [4]*upset some boiling ghee* on to a fire in one of the huts and the walls were *very soon* [6] *in flames*. *The whole of the huts were in* [7] *great danger of being burnt down for they consisted of nothing but frames of bamboo covered with grass* Luckily the [8] *fire-picquet* happened to be near. The havildar in charge at once divided his men into two parties. One of them tried to put out the flames by throwing water on to the burning hut, whilst the others [9] *pulled down* one or two huts on each side and so prevented the fire from spreading. One poor woman who was passing was [10] *severely hurt* by a piece of burning wood which fell on her shoulder.

1 ਅੱਗ ਲਗ ਗਈ 2 ਬਾਰਕਾਂ ਵਿੱਚ 3 ਤੇ ਜੇਹੜੀ ਉਸ ਵੇਲੇ ਪਸ਼ੌਰ ਵਿਚ ਰਹਿੰਦੀ ਸੀ 4 ਡੋਲਨਾ 5 ਤਾਇਆ ਹੋਇਆ ਘਿਓ 6 ਛੇਤੀ ਕੰਧਾਂ ਨੂੰ ਅਗ ਲਗ ਗਈ 7 ਸਾਰੀਆਂ ਝੁੱਗੀਆਂ ਦੇ ਸੜ ਜਾਣ ਦਾ ਡਰ ਸਾ ਕਿਓਂ ਜੋ ਓਹ ਨਿਰੇ ਫੂਸ ਨਾਲ ਢੱਕੇ ਹੋਏ ਬਾਂਸਾਂ ਦੇ ਠਾਠ ਸੇ 8 ਅਗ ਬੁਝਾਉਣ ਵਾਲੀ ਟੋਲੀ (f) 9 ਢਾ ਦੇਣਾ 10 ਵੱਡੀ ਸੱਟ ਲੱਗੀ ॥

No. 11.

As we got nearer to the [1] *Frontier* we found the country becoming [2] *wilder and wilder*. The hill sides were covered with great [3] *boulders*, behind which a man might easily have hidden, and the only [4] *signs of vegetation* were a few [5] *stunted shrubs* about a foot high. If we had been in an enemy's country we should have had great difficulty [6] *in forcing our way* through some of the passes. The inhabitants although not so tall as those living [7] *further south* are much more [8] *sturdy* and as [9] *hardy* as the animals they [10] *tend*. They are quite a different race of people from those who live in the Punjab, being more [11] *fierce and warlike* and I could easily understand [12] *how hard our troops fought had before he hillmen were conquered*.

1 ਸਰਹੱਦ 2 ਉਜਾੜ ਹੀ ਉਜਾੜ 3 ਪਥਰ ਵਟਾ 4 ਸਬਜੀ ਦੇ ਨਸ਼ਾਨ 5 ਨਿਕੀਆਂ ਨਿਕੀਆਂ ਝਾੜੀਆਂ 6 ਆਪਣਾ ਰਾਹ ਬਨਾਉਣ ਵਿਚ 7 ਪਰੇ ਦੱਖਨ ਵਲ 8 ਤਕੜਾ 9 ਮੇਹਨਤੀ ਬਹਾਦਰ 10 ਪਾਲਨਾ 11 ਤੁੰਦ ਤੇ ਬਹਾਦਰ 12 ਸਾਡੀ ਫੌਜ ਨੇ ਇਨਾਂ ਪਹਾੜੀਆਂ ਨੂੰ ਵਡੀ ਭਾਰੀ ਲੜਾਈ ਲੜਕੇ ਜਿਤਿਆ ਹੋਣਾ ਹੈ

No. 12.

We started for the jungle about *five a. m.*[1] for we had several miles to go. The Raja's *chief huntsman*[2] promised me some excellent game and said that I should have a shot at *more than one*[3] tiger, for his men had *found traces*[4] of three near a small *clearing*[5] about two miles away and so he had surrounded the place with *beaters*[6] some *three days before.*[7] I was very sorry that His Highness could not accompany us, but state business of an important nature detained him at his palace. His two sons however came and *the day's sport was the best I ever had,*[8] for by sunset we had bagged two tigers and a great deal of smaller game.

1 ਪੰਜ ਵਜੇ ਸਵੇਰੇ 2 ਵਡਾ ਸ਼ਕਾਰੀ 3 ਇੱਕ ਤੇ ਵਧੀਕ 4 ਖੋਜ ਕਢਣਾ 5 ਖੁਲੀ ਜਗਾ 6 ਝਾੜਨ ਵਾਲੇ 7 ਤਿਨਾਂ ਦਿਨਾਂ ਤੇ ਹੀ 8 ਉਸ ਦਿਨ ਦਾ ਸ਼ਕਾਰ ਅਜਿਹਾ ਚੰਗਾ ਸੀ ਜੋ ਮੈਂ ਕਦੀ ਨਹੀਂ ਦੇਖਿਆ ॥

No. 13.

One morning I met a lame man in a lane. *He had not gone far*[1] when his stick broke. *Being helpless,*[2] he set by the side of a white gate and *did not know what to do.*[3] There was none to help him. *By chance*[4] a kind-hearted boy passed that way on the back of a black mare. He *took pity*[5] on the lame man and helped him to ride on her, while he went by his side to his hut which was a mile off. When the lame man reached home he was happy, and blessed the boy for what he had done.

1 ਓਹ ਦੂਰ ਨਹੀਂ ਗਿਆ ਸੀ 2 ਲਚਾਰ ਹੋਕੇ 3 ਸੋਚਦਾ ਸਾ ਜੋ ਮੈਂ ਕੀ ਕਰਾਂ 4 ਅਚਾਨਕ 5 ਤਰਸ ਖਾਧਾ from ਤਰਸ ਖਾਣਾ

No. 14.

Two women were quarrelling *with one another*[1] about a child and neither of them had any witness. Having gone before the Judge *one continued saying*[2] "The child is mine." The other also said "The child is mine, O *your worship*[3] give justice." The Judge being helpless, sent for the executioner and said to him "Of this child make two pieces, and give one to each of these women." On hearing the order of the Judge the executioner [4]*drew his sword* and was about to cut the child in two. [5]*On this* one of the women stood still, and said nothing, but the other woman, [6]*weeping aloud,* said "O, Sir, do not kill my child ; if such is justice, I [7]*give up my claim.* [8]*For God's sake* give her the child." On hearing this the Judge became convinced that she indeed was the real mother who spoke.

1 ਇਕ ਦੂਜੀ ਦੇਨਾਲ 2 ਇਕ ਆਖਦੀ ਰਹੀ 3 ਹੇ ਦੀਨ ਦਿਆਲ 4 ਤਲਵਾਰ ਸੂਤੀ from ਤਲਵਾਰ ਸੂਤਨਾ 5 ਇਹ ਸੁਣਕੇ 6 ਜੋਰ ਨਾਲ ਰੋਕੇ 7 ਮੈਂ ਆਪਨਾ ਦਾਵਾ ਛਡਦੀ ਹਾਂ 8 ਰਬਦੇ ਵਾਸਤੇ

No. 15.

* *Gulāb Singh* had left one son, a boy named *Attar Singh,* [1]*nearly four years old,* and, as the [2]*custom seemed to prevail in the Farīdkot family* this child was acknowledged as chief by the British Government ; the [3]*administration of affairs* remaining, [4]*until he should reach his majority,* in the hands of *Faujā Singh* and *Sirdārnī Dharam Kaur* the widow. *Pahāṛ Singh* and *Sāhib Singh* had [5]*during the life time* of their brother lived with him and [6]*enjoyed the estate in common,* and it was decided that they [7]*were at liberty to remain thus.*

* *Note.*—Proper names are also given in italic.

1 ਚਾਰਕੁ ਵਰਹੇ ਦਾ ਸੀ 2 ਫਰੀਦਕੋਟ ਦੇ ਖਾਨਦਾਨ ਵਿਚ ਏਹ ਰੀਤ ਤੁਰੀ ਹੋਈ ਸੀ। 3 ਰਿਆਸਤ ਦਾ ਬੰਦੋਬਸਤ 4 ਜਦ ਤੀਕ ਓਹ ਜੁਆਨ ਨਾ ਹੋਵੇ 5 ਜੀਉਂਦੇ ਜੀ 6 ਜਗੀਰ ਦੀ ਆਂਮਦਨੀ ਸਾਂਝੀ ਖਾਂਦੇ ਰਹੇ 7 ਕਿ ਓਨਾਂ ਨੂੰ ਇਸ ਤਰਾਂ ਕਠੇ ਰਹਿਣ ਦਾ ਇਖਤਿਆਰ ਸੀ ॥

No. 16.

On the seventh of *June, Rājā Sarūp Singh* joined the British Camp at *Alīpore* and the [1]*following day* the battle of *Badlī Sarāe* was fought in which the *Jhīnd* troops [2]*behaved well,* and [3]*were complimented on the field by the Commander-in-Chief,* who sent one of the captured guns to the *Rājā* as a present. On the 19th June the *Jhīnd* troops aided in repulsing the *Nasīrābād* force which attacked the camp, and on the 21st were sent to *Bhāgpat* to repair the bridge of boats, [4] *which had been destroyed.* In three days the bridge was completed, but had to be again destroyed as the [5] *mutineers attacked the Rājā in overwhelming numbers compelling him to retire*

1 ਅਗਲੇ ਦਿਨ 2 ਚੰਗੀਤਰਾਂ ਲੜੇ 3 ਤੇ ਜੰਗੀ ਲਾਟ ਸਾਹਿਬ ਨੇ ਉਨ੍ਹਾਂ ਦੀ ਲੜਾਈ ਦੇ ਮਦਾਨ ਵਿਚ ਤਰੀਫ ਕੀਤੀ। 4 ਜੋ ਢਾ ਦਿਤਾ ਗਿਆ ਸੀ 5 ਦੰਗਈਆਂ ਨੇ ਵਡੀ ਫੌਜ ਨਾਲ ਹੱਲਾ ਕੀਤਾ ਜਿਸ ਤੇ ਰਾਜੇ ਨੂੰ ਪਿਛੇ ਹਟਨਾ ਪਿਆ ॥

No. 17.

[1] *Early in the month of November* 1845 *Sarūp Singh* was [2] *called upon* to send 150 camels for the use of the *Sirhind* Division, but this, in spite of promises and repeated orders, he neglected to do, [3] *and the result was great inconvenience to the troops* called upon to march. A fine of Rs. 10,000 was levied upon him by *Major Broadfoot*, which was [4] *realized* in the following year. After the [5] *warning* the conduct of the *Rājā* was quite satisfactory. The [6] *exertions of his people in providing supplies and carriage were great*; his contingent served with the British troops; and a detachment of it, which accompanied the *Patyālā* contingent to *Ghūmgarānā* under *Captain Hay* was highly praised by that officer, [7] *for its steady conduct and discipline.*

1 ਸਨ. ੧੮੪੫ ਨਵੰਬਰ ਮਹੀਨੇ ਚੜਦੇ ਹੀ 2 ਹੁਕਮ ਮਿਲਿਆ 3 ਇਸਤੇ ਫੌਜ ਨੂੰ ਵਡੀ ਤਕਲੀਫ ਹੋਈ 4 ਲੀਤਾ ਗਿਆ from ਲੀਤਾ ਜਾਣਾ 5 ਸਜਾ (ਧਮਕੀ) 6 ਭਾਰਬਰਦਾਰੀ ਤੇ ਰਸਤ ਦੇਨ ਵਿਚ ਓਸਦੇ ਲੋਕਾਂ ਨੇ ਵੱਡਾ ਜਤਨ ਕੀਤਾ 7 ਉਸਦੇ ਠੀਕ ਚਾਲ ਚਲਨ ਤੇ ਕਵੈਦ ਦੀ ॥

No. 18.

[1] *When the mutiny broke out in May* 1857 *Rājā Sarūp Singh was not behind the* [2] *Rājā of Patyālā in active loyalty.* When the news reached him in *Sangrūr*, of the revolt at Delhi, he at once collected all his troops and [3] *by forced marches* reached *Karnā* on the 18th, where he [4] *undertook the defence* of the City and Cantonments. His contingent did not exceed 800 men, but it was orderly and well disciplined and *its*

presence[5] *at Karnāl gave confidence,* and secured that station from plunder. From *Karnāl* the *Rājā* sent a detachment *to secure*[6] the bridge of boats at *Bhāgpat,* twenty miles north of Delhi, to enable the *Meerat* force to cross the *Jamnā* and join Sir H. *Barnard's* column. The town of *Pānīpat which was in a most excited*[7] *state was restored to order* and the *Jīndh* force marched in advance of the British columns.

1 ਜਦ ਸਨ ੧੮੫੭ ਵਿਚ ਗਦਰ ਉਠਿਆ 2 ਨਿਮਕ ਹਲਾਲੀ ਦੇ ਕੰਮਾਂ ਵਿਚ ਰਾਜੇ ਪਟਿਆਲੇ ਨਾਲੋਂ ਕੁਝ ਘਟ ਨਹੀਂ ਸਾ 3 ਦੋ ਪੜਾਵਾਂ ਦਾ ਇਕ ਕਰਕੇ (ਡਬਲ ਕੂਚ ਕਰਕੇ) 4 ਬਚਾਉ ਦਾ ਕੰਮ ਆਪਨੇ ਉਪਰ ਲਿਆ 5 ਓਹ ਦੇ ਕਰਨਾਲ ਜਾਨਤੇ ਲੋਕਾਂ ਦਾ ਦਿਲ ਜਮ ਗਿਆ 6 ਕਬਜਾ ਕਰਨਾ 7 ਜਿਥੇ ਬਹੁਤ ਹਲ ਚਲੀ ਪਈ ਹੋਈ ਸੀ ਅਮਨ ਹੋਗਿਆ ॥

No. 19.

(Higher Standard Punjábi 12th January 1890.

Two fellows by name *Heerā* and *Faujā Singh* stated, *that they had seen Dyāl Singh seize the ill fated lad*[1] *from behind and strangle him.* Owing to their being behind a *hedge*[2] he did not notice them. Their bullocks were resting, in fact one bullock had *got loose*[3] *from the yoke and was lying down.* There was not the least doubt that it was *Dyāl Singh* because he was *club-footed*[4] and *limped*[5] with the left leg, and they would know him by that at any time. This *Dyāl Singh* was a well known *bad character*[6] and cattle thief. He had already been several times in prison. On one occasion he had been *detected*[7] carrying off a cart and pair of bullocks, which were left standing near the gate of the village while the cart man was *getting some grain parched.*[8] He had been imprisoned for two years. *When the*[9] *head Lambardār heard what Faujā Singh had to say he sent for some trackers,* who lived in the next village, to trace *Dyāl Singh's* foot steps and catch him if possible. When they arrived at the place the foot steps of the club-footed man were easily traced, through the cultivation but afterwards they *were lost in the fallow land*[10] as the ground was so hard that no *impression*[11] was left. As it was of no use to try further, they returned home and reported the matter to the *Thānā*.

1 direct form ਕਿ ਅਸਾਂ ਦਯਾਲ ਸਿੰਘ ਨੂੰ ਉਸ ਅਭਾਗੀ ਮੁੰਡੇ ਨੂੰ ਪਿਛੇ ਤੇ ਫੜਦੇ ਤੇ ਗਲ ਘੁੱਟਦੇ ਦੇਖਿਆ 2 ਝਾੜੀ (ਵਾੜ)(*f*) 3 ਪੰਜਾਲੀ ਵਿਚੋਂ ਨਿਕਲਕੇ ਬੈਠਾ (ਲੇਟਿਆ) ਹੋਇਆ ਸੀ 4 ਭੁਬਾ 5 ਲੰਗੜਾਉਂਦਾ from ਲੰਗੜਾਉਨਾ 6 ਲੁੱਚਾ 7 ਪਕੜਿਆ ਗਿਆ 8 ਕੁਝ ਦਾਨੇ ਭੁਨਾਉਂਦਾ ਸਾ 9 ਜੈਲਦਾਰ ਨੇ ਫੌਜਾ ਸਿੰਘ ਦਾ ਹਾਲ ਸੁਣਕੇ ਕੁਝ ਖੋਜੀਆਂ ਨੂੰ ਬੁਲਾਇਆ 10 ਬੰਜਰ ਵਿਚ ਜਾਕੇ ਪੈੜ ਜਾਂਦੀ ਰਹੀ 11 ਪੈਰ ਦਾ ਨਸ਼ਾਨ

No. 20.

(Higher Standard Punjábi 10th July 1890.)

The wounded thief was unable to walk, so he was put in the cart with the [1] *dead body*. The boy's arms [2] *were fastened behind his back* and a cord passed round his neck, wihch I tied to my own saddle. Leaving twenty men to guard the wounded, we then quickly proceeded. We arrived at a large village before the sun rose, but the villagers [3] *were up*, and the [4] *herds of cattle were pouring out of the gates on their way to pasture.* We ordered our men to pitch the camp under some tall *shisham* trees. My father's brother-in-law and myself went to the gates and requested to see the head man. After waiting a long time we were [5] *ushered into* the house. He was a *Sikh* of high caste but of a [6] *proud disposition.* My father was spokesman, and having given him the usual [7] *salutation of the Sikhs* introduced himself as a merchant. He told him of the attack the robbers made on us, [8] *of which however he seemed to be perfectly incredulous.* He replied at once " [9] *you must be under some mistake* there has not been a high way robbery here for years.

1 ਲੋਥ 2 ਮੁਸ਼ਕਾ ਬੰਨ੍ਹੀਆਂ ਹੋਈਆਂ ਸੀ 3 ਜਾਗੇਹੋਏ ਸੀ 4 ਡੰਗਰਾਂ ਦੇ ਇੱਜੜ ਦਰਵਜਿਆਂ ਦੇ ਬਾਹਰ ਬੀੜ ਨੂੰ ਜਾ ਰਹੇਸੀ 5 ਵਾੜੇ ਗਏ from ਵਾੜਿਆ ਜਾਣਾ Passive voice 6 ਮਜਾਜੀ 7 ਵਾਹ ਗੁਰੂ ਜੀ ਕੀ ਫਤੇ lit: victory of God 8 ਪਰ ਮਲੂਮ ਹੁੰਦਾਸੀ ਉਸ ਨੂੰ ਸਾਡੀ ਗਲ ਦਾ ਬਿਲਕੁਲ ਜਕੀਨ ਨਹੀ ਆਇਆ 9 ਤੁਸੀ ਭੁਲਦੇ ਹੋਵੋਗੇ।

No. 21.

At that time he took his rifle in his hand and told the woman he was going to shoot her as she refused to marry him on account of his poverty. She, imagining he was joking, [1]*laughed at him.* He then [2]*deliberately* put his gun up to his shoulder, and, [3]*aiming at her head,* fired. [4]*The bullet penetrated the left eye and brain,* and came out at the back of the head. [5]*After satisfying himself that the woman was dead,* he stepped out of the house, and [6]*standing up against the wall shot himself through the heart.* The murderer and his victim [7]*were both very young,* neither of them being over 23 years of age, and the [8]*neighbours* say, the *only time they had any* [9]*high words, was, when the question of her turning Mohammadan was discussed.*

1 ਉਸ ਦੀ ਗਲ ਪੁਰ ਹੱਸੀ 2 ਜਾਨ ਬੁਝ ਕੇ 3 ਉਸ ਦੇ ਸਿਰ ਦੀ ਵਲ ਸ਼ਿਸਤ ਲਾਕੇ 4 ਗੋਲੀ ਖਬੀ ਅੱਖ ਤੇ ਮਗਜ ਵਿਚ ਵੜ ਗਈ। 5 ਇਸ ਬਾਤ ਦੀ ਪੂਰੀ ਤਸੱਲੀ ਕਰਕੇ ਜੋ ਤੀਵੀਂ ਮਰ ਗਈ ਹੈ 6 ਕੰਧ ਦੇ ਸਹਾਰੇ ਖੜੇ ਹੋਕੇ ਆਪਨੇ ਕਲੇਜੇ ਵਿਚ ਗੋਲੀ ਮਾਰੀ 7 ਦੋਵੇਂ ਛੋਟੀ ਉਮਰ ਦੇ ਸੀ 8 ਗੁਆਂਢੀ 9 ਕਿ ਓਹ ਨਿਰਾ ਇਕ ਵਾਰੀ ਉੱਚੀ ਬੋਲੇ ਸੇ ਜਦ ਉਸ ਤੀਮੀ ਦੇ ਮੁਸਲਮਾਨ ਹੋਨ ਪੁਰ ਬਹੁਤ ਝਗੜਾ ਹੋਇਆ ਸੀ।

No. 22.

(Higher Standard Punjábi 10th July 1887.)

One dark night *Lahnā Singh* and *Gujar Singh,* with two hundred men [1]*determined to surprise Lahore.* They found all the gates closed, but one *Dyāl Singh,* showed them a drain by which [2]*it was possible to enter with some squeezing,* *Gujar Singh,* [3]*led the way,* *Lahnā Singh,* followed and the other *Sikhs.* The *fort* [4]*was taken by surprise.* *Amīr Singh,* the Deputy Governor was captured at *a "Nautch"* and [5]*put in irons,* and *before* [6]*morning* the whole city was in the possession of the confederates. Early the next day *Sobhā Singh Kanhīyā,* nephew of *Jai Singh,* arrived. He had been in hiding at his native village of *Kānāh.* [7]*He was one of the confederates* and, [8]*although too late to aid in the capture was allowed a share of the prize.* Then came the other *Bhangi* and *Ghanayā* Sardárs and lastly *Charat Singh Sukar Chakīā who was*[9] *very hard to please* and would not go away till the *Bhangies* had given him the *Tamzamā gun* which he carried to *Gujrānwālā.*

1 ਲਹੌਰ ਪੁਰ ਛਾਪਾ ਮਾਰਨ ਦਾ ਅਰਾਦਾ ਕੀਤਾ 2 ਮੁਗਤ ਕੇ ਲੰਘ ਸਕਦੇ ਸੇ 3 ਅਗੇ ਅਗੇ ਚਲਿਆ 4 ਕਿਲਾ ਚੁਪ ਚੁਪਾਤੇ ਫਤੇ ਕੀਤਾ ਗਿਆ। 5 ਬੇੜੀਆਂ ਪਾਈਆਂ ਗਈਆਂ 6 ਦਿਨ ਚੜ੍ਹਨ ਤੇ ਪੈਹਲਾਂ 7 ਓਹ ਵੀ ਸਾਂਝੀਆਂ ਵਿਚੋਂ ਇਕ ਸੀ। 8 ਭਾਵੇਂ ਓਹ ਸ਼ਹਿਰ ਦੇ ਲੈਨ ਵਿਚ ਸਹਾਇਤਾ ਦੇਨ ਦੇ ਵੇਲੇ ਨਹੀ ਆਇਆ ਤਾਂ ਵੀ ਉਹ ਨੂੰ ਲੁਟਮਾਰ ਦਾ ਹਿੱਸਾ ਦਿਤਾ ਗਿਆ 9 ਜਿਸ ਦਾ ਰਾਜੀ ਕਰਨਾ ਵਡਾ ਔਖਾ ਸੀ

No. 23.

(Higher Standard Punjábi January 1888.)

About the same time[1] *Ranjīt Singh likewise found reasons to distrust the possessions of strong places* and *Fateh Singh Ahlūwālīā* was *persuaded*[2] by his *old brother in arms*[3] *to leave a massonary fort unfinished*[4] and *was further induced by his own fears to fly*[5] *to the south of the Sutlej.* He *was assured*[6] of English protection in his *family estates*[7] in the *Sirhind* province, but *Ranjīt Singh,* remembering perhaps the *treaty,*[8] with Lord *Lake earnestly endeavoured to allay the fear of the fugitive*[9] *and to recall a chief so dangerous in the hands of his allies. Fateh Singh* returned to *Lahore,* in 1827 ; he was received with *marked honour*[10] and *was confirmed in*[11] *nealy all his possessions.*

1 ਉਸੇ ਵੇਲੇ ਰੰਜੀਤ ਸਿੰਘ ਨੂੰ ਭੀ ਇਹੀ ਜਿਹੀ ਗਲ ਮਲੂਮ ਹੋਗਈ ਜਿਸ ਤੇ ਉਸ ਨੂੰ ਪਕਿਆਂ ਕਿਲਿਆਂ ਦਾ ਦੂਜਿਆਂ ਦੇ ਕਬਜੇ ਵਿਚ ਰਹਿਨ ਦਾ ਸ਼ਕ ਹੋਗਿਆ 2 ਸਮਝਾਯਾਗਿਆ 3 ਪੁਰਾਨਾ ਲੜਾਈ ਦਾ ਸਾਥੀ 4 ਪੱਕੇ ਕਿਲੇਨੂੰ ਅਧੂਰਾ ਛਡਨਾ 5 ਤੇ ਆਪਨੇ ਮਨ ਦੇ ਭੈ ਦਾ ਮਾਰਿਆ ਸਤਲੁਜ ਦੇ ਦਖਨ ਦੀ ਵਲ ਭਜ ਗਿਆ 6 ਭਰੋਸਾ ਦਿੱਤਾ ਗਿਆ 7 ਜੱਦੀ ਜਗੀਰ 8 ਅਹਿਦ ਨਾਮਾ 9 ਉਸ ਭਗੌੜੇ ਦਾ ਡਰ ਮਿਟਾਉਨ ਵਾਸਤੇ ਤੇ ਓਹ ਨੂੰ ਮੁੜਕੇ ਬੁਲਾਉਨ ਵਾਸਤੇ ਵਡਾ ਜਤਨ ਕੀਤਾ ਕਿਉਂ ਜੋ ਓਸਨੂੰ ਜਾਨਦਾ ਸਾ ਕਿ ਅਜਿਹੇ ਸ੍ਦਾਰ ਦਾ ਅੰਗਰੇਜਾਂ ਦੇ ਹਥ ਵਿਚ ਹੋਣਾ ਵਡਾ ਨਕਸਾਨ

ਪੁਚਾਉਣਾ ਹੈ 10 ਵਡੀ ਇਜ਼ੱਤ 11 ਤੇ ਉਸ ਨੂੰ ਲਗ ਭਗ ਸਾਰੀਆਂ ਜਗੀਰਾਂ ਫੇਰ ਦਿਤੀਆਂ ਗਈਆਂ।

No. 24.

(Higher Standard Punjábi 10th July 1888)

On his arrival in the *Punjāb*, to *the presence*[1] while *Humāyūn had summoned him* *Sikandar* found that *Tātār Khān* whom he left in command had fled from the new fortress of *Rohās* to *Delhi* and the *Mugals* had without *opposition*[2] recovered all the country as far as *Lahore*, *Sikandar* dispatched forty thousand horse to *oppose*[3] *their further progress*. This army suffered a great defeat. The baggage and elephants became the prey of his *adversaries*[4] and the *fugitives never drew rein till*[5] *they reached Delhi*. This defeat *did not deprive Sikandar Shāh of all hope of retrieving*[6] *his fortunes*.

1 ਜਿਥੇ ਆਉਣ ਵਾਸਤੇ ਓਹ ਨੂੰ ਹਮਾਯੂਨ ਨੇ ਸਦਿਆ ਸੀ 2 ਸਾਮਣਾ 3 ਕਿ ਓਨਾਂ ਨੂੰ ਅਗੇ ਨਾਂ ਵਧਨ ਦੇਨ 4 ਵੈਰੀ 5 ਭਗੌੜੇ ਦਿਲੀ ਪਹੁੰਚਨ ਤੀਕ ਨਾਂ ਰੁਕੇ 6 ਪਰ ਇਸ ਹਾਰ ਤੇ ਸਿਕੰਦਰ ਸਾਹ ਫੇਰ ਜਿਤਨ ਤੇ ਨਰਾਸ ਨਾਹੋਇਆ।

No. 25.

(Higher Standard Punjábi 12th July 1888.)

However much[1] *Gujar Singh may have wished to exclude his eldest son from the succession*, the *Sardār* of the *Khālsā would not admit*[2] his right to do so, and *Sāhib Singh took possession*[3] of his father's estates *without active*[4] *opposition* from *Fateh Singh*, who went to him, with *Mahān Singh* at *Gujrānwālā*. For some time there was peace *between the brother-in-law*[5] *Mahān Singh* and *Sāhib Singh*. But in 1789 they *openly quarrelled*[6] and for two years remained in *constant hostility*[7]. At length, in 1791, *Mahān Singh* shut up *Sāhib Singh* in the fort of *Sobia* and *reduced him to great*[8] *straits*. The *Bhangī* chief called to his assistance *Lahnā Singh* of *Lahore* and *Karm Singh* of *Doolo*. The former would not move, but *Karm Singh* came with a large force, to *raise*[9] *the siege*, and an engagement took place between him and *Mahān Singh*. The *Sukar Chakiān* chief was at this time very ill, and during the fight fainted on his elephant, the *Mahāwat* of which turned, and carried his master from the field: His forces, on seeing their leader depart fled, and the siege was raised *Mahān Singh* returned to *Gujrāṅwālā*, where he died three days afterwards, the [10] *desertion of his old friend Jodh Singh Wazirābādīā hastening his death.*

1 ਭਾਵੇਂ ਗੁਜਰ ਸਿੰਘ ਨੇ ਕਿਨੰਾ ਹੀ ਚਾਹਿਆ ਕਿ ਮੇਰਾ ਵਡਾ ਪੁਤ੍ਰ ਗਦੀ ਤੇ ਨਾ ਬੈਠੇ 2 ਨਾ ਮੰਨਿਆ 3 ਕਬਜਾ ਕਰਨਾ 4 ਲੜਾਈ ਤੇ ਬਿਨਾ 5 ਸਾਲੇ ਭਨਵਈਏ ਦੇ ਵਿਚਕਾਰ 6 ਖੁਲਮ ਖੁਲਾ ਝਗੜਾ ਹੋਇਆ 7 ਅਨਟੁਟ ਵੈਰ 8 ਓਹ ਨੂੰ ਵਡਾ ਤੰਗ ਕੀਤਾ 9 ਘੇਰਾ ਹਟਾਓਣਾ 10 ਆਪਣੇ ਪੁਰਾਨੇ ਮਿਤ੍ਰ ਜੋਧ ਸਿੰਘ ਵਜੀਰਾਬਾਦੀਏ ਦੇ ਸਾਥ ਛਡਨ ਦੇ ਗਮ ਵਿਚ ਛੇਤੀ ਮਰਗਿਆ

No. 26.

The *Patyālā Sirdārs* and the *Rājās* of *Jhindh* and *Nābhā*, who had benefitted so much by the [1] *late visit of Ranjīt Singh*, [2] *again invited his assistance*, which he very willingly promised. He collected a large body of horse under the command of his [3] *famous* general *Dīwān Mohkam Chand*, and Sirdār *Fateh Singh*, *Ahlūwālīā*, and *Ghurbā* Singh and in September 1807 he appeared before *Patyālā*, [4] *where the intrigues of the former year were repeated* [5] *in order to induce him to espouse the cause of one party or the other.* It [6] *was a mere question of money*, and the [7] *Rānī bribed highest*. Besides money and diamonds she gave *Ranjīt Singh* a brass gun named *Khūrī Khān*, afterwards taken by the English during the campaign of the *Satlej*.

1 ਪਿਛਲਾ ਮਿਲਾਪ 2 ਫੇਰ ਉਸਤੇ ਸਹਾਇਤਾ ਮੰਗੀ 3 ਨਾਮੀ 4 ਜਿਥੇ ਪਹਿਲੇ ਸਾਲ ਵਰਗੇ ਜੋੜ ਤੋੜ ਹੋਨ ਲਗੇ 5 ਇਸ ਕਰਕੇ ਕਿ ਓਹ ਕਿਸੇ ਨਾ ਕਿਸੇ ਧੜੇ ਦਾ ਪਖ ਕਰੇ idiom ਰੰਜੀਤ ਸਿੰਘ ਨੂੰ ਆਪਨੇ ਧੜੇ ਵਲ ਲਿਆਉਨ ਵਾਸਤੇ ਨਿਰਾ ਰੁਪਈਆ ਚਾਹੀਦਾ ਸੀ 7 ਰਾਨੀ ਨੇ ਵਡੀ ਭਾਰੀ ਵੱਢੀ ਦਿਤੀ।

No. 27.

Two men gave same [1] *property* in charge of an old woman and said "When we both come back, we will take our property." After a short time one of them came to the old woman and said," My *partner*[2] is dead, give me all the property." The old woman being helpless gave it to him. Soon after the other man came and demanded his property. Then the old woman said "Your partner came to me and said that you were dead; although I told him, I *did not believe him*,[3] he would not listen to what I said and took away all the property." The man *dragged*[4] the old woman before the judge, and demanded justice. The Judge after much consideration found out that the *old woman was blameless*,[5] and said to the man, "Your first agreement was when we both come we will take away the property. How can you take it away without him." The man being helpless went his way.

I ਮਾਲ ਮਤਾ 2 ਭਾਈ ਵਾਲ 3 use the direct Form ਮੈ ਤੇਰਾ ਅਤਬਾਰ ਨਹੀਂ ਕਰਦੀ 4 ਘਸੀਟਿਆ from ਘਸੀਟਣਾ 5 ਬੁਢੀ ਬੇਦੋਸ ਸੀ

No. 28.

On we marched for miles and miles over the desolate looking country[1] not a *blade of grass*[2] or a *sign of habitation*[3] anywhere. As night began to fall we halted at a *solitary*[4] hut, *shadowed by a clump of date trees*.[5] Close by there was a well of *fresh water*.[6] My quarters were a room twelve feet square without windows or *chimney*.[7] After a while it came on to rain. Then the *escort*[8] and donkey man *came in for shelter*.[9] The *Hājī* now *clad in more humble style*[10] sat on the floor and lit a fire, the *smoke*[11] of which found its way out through the open doorway. The next morning we started about three hours after sunrise and travelled along until evening, when we again halted. *When we came to a bad bit of road*,[12] the *animals had to be unloaded, and helped down by hand and by ropes*.[13]

1 ਅਸੀ ਕੋਹਾਂ ਤੀਕ ਉਸ ਉਜਾੜ ਦੇਸ ਵਿਚ ਅਗੇ ਅਗੇ ਚਲਦੇ ਗਏ 2 ਘਾ ਦਾ ਪਠਾ 3 ਅਬਾਦੀ ਦੀ ਨਸ਼ਾਨੀ 4 ਕਲੀ 5 ਖਜੂਰਾਂ ਦੇ ਝੁੰਡ ਨਾਲ ਢਕੀ ਹੋਈ ਸੀ 6 ਮਿਠਾ ਪਾਨੀ 7 ਅੰਗੀਠੀ (f) 8 ਰਾਖੇ 9 ਮੀਹ ਤੇ ਬਚਨ ਵਾਸਤੇ ਅੰਦਰ ਆਏ 10 ਮੈਲੇ ਕਚੈਲੇ ਕਪੜੇ ਪਾਕੇ 11 ਧੂਆਂ 12 ਜਦ ਅਸੀ ਸੜਕ ਦੇ ਖਰਾਬ ਟੁਕੜੇ ਪੁਰ ਆਏ

13 ਸਾਨੂੰ ਪਸੂਆਂ ਤੋ ਭਾਰ ਲਾਹਨਾ ਤੇ ਓਨਾ੍ਹ ਨੂੰ ਹਥਾਂ ਤੇ ਰਸੀਆਂ ਦੇ ਸਹਾਰੇ ਹੇਠ ਲਿਆਉਣਾ ਪਿਆ

No. 29.

When Sāhib Singh [1]*succeeded* his father at *Patiālā*, *Rājā Gujpat Singh did* [2]*his best to restore order* and assisted *Diwān Nānū Mall to put down the* [3]*rebellion* of Sirdār *Mahān* Singh *who had* [4]*proclaimed himself independent at Bhawānigurh.* He also, in person, marched against *Ālā* Singh of *Talwandī*, who had [5]*thrown off the authority of Patiālā.* In 1786 while engaged in an expedition against [6]*refractory villages* in the neighbourhood of *Umbāllā*, with *Diwān Nānū Mall* and *Bibi Rājindar* the sister of *Rājā Patiālā*, [7]*he fell ill with fever* and was carried to *Safidon*, where he died aged 51. His eldest son *Mehar* Singh died in A. D. 1780, leaving one son, *Hari* Singh, who was put in possession of *Safidon* by *Rājā Gajpat* Singh. But he was of [8]*dissipated habits* and in a state of intoxication fell from the roof of his house, and was killed.

1 ਗੱਦੀ ਤੇ ਬੈਠਾ 2 ਤੈਹ ਬਠਾਉਨ ਵਾਸਤੇ ਵਡਾ ਜਤਨ ਕੀਤਾ 3 ਬਲਵਾ ਮਿਟਾਉਨ 4 ਜਿਸ ਨੇ ਭਵਾਨੀ ਗੜ੍ਹ ਵਿਚ ਆਪਨੇ ਆਪ ਨੂੰ ਆਕੀ ਬਨਾ ਲਿਆਸੀ। 5 ਜਿਸ ਨੇ ਪਟਿਆਲੇ ਦਾ ਹੁਕਮ ਤੋੜ ਦਿਤਾ ਸਾ 6 ਆਕੀ ਪਿੰਡ 7 ਓਹ ਨੂੰ ਤਪ ਚੜ੍ਹਗਿਆ note the construction 8 ਉਜਾੜੂ, ਲੁੱਚਾ

No. 30.

To please my father I mounted the horse and as soon as I was upon his back I put my hand upon a [1]*peg*, as I had already seen the Indian do, to [2]*make the horse ascend into the air.* This I did without waiting to receive [3]*instructions* from the owner. The instant I touched the peg the horse mounted with me into the air, as swift as an arrow shot out of a bow, and I was soon at such a distance from the earth that [4]*I could not distinguish any object.* By the swiftness of [5]*the motion* I was for sometime [6]*unapprehensive of the danger* to [7]*which I was exposed*, but when I grew sensible of it I endeavoured to turn the peg the [8]*contrary way.* But the *experiment would not* [9]*answer my expectation* and still the horse ascended with me and carried me a greater distance from the earth.

1 ਕਿਲੀ (f) 2 ਘੋੜੇ ਨੂੰ (ਹਵਾ) ਅਕਾਸ ਉਪਰ ਚੜ੍ਹਾਓਨ ਲਈ 3 ਹੁਕਮ

4 ਮੈਂ ਕਿਸੇ ਚੀਜ ਨੂੰ ਪਛਾਨ ਨਹੀ ਸਕਦਾ ਸਾ 5 ਚਲਣ 6 ਫਿਕਰ ਵਿਚ ਗਲਤਾਂਨ
7 ਜੇੜ੍ਹਾ ਮੈਂ ਨੂੰ ਆਉਨ ਵਾਲਾਸਾ 8 ਪੁਠੇ ਪਾਸੇ, ਉਲਟੇ ਪਾਸੇ। 9 ਪਰ ਇਸ
ਪਰੀਖਯਾ ਤੇ ਮੇਰੀ ਆਸ ਪੂਰੀ ਨਾ ਹੋਈ (ਘੋੜ੍ਹਾ ਹੇਠਾ ਨਾ ਉਤ੍ਰਿਆ)

No. 31.

In January 1841, Sher Singh became *Mahārājā* of *Lahore* and some months later the *Rājā* of *Mandī* was released from confinement and permitted to return to his country, taking with him the silver image of the goddess (Devi) [1]*which was the object of general veneration in the hills*, and which the *Sikhs* had carried away from her temple at *Kamālgarh*. The release of the *Rājā* was a [2]*spontaneous act* of *Mahārājā* Sher Singh who was of a [3]*kindly disposition* and was exceedingly displeasing to the minister *Dhyān* Singh, who [4]*found himself disappointed of a very large present to himself and a Nazarānā to the state treasury, that had for* [5]*months past formed the object of a secret negotiation between him and certain Gosāīn bankers of Mandī.*

1 ਜਿਸ ਨੂੰ ਓਨਾਂ ਪਹਾੜੀਆਂ ਵਿਚ ਸਾਰੇ ਲੋਕ ਪੂਜ ਦੇ ਸੀ 2 ਮਰਜੀ ਦਾ ਕੰਮ
3 ਦਿਲ ਦਾ ਦਯਾਵਾਨ 4 ਜੋਕੇ ਆਪਨੇ ਆਪਨੂੰ ਇਕ ਵਡੀ ਨਜਰ ਤੇ ਰਿਆਸਤ ਦੇ
ਖਜ਼ਾਨੇ ਨੂੰ ਨਜਰਾਨਾ ਮਿਲਨ ਤੋ ਨਰਾਸ ਹੋ ਗਿਆ 5 ਜਿਸਦੀ ਖਾਤਰ ਓਹ ਕਈ
ਮਹੀਨਿਆਂ ਤੇ ਚੋਰੀ ਚੋਰੀ ਮੰਡੀ ਦੇ ਕਈ ਗੁਸਾਈਂ ਸਰਾਫਾਂ ਨਾਲ ਬੰਦੋਬਸਤ
ਕਰ ਰਿਹਾ ਸੀ।

No. 32.

(Higher Standard Punjábi 10th January 1895.)

When *Hīrā Singh* was killed by the army, the Colonel, who was considered a [1]*protsge* of the *Rājā*, was turned out of the Regiment by his own men, and he then [2]*entered the force* of *Sardār Shām Singh Attārīwālā*. When the Regiment was in front of the enemy at *Sabrān* the men finding that they could not fight without their old Colonel insisted upon his returning to command them, which he did, with [3]*distinguished gallantry* throughout the bettle. *Farn Shāh* had been sent with a [4]*deputation* from the *Panchāits* of the Army to *Rājā Gulāb Singh* to implore him to join them without delay [5] *but the Rājā had other designs*

1 ਪਾਲਿਆ ਪਲੋਸਿਆ ਹੋਯਾ 2 ਫੌਜ ਵਿਚ ਰਲਿਆ 3 ਵਡੀ ਬਹਾਦੁਰੀ 4 ਵਕੀਲਗੀ
5 ਪਰ ਰਾਜੇ ਦਾ ਮਤਲਬ ਹੋਰ ਸੀ।

No. 33.

(Higher Standard Punjābi 10th July 1895.

After the death of *Shām Singh* in 1813, *Dharam Singh* received a portion of his *Jāgīrs*. He served at *Multan, Kashmīr, Peshāwar*, and in other campaigns, and [1] *when he grew old* the *Mahārājā*, [2] *resuming his Jāgīrs*, gave him a cash pension of Rs. 2,000 and placed his son *Gandā Singh* with prince *Sher Singh*, who gave him a *Jāgīr* of Rs. 3,000 from his own estate. [3] *He was a great favorite with the prince* whom he accompanied to *Yūsafzaī*, where he was wounded, and afterwards to *Kulū*. When the prince was *Nizām* of *Kashmīr, Gandā Singh* held both [4] *civil and military* appointments under him and was employed [5] *to reduce the Rājās Bhambā and Khākhā to obedience.* He afterwards served at *Naushera* and *Banūn*.

1 ਜਦ ਓਹ ਬੁਢਾ ਹੋ ਗਿਆ 2 ਆਪਨੀ ਜਗੀਰ ਨਵੇਂ ਸਿਰੇ ਲੈਕੇ 3 ਕੰਵਰ ਉਸ ਨੂੰ ਵਡਾ ਪਿਆਰ ਕਰਦਾ ਸੀ 4 ਮੁਲਕੀ ਤੇ ਜੰਗੀ 5 ਰਾਜੇ ਭੰਬੇ ਤੇ ਖਾਖੇਂ ਨੂੰ ਤੰਗ ਕਰਕੇ ਸਰ ਕਰਲਿਆ

No. 34.

Nānūn Mul was on his road back from *Karnāl* [1] *when he heard* of all *that his enemies had accomplished against him.* Understanding, that *till fortune changed, it would be madness* [2] *to return to Patyālā*, where he could only expect imprisonment or death, he [3] *took refuge* with Sirdār *Karm Singh* of *Shāhābād.*

[4] *The chief promised him not only protection but assistance to recover his power in Patiālā* ; but treacherously wrote to *Rājā Sāhib Singh*, telling him of the arrival of the fugitive, and urging him to take *Ghanor* before the *Dīwān* could raise troops and come

to the help of his relative. [5] *Nānūn Mul with difficulty* collected a small force and marched [6] *to the relief of the fort*; but on the road he heard of its capture. His men deserted, and he was obliged to seek a new asylum in the *Kythal* territory where he took up his residence at the little village of *Chikah* close to the *Putyālā* frontier. All his estates were confiscated, his property seized, and his relations expelled from office or placed in confinement.

1 ਜਦ ਉਸ ਨੇ ਸਭ ਜੋ ਕੁਝ ਵੈਰੀਆਂ ਨੇ ਉਸ ਦੇ ਵਿਰੁਧ ਕੀਤਾ ਸੀ ਸੁਨ ਲਿਆ
2 ਜਦ ਤਾਂਈ ਭਾਗ ਨਾ ਮੁੜਨ ਪਟਿਆਲੇ ਮੁੜਨਾ ਮਹਾਂ ਮੂਰਖਪੁਣਾਹੈ 3 ਸਰਨ ਲੀਤੀ
4 ਸ੍ਰਦਾਰ ਨੇ ਓਹ ਦੇ ਨਾਲ ਨਾ ਨਿਰਾ ਪਨਾਹ ਦੇਨ ਦਾ ਕਰਾਰ ਕੀਤਾ ਸਗਵਾਂ ਇਹ
ਕਿਹਾ ਕਿ ਮੈਂ ਤੇਰੀ ਸਹਾਇਤਾ ਕਰਕੇ ਪਟਿਆਲੇ ਵਿਚ ਅਗੇ ਜਿਹਾ ਜੋਰ ਕਰਾ ਦੇਵਾਂਗਾ
note the construction 5 ਔਖੇ ਸੁਖਾਲੇਂ 6 ਕਿਲੇ ਨੂੰ ਛੁਡਾਉਨ ਲਈ

No. 35.

Jagut Singh joined the *Sikh* army in 1763, when *Zīn khān*, the *Afghān* Governor of *Sirhind*, was defeated and slain. He then seized a [1] *large tract of country*, including the districts of *Jhind* and *Sufidon*, [2] *overrunning Pānīpat* and *Karnāl*, [3] *but he was not sufficiently strong to hold them*. Yet, [4] *in spite of this rebellion*, he did not deny altogether the [5] *authority* of the *Delhi* Court. He remained, as before, a *Mālguzār* of *Delhi*, paying revenue to the Emperors; and in 1767, [6] *having fallen a lakh and half into arrears*, he was taken prisoner by *Najīb Khān*, the Muhammadan Governor, and carried to *Delhi*, where he remained a prisoner for three years, [7] *only obtaining release by leaving his son Mehr Singh as a hostage for the punctual payment of what was due,*

1 ਬਹੁਤ ਸਾਰਾ ਮੁਲਕ 2 ਫਤੇ ਕਰਕੇ 3 ਪਰ ਓਹਦੇ ਕੋਲ ਇਨੀ ਫੌਜ ਨਹੀਂ ਸੀ
ਜੋ ਇਨਾਂ ਜਗਾਂ ਨੂੰ ਸੰਭਾਲ ਸਕੇ 4 ਭਾਵੇਂ ਓਹਨੇ ਬਲਵਾ ਕੀਤਾ 5 ਈਨ (f) 6 ਜਦ
ਡੂਢ ਲਖ ਰੁਪਈਆ ਓਹ ਦੇ ਸਿਰ ਚੜ੍ਹ ਗਿਆ 7 ਅਰ ਓਹ ਤਦ ਛੁਟਿਆ ਜਦ ਓਹ
ਨੇ ਜੋ ਕੁਝ ਓਹ ਦੇ ਉਤੇ ਚੜ੍ਹਿਆ ਹੋਇਆ ਸੀ ਓਹ ਦੇ ਲਵੇ ਸਿਰ ਦੇਨ ਦੇ ਥਾਂ ਆਪਨੇ
ਪੁਤ੍ਰ ਮੇਹਰ ਸਿੰਘ ਨੂੰ ਵਕ ਕਰਕੇ ਛਡਿਆ।

No. 36.

In 1826, *Rājā Sangat Singh* paid a visit to *Mahārājā Ranjīt Singh*. He was met at *Amritsar* by some *Sirdārs* of the Court, and conducted *with honor*[1] to *Lahore*, where the *Mahārājā received him very kindly*[2] and on the festival of the *Holī* made his officials present nazar to him. *Ranjīt Singh* invited the *Rājā* to accompany him to *Jawālā Mukhī, a place of pilgrimage*[3] in the *Kāngrā* hills, and he *consented* to go as far as *Dīnāngar*, where he waited for the *Mahārājā's* return, when he received the grant of the *Jāgir* in the *Jalandhar Doāb*. In 1827, he again visited *Lahore*. *Mahārājā Ranjīt Singh* seems to *have taken a great liking for him*[4] and gave him many *presents*[5], one of which brought him into some trouble with the British Government.

1 ਆਦਰ ਮਾਨ ਨਾਲ 2 ਵਡੀ ਦਯਾ ਨਾਲ ਆਓ ਭਗਤ ਕੀਤੀ 3 ਤੀਰਥ 4 ਉਸ ਨੂੰ ਵਡਾ ਚਾਹੁਨ ਲਗ ਪਿਆਸਾ 5 ਅਨਾਮ

No 37.

(Higher Standard Punjábí January 1896.)

Prince *Nau Nihāl Singh, indignant*[1] with *Misar Belī Rām* for having *supported*[2] his father's favourite *Chet Singh*, threw him and his brother into prison, where they remained for six months, till, at *the intercession of*[3] *Mahārājā Kharak Singh* they were released. *Belī Rām* was a *zealous supporter*[4] of Prince *Sher Singh* who when he ascended the throne, restored the *Misr* to his old post of *Toshā Khānā*. *Rūp Lāl* was made Governor of *Kalānaur* and the lands of *Lahore* State south of the *Satlej* with orders to resume the fort of *domain*[5] *Bhratpur* from *Jamādār Khushāl Singh*.

1 ਗੁਸੇ ਹੋਕੇ 2 ਸਹਾਇਤਾ ਦਿਤੀ 3 ਮਹਾਰਾਜੇ ਦੇ ਵਿਚ ਪੈਣ ਨਾਲ 4 ਜ਼ੋਰ ਨਾਲ ਸਹਾਇਤਾ ਕਰਨ ਵਾਲਾ ਸਾ 5 ਇਲਾਕਾ

No. 38.

(Punjábí Examination July 1896.)

[1] *A great famine desolated* Sirsā; in 1783, and the Sirdar returned to the Punjab, At *Ludihānā* he met messengers from Sirdar *Mahān Singh Sukarchakīā* and Rájá *Sansār Chand* of *Kāngṛā* [2] *offering to reinstate him in his possessions* if he would join them against Sirdar *Jai Singh, Kanhīyā, Jassā Singh* consented readily enough [3] *and having joined forces, the allies marched to Battālā, Gurbakhsh Singh,* son of *Jai Singh,* advanced against them, with 8,000 men, but he was defeated and slain, and the *Kanhīyā* chief was [4] *compelled to give up* the *Ramghaṛīā* estate to their old owner, and the fort of Kāngṛā which he had held for four years, to Sansār *Chand.* [5] *But Jassā Singh was not destined to enjoy peace,* and for many years he was engaged in disputes with *Kanhīyā* misal, in which he was sometimes successful sometimes defeated.

1 ਵਡੇ ਕਾਲ ਨੇ ਸਰਸੇ ਨੂੰ ਵਗਾਨ ਕਰਦਿਤਾ 2 ਓਹ ਨੇ ਕਿਹਾ ਕਿ ਮੈਂ ਤੇਰੀ ਜਗੀਰ ਫੇਰ ਦੇ ਦੇਵਾਂਗਾ 3 ਫੌਜ ਕਠੀ ਕਰਕੇ ਦੋਹਾਂਨੇ ਰਲਕੇ ਬਟਾਲੇ ਨੂੰ ਕੂਚ ਕੀਤਾ 4 ਛਡਣੀਆਂ ਪਈਆਂ 5 ਪਰ ਜਸਾ ਸਿੰਘ ਦੇ ਭਾਗ ਵਿਚ ਅਰਾਮ ਨਾਲ ਜਿੰਦਗੀ ਭੋਗਨੀ ਨਹੀ ਲਿਖੀ ਸੀ

No 39.

(Punjábí Examination January 1897.)

Early in June 1842, *Sher Singh,* with most of the Chiefs and a large force, marched to *Wazīrābād. Rājā Dhiyān Singh* remaining behind in *Lahore. Chand Kaur* has been ordered to [1] *take up her quarters* again in the fort, of which *Mīān Singh* was in charge and on the 12th of *June,* her slave girls who had received their orders attempted to kill her by mixing poison in a [2] *beverage* which they offered her. She tasted it and threw it away and the girls, then fearing, [3] *their design was discovered* fell [4] *upon her with stones,* fractured her skull and left her [5] for dead. *Rājā Dhiyān Singh* attended his victim immediately and *had her wounds dressed Faqīr Nūr-ud-dīn* thought at one time there was some hope of her life but *she never recovered her senses* and died within two days. The assessins were heavily ironed *and it is said that when threatend with mutilation they accused Dhiyān Singh openly of having instigated*[8] *the murder and of having promised them great rewards for effecing it. Their fate*[9] *is unknown,* but it is supposed were *made away*[10] *with* by order of the Rāja.

1 to take up quarters ਜਾ ਵਸਨਾ 2 ਸ਼ਰਬਤ (*m*) 3 direct form ਸਾਡੀ ਤਜਵੀਜ ਮਲੂਮ ਹੋ ਗਈ 4 ਓਹ ਦੇ ਉਤੇ ਪੱਥਰ ਬਰਸਾਉਨ ਲਗ ਪਈਆਂ 5 ਓਹ ਨੂੰ ਮਰੀ ਹੋਈ ਸਮਝ ਕੇ ਛਡ ਗਈਆਂ 6 ਓਹ ਦੇ ਜਖਮਾਂ ਉਤੇ ਮੱਲਮ ਪੱਟੀ ਕਰਵਾਈ 7 ਓਹ ਨੂੰ ਬਿਲਕੁਲ ਹੋਸ਼ ਨਾ ਆਈ 8 ਆਖਦੇ ਹਨ ਕਿ ਜਦ ਓਨ੍ਹਾਂ ਦੇ ਅੰਗ ਅੰਗ ਤੋੜਨ ਦੀ ਧਮਕੀ ਦਿਤੀ ਗਈ ਤਾਂ ਉਨਾਂ ਨੇ ਖੁਲਮ ਖੁਲਾ ਧਿਆਨ ਸਿੰਘ ਉਤੇ ਦੋਸ ਲਾਇਆ ਕਿ ਉਹ ਨੇ ਸਾਨੂੰ ਰਾਨੀ ਦੇ ਮਾਰਨ ਵਾਸਤੇ ਵਡੇ ਇਨਾਮ ਦੇਣ ਦਾ ਕਰਾਰ ਕਰਕੇ ਚੁਕਿਆ (ਉਕਸਾਇਆ)ਸੀ 9 ਪਤਾ ਨਹੀਂ ਓਹਨਾਂ ਦਾ ਕੀ ਹਾਲ ਹੋਇਆ 10 ਮਰਵਾਈਆਂ ਗਈਆਂ ਸੀ ॥

No. 40.

Punjābi Examination, 12th January 1898.

On the 12th of June the force was at *Chichāwatni* and *ready to proceed*[1]; but it was not thought *expedient*[2] to hasten its march until *some decided advantage*[3] *had been gained over Mulrāj,* by Edwards and the *Bahāwalpur* troops. *Sher Singh* and his *colleagues*[4] had no thought of *treason*[5], but their troops *sympathised*[6] with the rebels, and would have been only too glad to have joined them. On the 22nd June, *Sher Singh* reached *Talambā.* He was ordered to stop here, *but either his troops were*[7] *no longer under command* or *fancying that he could not trust to their fidelity* he wished to join in the *successes*[8] of the British, for the battle of *Kaneri* had now been fought. He advanced to *Gugrān,* nine miles from the city of *Multān. Lieutenant Edwardes* then directed *Sher Singh* to join him, which he did, *pitching*[9] *his camp* at *Sūrajkund* 3 miles from *Tibī,* where *Lieutenant Edwardes* was encamped. He arrived at this place on the 6th July.

1 ਅਗੇ ਵਧਨ ਨੂੰ ਤਿਆਰ ਸੀ 2 ਮੁਨਾਸਬ 3 ਜਦ ਤੀਕ ਮੁਲਕ ਰਾਜ਼ ਪਰ ਪੂਰੀ ਪੂਰਾ ਫਤ ਨਾ ਹੋ ਜਾਵੇ 4 ਸਾਥੀ 5 ਧੋਖਾ (m) 6 ਦਯਾ ਕੀਤੀ 7 ਪਰ ਜਾਂ ਤਾ ਫੌਜ ਉਸਦੇ ਵਸਵਿਚ ਨਹੀਂ ਸੀ ਜਾਂ ਇਹ ਸੋਚਕੇ ਕਿ ਉਨਾਂ ਦੀ ਅਮਾਨ ਦਾਰੀ ਪਰ ਭਰੋਸਾ ਨਹੀਂ 8 ਜਿਤ from ਜਿਤਨਾਂ 9 ਡੇਰਾ ਗੱਡਕੇ From ਡੇਰਾ ਗਡਨਾਂ ।

No. 41.

(Punjábi Examination, July 1898.)

The chief of *Sayyidwālā Karm Singh*, was the *rival*[1] of *Rām Singh and they fought with varying success*[2] *for some years* till at length *Rām Singh obtained a decided advantage*[3] and took possession of *Sayyidwālā*. *Sārdār Rām Singh* died in 1781 and his eldest son *Bhagwān Singh* who succeeded to the command of the *misals* was not able to hold the territory, his father had acquired *Sayyadwālā* was recovered by *Wazīr Singh* brother of *Karm Singh* who also took some of the *nakaī* villages, but these he *eventually gave up*[4]. *Bhagwān Singh*, now percieved that unless he made powerful friends he would probably loose his territory altogether, so he *betrothed*[5] his sister *nakkāin* generally known as *Rāj Kaurāṅ* to *Ranjīt Singh* son of *Mahān Singh Sukkarchakīā* who was then one of the most powerful chief in the Punjāb.

1 ਵੈਰੀ —2 ਕਈ ਵਰਿਹਾਂ ਤੀਕ ਉਨਾਂਦੀ ਆਪਸ ਵਿਚ ਦੀ ਹਾਰ ਜਿਤ ਰਹੀ 3 ਰਾਮ ਸਿੰਘਨੂੰ ਪੂਰੀ ਪੂਰੀ ਜਿਤ ਹੋਗਈ 4 ਪਰ ਅੰਤ ਨੂੰ ਓਹ ਉਸਨੇ ਛਡ ਦਿਤੇ 5 ਕੁੜਮਾਈ ਕੀਤੀ ।

No. 42.

(Punjábi Examination 10th July 1900.)

When he arrived at *Mooltān*, he issueu orders that 4,000 boats should be built and *that for each of these boats excessively*[1] *strong iron spikes should be constructed. One spike in the bows*[2] *of the vessel*, so that *whatever came into contact*[3] *with them, should not thereafter remain in tact*. They *launched*[4] them all in the stream, and embarked 20 men with arrows bows and other muniteons of war in each separate boat, and proceeded to *exterminate*[5] the *Jats*. *When the Jats were aware of this*[6]; they sent their women and children to the islands, and the men alone remained prepared *for*[7] *combat*.

1 ਕਿ ਹਰ ਇਕ ਬੇੜੀ ਵਾਸਤੇ ਬਹੁਤ ਮੋਟੀਆਂ ਲੋਹੇ ਦੀਆਂ ਮੇਖਾਂ ਬਨਾਈਆਂ ਜਾਨ 2 ਬੇੜੀ ਦੇ ਮਥੇ ਪੁਰ ਇਕ ਮੇਖ ਲਾਈ ਜਾਵੇ 3 ਜਿਸ ਚੀਜ ਦੀ ਉਸ ਨੂੰ ਟਕਰ ਲਗੇ ਉਹ ਨਾਲ ਨਾ ਲਗੀ ਰਹੇ। 4 ਤਰਾਇਆ From ਤਰਾਉਨਾ 5 ਖੁਰਾ ਖੋਜ ਪੁਟਣਾ, ਜੜ ਪੁਟਣਾ 6 ਜਦ ਜਟਾਂ ਨੂੰ ਇਹ ਹਾਲ ਮਲੂਮ ਹੋਇਆ 7 ਜੁਧ

No. 43.

(Punjábí Examination 10th July 1901.)

When *Ranjit Singh* had obtained leisure from his *funeral obsequsies*,[1] then during the month of *Chet*, he succeeded to the *seat*[2] of his father. As, at that time, he was only of 12 years of age, for this reasen, he was not fit for the *business of Government*[3]; and although he was at that time seated on the throne of the kingdom, still his mother did not approve of his conducting the affairs of the kingdom. *When he reached seventeen years of age*,[4] then by the mercy of God, every one, *of their own accord*[5] became *subservient*[6] to him. Accordingly, in the year 1796, a king, named *Shāh Zamān*, who ascended the throne after the death of *Timūr Shāh*, setting forth from *Khurāsān*, came to the Punjab. As no chief opposed him, he entered *Lahore through open gates*.[7] Having come to *Lahore*, and seeing that the Punjab could not for many reasons be controlled by him, he returned back. Afterwards he said to the chief *of his ordnance*[8] named *Sahānchi*, "Do you efface the name and trace of the Sikhs." On this he taking some artillery with him attacked *Rām Nagar*, But the *Khālsā* fought well with them from that day moreover, the *dread*[9] of *Puthāns* was entirely removed from the hearts of the Sikhs. As, at that time, the renown of *Mahārājā Ranjit Singh* was daily on the increase many people, from seeing it, became very *jealous*[10] at heart.

1 ਕਿਰਿਆ ਕਰਮ 2 ਗੱਦੀ (f) 3 ਰਾਜ ਦਾ ਕੰਮਕਾਰ 4 ਜਾਂ ਇਹ ਸਤਰਾਂ ਬਰਸਾਂ ਦਾ ਹੋਇਆ or ਜਾਂ ਇਸਦੀ ਉਮਰ ਸਤਾਰਾਂ ਬਰਸਾਂ ਦੀ ਹੋਈ note the construction 5 ਆਪਨੇ ਆਪ ਹੀ 6 ਅਧੀਨ 7 ਖੁਲੀ ਦਰਵਜੀਂ 8 ਮੀਰਆਤਸ਼ੀ 9 ਭੌ, ਭੈ 10 ਖਾਰ ਖਾਧੀ From ਖਾਰ ਖਾਨਾ to be jealous

No. 44.

(Punjābī Examination, 10th January 1900.)

During the [1]*last year of Ranjīt Singh's life,* Bhai *Rām Singh's* [2]*influence* continually increased ; and when the *Mahārājā* died *Nou Nihal Singh,* who had received the *pahul* from the *Bhāi* [3]*entrusted him with still greater power* for he was himself very [4]*averse* to conduct the details of business. He was one of the chief [5]*conspirators* with *Rājā Gulāb Singh Dhiān Singh* and others, in the murder of Sirdar *Chet Singh* the minister of *Khṛak Singh,* and it was at his house the conspirators assembled before proceeding to the palace to commit the murder. Neither *Nihāl Singh* nor the *Bhāī* were popular with the chief. The former compelled all the *Sirdārs, jagirdārs* to fulfil their services ; and to keep their contingents in good order, which was most [6]*irksome* to the men who during the last years of *Ranjīt Singh's* life had done much as they liked and been responsible to no one.

1 ਰੰਜੀਤ ਸਿੰਘ ਦੀ ਅਵਸਥਾ ਦੇ ਪਿਛਲੇ ਵਰਹੇ 2 ਜ਼ੋਰ 3 ਉਸਦਾ ਹੋਰਵੀ ਦਰਜਾ ਵਧਾ ਦਿਤਾ 4 ਘਿਨ ਕਰਨਾ 5 ਸਾਥੀ 6 ਦੁਖ ਦੇਨ ਵਾਲਾ ।

No. 45.

(Punjábí Examination 10th January 1901.)

General Franks had [1]*begun to move* just five weeks earlier. He had [2]*taken up his position* with a portion of his army at a town called *Badlāpur,* where he heard that, a rebel chief named *Medī Hossain* with a force of 15,000 watchmen, of whom only 5,000 deserved to be called soldiers, intended to oppose his entrance into Oudh. As soon as his preparations were complete, he marched out, defeated one of *Medī Hossain's* Lieutenants and then returned. On the 14th of February he again moved forward to a point, within a few miles of the frontier. [3]*Then he made up his mind to halt,* until the news should arrive that *Jān Bahādur* was ready to work with him. This news reached him on the 19th he advanced instantly crossed the frontier and before night, had gained two victories over detachments of *Medī Hossain's* army.

1 ਕੂਚ ਕਰਨ ਦਾ ਅਰੰਭ ਕੀਤਾ 2 ਓਹਨੇ ਆਪਨਾ ਮੋਰਚਾ ਲਾਇਆ
3 ਤਦ ਉਸਨੇ ਡੇਰਾ ਲਾਉਨ ਦੀ ਮਨ ਵਿਚ ਠਰਾਈ ।

Translate into English.

No. 1.

*ਸ਼ਾਹ ਮਹੀਮਦ ਦੇ ਵੇਲੇ ਤਾਂਈ ਸਾਰਾ ਟੱਬਰ ਨਿਰਾ ਖੇਤੀ ਪੱਤੀ ਦਾ ਕੰਮ ਕਰਦਾ ਰਿਹਾ ਓਹ ਵਡਾ ਬਲਵਾਨ ਸੀ ਤੇ ਉਸਨੇ ਅਹਮਦਸ਼ਾਹ ਦੁਰਾਨੀਦੀਫੌਜ ਵਿਚ ਨੌਕਰੀ ਕੀਤੀ ਜਦ ਉਸਨੇ ਹਿੰਦੁਸਤਾਨ ਪੁਰ ਕਈ ਧਾਵੇ ਕੀਤੇ ਸੰਨ ੧੭੭੨ ਵਿਚ ਓਹਨੇ ਮੁਲਤਾਂਨ ਦੇ ਸੂਬੇ ਸੁਜਾ ਖਾਂ ਨੂੰ ਝੰਡਾਸਿੰਘ ਤੇ ਗੰਡਾਸਿੰਘ ਭੰਗੀ ਸੂਦਾਰਾਂਦੇ ਵਿਰੁਧ ਸ਼ੈਹਰਨੂੰ ਬਚਾਉਨ ਵਿਚ ਸਹਾਇਤਾ ਦਿਤੀ ਪਰ ਉਨਾਂਨੇ ਸ਼ੈਹਰਨੂੰ ਫ਼ਤੇਕਰ ਲਿਆ ਭਾਵੇਂ ਉਨਾਂਨੂੰ ਬਹਾਦਰੀ ਨਾਲ ਬਚਾਇਆ। ਸੁਜਾ ਖਾਂ ਛੇਤੀਹੀ ਇਹ ਦੇ ਮਗਰੋਂ ਮਰਗਿਆ ਅਰ ਮੁਜ਼ਫ਼ਰਖਾਂ ਨੇ ਅਹਮਦ ਸ਼ਾਹ ਦੁਰਾਨੀ ਦੇ ਪੁਤ ਤੈਮੂਰ ਸ਼ਾਹ ਨੂੰ ਸਹਾਇਤਾ ਵਾਸਤੇ ਲਿਖਿਆ ਜਿਸਨੇ ਮੁਲਤਾਂਨ ਤੇ ਕੂਚ ਕੀਤਾ ਤੇਓਸਨੇ ਸੰ: ੧੭੭੭ ਵਿਚ ਚਾਲੀ ਦਿਨਦੇ ਘੇਰੇ ਬਾਦ ਸ਼ਹਿਰ ਨੂੰ ਫੇਰ ਲੈਲਿਆ। ਮੁਜ਼ਫ਼ਰਖਾਂ ਨੂੰ ਫੇਰ ਸੂਬਾ ਬਨਾ ਦਿਤਾ ਤੇ ਸ਼ਾਹ ਮਹੀਮਦ ਨੂੰ ਉਹਦੀ ਨੌਕਰੀ ਦੇ ਇਨਾਮ ਵਿਚ ਦੋ ਜਗੀਰਾਂ ਦਸਹਜ਼ਾਰ ਰੁਪਏ ਦੀ ਮਲਕੀਅਤ ਦੀਆਂ ਦਿਤੀਆਂ ਇਕ ਡੇਰਾ ਦਨਪਾਂਨ ਤੇ ਦੂਜੀ ਡੇਰਾ ਗਾਜ਼ੀ ਖਾਂ॥

No. 2.

ਜਦ ਰਨਜੀਤ ਸਿੰਘ ਦਾ ਜ਼ੋਰ ਵਧ ਗਿਆ ਤੇ ਓਹਨੇ ਲਾਹੌਰ ਅੰਮ੍ਰਿਤਸਰ ਕਬਜੇ ਕਰ ਲਏ ਕਰਮ ਸਿੰਘ ਨੇ ਭੀ ਓਹਦੀ ਹੇਠੀ ਮੰਨ ਲਈ ਅਰ ਫੇਰ ਸਦਾ ਦੇ ਲਈ ਮਹਾਰਾਜੇ ਦਾ ਵਡਾ ਆਗਿਆ ਕਾਰ ਨੌਕਰ ਰਿਹਾ ਪਰ ਇਕ ਵਾਰੀ ਜਰੂਰ ਉਨ੍ਹਾਂ ਵਿਚ ਝਗੜਾ ਹੋਇਆ ਕਰਮ ਸਿੰਘ ਰਨਜੀਤ ਸਿੰਘ ਦੀ ਖੁਲੀ ਫ਼ੌਜ ਦਾ ਕਪਤਾਨ ਸੀ ਕਿਉਂ ਜੋ ਇਨਾਂ ਪਹਿਲਿਆਂ ਹੀ ਦਿਨਾਂ ਵਿਚ ਰਨਜੀਤ ਸਿੰਘ ਪਾਸ ਬਹੁਤਾ ਫ਼ਾਲਤੂ ਰੁਪਯਾ ਨਹੀਂ ਸੀ। ਫੌਜ ਦੀ ਤਲਬ ਚੜ੍ਹ ਗਈ ਕਰਮ ਸਿੰਘ ਨੇ ਫੌਜ ਵਲ ਹੋਕੇ ਰਨਜੀਤ ਸਿੰਘ ਤੇ ਓਨਾਂਦੀ ਤਲਬ ਮੰਗੀ। ਜਿਨੂੰ ਇਸਡਰ ਨਾਲ ਕਿ ਫੌਜ ਬਿਗੜ ਨਾ ਜਾਵੇ ਆਪਣੀ ਵਹੁਟੀ ਮਤਾਬ ਕੌਰ ਦੀ ਟੂੰਬ ਟਲੀ ਗਹਿਣੇ ਧਰਨੀ ਪਈ। ਇਸਤੇ ਪਿਛੇ ਮਹਾਰਾਜੇ ਨੇ ਕਰਮ ਸਿੰਘ ਨੂੰ ਸਜਾ ਦਿਤੀ ਕਿ ਓਹਨੇ ਮਹਾਰਾਜ ਦੇ ਵਿਰੁਧ ਕੰਮ ਕੀਤਾ ਤੇ ਮਹਾਰਾਜ ਦੇ ਅੰਮ੍ਰਿਤਸਰ ਦੇ ਘਰ ਨੂੰ ਲੁਟਿਆ ਤੇ ਬਰਬਾਦ ਕੀਤਾ ਪਰ ਫੇਰ ਓਹ ਮੰਨ ਪਏ ਤੇ ਸਰਦਾਰ ਲਗਭਗ ਰਨਜੀਤ ਸਿੰਘ ਦੀਆਂ ਸਾਰੀਆਂ ਹੀ ਲੜਾਈਆਂ ਵਿਚ ਓਹਦੇ ਨਾਲ ਰਿਹਾ॥

* For words consult the vocabulary at the end.

No. 3.

ਸੰ: ੧੮੧੬ ਫਰਵਰੀ ਵਿਚ ਸਿਖਾਂ ਨੇ ਮੁਲਤਾਨ ਪਰ ਹੱਲਾ ਕਰ ਦਿਤਾ। ਇਕ ਵਡੀ ਫੌਜ ਬਹਾਵਲਪੁਰ ਤੇ ਮੁਲਤਾਂਨ ਨੂੰ ਦਕੇ ਉਗਰਾਹੁਨ ਘਲੀ ਗਈ। ਮੁਜ਼ਫ਼ਰ ਖਾਂ ਨੇ ਟਰੀ ਦੇਨ ਵਿਚ ਵਿਲਮਠ ਕੀਤੀ ਫੂਲਾ ਸਿੰਘ ਅਕਾਲੀ ਨੇ ਜੋ ਭੰਗ ਪੀਕੇ ਮਸਤ ਹੋਇਆ ਹੋਇਆ ਸੀ ਅਪਨੇ ਵਰਗੇ ਮਸਤ ਆਦਮੀਆਂ ਨਾਲ ਸ਼ਹਿਰ ਪੁਰ ਧਾਵਾ ਕਰ ਦਿਤਾ ਅਰ ਅਜੇਹੇ ਜੋਰ ਨਾਲ ਹੱਲਾ ਕੀਤਾ ਕਿ ਕਿਲੇ ਦੇ ਬਾਹਰਲੇ ਕਈ ਮੋਰਚੇ ਉਨ੍ਹਾਂ ਦੇ ਹਥ ਆਗਏ ਪਰ ਫ਼ਕੀਰ ਅਜੀਜਦੀਨ ਨੇ ਮਾਫ਼ੀ ਮੰਗ ਲਈ ਤੇ ਨਵਾਬ ਨੇ ਅਪਨੇ ਟਗੇ ਅਗੇ ਨਾਲੋਂ ਛੇਤੀ ਦੇ ਦਿਤੇ। ਸਿਖਾਂ ਦੀ ਫੌਜ ਮੁਕੇਰਾਂ ਵਲ ਅਗੇ ਵਧੀ ਸੰਨ ੧੮੧੭ ਵਿਚ ਸਿਖਾਂ ਦੀ ਫੌਜ ਨੇ ਦੀਵਾਨਚੰਦ ਦੇ ਹੇਠ ਮੁਲਤਾਨ ਪੁਰ ਧਾਵਾ ਕਰਨ ਨੂੰ ਕੂਚ ਕੀਤਾ ਤੇ ਕਿਲੇ ਤੇ ਹੱਲਾ ਕੀਤਾ ਪਰ ਪਿਛੇ ਹਟਾਏ ਗਏ ਅਰ ਫੇਰ ਓਹ ਦਸ ਹਜਾਰ ਰੁਪਈਆ ਲੈਕੇ ਓਥੋਂ ਮੁੜ ਗਏ ਪਰ ਇਹ ਹੱਲੇ ਵਡੇ ਜ਼ੋਰ ਸ਼ੋਰ ਨਾਲ ਨਹੀਂ ਕੀਤੇ ਗਏ ਸੀ॥

No. 4.

ਸ੍ਰਦਾਰ ਨਿਧਾਂਨਸਿੰਘ ਚਾਰ ਰੁਪਏ ਰੋਜ਼ ਤੇ ਘੋੜ ਚੜ੍ਹਿਆਂ ਵਿਚ ਭਰਤੀ ਹੋਇਆ। ਤੇ ਉਹਨੇ ਕਈਆਂ ਲੜਾਈਆਂ ਵਿਚ ਕੰਮ ਕੀਤਾ (or ਓਹ ਲੜਿਆ) ਸੰਨ ੧੮੨੩ ਦੀ ਤੇਰਹੀ ਦੀ ਲੜਾਈ ਵਿਚ ਜਿਥੇ ਵਡੀ ਭਾਰੀ ਝੜਪਾ ਝੜਪੀ ਹੋਈ ਉਹਨੇ ਵਡਾ ਨਾਓ ਪਾਇਆ। ਕਈ ਵਾਰੀ ਓਹ ਘਾਇਲ ਹੋਇਆ। ਤੇ ਓਹਦਾ ਘੋੜਾ ਮਾਰਿਆ ਗਿਆ। ਅਰ ਮਹਾਰਾਜੇ ਨੇ ਓਹਨੂ ਗੁਰਦਾਸ ਪੁਰ ਦੇ ਜਿਲੇਵਿਚ ਕੋਈ ੧੪ ਪਿੰਡਾਂ ਦੀ ਜਾਗੀਰ ਜਿਹਦੀ ਆਓਂਦਣ ੧੪੦੦੦ ਰੁਪਯੇ ਦੇ ਲਗ ਭਗ ਸੀ ਬਖ਼ਸ਼ੀ। ਗੁੱਜਰਸਿੰਘ ਤੇ ਮੂਲ ਸਿੰਘ ਨੂੰ ਵੀ ਜਰਨੈਲੀ ਦੇ ਉਹਦੇ ਮਿਲੇ। ਨਿਹਾਲਸਿੰਘ ਉਨਾਂ ਵਕੀਲਾਂਦੇ ਨਾਲ ਗਿਆ ਜੋ ਲਾਹੌਰ ਦੇ ਰਾਜੇ ਨੇ ਸੰ: ੧੮੩੧ ਵਿਚ ਲਾਟ ਵੀ. ਬੀ. ਐਮ. ਬੈਂਟਿੰਗ ਕੋਲ ਸ਼ਿਮਲੇ ਭੇਜੇ ਤੇ ਤਿੰਨ ਸਾਲ ਦੇ ਪਿਛੇ ਉਹ ਸ੍ਰਦਾਰ ਹਰੀ ਸਿੰਘ ਨਲੂਏ ਤੇ ਕੌਰ ਨਿਹਾਲ ਸਿੰਘ ਨਾਲ ਪਸ਼ਾਵਰ ਦੀ ਲਾਂਮ ਵਿਚ ਜਾ ਰਲਿਆ। ਉਹ ਸੰਨ੧੮੩੦ ਤਾਂਈ ਸਾਰੀ ਲੜਾਈ ਵਿਚ ਲੜਦਾ ਰਿਹਾ। ਜਦ ਹਰੀਸਿੰਘ ਦੇ ਮਰਨੇ ਤੇ ਪਠਾਨਾਂ ਦੀ ਫੌਜ ਦੇ ਭੱਜਨ ਨਾਲ ਉਹ ਲੜਾਈ ਪੂਰੀ ਹੋਗਈ ਇਸਤੇ ਦੋ ਵਰ੍ਹੇ ਪਿਛੇ ਉਹ ਆਪਣੇ ਬੁਢਾਪੇ ਦੇ ਪਹਿਲਾਂ

ਪਹਿਲਾਂ ਮਾਂਦਾ ਹੋਕੇ ਮਰਗਿਆ॥

No. 5.

ਸੋਧਰੇ ਦੇ ਘੇਰੇ ਵਿਚ ਆਖਦੇ ਹਨ ਜੋਧਸਿੰਘ ਨੇ ਆਪਨੇ ਮਿਤ੍ਰ ਸਾਹਿਬਸਿੰਘ ਨਾਲ ਧ੍ਰੋਹ ਕਮਾਇਆ। ਸਾਹਿਬਸਿੰਘ ਜੋ ਕਿਲੇ ਵਿਚ ਘੇਰਿਆ ਹੋਇਆ ਸੀ। ਉਹਦੇ ਕੋਲ ਬਰੂਦ ਦਾ ਤੋੜਾ ਹੋਗਿਆ। ਤੇ ਉਸਦਾ ਸ਼ਰਨ ਪੈਨਾਂ ਅਵਸ਼ ਸੀ। ਪਰ ਜੋਧ ਸਿੰਘ ਨੇ ਜਿਸ ਨੂੰ ਡਰਸੀ ਜੇ ਸਾਹਿਬਸਿੰਘ ਮਾਰਿਆ ਜਾਊ ਤਾਂ ਮਹਾਂਸਿੰਘ ਵਡਾ ਬਲਵਾਨ ਹੋ ਜਾਊ। ਸਾਹਿਬਸਿੰਘ ਨੂੰ ਗੋਲੀ ਸ਼ਿਕੇ ਦੀ ਸਹਾਇਤਾ ਦਿਤੀ। ਜਦ ਤਾਂਈ ਘੇਰਾ ਪਿਆ ਰਿਹਾ। ਮਹਾਂ ਸਿਘ ਡਾਢਾ ਮਾਂਦਾ ਰਿਹਾ। ਅਰ ਧੋਖੇ ਨਾਲ ਉਹ ਥੋੜੇ ਹੀ ਦਿਨਾਂ ਵਿਚ ਮਾਰਿਆ ਗਿਆ। ਆਖਦੇ ਹਨ ਕਿ ਜੋਧਸਿੰਘ ਦੀ ਇਸ ਕਰਤੂਤ ਤੇ ਰੰਜੀਤ ਸਿੰਘ ਉਹਦਾ ਵੈਰੀ ਬਨ ਗਿਆ। ਪਰ ਮਹਾਂਰਾਜ ਦੇ ਸਲੂਕ ਦਾ ਕਾਰਨ ਨਿਰੀ ਉਹਦੀ ਰਾਜ ਦੀ ਚਾਹ ਸੀ। ਕਈ ਵਰਿਹਾਂ ਤਾਈ ਉਹਨੇ ਦੇਖਿਆ ਕਿ ਵਜੀਰਾ ਬਾਦ ਦੇ ਰਾਜੇ ਉਤੇ ਹੱਲਾ ਕਰਨਾਂ ਔਖਾ ਸੀ। ਕਿਉਂਜੋ ਉਹ ਬਲਵਾਨ ਸੀ। ਅਰ ਉਸਨੇ ਇਕ ਵਾਰੀ ਇਹਵੀ ਜਤਨ ਕੀਤਾ ਕਿ ਉਹ ਉਹਦੇ ਰਾਜ ਨੂੰ ਜੇਹੜਾ ਜੋਰ ਨਾਲ ਨਹੀਂ ਲੈ ਹੁੰਦਾ ਸਾ ਧੋਖੇ ਨਾਲ ਲੈਲਵੇ।

No. 6.

ਰਾਨੀ ਚੰਦਕੌਰ ਦੀ ਥੋੜੀ ਜੇਹੀ ਹੋਰਬੀ ਗਲ ਹੈ। ਰਾਜਾ ਗੁਲਾਬ ਸਿੰਘ ਨੇ ਰਾਨੀ ਸਾਹਿਬ ਕੌਰਨੂੰ ਆਪਨੇ ਨਾਲ ਲਜਾਨ ਦੀ ਸਲਾਹ ਕੀਤੀ। ਪਰ ਇਹ ਗਲ ਸ਼ਰ ਸਿੰਘ ਨੇ ਨਾਂ ਮੰਨੀ। ਉਹ ਅਪਨੇ ਵੈਰੀ ਦੇ ਹਥਾਂ ਵਿਚ ਹਥਿਆਰ ਨਹੀਂ ਦੇਨੇ ਚਾਹੁੰਦਾ ਸਾ। ਚੰਦਕੌਰ ਨੂੰ ਹੁਕਮ ਮਿਲਿਆ। ਕਿ ਤੂੰ ਸੰਮਨ ਬੁਰਜ ਨੂੰ ਛਡਕੇ ਅਪਨੇ ਸ਼ਹਿਰ ਵਾਲੇ ਘਰ ਵਿਚ ਜਾਰਹੁ। ਅਰ ਓਥੇ ਓਹ ਫੌਜ ਤੇ ਸਰਦਾਰ ਨਾਲ ਗੋਂਦਨੇ ਗੁੰਦਦੀ ਰਹੀ। ਉਹਨੇ ਸ੍ਰਦਾਰ ਅਜੀਤਸਿੰਘ ਨੂੰ ਕਲਕੱਤੇ ਭੇਜਿਆ। ਜੋ ਓਹ ਮੁਲਕੀ ਲਾਟ ਨੂੰ ਓਹਦਾ ਹੱਕ ਜਤਾਏ ਅਰ ਉਹਦੇ ਏਲਚੀ ਸਾਰੇ ਦੇਸ ਵਿੱਚ ਵਡੀ ਤੇਜੀ ਨਾਲ ਕੰਮ ਕਰਦੇ ਸੇ। ਸੰ: ੧੯੪੧ ਦੇ ਅਕਤੂਬਰ ਮਹੀਨੇ ਵਿਚ ਸ੍ਰਦਾਰ ਅਤਰ ਸਿੰਘ ਓਹਦੇ ਬੁਲਾਵੇ ਤੇ ਥਨੇਸਰ ਤੇ ਫੀਰੋਜਪੁਰ ਆਇਆ ਏਥੇ ਉਹ ਤਕਦਾ ਰਹਿਆ ਕਿ

ਮੈਨੂੰ ਪੰਜਾਬ ਵਿਚ ਬੜਨ ਦਾ ਕੁਝ ਚੰਗਾ ਵੇਲਾ ਮਿਲੇ। ਮਾਈ ਵਲੋਂ ਇਸ ਵੇਲੇ ਕੋਈ ਬਾਰਾਂ ਹਜਾਰ ਫੌਜੀ ਤੇ ਕਈ ਬਲਵਾਨ ਸਰਦਾਰਸੇ। ਸੈਨਾਂ ਦਾ ਦਿਲ ਸ਼ੇਰਸਿੰਘ ਤੋਂ ਫਿਰ ਗਿਆ। ਕਿਉਂ ਜੋ ਉਹ ਓਨ੍ਹਾਂ ਦੀਆਂ ਲੋੜਾਂ ਨੂੰ ਪੂਰਾ ਨਾਂ ਕਰ ਸਕਿਆ। ਅਰ ਮਾਈ ਵਲ ਵਧ ਗਿਆ। ਤੇ ਅਪਰੈਲ ਸੰ: ੧੮੪੨ ਵਿਚ ਸੈਨਾਂ ਸਾਰੀ ਦੇ ਲਗ ਭਗ ਮਾਈ ਵਲ ਹੋਗਈ।

No. 7.

ਗੁਲਾਬ ਸਿੰਘ ਸਤਲੁਜ ਦੀ ਲੜਾਈ ਵਿਚ ਨਾ ਰਲਿਆ ਤੇ ਓਹਦੀ ਫੌਜ ਮਹਾਰਾਜ ਦੀ ਰਖਿਆ ਕਰਨ ਲਈ ਲਾਹੌਰ ਵਿਚ ਰਹੀ ਤੇ ਸੰ: ੧੮੪੭ ਅਪਰੈਲ ਵਿਚ ਓਹ ਰੈਜੀਡੈਂਟ ਦੀ ਸਪਾਰਸ਼ ਪੁਰ ਪਸ਼ਾਵਰ ਦਾ ਸੂਬਾ ਬਣਾਇਆ ਗਿਆ ਅਰ ਕਿਉਂ ਜੋ ਇਸ ਵੇਲੇ ਓਹ ਸਭ ਤੋਂ ਵੱਡਾ ਜਰਨੈਲ ਸਾ ਓਹਨੂੰ ਪਸ਼ਾਵਰ ਦੀ ਫੌਜ ਦਾ ਕਮਾਨ ਅਫਸਰ ਬਨਾ ਦਿਤਾ ਗੁਲਾਬ ਸਿੰਘ ਦੇ ਇਸ ਵਡੇ ਹੁਦੇ ਤੇ ਚੜਨ ਤੇ ਖਾਲਸਾ ਫੌਜ ਨੂੰ ਵਡੀ ਖੁਸ਼ੀ ਹੋਈ ਕਿਉਂ ਜੋ ਓਹ ਉਸ ਬਹਾਦਰ ਬੁਢੇ ਦੀ ਵਡੀ ਇਜ਼ਤ ਤੇ ਪਿਆਰ ਕਰਦੀ ਸੀ ਓਹਨੂੰ ਸਰਦਾਰ ਬਨਾ ਦਿਤਾ ਤੇ ਇਕ ਦਰਬਾਰ ਵਿਚ ਜੇਹੜਾ ੧੮੪੭ ਸੰਨ ਦੇ ੨੯ ਨਵੰਬਰ ਨੂੰ ਲਾਹੌਰ ਹੋਇਆ ਉਹਨੂੰ ਬਹਾਦਰ ਦਾ ਖਤਾਬ ਮਿਲਿਆ ਸਰਦਾਰ ਗੁਲਾਬ ਸਿੰਘ ਨੇ ਆਪਣੇ ਨਵੇਂ ਹੁੱਦੇ ਦੇ ਕੰਮਾਂ ਨੂੰ ਲਿਆਕਤ ਤੇ ਸਿਆਨਪ ਨਾਲ ਪੂਰਾ ਕੀਤਾ ਤੇ ਜਦ ਮੁਲਤਾਨ ਵਿਚ ਗਦਰ ਫੁਟਿਆ ਤਾਂ ਉਸਨੇ ਲਾਰਨਸ ਸਾਹਿਬ ਨੂੰ ਜਿਦਾ ਪਸ਼ਾਵਰ ਵਿਚ ਚਾਰਜ ਸਾ ਉਸ ਜਿਲੇ ਦਾ ਅਮਨ ਰਖਨ ਲਈ ਤਨ ਮਨ ਨਾਲ ਸਹਾਇਤਾ ਦਿਤੀ॥

No. 8.

ਮਹਾਰਾਜਾ ਰੰਨਜੀਤ ਸਿੰਘ ਨੇ ਦੋਵਾਂ ਭਰਾਵਾਂ ਨੂੰ ਨੌਕਰ ਕਰ ਲਿਆ ਅਰ ਸ਼ਾਹਜ਼ਾਦੇ ਖੜਕ ਸਿੰਘ ਦੇ ਹੇਠ ਉਨਾਂਨੂੰ ੫੦੦ ਸਵਾਰ ਦਾ ਕਮਾਨ ਦੇ ਦਿਤਾ ਕਿਸ਼ਨ ਸਿੰਘ ਸੰਨ ੧੮੨੭ ਵਿਚ ਇਕ ਲੜਾਈ ਵਿਚ ਮਾਰਿਆ ਗਿਆ ਅਰ ਓਹਦੇ ਭਰਾ ਨੂੰ ਜਿਸਨੇਂ ਓਸੇ ਲੜਾਈ ਵਿਚ ਵਡੀ ਬਹਾਦਰੀ ਦਖਾਈ ਸੀ ਅੰਮ੍ਰਿਤਸਰ ਦੇ ਜ਼ਿਲੇ ਵਿਚ ਸੱਤ ਪਿੰਡ ਮਿਲੇ। ਜਦ ਚੇਤ ਸਿੰਘ ਖੜਕ ਸਿੰਘ ਦਾ ਮਿਤ੍ਰ ਮਾਰਿਆ ਗਿਆ ਤਾਂ ਸਜਾਦੇ ਨੇ ਰਾਮ

ਸਿੰਘ ਨੂੰ ਜਿਸ ਨਾਲ ਬਹੁਤ ਪਿਆਰ ਕਰਦਾ ਸਾ ਅਪਨੀ ਖਾਸ ਮੋਹਰ ਸਪੁਰਦ ਕਰ ਦਿਤੀ ਅਰ ਸ਼ਾਹਪੁਰ ਤੇ ਅੰਮ੍ਰਿਤਸਰ ਦਿਆਂ ਜਿਲਿਆਂ ਵਿਚ ਜਗੀਰਾਂ ਦਿਤੀਆਂ ਨੌਨਿਹਾਲ ਸਿੰਘ ਖੜਕ ਸਿੰਘ ਦੇ ਪੁਤ੍ਰ ਨੂੰ ਆਪਣੇ ਪਿਤਾ ਦੇ ਮਿਤ੍ਰਾਂ ਨਾਲ ਕੁਝ ਪਿਆਰ ਨਾ ਸਾ ਕਿ ਓਹਨੇ ਰਾਮ ਸਿੰਘ ਨੂੰ ਕੈਦ ਕਰਨ ਦੀ ਧਮਕੀ ਦਿਤੀ ਸ਼ਾਇਦ ਓਹ ਇਸ ਧਮਕੀ ਨੂੰ ਪੂਰਾ ਕਰ ਦਿੰਦਾ ਜੇ ਕਰ ਓਹ ਅਪਨੇ ਬਾਪ ਦੇ ਮਰਨ ਦੇ ਦਿਨ ਨਾ ਮਾਰਿਆ ਜਾਂਦਾ ਇੰਦ੍ਰ ਸਿੰਘ ਤੇ ਰਾਮ ਸਿੰਘ ਨੂੰ ਸਪਾਰਸ਼ ਨਾਲ ਕਈ ਜੰਗੀ ਕਮਾਨ ਮਿਲੇ ਜਿਸਨੂੰ ਓਹ ਮਹਾਰਾਜਾ ਖੜਕ ਸਿੰਘ ਦੀਆਂ ਚੋਰੀ ਖਬਰਾਂ ਰਾਜਾ ਧਿਆਨਸਿੰਘ ਦੇ ਵਿਰੁਧ ਦਿੰਦਾ ਸਾ ਅਰ ਓਹਦੀ ਅਪਨੀ ਜਗੀਰ ੧੫੦੦੦ ਰੁਪਏ ਸਾਲਾਨਾ ਕਰ ਦਿਤੀ ਗਈ॥

No. 9.

ਮਤਾਬ ਸਿੰਘ ਸਨ ੧੭੧੧ ਵਿਚ ਜੰਮਿਆ ਅਤੇ ਜਦੋਂ ਬਿਲਕੁਲ ਮੁੰਡਾ ਹੀ ਸੀ ਕੱਚੇ ਰਸਾਲੇ ਵਿਚ ਸੂਬੇਦਾਰ ਕਰਕੇ ਰਖਿਆ ਗਿਆ ਸਨ ੧੭੩੧ ਵਿਚ ਮਹਾਰਾਜੇ ਦੇ ਰੋਪੜ ਨੂੰ ਆਉਣ ਤੇ ਥੋੜਾ ਚਿਰ ਅਗੋਂ ਉਹ ਕਰਨੈਲ ਬਨਾਇਆ ਗਿਆ ਤੇ ਦੋ ਪਲਟਣਾ ਉਤੇ ਕਮਾਨ ਕਰਦਾ ਹੋਇਆ ਅੰਬਰ ਸਰ ਅਟਕਿਆ ਰਿਹਾ ਸਨ ੧੮੩੪ ਵਿਚ ਉਹ ਅਪਣੇ ਪਿਉ ਅਮਰ ਸਿੰਘ ਨਾਲ ਪੇਸ਼ਾਵਰ ਨੂੰ ਗਿਆ, ਤੇ ਲਾਮ ਵਿਚ ਬੜੇ ਭਲਮਣ-ਸਊ ਨਾਲ ਕੰਮ ਕਰਦਾ ਰਹਿਆ, ਉਸੇ ਬਰਹੇ ਵਿਚ ਉਹਦਾ ਭਰਾ ਗੁਰਦਿਤ ਸਿੰਘ ਮਹਾਰਾਜ ਦਾ ਨੌਕਰ ਹੋਗਿਆ, ਸਨ ੧੮੩੯ ਵਿਚ ਮਤਾਬ ਸਿੰਘ ਸਰਦਾਰ ਤੇਜਾ ਸਿੰਘ ਦੇ ਹੇਠ ਅਫਰੀਦੀਆਂ ਦੀ ਲਾਮ ਵਿਚ ਲੜਦਾ ਰਹਿਆ, ਸਨ ੧੮੪੧ ਵਿਚ ਮਹਾ ਰਾਜੇ ਸ਼ੇਰ ਸਿੰਘ ਨੇ ਉਹਨੂੰ ਜਰਨੈਲ ਬਣਾ ਦਿਤਾ ਤੇ ਪੇਸ਼ਾਵਰ ਵਿਚ ਕਮਾਨ ਕਰਦਾ ਰਹਿਆ ਉਹਦੇ ਹੇਠ ਚਾਰ ਪਲਟਨਾਂ, ਛੱਬੀ ਤੋਪਾਂ ਅਰ ਇਕ ਅਕਾਲੀਆਂ ਦੀ ਪਲਟਣ ਸੀ।

No. 10.

ਸਨ ੧੮੪੨ ਤੇ ਜੂਨ ਚੜ੍ਹਦਿਆਂਹੀ ਸ਼ੇਰਸਿੰਘ ਨੇ ਬਹੁਤ ਸਾਰੇ ਸਰਦਾਰਾਂ ਤੇ ਵਡੀ ਸੈਨਾ ਨਾਲ ਵਜੀਰਾਬਾਦ ਦੀ ਵਲ ਕੂਚ ਕੀਤਾ। ਚਾਚਾ ਧਿਆਨ ਸਿੰਘ ਪਿਛੇ ਲਾਹੌਰ ਰਹਿ ਗਿਆ। ਚੰਦਕੌਰ ਨੂੰ ਫੇਰ ਹੁਕਮ ਮਿਲ ਚੁੱਕਾ ਸੀ। ਕਿ ਉਹ ਕਿਲੇ ਵਿਚ ਜੋ

ਸ਼ਾਨ ਸਿੰਘਦੇ ਹਥ ਹੇਠਸੀ ਆਪਨੇਘਰ ਚਲੀ ਜਾਵੇ। ਜੂੰਨਦੀ ਬਾਰਵੀਂ ਨੂੰ ਉਹਦੀਆਂ ਟਹਿਲਣਾਂ ਨੇ ਜੋ ਪਹਿਲਾਂ ਸਿਖਾਈਆਂ ਹੋਈਆਂ ਸੀਆਂ। ਮਾਈ ਚੰਦਕੌਰ ਨੂੰ ਸ਼ਰਬਤ ਦੇਕੇ ਜ਼ੈਹਿਰ ਰਲਾਕੇ ਉਹਨੂੰ ਮਾਰਨ ਦਾ ਜਤਨ ਕੀਤਾ। ਉਹਨੇ ਸੁਆਦ ਚਖਕੇ ਪਰੇ ਸੁਟ ਦਿਤਾ। ਤੇ ਟਹਿਲਨੀਆਂ ਨੇ ਫੇਰ ਇਹ ਭੈ ਕਰਕੇ ਕਿ ਸਾਡਾ ਭੇਤ ਖੁਲ ਗਿਆ ਅਤੇ ਉਹਦੇ ਪੁਰ ਪਥਰ ਵਰਸਾਉਨ ਲਗੀਆਂ। ਤੇ ਉਹਦੀ ਖੋਪਰੀ ਤੋੜ ਦਿਤੀ ਅਤੇ ਉਹਨੂੰ ਮੁਰਦਾ ਸਮਝਕੇ ਛਡ ਗਈਆਂ। ਰਾਜਾ ਧਿਆਨ ਸਿੰਘ ਉਸੀ ਵੇਲੇ ਆਪਨੇ ਸ਼ਕਾਰ ਕੋਲ ਆਇਆ। ਤੇ ਉਹਦੇ ਜਖਮਾਂ ਉੱਤੇ ਮਲਮ ਪਟੀ ਕਰਵਾਈ। ਫਕੀਰ ਨੂਰਦੀਨ ਨੂੰ ਇਕ ਵਾਰੀ ਖਿਆਲ਼ ਹੋਇਆ ਕਿ ਭਾਂਵੇਂ ਇਹ ਬਚ ਜਾਏ। ਪਰ ਫੇਰ ਉਹਨੂੰ ਸੁਰਤ ਮੂਲੋਂ ਨਾਂ ਆਈ। ਅਰ ਦੋ ਦਿਹਾੜੇ ਵਿਚ ਵਿਚ ਮਰਗਈ। ਮਾਰਨ ਵਾਲੀਆਂ ਟਹਿਲਨਾਂ ਦੇ ਵਡੀਆਂ ਭਾਰੀ ਬੇੜੀਆਂ ਪਾਈਆਂ ਗਈਆਂ। ਅਰ ਆਖਦੇ ਹਨ ਕਿ ਜਦ ਉਹਨਾਂ ਨੂੰ ਇਹ ਧਮਕੀ ਦਿਤੀ ਗਈ। ਕਿ ਤੁਹਾਡਾ ਬੰਦ ਬੰਦ ਜੁਦਾ ਕੀਤਾ ਜਾਊ। ਤਾਂ ਉਨਾਂ ਨੇ ਖੁਲਮਖੁਲਾ ਆਖ ਦਿਤਾ। ਕਿ ਸਾਨੂੰ ਧਿਆਨ ਸਿੰਘ ਨੇ ਚੁਕਿਆਸਾ। ਤੇ ਉਹਨੇ ਮਾਰਨ ਦੇ ਲਈ ਸਾਂਨੂੰ ਵਡੇ ਅਨਾਂਮ ਦਾ ਕਰਾਰ ਕੀਤਾ ਸਾ। ਉਹਨਾਂ ਦੀ ਇਹ ਖਬਰ ਨਹੀਂ। ਜੋ ਫੇਰ ਟਹਿਲਣਾਂ ਦਾ ਕੀ ਹਾਲ ਹੋਇਆ। ਪਰ ਇਹ ਸੋਚਦੇ ਹਾਂ। ਜੋ ਰਾਜੇ ਦੇ ਹੁਕਮ ਨਾਲ ਉਹ ਮਾਰੀਆਂ ਗਈਆਂ ਸੀਆਂ।

No. 11

ਸੰਨ ੧੭੬੬ ਝੰਡਾ ਸਿੰਘ ਤੇ ਗੰਡਾ ਸਿੰਘ ਨੇ ਵੱਡੀ ਫੌਜ ਨਾਲ ਮੁਲਤਾਂਨ ਤੇ ਚੜ੍ਹਾਈ ਕੀਤੀ ਸ਼ੁਜਾਖਾਂ ਉਥੇ ਦੇ ਸੂਬੇ ਤੇ ਬਹਾਵਲ ਪੁਰ ਦੇ ਮੁਬਾਰਕ ਖਾਂ ਨੇ ਸਤਲੁਜ ਦੇ ਕੰਢੇ ਪੁਰ ਓਨਾਂ ਨਾਲ ਲੜਾਈ ਕੀਤੀ ਕਿਸੀ ਧਿਰ ਦੀ ਜਿਤ ਨਾਂ ਹੋਈ ਪਰ ਇਕ ਰਾਜੀ ਨਾਮਾ ਇਨਾਂ ਸ਼ਰਤਾਂ ਤੇ ਹੋਗਿਆ ਕਿ ਸਿਖਾਂ ਤੇ ਪਠਾਨਾਂ ਦੇ ਰਾਜ ਵਿਚ ਪਾਕਪਟਨ ਹਦ ਹੋਜਾਏ ਇਸਤੇ ਬਾਦ ਫੇਰ ਝੰਡਾ ਸਿੰਘ ਅੰਮ੍ਰਿਤਸਰ ਨੂੰ ਮੁੜ ਆਇਆ ਅਰ ਓਹਦੇ ਪੂਰਾ ਕਰਨ ਵਿਚ ਲਗ ਗਿਆ ਭੰਗੀਆਂ ਦੇ ਕਿਲ਼ੇ ਨੂੰ ਜਿਦਾ ਅਰੰਭ ਹਰੀ ਸਿੰਘ ਨੇ ਕੀਤਾ ਸਾ ਤੇ ਜਿਸਦੇ ਖੰਡਰ ਲੂਣ ਮੰਡੀ ਬਜਾਰ ਨਜਰ ਆਉਂਦੇ ਹਨ ਉਸਤੇ ਪਿਛੇ ਛੇਤੀ ਹੀ ਝੰਡਾ ਸਿੰਘ ਨੇ ਮੁਲਤਾਂਨ ਦੇ ਸਰਦਾਰ ਦੇ ਨਾਲ ਰਾਜ਼ੀ ਨਾਮੇ ਦੀ ਸ਼ਰਤ ਤੋੜ

ਦਿਤੀ ਅਰ ੧੭੭੧ ਵਿਚ ਓਹਦੇ ਮੁਲਕ ਪੁਰ ਹਲਾ ਕਰ ਦਿਤਾ ਉਹਨੇ ਛੇਵ ਮਹੀਨੇ ਤੀਕ ਕਿਲੇ ਪੁਰ ਘੇਰਾ ਪਾ ਰਖਿਆ ਪਰ ਕੁਝ ਲਾਭ ਨਾਂ ਹੋਇਆ ਅਰ ਫੇਰ ਪਠਾਨਾਂ ਦੀ ਇਕ ਫੌਜ ਜਹਾਂਨਖਾਂ ਦੀ ਕਮਾਂਨ ਹੇਠਾਂ ਐਨੀ ਨੇੜੇ ਪਹੁੰਚ ਆਈ ਕਿ ਓਹ ਨੂੰ ਘੇਰਾ ਚਦਾਉਨਾ ਪਿਆ।

No. 12

(ਵਡਾ ਤੁਫਾਨ)

ਪਿਛਲੇ ਸ਼ੁਕਰ ਵਾਰ ਨੂੰ ੩ ਬਜੇ ਦੁਪੈਹਰ ਦੇ ਪਿਛੋਂ ਦਖਣ ਤੇ ਲੈਂਦੇ ਪਾਸਿਓਂ ਹਨੇਰੀ ਇਸ ਜੋਰ ਸ਼ੋਰ ਨਾਲ ਉਤਰੀ ਕਿ ਤੁਰਤ ਫੁਰਤ ਹਨੇਰਾ ਹੋਗਿਆ ਅਰ ਹਜਾਰਾਂ ਬ੍ਰਿਛ ਢੈਕੇ ਢੇਰੀ ਹੋਗਏ । ਬਥੇਰਿਆਂ ਲੋਕਾਂ ਨੂੰ ਡਾਢੀਆਂ ਸਟਾਂ ਲਗੀਆਂ। ਮੇਰਾ ਇਕ ਮਿਤਰ ਜਲੰਧਰ ਗਿਆ ਹੋਇਆ ਸੀ ਜਦ ਦੋ ਕੋਹਾਂ ਦੇ ਲਗ ਭਗ ਇਧਰ ਮੁੜ ਆਇਆ ਤਾਂ ਹਨੇਰੀ ਨੇ ਆ ਘੇਰਿਆ ਜੇੜ੍ਹੇ ਬ੍ਰਿਛ ਦੀ ਓਟ ਲਈ ਸੀ ਉਹ ਜੜ ਤੋਂ ਉਖੜਕੇ ਦੂਰ ਜਾ ਪਿਆ ਅਤੇ ਯਕਾ ਅਰ ਘੋੜਾ ਪੁਰਜੇ ਪੁਰਜੇ ਹੋਣ ਲਗੇ। ਯਕੇ ਵਾਲਾ ਚਾਤਰ ਸੀ ਘੋੜਾ ਖੋਲ ਲਿਆ ਅਰ ਯਕੇ ਨੂੰ ਆਪਣੇ ਸਾਮਣੇ ਪੁਰਜੇ ਪੁਰਜੇ ਹੁੰਦੇ ਵੇਖਿਆ ਜਦ ਹਨੇਰੀ ਦੇ ਪਿਛੇ ਮੀਂਹ ਪੈਣ ਲਗਾ ਤਾਂ ਮੇਰਾ ਮਿਤਰ ਅਰ ਨਾਲ ਦੀਆਂ ਸਵਾਰੀਆਂ ਇਕ ਉਜਾੜ ਦੀ ਕੋਠੀ ਵਿਚ ਓਟ ਲੈਣ ਲਈ ਜਾਵੜੇ ਜਿਥੇ ਧਮੋੜੀਆਂ (ਭੂੰਡ A wasp) ਅਕਠੀਆਂ ਸੀਆਂ ਓਨਾਂ ਨੇ ਐਹੋ ਜਹੀ ਟਹਿਲ ਤੇ ਆਦਰ ਕੀਤਾ ਕਿ ਸਭਨਾਂ ਨੂੰ ਵਢ ਵਢ ਕੇ ਕੁੱਪਾ ਬਨਾ ਦਿਤਾ ਅਰ ਨਸਦਿਆਂ ਨੂੰ ਰਾਹ ਨਾ ਲਭਾ ਅਤੇ ਡਿਗਦੇ ਢੈਂਦੇ ਜਲੰਧਰ ਪੁਜਕੇ ਦੂਜੀ ਵਾਰੀ ਯਕਾ ਕੀਤਾ ਅਰ ਕਪੂਰਥਲੇ ਪੁਜੇ। ਇਹ ਬ੍ਰਿਤਾਂਤ ਹੈ ਨਹੀ ਤੇ ਜਿਨੇਕੁ ਬ੍ਰਤਾਂਤ ਸੁਣੇ ਗਏ ਹੈਨ ਜੇਕਰ ਵਖਰੇ ਵਖਰੇ ਲਿਖੇ ਜਾਣ ਤਾਂ ਦਫਤਰ ਚਾਹੀਦਾ ਹੈ। ਸੁਣਿਆਂ ਹੈ ਕਿ ਇਕ ਹਿੰਦੂਆਂ ਦੀ ਜੰਜ ਇਸ ਤੁਫਾਨ ਨੇ ਸਿਰੀ ਹਰਿਗੋਬਿੰਦ ਪੁਰ ਦੇ ਪਤਣ ਵਿਚ ਪਾਣੀ ਦੇ ਵਿਚ ਗਰਕ ਕਰ ਦਿਤੀ। ਚਾਰਪੰਜ ਗੇਣਤੀ ਦੇ ਆਦਮੀ ਬਚੇ ਅਤੇ ਸਾਰਿਆਂ ਦਾ ਖੋਜ ਨਹੀ ਲਭਾ। ਸੋਚਣਾਂ ਚਾਹੀਏ ਕਿ ਕਿਨੇਈ ਛੋਟੇ ਵਡੇ ਘਰਾਣੇ ਇਕ ਪਲ ਵਿਚ ਪਰਲੋਕ ਨੂੰ ਚਲੇ ਗਏ ਅਰ ਪਿਛਲ੍ਹਿਆਂ

ਨੂੰ ਦਾਗ ਦੇ ਗਏ ਕੀ ਹਨੇਰੀ ਸੀ ਪਰਮੇਸ਼ਰ ਦੀ ਕਰੋਪੀ ਸੀ ਕੈਂਹਦੇ ਹੈਨ ਕਿ ਸ਼ੁਕਰ ਨੂੰ ਆਪ ਜੁਮੇਸ਼ਾਹ ਸੁਵਾਰ ਸਾ ਜੋਹੜਾ ਸਦਾਈ ਇਸ ਰੁਤ ਵਿਚ ਦੌਰਾ ਕਰਦਾ ਹੈ ਬਰਖਾ ਦੇ ਸਬਬ ਦੋ ਦਿਨ ਠੰਡ ਰਹੀ ਹੁਨ ਫੇਰ ਗਰਮੀ ਦਾ ਜੋਰ ਹੈ। ਕਣਕ ਦਾ ਭਾ ਸਸਤਾ ਹੋਗਿਆ ਹੈ ਖਵਰੇ ਬਾਹਰ ਦੀ ਖ਼ਰੀਦਾਰੀ ਨਹੀ ਹੋਈ।

No. 13

ਅਸਾਂ ਵੀ ਵਡੇ ਜ਼ੋਰ ਸ਼ੋਰ ਨਾਲ ਓਨਾਂ ਦਾ ਪਿਛਾ ਕੀਤਾ ਓਹ ਕਿਲੇ ਦੇ ਬੂਹੇ ਦੇ ਅਗੋਂ ਲੰਘ ਪਏ ਸੋ ਓਥੇ ਮਸ਼ੀਨਾਂ ਦੀ ਅਜਿਹੀ ਬੁਛਾੜ ਹੋਈ ਜੋ ਓਹਨਾਂ ਦੇ ਹਜਾਰਾਂ ਆਦਮੀਂ ਭੁਜ ਗਏ ਤੇ ਹਜਾਰਾਂ ਆਪਸ ਵਿਚ ਕਟ ਮੋਏ। ਉਸ ਵੇਲੇ ਦੀ ਗੱਲ ਲਿਖਣ ਤੋ ਬਾਹਰ ਹੈ ਰੋਨ ਪਿਟਨ ਦਾ ਹੀ ਅਵਾਜ ਆਉਂਦਾ ਸੀ। ਅੰਤ ਨੂੰ ਪਿਛਲੀ ਰਾਤੀ ਵੈਰੀ ਸਾਰੇ ਹੀ ਨਸ ਗਏ ਤਿਨ ਚਾਰ ਹਜਾਰ ਓਨਾਂ ਦੀ ਲਾਸ਼ ਪਈ ਰਹੀ। ਸਾਡੀ ਵਲ ਹੋਰ ਤਾਂ ਸਭ ਤਰਾਂ ਸੁਖ ਰਹੀ ਪਰ ਜੀਟਨ ਸਾਹਿਬ ਦੀ ਭੱਜਨ ਲਗਿਆਂ ਬੂਟ ਦੇ ਫਿਸਲਨ ਕਰਕੇ ਸੱਜੀ ਲਤ ਟੁਟ ਗਈ ਹੁਨ ਸਾਹਿਬ ਹਸਪਤਾਲ ਵਿਚ ਹੈ ਤੇ ਡਾਕਦਾਰ ਸਾਹਿਬ ਨੇ ਮਲਹਮ ਪੱਟੀ ਕਰਕੇ ਲੱਤ ਬਨ ਦਿਤੀ ਹੈ। ਆਖਦੇ ਹਨ ਜੋ ਛੇਤੀ ਹੀ ਲੱਤ ਜੁੜ ਜਾਵੇਗੀ। ਇਹ ਗੁਰੂ ਮਹਾਰਾਜ ਦੇ ਉਸ ਵਾਕ ਮੂਜਬ ਗਲ ਹੋਈ "ਸਵਾਲਾਖ ਸੇ ਏਕ ਲੜਾਊਂ" ਸੋ ਸਾਡੇ ਵੀਹ ਆਦਮੀ ਕਈ ਹਜਾਰਾਂ ਵੈਰੀਆ ਨਾਲ ਲੜੇ ਤੇ ਓੜਕ ਨੂੰ ਫਤੇ ਪਾਈ। ਬਾਕੀ ਫੇਰ।

No. 14

ਜਦ ਔਰੰਗਜੇਬ ੧੬੫੯ ਸਾਲ ਵਿਚ ਗੱਦੀ ਤੇ ਬੈਠਾ ਤਾਂ ਹੁਸੈਨ ਖਾਂ ਨੂੰ ਆਪਨੀ ਜਾਗੀਰ ਮਿਲਗਈ। ਪਰ ਉਹਦੇ ਤੇਜ ਸੁਭਾਉ ਦੇ ਕਾਰਨ ਫੇਰ ਛੇਤੀ ਓਹਦੀ ਵਡੀ ਨਰਾਦ੍ਹੀ ਹੋਈ। ਇਕ ਅਭਾਗੀ ਦਿਨ ਸ਼ਹਿਨਸ਼ਾਹ ਕੁਝ ਘੋੜਿਆਂ ਨੂੰ ਦੇਖ ਰਹਿਆਸਾ ਜੋ ਉਸਦੀ ਸੇਵਾ ਵਿਚ ਹਾਜਰ ਕੀਤੇ ਗਏਸੀ। ਓਹਨਾਂ ਵਿਚੋਂ ਇਕ ਵਲ ਉਂਗਲ ਕਰਕੇ ਉਹਨੇ ਹੁਸੈਨਖਾਂ ਤੇ ਪੁਛਿਆ। ਉਹਦੀ ਕੀ ਨਸਲ ਹੈ ਉਸ ਸਰਦਾਰ ਨੇ ਕੁਝ ਢਿਲ ਮਠ ਕੀਤੀ। ਤੇ ਇਕ ਸੋਹਣੇ ਸਜਾਏ ਪਠਾਂਨ ਨੇ ਜੋ ਕੋਲ ਖਲੋਤਾ ਸੀ। ਉਤਰ ਦਿਤਾ। ਹੁਸੈਨਖਾਂ ਨੇ ਵਡੇ ਗੁੱਸੇ ਵਿਚ ਆਕੇ ਕਿਹਾ ਓਏ ਗੋਲਿਆ ਜਦ ਬਾਦਸ਼ਾਹ

ਮੇਰੇ ਨਾਲ ਗਲ ਕਰਦਾ ਹੈ ।ਤੂੰ ਕਿਉਂ ਬੋਲਦਾ ਹੈਂ । ਉਹਨੇ ਉਤਰ ਦਿਤਾ। ਕਿ ਗੋਲੇ ਕਮੀਨੀਆਂ ਸ਼ਕਲਾਂ ਤੋਂ ਹੀ ਨਜ਼ਰ ਆ ਜਾਂਦੇ ਹਨ। ਹੁਸੈਨਖਾਂ ਜੋ ਮਧਰਾ ਤੇ ਭਾਵਾ ਕਾਲੇ ਰੰਗਦਾ ਸੀ । ਉਹਨੂੰ ਇਸਪੁਰ ਇਨਾਂ ਕ੍ਰੋਧ ਆਇਆ । ਕਿ ਉਹਨੇ ਆਪਨੀ ਖੰਜਰ ਸੂਤ ਲਈ ਤੇ ਉਸ ਬੇਧੜਕ ਬੋਲਨ ਵਾਲੇ ਪਠਾਂਨ ਦੇ ਜਿਗਰ ਵਿਚ ਮਾਰਕੇ ਖੂੰਨ ਕਰ ਦਿਤਾ। ਇਸ ਦੋਸਦੇ ਬਦਲੇ ਜੇਹੜਾ ਉਹਨੇ ਬਾਦਸ਼ਾਹ ਦੇ ਸਾਮਨੇ ਕੀਤਾ। ਹੁਸੈਨਖਾਂ ਕੈਦ ਕੀਤਾ ਗਿਆ। ਤੇ ਭਾਵੇਂ ਥੋੜੇ ਚਿਰ ਪਿਛੋਂ ਛੁਟ ਗਿਆ ਪਰ ਦਰਬਾਰ ਤੇ ਉਮਰ ਭਰ ਵਾਸਤੇ ਕਢਿਆ ਗਿਆ ।

PUNJABI DIALOGUES.

SECTION I.—General Orders and Questions

1.	Stand up.	ਉਠਕੇ ਖੜੋ । *uṭh ke kharo.*
2	Sit down.	ਬੈਠ ਜਾ । *baiṭh jā.*
3.	Come quickly.	ਛੇਤੀ ਆ । *chheṭī ā.*
4	Go in.	ਅੰਦਰ ਜਾ *aṅdar jā.*
5.	Make haste.	ਛੇਤੀ ਕਰ । *chhetī kar.*
6.	Come back.	ਮੁੜ ਆ । *muṛ ā.*
7.	Go soon.	ਛੇਤੀ ਜਾ । *chhetī jā.*
8.	Be quiet.	ਚੁਪਕਰ *chup kar.*
9	Speak out.	ਉੱਚੀ ਬੋਲ । *uchchī bol*
10.	Come here.	ਉਰੇ ਆ । *ure ā.*
11.	Go away.	ਚਲਿਆ ਜਾ । *chaliā jā.*
12.	Come near.	ਨੇੜੇ ਆ । *neṛe ā.*
13	Be careful.	ਖਬਰਦਾਰ । *khabardār.*
14.	Have patience.	ਸਾਹ ਲੈ । *sāh lai.*
15.	Stand still.	ਖੜਾ ਰਹੁ । *khaṛā rahu.*
16.	Don't forget.	ਭੁਲੀਂ ਨਾ । *bhulīṅ nā.*
17.	Do not move.	ਹਿੱਲ ਨਾ । *hill nā.*
18.	Stand back.	ਪਿਛੇ ਹਟਕੇ ਖੜੋ । *pichhe haṭ ke kharo*
19.	Take this letter to the fort.	ਏਹ ਅਰਦਾਸ ਕਿਲੇ ਨੂੰ ਲੈ ਜਾਹ । *ih ardās kile nūṅ laijāh.*
20.	Bring an answer.	ਜਵਾਬ ਲਿਆ । *jawāb liā.*
21.	First turn to the right and then to the left.	ਪਹਿਲਾਂ ਸੱਜੇ ਹਥ ਵੱਲ ਅਰ ਫੇਰ ਖੱਬੇ ਹਥ ਵੱਲ ਮੁੜ । *pahilāṅ sajje hath wall ar pher khabbe hath wall muṛ.*
22.	Call the cook and the groom.	ਲਾਂਗਰੀ ਅਤੇ ਸਹੀਸ ਨੂੰ ਸੱਦ । *lāṅgrī ute sahīs nūṅ sad.*
23.	They are gone to the Bazar.	ਓਹ ਬਜਾਰ ਨੂੰ ਗਏ ਹਨ । *oh bajār nūṅ gae han.*

24. Don't make a noise.	ਰੌਲਾ ਨਾ ਪਾ । *raulā nā pā.*
25. Do as I say.	ਜਿਹਾ ਮੈਂ ਆਖਾਂ ਤਿਹਾ ਕਰ । *jihā maiṅ ākhāṅ tihā kar.*
26. Mind your own business.	ਆਪਣਾ ਕੰਮ ਕਰ । *āpnā kam kar.*
27. What is your name?	ਤੇਰਾ ਨਾਂ ਕੀ ਹੈ ? *terā nāṅ kī hai.*
28. My name is *Bhagwān Singh.*	ਮੇਰਾ ਨਾਂ ਭਗਵਾਨ ਸਿੰਘ ਹੈ । *merā nāṅ Bhagwān Singh hai.*
29 What is your occupation?	ਤੁਸੀਂ ਕੀ ਕੰਮ ਕਰਦੇ ਹੋ ? *tusīṅ kī kanm karde ho.*
20. I am a horse dealer.	ਮੈਂ ਘੋੜਿਆਂ ਦਾ ਸੌਦਾਗਰ ਹਾਂ । *maiṅ ghoṛiāṅ dā saudāgar hāṅ.*
21. Where have you come from?	ਤੁਸੀ ਕਿਧਰੋਂ ਆਏ ਹੋ ? *tusī kidhroṅ āe, ho.*
32. I have come from *Lahore.*	ਮੈਂ ਲਹੌਰੋਂ ਆਇਆ ਹਾਂ। *maiṅ lahauroṅ āiā hāṅ.*
33. Where do you live?	ਤੁਸੀਂ ਕਿਥੇ ਰਹਿੰਦੇ ਹੋ ? *tusī kiththe rahiṅde ho.*
34. In the *Saddar Bazar.*	ਸਦਰ ਬਜਾਰ ਵਿਚ । *sadar bajār wich.*
35. How far is it from here?	ਓਹ ਏਥੋਂ ਕਿੱਨੀ ਦੂਰ ਹੈ ? *oh ethon kinnī dūr hai.*
36. Is any one there?	ਕੋਈ ਹੈ । *koī hai.*
37. Where is my servant?	ਮੇਰਾ ਨੌਕਰ ਕਿੱਧਰ ਹੈ ? *merā naukar kidhdhar hai.*
38. Do you recognise him?	ਤੁਸੀ ਉਸ ਨੂੰ ਸਿਆਣਦੇ ਹੋ? *tusī usnūṅ siānde ho.*
39. Make haste.	ਛੇਤੀ ਕਰ *chheti kar.*
40. The village has been demolished on account of a raid made by its inhabitants.	ਪਿੰਡ ਦੇ ਵਸਕੀਨਾਂ ਦੇ ਧਾਵੇ ਕਰਨ ਕਰ-ਕੇ ਨਗਰ ਢਾ ਦਿਤਾ ਗਿਆ ਹੈ । *piṅd de waskīnāṇ de dhāwe karan karke nagar dhhā dittā giā hai.*

41. Speak slowly, I shall then understand all you say.
ਹੌਲੀ ਹੌਲੀ ਬੋਲ ਤਾਂ ਜੋ ਕੁਝ ਤੂੰ ਆਖਨਾ ਹੈ ਮੈਂ ਸਮਝਾਂਗਾ। *haulī haulī bol tāṇ jo kujh tūṅ ākhnā hai maiṅ samjhāṅgā.*

42. How many men have been captured bring them all before me.
ਕਿਨੇ ਮਨੁੱਖ ਪਕੜੇ ਗਏ ਹਨ ਉਨਾਂ ਨੂੰ ਮੇਰੇ ਸਾਹਮਣੇ ਲਿਆ। *kinne manukh pakṛe gaye han unhāṅ nūṅ mere sāmhne liā.*

43. Let the men who have received their pay stand on one side, and those who have not been paid stop to the front.
ਓਹ ਆਦਮੀ ਜੇਹੜੇ ਤਲਬ ਲੈ ਚੁਕੇ ਹਨ ਓਨਾਂ ਨੂੰ ਇਕ ਪਾਸੇ ਖੜੇ ਹੋਨ ਦੇ ਤੇ ਦੂਜੇ ਜਿਨਾਂ ਅਜੇ ਨਹੀਂ ਲੀਤੀ ਅਗੇ ਵਧਕੇ ਖੜੇ ਹੋਨ। *oh ādmī jehṛe talab lai chuk han unhāṅ nūṅ ik pāse khaṛe hon de te dūje jinhāṅ aje nahīṅ lītī age wadh ke khaṛe hon.*

44. Has he come alone or is there anyone with him?
ਓਹ ਕੱਲਾ ਆਇਆ ਹੈ ਜਾਂ ਕੋਈ ਹੋਰ ਵੀ ਉਸਦੇ ਨਾਲ ਹੈ। *oh kallā āiā hai jāṅ koī hor wī usde nāl hai.*

45. Do this, and don't do that.
ਇਹ ਕੰਮ ਕਰ ਤੇ ਉਸਨੂੰ ਛੱਡ ਦੇ। *ih kanm kar te usnūṅ chhaḍ de.*

46. What do you mean by talking so to me?
ਤੇਰਾ ਮੇਰੇ ਨਾਲ ਇਸ ਤਰਾਂ ਗਲ ਕਰਨ ਥੀਂ ਕੀ ਮਤਲਬ ਹੈ। *terā mere nāl istarāṇ gal karan thīṅ kī matlab hai.*

47. Don't walk about on the grass, lest you tread on a snake.
ਘਾ ਉੱਤੇ ਨਾ ਤੁਰ ਫਿਰ ਕਿਧਰੇ ਸਪ ਤੇ ਪੈਰ ਨਾ ਆਜਾਵੇ। *ghā utte nā tur phir kidhre sapp te pair nā ājāwe.*

48. Is there a spring near the village?
ਪਿੰਡ ਦੇ ਨੇੜੇ ਕੋਈ ਸੁੰਬ ਹੈ। *piṅd d nere koī sumb hai.*

49. Is the water clean and cool, and fit for the men to drink?
ਪਾਣੀ ਠੰਢਾ ਤੇ ਸਾਫ ਅਤੇ ਆਦਮੀਆਂ ਦੇ ਪੀਨ ਲੈਕ ਹੈ। *pānī ṭhaṅḍā te sāf ate admīāṅ de pīn laik hai.*

50. No sir it is only fit for the mules to drink, for the washermen to wash clothes in, or for the soldiers to bathe in. — ਨਹੀਂ ਜੀ ਓਹ ਨਿਰਾ ਖਚਰਾਂ ਦੇ ਪੀਨ ਲੈਕ ਤੇ ਧੋਬੀਆਂ ਦੇ ਕਪੜੇ ਧੋਨ ਲਈ ਤੇ ਸਪਾਹੀਆਂ ਦੇ ਨ੍ਹਾਉਣ ਦੇ ਕੰਮਦਾ ਹੈ। *nāhin jī oh nirā khachrān de pīn laik te dhobīān de kappre dhon laī te sapāhīān de nhāun de kam dā hai.*

51. Is the master at home ? — ਸਾਹਬ ਘਰ ਹੈ ? *sāhib ghar hai ?*

52. Yes, Sir. — ਹਾਂ, ਜੀ। *hān jī.*

53. Is he awake ? — ਓਹ ਜਾਗਦਾ ਹੈ ? *oh jāgdā hai ?*

54. He is asleep. — ਓਹ ਸੁਤਾ ਪਿਆ ਹੈ। *oh suttā piā hai*

55. What is the matter ? — ਕੀ ਹੋਇਆ ਹੈ ? *kī hoiyā hai ?*

56. Where did you hear this news ? — ਇਹ ਖਬਰ ਤੂੰ ਕਿਥੋਂ ਸੁਣੀ ? *eh khabar tūn kithon sunī ?*

57. I heard from that soldier. — ਮੈਂ ਉਸ ਸਪਾਹੀ ਕੋਲੋਂ ਸੁਣੀ। *main us sapāhī kolon suṇī.*

58. How do you know that it is true ? — ਤੂੰ ਕੀਕਰ ਜਾਣਦਾ ਹੈਂ ਕਿ ਇਹ ਸਚ ਹੈ? *tūn kīkar jāṇdā hain ki eh sach hai.*

59. What do you call this ? — ਤੁਸੀ ਇਸਨੂੰ ਕੀ ਸਦਦੇ ਹੋ? *tusīn isnūn kī sadde ho.*

60. We call it (bhālā) a lance. — ਅਸੀਂ ਇਸਨੂੰ ਭਾਲਾ ਸਦਦੇ ਹਾਂ। *asīn isnūn bhālā sadde hān.*

61. Is there any fresh news ? — ਕੁਝ ਤਾਜੀ ਖਬਰ ਹੈ ? *kujh tājī khabar hai ?*

62. A new regiment is coming into the station to-morrow. — ਕਲ ਇਕ ਨਵੀਂ ਪਲਟਨ ਛੌਣੀ ਵਿਚ ਆਉਂਦੀ ਹੈ। *kal ikk nawīn palṭaṇ chhauṇī wich āundī hai.*

63. Is this right or wrong ? — ਇਹ ਠੀਕ ਹੈ ਜਾਂ ਝੂਠ ? *ih ṭhīk hai jān jhūṭh.*

64. Say it again. — ਇਸ ਨੂੰ ਫੇਰ ਆਖ। *is nūn pher ākh.*

65. How far is your birth place ? — ਤੁਹਾਡੀ ਜਨਮ ਭੂਮੀ ਕਿਨੀ ਦੂਰ ਹੈ ? *tuhāḍī janam bhūmī kiṇṇī dūr hai ?*

66. About one hundred and twenty miles — ਕੋਈ ਸਠਕੁ ਕੋਹ **koī saṭhku koh.*

* ਕੋਹ is equal to two miles.

67. Where is your family ?	ਤੁਹਾਡਾ ਕਬੀਲਾ (ਟੱਬਰ) ਕਿਥੇ ਹੈ *tuhāḍā kabīlā (ṭabbar) kithe hai.*
68. My wife is with her parents.	ਮੇਰੀ ਵਹੁਟੀ ਆਪਣੇ ਪੇਕਿਆਂ ਦੇ ਨਾਲ ਹੈ । *merī wahuṭī āpne pekiyāṅ de nāl hai.*
69. I want a good servant.	ਮੈਨੂੰ ਇਕ ਚੰਗੇ ਟਹਿਲੂਏ ਦੀ ਲੋੜ ਹੈ *maiṇūn ikk change ṭahlūe dī loṛ hai.*
70. What wages will you take ?	ਤੂੰ ਕੀ ਤਲਬ ਲਵੇਂਗਾ ? *tūṇ ki talab lawengā ?*
71. I will take ten rupees a month.	ਮੈਂ ਦਸ ਰੁਪੈ ਮਹੀਨਾ ਲਵਾਂਗਾ । *main das ropaye mahīṇā lawāṅgā.*
72. Why did you not come earlier ?	ਤੁਸੀ ਜਰਾ ਅਗੇ ਕਿਉਂ ਨਾ ਆਏ? *tusīṅ jarā agge kiyoṅ ṇā āe.*
73. Sir, I was busy.	ਸਾਹਬ, ਮੈਨੂੰ ਕੰਮ ਸੀ । *sāhib maiṇūṅ kaṅm sī.*
74. Did the washerman come to-day ?	ਅਜ ਧੋਬੀ (ਛੀਂਬਾ) ਆਇਆ ਸੀ । *aj ḍhobī (chhīṅbā) āiyā sī ?*
75. Yes, he has taken away the dirty clothes.	ਹਾਂ, ਓਹ ਮੈਲੇ ਕਪੜੇ ਲੈ ਗਿਆ ਹੈ । *hāṅ oh maile kapṛe lai giyā hai.*
76. Has the cook returned yet from the market ?	ਲਾਂਗਰੀ ਅਜੇ ਬਜਾਰੋਂ ਮੁੜਿਆ ਹੈ ਕਿ ਨਹੀਂ? *lāṅgrī aje bajāroṅ muṛiyā hai ki nahīṅ*
77. Let me know when he comes.	ਜਦ ਓਹ ਆਵੇ ਮੈਨੂੰ ਦਸੀਂ । *jad oh āwe maiṅ ṇūṅ dasīṅ.*
78. Open this box and empty it.	ਇਸ ਸੰਦੂਕ ਨੂੰ ਖੋਲਕੇ ਵੇਹਲਾ ਕਰ *is sandūk ṇūṅ khol ke wehlā kar.*
79. Lock it up and give me the key.	ਜੰਦਰਾ ਮਾਰਕੇ ਕੁੰਜੀ ਮੈਨੂੰ ਦੇਦੇ । *jaṅdrā mārke kuṅjī maiṅ ṇūṅ dede.*
80. Have you lighted the lamp ?	ਦੀਵਾ ਜਗਾਇਆ ਹਈ ? *dīwā jagāiyā haī ?*
81. I am going to light it.	ਮੈਂ ਬਾਲਣ ਲਗਾ ਹਾਂ । *maiṅ bālaṇ lagā hāṅ.*
82 Shut all the doors.	ਸਾਰੇ ਬੂਹੇ ਮਾਰ ਦੇ । *sāre būhe mār de.*
83 That will do you can go now.	ਬਸ ਕਰ ਹੁਣ ਜਾਹ । *bas kar hun jāh.*

84. Are you at leasure now? — ਹੁਣ ਤੈਨੂੰ ਵੇਹਲ ਹੈ? *hun taiṇūn wehal hai.*

85. I have nothing to do now. — ਹੁਣ ਮੈਨੂੰ ਕੁਝ ਕੰਮ ਨਹੀਂ। *hun main ṇūṅ kujh kanm nahīn.*

86. Clean all the house well. — ਸਾਰਾ ਘਰ ਚੰਗੀਤਰਾਂ ਸਾਫ਼ ਕਰ। *sārā ghar changī tarāṅ sāph kar.*

87. Bring my clothes I will go out. — ਮੇਰੇ ਲੀੜੇ ਲਿਆ ਮੈਂ ਬਾਹਰ ਜਾਵਾਂਗਾ *mere līṛe liyā main bāhar jāwāngā.*

88. Wake me very early to-morrow morning. — ਕਲ ਸਵੇਰੇ ਮੈਨੂੰ ਵੱਡੀਛੇਤੀ ਜਗਾਵੀਂ। *kal sawere maiṇūn waḍḍī chhetī jagāwīn*

89. At what time? — ਕਿਸ ਵੇਲੇ? *kis wele.*

90. At about 6 o'clock. — ਕੋਈ ਛੀਕੁ ਵਜੇ। *koī chhīku waje.*

91. Bring some water that I may wash my hands and face. — ਕੁਝ ਪਾਣੀ ਲਿਆ ਜੋ ਮੈਂ ਆਪਣੇ ਹਥ ਤੇ ਮੂੰਹ ਧੋਵਾਂ। *kujh pāṇī liyā jo main āpṇe hathh te mūnh dhowān.*

92. Shall I bring hot or cold water? — ਤਤਾ ਜਾਂ ਠੰਡਾ ਪਾਣੀ ਲਿਆਵਾਂ? *tattā jāṇ ṭhanḍā pāṇī liāwān?*

93 Put these rupees in the bag and hang it on the peg. — ਇਹ ਰੁਪੈ ਥੈਲੀ ਵਿਚ ਪਾਕੇ ਕਿੱਲੀ ਨਾਲ ਟੰਗ ਦੇ। *ih rupai thailī wich pā ke killī ṇāl ṭaṅg de.*

94. There is no oil in the lamp. — ਦੀਵੇ ਵਿਚ ਤੇਲ ਨਹੀਂ। *diwe wich tel nahīn.*

95. I am going to put some. — ਮੈਂ ਕੁਝ ਪਾਉਣ ਲਗਾ ਹਾਂ। *main kujh pāoṇ laggā hān.*

96. Have you a new suit of clothes? — ਤੁਹਾਡੇ ਕੋਲ ਨਵਾਂ ਕਪੜਿਆਂ ਦਾ ਜੋੜਾ ਹੈ? *tuhāde kol nawān kapṛiān dā joṛā hai?*

97. I am going to the washerman to bring it. — ਮੈਂ ਧੋਬੀ ਕੋਲੋਂ ਇਕ ਜੋੜਾ ਲੈਨ ਲਈ ਜਾਂਦਾ ਹਾਂ। *main dhobī kolon ikk joṛā lain laī jāndā hān.*

98. This cloth is coarse, I want something finer. — ਇਹ ਕਪੜਾ ਮੋਟਾ ਹੈ ਤੇ ਮੈਨੂੰ ਮਹੀਨ ਲੋੜੀਦਾ ਹੈ। *ih kapṛā moṭā hai te main nūṇ mahīn loṛīdā hai.*

99. I shall be able to give you good cloth to-morrow.	ਕਲ ਮੈਂ ਤੁਹਾਨੂੰ ਚੰਗਾ ਕਪੜਾ ਦੇ ਸਕਾਂਗਾ। *kal maiṅ tuhānūṅ changā kapṛā de sakāṅgā.*
100. This is a difficult business.	ਏਹ ਔਖਾ ਕੰਮ ਹੈ। *eh aukhā kaṅm hai.*
101. Why are you laughing?	ਤੁਸੀਂ ਕਿਸ ਕਰਕੇ ਹਸਦੇ ਹੋ? *tusīṅ kiskar ke hasde ho?*
102. It is my mistake Sir.	ਹਜ਼ੂਰ ਇਹ ਮੇਰੀ ਭੁਲ ਹੈ। *hajūr ih merī bhul hai.*
103. Tell him to bring a horse for me.	ਉਸਨੂੰ ਆਖ ਜੋ ਮੇਰੇ ਲਈ ਘੋੜਾ ਲਿਆਵੇ। *usnūṅ ākh jo mere laī ghoṛā liāwe.*
104. What time will the horse race begin?	ਘੋੜ ਦੌੜ ਕਿਸ ਵੇਲੇ ਹੋਵੇਗੀ *ghoṛdauṛ kis wele howegī.*
105. The first race will be at half past three.	ਪਹਿਲੀ ਦੌੜ ਸਾਢੇ ਤਿਨ ਵਜ ਹੋਵੇਗੀ। *pahilī dauṛ sāḍhe tin waje howegī.*
106. Take this chit to the Adjutant's Bungalow.	ਏਹ ਚਿੱਠੀ ਅਜੀਟਨ ਸਾਹਿਬ ਦੇ ਬੰਗਲੇ ਲੈ ਜਾਹ। *eh chiṭhī ajīṭan sāhib de baṅgle lai jāh.*
107. Will there be any answer?	ਕੁਝ ਉਤਰ ਹੋਵੇਗਾ? *kujh uttar howaegā*
108. Yes, wait for the answer.	ਹਾਂ ਜਵਾਬ ਦੇ ਲਈ ਠਹਿਰੀਂ *hāṅ jawāb de laī thahirīṅ.*
109 Open the door.	ਬੂਹਾ ਖੋਲ *būhā khol.*
110. Shut the window.	ਤਾਕੀ (ਬਾਰੀ) ਮਾਰ। *tākī (bārī) mār.*
111. Light the lamp.	ਦੀਵਾ ਬਾਲ। *dīwā bāl.*
112. Put out the candle.	ਮੋਮ ਵੱਟੀ ਬੁਝਾ। *mom waṭṭī bujhā.*

GENERAL.

1. Are there any good grazing grounds for camels near cantonment ?

ਛੌਨੀ ਦੇ ਨੇੜੇ ਤੇੜੇ ਊਠਾਂ ਦੇ ਚਰਨ ਲਈ ਕੋਈ ਚੰਗੀ ਥਾਂ ਹੈ । *chhauní de neṛe teṛe ūṭhāṅ de charan laī koī changī thāṅ hai.*

2. Three of the mules have sore backs they must not carry loads.

ਤਿੰਨਾਂ ਖਚਰਾਂ ਦੀ ਪਿਠ ਲਗੀ ਹੋਈ ਹੈ ਉਨ੍ਹਾਂ ਉਤੇ ਭਾਰ ਨਹੀਂ ਲਦਣਾ ਚਾਹੀਦਾ *tināṅ khachrāṅ dī piṭh laggī hoī hai unhāṅ ute bhār nahīṅ ladṇā chāhīdā.*

3. This mare has been lame since last month.

ਇਹ ਘੋੜੀ ਪਿਛਲੇ ਮਹੀਨੇ ਤੋਂ ਲੰਗੜੀ ਹੈ *ih ghoṛī pichhle mahīne toṅ langṛī hai.*

4. Show me the nearest road to the camp

ਮੈਨੂੰ ਕੰਪੂ ਦਾ ਸੁਖਾਲਾ ਰਸਤਾ ਦਸ। *maiṅ nūṅ kampū dā sukhālā rastā das.*

5 If you really had presented a petition I would have heard it at once.

ਜੇਕਰ ਤੂੰ ਸਚ ਮੁਚ ਅਰਜੀ ਕਰਦਾ ਤਾਂ ਮੈਂ ਤੁਰਤ ਤੇਰੀ ਅਰਜ਼ ਸੁਣਦਾ। *je kar tūṅ sach much arjī kardā tāṅ maiṅ turt terī arj suṇdā.*

6. Is it likely that the common people in your village will listen to the advice of their elders ?

ਏਹ ਹੋਸਕਦਾ ਹੈ ਕਿ ਤੁਹਾਡੇ ਪਿੰਡ ਵਿਚ ਆਮ ਲੋਕ ਵਡਿਆਂਦੀ ਸਲਾਹ ਸੁਨਣਗੇ। *ih hosakdā hai ki tuhāḍe piṅḍ wich ām lok waḍiāṅ dī salāh sunange.*

7. The watchman says that when he first saw the thieves, they were just leaving the merchant's shop.

ਪਹਿਰੇ ਵਾਲਾ ਆਖਦਾ ਹੈ ਕਿ ਜਦ ਮੈ ਪਹਿਲਾਂ ਚੋਰਾਂ ਨੂੰ ਡਿਠਾ ਓਹ ਉਸੇ ਵੇਲੇ ਸੁਦਾਗਰ ਦੀ ਹੱਟੀ ਤੋਂ ਚੱਲੇ ਸੀ । *pahire wālā ākhdā hai ke jad maiṅ pahilāṅ chorāṅ nūṅ ḍiṭhā oh use wele sudāga dī haṭṭī toṅ chale sī.*

8. It will, I think, be better for you to explain the whole circumstances

ਮੈਂ ਸੋਚਦਾ ਹਾਂ ਕਿ ਤੇਰੇ ਲਈ ਚੰਗਾ ਹੋਵੇ ਗਾ ਜੋ ਸਾਰਾ ਵਰਤਾਂਤ (ਹਾਲ) ਜਿਸ ਤਰਾਂ ਹੋਇਆ ਹੈ ਦਸੇਂ ਝੂਠ ਬੋਲਨ ਤੇ

exactly as they occurred ; you will gain nothing by telling a lie.	ਤੈਨੂੰ ਕੁਝ ਲਾਭ ਨਹੀਂ ਹੋਵੇਗਾ। *main sochdā hān ki tere lai changā howegā jo sārā wartānt (hāl) jis tarān hoiā hai dasen jhūth bolan te tainūn kujh lābh nahīn howegā.*

CULTIVATION.

1. The wheat and barley harvests have been very good this year.	ਇਸ ਵਰਹੇ ਕਣਕ ਤੇ ਜੌਆਂ ਦੀ ਫਸਲ ਵਡੀ ਚੰਗੀ ਹੋਈ ਹੈ। *is warhe kanak te jauān dī phasal waḍḍī changī hoī hai.*
2. Tell me the approximate revenue got from irrigated and unirrigated land, respectively, in your village.	ਮੈਨੂੰ ਇਹ ਦਸ ਜੋ ਤੁਹਾਡੇ ਪਿੰਡ ਵਿਚੋਂ ਸਿੰਜੀ ਹੋਈ ਤੇ ਨਾ ਸਿੰਜੀ ਹੋਈ ਜਮੀਨ ਦਾ ਕਿਨਾਕੁ ਮਾਮਲਾ ਕਠਾ ਹੋਇਆ। *mainūn ih dass jo tuhāde piṇḍ wichon sinjī hoī te ṇā sinjī hoī jamīṇ dā kiṇṇā ku māmlā kaṭhḥā hoiā.*
3. Are there any water-mills near the village, or hand mills generally used ?	ਪਿੰਡ ਦੇ ਲਾਗੇ ਕੋਈ ਘਰਾਟ ਹਨ ਜਾਂ ਚੱਕੀਆਂ ਹੀ ਅਕਸਰ ਵਰਤਦੇ ਹਨ? *piṇḍ de lāge koī gharāṭ haṇ jān chakīān hī aksar wartde haṇ.*
4. When he had ploughed the field and sown the seed he went home.	ਜਦ ਓਹ ਖੇਤ ਵਾਹ ਤੇ ਬੀ ਪਾ ਚੁੱਕਾ ਤਾਂ ਘਰ ਨੂੰ ਚਲਾ ਗਿਆ। *jad oh khet wāh te bī pā chukkā ṭān ghar ṇūn chalā giyā.*
5. How many crops of wheat and barley do you reap in the year ?	ਵਰਹੇ ਵਿਚ ਕਣਕ ਤੇ ਜੌਆਂ ਦੇ ਕਿੱਨੇ ਫਸਲ ਵਢਦੇ ਹੋ। *warhe wich kaṇk te jauān de kiṇṇe phasal waḍhde ho.*
6. How many wells and ploughs has he got ?	ਉਸ ਕੋਲ ਕਿਨੇ ਹਲ ਤੇ ਖੂਹ ਹਨ। *us kol kiṇṇe hal te khūh haṇ.*
7. Two oxen are used in a plough.	ਇਕ ਹਲ ਵਿਚ ਦੋ ਬੈਲ ਜੋਤੇ ਜਾਂਦੇ ਹਨ *ikk hal wich do bail jote jānde haṇ.*
8, Since the *Jhelum* canal has been opened	ਜਦ ਤੇ ਜੇਹਲਮ ਦੀ ਨਹਿਰ ਖੁਲੀ ਹੈ *jad te jihlam dī nahr khulī hai*

	rice and sugar cane are sown to a large extent.	ਚੌਲ ਤੇ ਗੱਨੇ ਬਹੁਤ ਬੀਜੇ ਜਾਂਦੇ ਹਨ *chaul te gaṇṇe bahut bīje jāṅde haṇ.*
9.	How is revenue calculated and fixed?	ਕਿਸ ਤਰਾਂ ਮਾਮਲਾ ਗਿਣਿਆ ਤੇ ਲਾਇਆ ਜਾਂਦਾ ਹੈ । *kistarāṅ māmlā giṇiā te lāiyā jāṅḍā hai.*
10.	The fields are now full of barley and wheat.	ਖੇਤਾਂ ਵਿਚ ਹੁਣ ਜੌਂ ਤੇ ਕਨਕਾਂ ਭਰੀਆਂ ਹੋਈਆਂ ਹਨ । *khetāṅ wich hun jauṅ te kaṇkāṇ bhariāṅ hoīāṅ haṇ.*
11.	This year the locusts did much damage to the fruit trees and crops	ਐਤਕੀਂ ਟਿਡੀ ਨੇ ਫਲ ਦੇ ਦਰਖਤਾਂ ਤੇ ਫਸਲਾਂ ਨੂੰ ਬਹੁਤ ਜਾਨ ਪੁਚਾਇਆ। *aitkī ṭiḍḍī ne phal de darakhtāṅ te phaslāṅ nūṅ bahut jāṇ puchāiyā.*
12.	Are you a land owner, cultivator, or trader?	ਤੂੰ ਜਮੀਂਦਾਰ ਜਾਂ ਕਰਸਾਨ ਜਾਂ ਬਪਾਰੀ ਹੈਂ । *tūṅ jamīṅdār jāṅ karsāṇ jāṅ bapārī haiṅ.*
13.	This land produces millet, mustard gram, radishes and carrots.	ਇਸ ਜਮੀਨ ਵਿਚ ਬਾਜਰਾ, ਰਾਈ, ਛੋਲੇ, ਮੂਲੀਆਂ, ਗੋਂਗਲੂ ਤੇ ਗਾਜਰਾਂ ਵੀ ਹੁੰਦੀ-ਆਂ ਹਨ । *is jamīṇ wich bājrā, rāī, chhole, mūlīāṅ, goṅglū te gājrāṅ wī hundīān haṇ.*
14.	The village lands are both irrigated and unirrigated.	ਪਿੰਡ ਦੀ ਭੋਂ ਸੇਂਜੇ ਦੀ ਤੇ ਬਰਾਨੀ ਹੈ *pinḍ dī bhoṅ seṅje dī te barānī hai,*
15	The revenue is not very heavy and we ought to be rich.	ਮਾਮਲਾ ਬਹੁਤ ਕਰੜਾ ਨਹੀ ਹੈ ਇਸ ਕਰਕੇ ਸਾਨੂੰ ਧਨਵਾਨ ਹੋਣਾ ਚਾਹੀਦਾ ਹੈ *māmlā bahut karṛā nāhīṅ hai is karke sāṇūṅ dhaṇwāṇ hoṇā chahīdā hai.*

Section II.—Seasons and Weather.

THE SEASONS.

1.	When do you think the river will be in flood ?	ਤੇਰੀ ਸਮਝ ਵਿਚ ਦਰਿਆ ਵਿਚ ਕਦ ਹੜ ਆਊ । *terī samjh wichh daryā wich kad haṛ āū.*
2.	It was very hot last night, but it is cold and cloudy to-day.	ਕਲ ਰਾਤ ਵਡੀ ਗਰਮੀ ਸੀ ਪਰ ਅਜ ਠੰਡ ਤੇ ਝੜ ਹੈ । *kal rāt waḍḍī garmī sī par aj ṭhaṇḍ te jhaṛ hai.*
3.	A dust storm is upon us.	ਸਾਡੇ ਉਤੇ ਹਨੇਰੀ ਆਗਈ ਹੈ । *sāḍe utte hanerī āgāī hai.*
4.	The river came down in flood and carried away my water mill.	ਦਰਿਆ ਦਾ ਹੜ ਆਇਆ ਤੇ ਮੇਰਾ ਘਰਾਟ ਰੋੜ੍ਹਕੇ ਲੈਗਿਆ । *daryā dā haṛ āyā te merā gharāṭ roṛhke laigiā.*
5.	Here the water is shallow but further on it is very deep.	ਇਥੇ ਪਾਣੀ ਥੋੜਾ ਥੋੜਾ ਹੈ ਪਰ ਅਗਾਹਾਂ ਵੱਡਾ ਡੂਘਾ ਹੈ । *ithe pāṇī thoṛā thoṛā hai par agāhāṅ waḍḍā dūṅghā hai.*
6.	Has there been any rain lately ?	ਅਜ ਕਲ ਕੋਈ ਮੀਂਹ ਪਾਣੀ ਪਿਆ ਹੈ ? *aj kal koi mīṅh pāṇī piā hai.*
7.	My land is close to the canal ; for this reason I manage very well.	ਮੇਰੀ ਜਮੀਨ ਨਹਿਰ ਦੇ ਨੇੜੇ ਹੈ ਇਸ ਕਰਕੇ ਮੈਂ ਚੰਗੀ ਤਰਾਂ ਸਿੰਜ ਲੈਂਦਾ ਹਾਂ । *merī jamīṇ ṇahir de neṛe hai is karke maiṅ changī trāṅ sinj laiṅdā hāṅ.*
8.	In *Peshāwar* the hot weather lasts only for two or three months.	ਪਸ਼ੌਰ ਵਿਚ ਹੁਨਾਲ (ਗਰਮੀ ਦੀ ਰੁਤ) ਨਿਰੀ ਦੋ ਜਾਂ ਤਿੰਨ ਮਹੀਨੇ ਰਹਿੰਦੀ ਹੈ । *pashaur wichch hunāl (garmī dī rut) ṅirī do jāṅ tiṇ mahīṇe rahiṅdī hai.*
9.	The cold weather lasts for five or six months.	ਸਿਆਲ (ਠੰਢ ਦੀ ਰੁਤ) ਪੰਜ ਜਾਂ ਛੀ ਮਹੀਨੇ ਰਹਿੰਦੀ ਹੈ । *siāl (ṭhaṇḍ dī rut) pañj jāṅ chhī mahīne rahiṅdī hai.*

10.	The sky is clear to-day.	ਅਜ ਅਕਾਸ਼ ਨਿਰਮਲ ਹੈ । *aj akās nirmal hai.*
11.	It is warmor thau yesterday.	ਅਜ ਕਲ ਨਾਲੋਂ ਗਰਮੀ ਹੈ। *aj kal nāloṅ garmī hai.*
12.	Yesterday a great deal of hail fell.	ਕਲ ਬੜੇ ਗੜੇ ਪਏ । *kal baṛe gaṛe pae.*
13.	It rained for three days without stoping.	ਤਿਨ ਦਿਨ ਤੀਕ ਲਗਾ ਤਾਰ ਮੀਂਹ ਵਰਦਾ ਰਿਹਾ । *tin din tīk lagātār mīṅh wardā rihā.*
14.	The lightning is flashing, the clouds are roaring and the rain is falling.	ਬਿਜਲੀ ਲਿਸ਼ਕ ਦੀ ਹੈ ਬਦਲ ਗਜਦੇ ਹਨ ਤੇ ਮੀਂਹ ਪੈਂਦਾ ਹੈ । *bijlī lishakdī hai badal gajde haṇ te mīṅh paiṅdā hai.*
15.	Do not sleep out side as there is a heavy due at night.	ਬਾਹਰ ਨਾ ਸੌਂ ਕਿਉਂ ਜੋ ਰਾਤ ਨੂੰ ਬਹੁਤ ਤ੍ਰੇਲੀ ਪੈਂਦੀ ਹੈ । *bāhar nā sauṅ kyoṅ jo rāt nūṅ bahut telī paiṅdī hai.*
16.	The climate of Umballa is very good.	ਅੰਬਾਲੇ ਦਾ ਪਾਣੀ ਬੜਾ ਚੰਗਾ ਹੈ। *ambāle dā pāṇī baṛā changā hai.*
17.	There was a great storm in the hills the day before yesterday.	ਪਰਸੋਂ ਪੰਹਾੜ ਤੇ ਵਡਾ ਹੜ ਆਇਆ । *parsoṅ pahāṛ te waḍḍā haṛ āyā.*
18.	Do you like summer or winter ?	ਤੁਸਾਂ ਨੂੰ ਸਿਆਲ ਚੰਗਾ ਲਗਦਾ ਹੈ ਕਿ ਹੁਨਾਲ । *tusānūṅ syāl changā lagdā hai ki huṇāl.*
19.	The trees will blossom in the spring.	ਰੁਖ ਬਹਾਰ (ਬਸੰਤ) ਦੀ ਰੁਤੇ ਫੁਲਨਗੇ । *rukh bahār (basant) dī rutte phulaṇge.*
20.	It is very clouldy and I think it will rain soon.	ਅਜ ਬਹੁਤ ਝੜ ਹੈ ਅਤੇ ਮੈਂ ਸੋਚਦਾ ਹਾਂ ਕਿ ਛੇਤੀ ਮੀਂਹ ਵਰੇਗਾ । *aj bahut jhaṛ hai ate main sochdā hāṅ ki chhetī mīṅh warhegā.*

SECTION III.—Time and age.

1. What time is it ?	ਹੁਣ ਕੀ ਵੇਲਾ ਹੈ ? *huṇ kī welā hai ?*
2. It is half past one.	ਡੂੜ ਵਜਿਆ ਹੈ । *dūṛh wajiā hai.*
3. Wake me at 2-30.	ਮੈਨੂੰ ਢਾਈ ਵਜੇ ਜਗਾਵੀਂ । *maiṅ nūṅ dhāī waje jagāwīṅ.*
4. He has been sleeping for two hours.	ਓਹ ਦੋ ਘੰਟਿਆਂ ਦਾ ਸੁਤਾ ਹੋਇਆ ਹੈ । *oh do ghaṇṭiyāṅ dā suttā hoiā hai.*
5. That old man lived for forty years in the same village.	ਓਹ ਬੁਡਾ ਮਨੁਖ ਚਾਲੀਆਂ ਵਰਿਹਾਂ ਤਾਂਈ ਇਕੋ ਪਿੰਡ ਵਿਚ ਰਿਹਾ । *oh buḍhā manukh chālīāṅ warihāṅ tāīṅ ikko piṅḍ wich rihā*
6. Tell him to get the carriage ready at 2-45.	ਉਸ ਨੂੰ ਆਖ ਜੋ ਪੌਣੇ ਤਿਨ ਵਜੇ ਗੱਡੀ ਤਿਆਰ ਕਰੇ । *us nūṅ ākh jo pauṇe tin waje gaḍḍī tiyār kare.*
7. That child is only 3½ years old.	ਓਹ ਮੁੰਡਾ ਨਿਰਾ ਸਾਢੇ ਤਿੰਨਾ ਵਰਿਹਾਂ ਦਾ ਹੈ। *oh muṅḍā nirā sāḍhe tiṇā warihāṅ-dā hai.*
8, He is never late.	ਓਹ ਕਦੀ ਚਿਰ ਨਹੀਂ ਲਾਉਂਦਾ ਹੈ । *oh kadī chir nahīṅ lāuṅdā hai.*
9. Strike the gong exactly at twelve o'clock.	ਘੜਿਆਲ ਠੀਕ ਬਾਰਾਂ ਵਜੇ ਵਜਾਇਆ ਕਰ । *ghaṛiāl ṭhīk bārāṅ waje wajāiyā kar.*
10. There is great difference between this letter and that	ਇਸ ਚਿਠੀ ਤੇ ਉਸ ਵਿਚ ਵਡਾ ਵੇਰਵਾ ਹੈ *is chiṭhṭhī te us wich waḍḍā werwā hai.*
11. I took the fort with the assistance of the army.	ਮੈਂ ਉਸ ਫੌਜ ਦੀ ਕੁਮਕ ਨਾਲ ਕਿਲਾ ਲੈ ਲੀਤਾ । *maiṅ us fauj dī kumk nāl kilā lai lītā.*
12. You promised to come at ten and it is half past eleven now.	ਤੂੰ ਦਸ ਵਜੇ ਆਉਂਣ ਦਾ ਕਰਾਰ ਕੀਤਾ ਸੀ ਤੇ ਹੁਣ ਸਾਢੇ ਯਾਰਾਂ ਵਜੇ ਹਨ । *tūṅ das waje āoṅ dā karār kītā sī te huṇ sāḍhe yārāṅ waje haṇ.*

SECTION IV.—Money, Weight, and measure.

1. What is the price of this ? ਇਸ ਦਾ ਮੁਲ ਕੀ ਹੈ । *is dā mul kī hai ?*

2. What is the lowest price you will take ? ਘਟ ਤੋਂ ਘਟ ਕੀ ਲਵੇਂਗਾ । *ghaṭ toṅ ghaṭ kī lawengā.*

3. Why is the grain so dear here ? ਏਥੇ ਅੰਨ ਏਨਾ ਮਹਿੰਗਾ ਕਿਉਂ ਹੈ । *ethe aṇṇ aiṇā mahingā kiyon hai.*

4. It is very cheap at Ludhiana ! ਲੁਦਿਹਾਨੇ ਵਿਚ ਬਹੁਤ ਸਸਤਾ ਹੈ । *ludi-hāne wich bahut sastā hai.*

5. Go to the Bazar and get this rupee changed. ਬਜ਼ਾਰ ਜਾਕੇ ਇਸ ਰੁਪੈ ਦਾ ਭਾਨ ਲਿਆ । *bazār jā ke is rupaye dā bhān liyā.*

6. How many seers are there in a maund? ਇਕ ਮਨ ਵਿਚ ਕਿੱਨੇ ਸੇਰ ਹੂੰਦੇ ਹਨ ? *ikk maṇ wich kiṇṇe ser hunde haṇ?*

7. Get a seer and a half of rice and ¾ seer of ghee. ਡੇਢ ਸੇਰ ਚੌਲ ਤੇ ਤਿਨਪਾ ਘਿਓ ਲਿਆ । *ḍeḍh ser chaul te tin pā ghio liyā.*

8. Give the horse one seer and half of barley. ਘੋੜੇ ਨੂੰ ਡੇਢ ਸੇਰ ਜੌਂ ਦੇ । *ghoṛe nūṅ ḍeḍh ser jauṅ de.*

9. Ask the banker for a cheque for 250 rupees on Peshawar. ਸਰਾਫ ਤੋਂ ੨੫੦) ਰੁਪੈ ਦੀ ਹੁੰਡੀ ਪਸ਼ੌਰ ਲਈ ਕਰਾ ਲਿਆ । *sarāph toṅ 250 rupaye dī huṅḍī pashour laī karā liyā.*

10. Will you lend me a hundred rupees for a month ? ਤੁਸੀ ਮੈਨੂੰ ੧੦੦) ਰੁਪਈਆ ਇਕ ਮਹੀਨੇ ਲਈ ਹੁਦਾਰ ਦੇਉਗੇ ? *tusīṅ maiṅ ṇūṅ 100 rupaiyā ikk mahīne laī hudār dioge?*

11. Make up your accounts to the end of the last month. ਆਪਨਾ ਹਿਸਾਬ ਪਿਛਲੇ ਮਹੀਨੇ ਦੇ ਅੰਤ ਤੀਕ ਬਣਾ । *āpṇā hisāb pichhle mahīṇe de aṅt tīk banā.*

12. I will pay you what is due in cash. ਜੋ ਬਾਕੀ ਹੋਵੇਗਾ ਮੈਂ ਰੋਕ ਦੇਵਾਂਗਾ । *jo bākī howegā maiṅ rok dewāṅgā.*

SECTION V.—Books and Office Work.

1. I want to write a letter.	ਮੈਂ ਇਕ ਅਰਦਾਸ ਲਿਖਣੀ ਚਾਹੁੰਦਾ ਹਾਂ *main ikk ardās likhṇī chāhundā hāṅ.*
2. Bring paper, ink and pen.	ਕਾਗਤ ਤੇ ਲਿਖਣ ਦੁਵਾਤ ਲਿਆ। *kāgat te likhan dwāt liyā.*
3. Write clearly so that I may be able to read it.	ਸਾਫ ਲਿਖ ਜੋ ਮੈ ਪੜ੍ਹ ਸਕਾਂ। *sāph likh jo main paṛh sakāṅ.*
4. Mend the pen nicely.	ਲਿਖਣ ਚੰਗੀ ਤਰਾਂ ਘੜ। *likhaṇ changī tarāṅ ghaṛ.*
5. You will find that story in the 2nd chapter of that book.	ਤੁਹਾਨੂੰ ਓਹ ਕਹਾਨੀ ਉਸ ਪੋਥੀ ਦੇ ਦੂਜੇ ਭਾਗ ਵਿਚ ਮਿਲੇਗੀ। *tuhānū oh kahānī us pothī de dūje bhāg wich milegī.*
6. The messenger has arrived.	ਹਲਕਾਰਾ ਆ ਗਿਆ ਹੈ। *halkārā ā giyā hai.*
7. That book was printed at Lucknow.	ਉਹ ਪੋਥੀ ਲਖਨਊ ਵਿਚ ਛਪੀ ਸੀ। *oh pothī lakhnow wich chhapī sī.*
8. Post this letter.	ਇਹ ਚਿਠੀ ਡਾਕ ਵਿੱਚ ਪਾਇਆ। *ih chiṭhī ḍāk wich pāiā.*
9. The printer of the news paper is ignorant.	ਅਖਬਾਰ ਛਾਪਣਵਾਲਾ ਅਣਜਾਨ ਹੈ। *akhbār chhāpan wālā anjāṇ hai.*
10. Write a letter for me in Gurmukhi.	ਮੈਂਨੂੰ ਗੁਰਮੁਖੀ ਵਿਚ ਇਕ ਚਿੱਠੀ ਲਿਖਦੇ। *main nūṅ gurmukhī wich ikk chiṭhhī likhde.*
11. Is there any orderly outside ?	ਬਾਹਰ ਕੋਈ ਅੜਦਲੀ ਹੈ ? *bāhir koī aṛdalī hai ?*
12. Tell him to wait.	ਉਸ ਨੂੰ ਆਖ ਜੋ ਠਹਿਰੇ। *us nūn ākh jo ṭhahre.*
13. Why have you been so long ?	ਤੂੰ ਐਨਾ ਚਿਰ ਕਿਓਂ ਲਾਇਆ ਹੈ। *tūṅ aiṇā chir kiyoṅ lāiyā hai.*

14. If you do so again you will be fined. — ਜੇ ਫੇਰ ਅਜਿਹਾ ਕਰੇਂਗਾ ਤਾਂ ਜਰਮਾਨਾ ਲਗੇਗਾ। *je pher ajihā karengā tāṅ jarmāṇā lugegā.*

15. Come to your work punctually. — ਵੇਲੇਸਿਰ ਕੰਮ ਤੇ ਹਾਜਰ ਹੋਇਆ ਕਰ। *wele sir kaṅm te hājar hoiā kar.*

SECTION VI.—Travelling, &c.

1. Which is the way to Karnal? — ਕਰਨਾਲ ਦਾ ਰਾਹ ਕਿਧਰ ਹੈ? *karnāl dā rāh kidhar hai?*

2. Where does this road lead to? — ਇਹ ਰਾਹ ਕਿਧਰ ਨੂੰ ਜਾਂਦਾ ਹੈ? *ih rāh kidhar ṇūṅ jāṅdā hai?*

3. Tie the horse under the shade of that tree. — ਘੋੜੇ ਨੂੰ ਉਸ ਰੁਖਦੀ ਛਾਂਹੇਠ ਬਨ੍ਹ। *ghoṛe ṇūn us rukhkh dī chhāṅ heṭh baṇh.*

4. Who lives in that house? — ਉਸ ਘਰ ਵਿਚ ਕੌਨ ਰਹਿੰਦਾ ਹੈ? *us ghar wich kauṅ rahiṅdā hai?*

5. Bring some grass and gram from that village. — ਉਸ ਪਿੰਡੋਂ ਕੁਝ ਘਾ ਤੇ ਦਾਨਾ ਲਿਆ। *us piṅḍoṅ kugh ghā te dāṇā liyā.*

6. Who is coming from the city? — ਉਸ ਸ਼ਹਿਰੋਂ ਕੌਣ ਆਉਂਦਾ ਹੈ? *us shahroṅ kauṇ āuṅdā hai.*

7. Walk the pony about. — ਟੱਟੂ ਨੂੰ ਏਧਰ ਓਧਰ ਫਰਾ। *ṭaṭṭū ṇūṅ edhar odhar pharā.*

8. Tie the head and heel ropes. — ਅਗਾੜੀ ਤੇ ਪਛਾੜੀ ਬੰਨ੍ਹ ਦੇ। *agāṛī te pachhāṛī baṇh de.*

9. Pack up the tents, put them in the bags, and load the camels with them. — ਤੰਬੂਆਂ ਨੂੰ ਲਪੇਟ ਕੇ ਥੈਲਿਆਂ ਵਿੱਚ ਪਾਓ ਅਤੇ ਊਠਾਂ ਤੇ ਲਦਦਿਓ। *taṇbūāṅ ṇūṅ lepeṭ ke thailiāṅ wich pāo ate ūṭhāṅ te lad dio.*

10. Is the boat ready? — ਬੇੜੀ ਤਿਆਰ ਹੈ? *beṛī tiyār hai?*

11. Loosen the girths. — ਤੰਗ ਢਿੱਲੇ ਕਰ। *taṅg dhille kar?*

12. Will you let me have a pony on hire ? — ਮੈਨੂੰ ਇਕ ਟੱਟੂ ਭਾੜੇ ਉਤੇ ਦੇਓਗੇ ? *maiṅ ṇūṅ ikk ṭaṭṭū bhāṛe utte dioge.*

13. Is the horse quite or vicious ? — ਘੋੜਾ ਗਰੀਬ ਹੈ ਜਾਂ ਬਦਮਾਸ ? *ghoṛā gārīb hai jāṅ badmāsh.*

14. We shall rest till the afternoon. — ਅਸੀ ਲੌਡਿਵੇਲੇ ਤੀਕਰ ਰਾਮ ਕਰਾਂਗੇ । *asiṇ lauḍe wele tīkar rām karāṅge.*

15. Call a farrier at once. — ਕਿਸੇ ਨਾਲਬੰਦ ਨੂੰ ਛੇਤੀ ਸੱਦ । *kise nāl-baṅd ṇūṅ chhetī sadd*

16. What is the price of the grey mare ? — ਸਬਜੀ ਘੋੜੀ ਦਾ ਕੀ ਮੁਲ ਹੈ । *sabjī ghoṛī dā kī mul hai.*

17. What will you take for the bay ? — ਕੁਮੈਤ ਦਾ ਕੀ ਲਵੋਗੇ । *kumait dā kī lawoge.*

18. Is he a gelding ? — ਕੀ ਓਹ ਖੱਸੀ ਹੈ । *kī oh khasī hai.*

Section VII.—Military terms.

1. When was this regiment raised ? — ਇਹ ਪੜਤਲ (ਪਲਟਨ) ਕਦ ਖੜੀ ਹੋਈ ਸੀ ? । *ih paṛtal (paltan) kad khaṛī hoī sī.*

2. How long is it since you were enlisted ? — ਤੈਨੂੰ ਭਰਤੀ ਹੋਇਆਂ ਕਿਨਾਂ ਚਿਰ ਹੋਇਆ ਹੈ ? । *taiṅ nūṅ bhartī hoyāṅ kinnā chir hoyā hai ?*

3. I have served seven years with this regiment. — ਇਸ ਪਲਟਨ ਵਿਚ ਮੈਂ ਸਤ ਵਰਹੇ ਨੌਕਰੀ ਕੀਤੀ ਹੈ । *is paltaṇ wichch maiṅ sat warhe naukrī kītī hai.*

4. What is his rank in the army ? — ਫੌਜ ਵਿਚ ਉਸਦਾ ਹੁਦਾ ਕੀ ਹੈ ? । *phauj wich usdā hudā kī hai ?*

5. One Havildar and ten men to be on duty to-night in the fort. — ਅਜ ਰਾਤ ਕਿਲੇ ਵਿਚ ਇਕ ਹੌਲਦਾਰ ਅਤੇ ਦਸ ਸਪਾਹੀਆਂ ਦੀ ਨੌਕਰੀ ਹੈ। *ajj rāt kile wich ikk havildār ate das sapāhīyāṅ dī naukarī hai.*

6. The hammer of your rifle is dirty.

ਤੇਰੀ ਬੰਦੂਕ ਦਾ ਘੋੜਾ ਮੈਲਾ ਹੈ । *teri bandūk dā ghoṛā mailā hai.*

7. How is it that my sword is rusty ?

ਮੇਰੀ ਕਿਰਚ ਨੂੰ ਜੰਗਲ ਕੀਕੂੰ ਲਗਾ ਹੈ ? *merī kirach nūn jangāl kikūn lagī hai ?*

8. That rifle will carry 1000 paces.

ਉਸ ਰਫਲ (ਬੰਦੂਕ) ਦੀ ੧੦੦੦ ਕਦਮ ਮਾਰ ਹੈ । *us rafal (bandūk) dī hajār kadam mār hai.*

9. Clean the inside of the barrel.

ਨਾਲੀ ਨੂੰ ਅੰਦਰੋਂ ਸਾਫ ਕਰ । *nālī nūn andron sāf kar.*

10. Draw your sword from its scabbard.

ਕਿਰਚ ਨੂੰ ਮਿਆਨ ਵਿਚੋਂ ਸੂਤ । *kirach nūn miān wichon sūt.*

11. How many cartridges are there in your pouch ?

ਤੇਰੀ ਖੀਸੀ ਵਿਚ ਕਿੱਨੇ ਰੌਂਦ ਹਨ । *teri khīsī wich kinne raund han ?*

12. Give me the waste-belt and cross-belt.

ਮੈਨੂੰ ਪੇਟੀ ਤੇ ਪੜਤਲਾ ਦਿਓ । *main nūn peṭī te paṛtlā dio.*

13. The regiment must march an hour before day break.

ਪਲਟਨ ਨੂੰ ਦਿਨ ਚੜ੍ਹਨ ਤੋਂ ਇਕ ਘੰਟਾ ਅਗੇ ਕੂਚ ਕਰਨਾ ਚਾਹੀਏ । *palṭan nūn din chaṛhan ton ikk ghanṭā agge kūch karnā chāhie.*

14. When you are within 200 paces from the enemy charge them.

ਜਦ ਤੁਸੀਂ ਵੈਰੀ ਤੋਂ ੨੦੦ ਕਦਮਾਂ ਤੇ ਰਹਿਜਾਓ ਤਾਂ ਹੱਲਾ ਕਰਦਿਓ । *jad tusīn wairī ton 200 kadmān te rah jāo tān hallā kardio.*

15. Load your pistol and shoot that mucineer.

ਪਸਤੌਲ ਭਰਕੇ ਉਸ ਬਾਗੀ ਨੂੰ ਮਾਰ । *pastaul bharke us bāghī nūn mār.*

16. The sepoy quickly loaded his gun and from a distance of 100 paces, fired at the deceased who was standing with his back to him.

ਸਪਾਹੀ ਨੇ ਛੇਤੀ ਨਾਲ ਆਪਣੀ ਬੰਦੂਕ ਭਰੀ ਅਰ ੧੦੦ ਕਦਮ ਤੋਂ ਮਰਣ ਵਾਲੇ ਵਲ ਚਲਾਈ, ਜੋ ਉਸ ਵਲ ਆਪਣੀ ਪਿਠ ਕਰੀ ਖੜਾ ਸਾ । *sapāhī ne chhetī nāl āpnī bandūk bharī ar 100 kadam ton maran wāle wal chalāī jo us wal āpnī piṭh karī khaṛā sā.*

17. The hill men attacked them.

ਪਹਾੜੀਆਂ ਨੇ ਓਹਨਾਂ ਉਤੇ ਹੱਲਾ ਕੀਤਾ *pahāṛīān ne ohnā utte hallā kītā.*

18. After firing two rounds they fled.

ਦੋ ਦੋ ਰੌਂਦ ਚਲਾਕੇ ਓਹ ਨਸ ਗਏ। *do do raund chalāke oh nas gaye.*

19. Two corporals were wounded and one soldier killed.

ਦੋ ਨੈਕ ਘਾਇਲ ਹੋਏ ਅਤੇ ਇਕ ਸਪਾਹੀ ਮਾਰਿਆ ਗਿਆ। *do naik ghāil hoe te ikk sipāhī māṛiā giā.*

20. One dangerously wounded and the other slightly.

ਇਕ ਕਾਰੀ ਘਾਇਲ ਹੋਇਆ ਅਤੇ ਦੂਜਾ ਥੋੜਾ ਜਿਹਾ। *ikk kāṛī ghāil hoyā te dūjā thoṛā jihā.*

21. The enemy was completely defeated.

ਵੈਰੀ ਨੂੰ ਪੂਰੀ ਪੂਰੀ ਹਾਰ ਆਈ। *wairī nūṅ pūrī pūrī hār āī.*

22. Dig the entrenchment before the enemy's battery.

ਵੈਰੀ ਦੇ ਤੋਪਖਾਨੇ ਦੇ ਸਾਮ੍ਹਨੇ ਮੋਰਚਾ ਪਟੋ। *wairī de top khāne de sāmhne morchā paṭṭo.*

23. How does your Commanding Officer treat the regiment?

ਤੁਹਾਡਾ ਕਮਾਨ ਅਫਸਰ ਪਲਟਨ ਨਾਲ ਕਿਸਤਰਾਂ ਵਰਤਦਾ ਹੈ ? *tuhāḍā kamān afsar paltaṇ nāl kistrāṅ wartdā hai ?*

24. What people is your regiment composed of?

ਤੁਹਾਡੀ ਪਲਟਨ ਵਿਚ ਕਿਸ ਕਿਸ ਜਾਤ ਦੇ ਆਦਮੀ ਹਨ ? *tuhāḍī paltaṇ wich kis kis jāt de ādmī han ?*

25. What is the rule for promotion in your regiment?

ਤੁਹਾਡੀ ਪਲਟਨ ਵਿਚ ਹੁੱਦੇ ਵਧਾਓਣ ਦਾ ਕੀ ਢੱਬ ਹੈ ? । *tuhāḍī paltaṇ wichch hudde wadhāuṇ dā kī ḍhab hai.*

26. Did you serve in the Kabul war?

ਤੂੰ ਕਾਬਲ ਦੀ ਲੜਾਈ ਵਿਚ ਗਿਆ ਸੀ ? *tūṅ kābul dī laṛāī wich giā sī ?*

27. Are there any Pathans in your regiment?

ਤੁਹਾਡੀ ਪਲਟਨ ਵਿਚ ਕੁਝ ਪਠਾਣ ਹਨ ? *tuhāḍī paltaṇ wich kujh paṭhāṇ han ?*

28. Are their rifles just like yours or different ?	ਉਨ੍ਹਾਂ ਦੀਆਂ ਬੰਦੂਕਾਂ ਤੁਹਾਡੇ ਵਾਂਙੂ ਜਾਂ ਨਿਆਰੀਆਂ ਹਨ ? *unhāṅ diāṅ bandūkāṅ tuhāḍe wāṅgū jāṅ niārīāṅ han.*
29. At what time do you go on parade in these days ?	ਅਜ ਕਲ ਤੁਸੀਂ ਕਿਸ ਵੇਲੇ ਪਰੇਟ (ਕਵੈਦ) ਤੇ ਜਾਂਦੇ ਹੋ । *aj kal tusīṅ kis wele paret (kawaid) te jānde ho.*
30. In the morning and afternoon.	ਸਵੇਰੇ ਤੇ ਲੌਡੇ ਵੇਲੇ । *savere te laude wele*
31. Does the Commanding Officer attend the parade or not ?	ਕਮਾਨ ਅਫਸਰ ਸਾਹਬ ਪਰੇਟ ਤੇ ਆਉਂਦਾ ਹੈ ਕਿ ਨਹੀਂ ? *kamān afsar sāhib pareṭ te āundā hai ki nahīn ?*
32. He attends every now and then.	ਓਹ ਕਦੀ ਕਦੀ ਆਉਂਦਾ ਹੈ । *oh kadī kadī āundā hai.*
33. Have you finished your course of musketry ?	ਤੁਸੀ ਆਪਣੀ ਚਾਂਦ ਮਾਰੀ ਪੂਰੀ ਕਰ ਲਈ ਹੈ ਕਿ ਨਹੀਂ ? *tusī āpnī chānd-mārī pūrī kar laī hai ki nahīn ?*
34. Do you remember the Indian Mutiny?	ਤੁਹਾਨੂੰ ਗਦਰ ਯਾਦ ਹੈ ? *tuhānūn gadar yād hai ?*
35. Tell the Subedar to chose a Naik and five sturdy sepoys and post them in the ravine at rear of the camp.	ਸੂਬੇਦਾਰ ਨੂੰ ਆਖ ਜੋ ਇਕ ਨੈਕ ਤੇ ਪੰਜ ਤਕੜੇ ਸਿਪਾਹੀ ਚੁਣਕੇ ਕੈਂਪੂ ਦੇ ਪਿਛੇ ਨਾਲੀ ਵਿਚ ਖੜੇ ਕਰੇ । *sūbedār nūn ākh jo ikk nāik te panj takṛ sipāhī chunke kanpū de pichhe nālī wich khaṛe kare.*
36. By how many days has this sepoy overstayed his leave ?	ਏਹ ਸਿਪਾਹੀ ਛੁਟੀ ਤੋਂ ਕਿਨੇ ਦਿਨ ਵਧੀਕ ਲਾ ਆਇਆ ਹੈ । *ih sipāhī chhuṭṭī toṅ kiṇne diṇ wadhīk lā āiā hai ?*

37. Any man who brings fifty recruits with horses for service in the regiment will receive a Jamadar's commission.

ਜੇਹੜਾ ਮਨੁਖ ਪੰਜਾਹ ਆਦਮੀ ਰਸਾਲੇ ਵਿਚ ਨੌਕਰੀ ਵਾਸਤੇ ਘੋੜਿਆਂ ਸਮੇਤ ਲਿਆਵੇ ਗਾ ਉਸਨੂੰ ਜਮਾਂਦਾਰੀ ਮਿਲੇ ਗੀ । *jehṛā manukh panjāh ādmī rasāle wich naukrī wāste ghoṛiāṅ smet liyāwegā us nūṅ jamādārī milegī.*

38. I noticed that the horses of those men that have just rejoined from leave are in a very poor condition.

ਮੈਂ ਦੇਖਿਆ ਹੈ ਕਿ ਉਨਾਂ ਸਵਾਰਾਂ ਦੇ ਘੋੜੇ ਜੋ ਹੁਣੇ ਛੁਟੀ ਤੋਂ ਆਕੇ ਰਲੇ ਹਨ ਵਡੇ *ਲਿਸੇ ਹਨ । *main dekhiā hai ki unhāṅ suwārāṅ de ghoṛe jo hune chhuṭṭī toṅ āke rale haṇ waḍḍe lisse haṇ.*

39 What supplies will you require on the March ?

ਕੂਚ ਤੇ ਤੁਹਾਨੂੰ ਕੇਹੜੀਆਂ ਚੀਜਾਂ ਦੀ ਲੋੜ ਪਵੇ ਗੀ । *kūch te tuhāṇūṅ kehṛīāṅ chījāṅ dī loṛ pawegī.*

40. I shall require gram, ata, rice, owls, milk, eggs, and firewood

ਮੈਨੂੰ ਦਾਨਾਂ ਆਟਾ ਚੌਲ ਕੁਕੜੀਆਂ ਦੁਧ ਆਂਡੇ ਤੇ ਬਾਲਣ ਦੀ ਲੋੜ ਪਵੇਗੀ । *main nūṅ dānā āṭā chaul kukṛīāṅ dudh āṅḍe te bālaṇ dī loṛ pawegī.*

41. Have all our tents quickly repaired as we expect to march soon.

ਸਾਡੇ ਤੰਬੂ ਛੇਤੀ ਮਰੰਮਤ ਕਰਵਾ ਦੇ (ਸਵਰਵਾਦੇ) ਕਿਉਂ ਜੋ ਸਾਨੂੰ ਛੇਤੀ ਕੂਚ ਕਰਨ ਦੀ ਆਸ ਹੈ । *sāḍe tanbū chhetī marmat karwāde (sawarwāde) kiyoṅ jo sāṇṇūṅ chhetī kūch karṇ dī ās hai.*

42. Can you tell how many tents you have with you ?

ਤੁਸੀਂ ਦਸ ਸਕਦੇ ਹੋ ਕਿ ਤੁਹਾਡੇ ਪਾਸ ਕਿੰਨੇਂ ਤੰਬੂ ਹਨ । *tusīṅ das sakde ho ki tuhāḍe pās kiṇṇe tanbū haṇ.*

* Note the construction ਲਿੱਸਾ = thin.

43. One tent for every eight men will be sufficient

ਅਠ ਅਠ ਸਪਾਹੀਆਂ ਦੇ ਲਈ ਇਕ ਤੰਬੂ ਬਥੇਰਾ ਹੈ। *aṭh aṭh sipāhīāṅ de laī ikk ikk tanbū batherā hai.*

44. A force has crossed the river.

ਫੌਜ ਦਰਿਆਓਂ ਪਾਰ ਹੋਗਈ ਹੈ। *fauj dariyāoṅ pār ho gaī hai.*

45. How long did it take to cross the river?

ਪਾਰ ਜਾਨ ਵਿਚ ਕਿੰਨਾ ਚਿਰ ਲੱਗਾ। *pār jāṅ wich kiṇṇā chir laggā.*

46. It has taken the troops 2 hours to cross over.

ਸੈਨਾ ਨੂੰ ਪਾਰ ਜਾਨ ਵਿਚ ਦੋ ਘੰਟੇ ਲਗੇ। *sainā nūṅ pār jāṅ wich do ghaṅṭe lage.*

47. If the half battalion starts at dawn, it will reach the next encamping ground by 7 o'clock.

ਜੇਕਰ ਅਧੀ ਪਲਟਨ ਦਿਨ ਚੜ੍ਹੇ ਕੂਚ ਕਰੇ ਤਾਂ ਓਹ ਦੂਜੇ ਪੜਾ ਤੇ ਸਤ ਵਜੇ ਪੁਜੇਗੀ। *jekar adhī palṭaṇ diṇ chaṛhe kūch kare tāṅ oh dūje paṛā te sat waje pujegī.*

48. The mens' tents should be pitched at once and sentries posted all round the camp.

ਸਪਾਹੀਆਂ ਦੇ ਤੰਬੂ ਤੁਰਤ ਲਾਏ ਤੇ ਕੈਂਪੂ ਦੇ ਚਾਰੇ ਪਾਸੇ ਸੰਤਰੀ ਖਲਿਆਰੇ ਜਾਣੇ ਚਾਹੀਦੇ ਹਨ। *sipāhīāṅ de tanbū turt lāe te kanpū de chāre pāse santrī khaliāre jāṇe chāhīde haṇ.*

49. The trooper made a cut at me with a sword, but I warded it off with my rifle.

ਸਵਾਰਨੇ ਮੈਨੂੰ ਤਲਵਾਰ ਦਾ ਵਾਰ ਮਾਰਿਆ ਪਰ ਮੈਂ ਉਸਨੂੰ ਬੰਦੂਕ ਨਾਲ ਰੋਕਿਆ। *sawār ne maiṅ nūṇ talwār dā wār māriā par maiṇ us nūṅ bandūk nāl rokiyā.*

50. He then rode at me with his lance, but I fired at him and the bullet lodged in his chest.

ਤਦ ਓਹਨੇ ਮੇਰੇ ਉਤੇ ਬਰਛੇ ਨਾਲ ਧਾਵਾ ਕੀਤਾ ਤਾਂ ਮੈਂ ਉਸ ਵਲ ਗੋਲੀ ਚਲਾਈ ਤੇ ਗੋਲੀ ਉਸਦੀ ਛਾਤੀ ਵਿਚ ਲਗੀ। *tad oh ne mere utte barchhe nāl dhāwā kītā tāṅ main us wal golī chalāī te golī us dī chhātī wich lagī.*

51. This old man is no doubt spy, take him away and shoot him.

ਏਹ ਬੁੱਢਾ ਜਰੂਰ ਜਸੂਸਹੈ ਇਸਨੂੰ ਲਜਾਕ ਜਰੂਰ ਗੋਲੀ ਨਾਲ ਮਾਰ ਸੁਟੋ। *eh budhhā jarūr jasūs hai is nūṅ lajā ke jarūr golī nāl mār suṭo.*

52. I examined the Havildar's pouch, it contained 7 cartridges.

ਮੈਂ ਹੌਲਦਾਰ ਦੇ ਤੋਸ਼ਦਾਨ ਦਾ ਝਾੜਾ ਲੀਤਾ ਤੇ ਉਸਵਿਚ ੭ ਕਾਰਤੂਸ ਸੀ। *maiṅ hauldār de toshdāṅ dā jhāṛā lītā te us wich 7 kārtūs sī.*

53. I also examined the target and found he had a hit it four times and missed it six times.

ਮੈਂ ਚੰਦ ਨੂੰ ਵੀ ਦੇਖਿਆ ਤੇ ਮਲੂਮ ਕੀਤਾ ਜੋ ਉਸਨੇ ਚਾਰ ਵਾਰੀ ਮਾਰਿਆ ਤੇ ਛੀ ਵਾਰੀ ਖਾਲੀ ਗਿਆ। *maiṅ chand nūṅ wī dekhiā te malūm kītā jo us ne chār wārī māriā te chhī wārī khālī giā.*

54. Sir, these blankets require repairing.

ਹਜੂਰ ਏਨਾਂ ਭੂਰਿਆਂ ਦੀ ਮਰੰਮਤ ਦੀ ਲੋੜ ਹੈ। *hajūr eṇāṅ bhūriāṅ dī marmat dī loṛ hai.*

55. You also say that you have two medals and three clasps, and have been wounded twice.

ਤੂੰ ਏਹ ਵੀ ਆਖਦਾ ਹੈਂ ਕਿ ਮੇਰੇ ਪਾਸ ਦੋ ਤਕਮੇ ਤੇ ਤਿੰਨ ਕੜੀਆਂ ਹਨ ਤੇ ਮੈਂ ਦੋ ਵਾਰੀ ਜਖਮੀ ਹੋ ਚੁਕਾ ਹਾਂ। *tūṅ ih wī ākhdā haiṅ ki mere pās do takme te tiṇ kaṛiāṅ haṇ te maiṅ do wārī jakhmī ho chukā hāṅ.*

SECTION VIII.—Medical.

1.	Let me feel your pluse.	ਆਪਣੀ ਨਬਜ਼ (ਨਾੜ) ਦਖਾ । *āpṇi nabaj (nāṛ) dukhā.*
2.	Open your tongue.	ਜੀਭ ਖੋਲ । *jibh khol.*
3.	How long is it since you are ill ?	ਤੂੰ ਕਦ ਤੇ ਮਾਂਦਾ ਹੈਂ । *tūṅ kad te māṅdā haiṅ.*
4.	He fell down and hurt his fore-head.	ਓਹ ਡਿਗ ਪਿਆ ਤੇ ਉਸਦਾ ਮਥਾ ਭਜ ਗਿਆ (ਉਸਦੇ ਮਥੇ ਨੂੰ ਸੱਟ ਲਗੀ) *oh ḍig piā te us dā mathā bhaj giyā (us de mathe nūṅ saṭṭ lagī).*
5.	He has the liver complaint.	ਉਸਨੂੰ ਜਿਗਰੀ ਰੋਗ ਹੈ । *us nūṅ jigrī rog hai.*
6.	The people of this village suffer from fever and rheumatism.	ਇਸ ਪਿੰਡ ਦੇ ਲੋਕਾਂ ਨੂੰ ਤਪ ਤੇ ਗਠੀਏ (ਬਾਈ) ਦੀ ਬਮਾਰੀ ਹੈ । *is piṅḍ de lokāṅ nūṅ tap te gaṭhīe (bāī) dī bamārī hai.*
7.	What is the matter with you ?	ਤੈਨੂੰ ਕੀ ਹੋਇਆ ਹੈ ? *taiṅ nūṅ kī hoiā hai ?*
8.	I have a headache.	ਮੈਨੂੰ ਸਿਰ ਪੀੜ ਹੈ । *maiṅ nūṅ sir pīṛ hai.*
9.	He has fever and pain in his libmbs.	ਉਸਨੂੰ ਤਾਪ ਅਰ ਜੋੜਾਂ ਵਿਚ ਪੀੜ ਹੈ । *us nūṅ tāp ar joṛāṅ wich pīṛ hai.*
10.	Have you any pain in your stomach ?	ਤੇਰੇ ਢਿਡ ਵਿਚ ਕੁਝ ਪੀੜ ਹੈ *tere ḍhiḍ wich kujh pīṛ hai ?*
11.	When I touch here do you feel any pain ?	ਜਦ ਮੈਂ ਏਥੇ ਟੋਹੰਦਾ (ਹਥ ਲਾਉਂਦਾ) ਹਾਂ ਤਾਂ ਤੈਨੂੰ ਪੀੜ ਹੁੰਦੀ ਹੈ । *jad maiṅ ethe tohaṅdā (hath lāuṅdā) hāṅ tāṅ taiṅ nūṅ pīṛ huṅdī hai.*
12.	That does not hurt me.	ਉਸ ਨਾਲ ਮੈਨੂੰ ਕੁਝ ਪੀੜ ਨਹੀਂ ਹੁੰਦੀ । *us nāl maiṅ nūṅ kujh pīṛ nahīṅ huṅdī.*

13. Have you any pain in your liver or any cough ?	ਤੇਰੇ ਕਲੇਜੇ ਵਿਚ ਪੀੜ ਹੈ ਜਾਂ ਖੰਘ ਆਉਂਦੀ ਹੈ *tere kaleje wich kujh pīṛ hai jāṅ khaṅgh āūṅdī hai ?*
14. That man has a cold.	ਉਸ ਮਨੁਖ ਦੇ ਨਕ ਨੂੰ ਵਾ ਲਗ ਗਈ ਹੈ। *us manukh de nak nūṅ wā lag gaī hai.*
15. Have you had any shivering ?	ਤੈਨੂੰ ਕਾਂਬਾ ਆਇਆ ਸੀ। *taiṅ nūṅ kāṅbā āiā sī ?*
16 I suffer from indigestion.	ਮੈਨੂੰ ਰੋਟੀ ਨਹੀਂ ਪਚਦੀ। *maiṅ nūṅ roṭī nahīṅ pachdī.*
17. I have hurt my ankle.	ਮੇਰੇ ਗਿਟੇ ਨੂੰ ਸਟ ਲਗੀ ਹੈ। *mere giṭṭe nūṅ saṭ laggī hai.*
18. Bathe it with hot water four times a day.	ਦਿਨ ਵਿਚ ਚਾਰ ਵਾਰੀ ਤੱਤੇ ਪਾਣੀ ਨਾਲ ਉਸਨੂੰ ਧੋ। *diṇ wich chār wārī tatte pāṇī nāl us nūṅ dho.*
19. Have you got spleen ?	ਤੈਨੂੰ ਤਿਲੀ ਹੈ। *taiṅ nūṅ tillī hai,*
20. Is there any cholera in the neighbourhood of Lahore ?	ਲਾਹੌਰ ਦੇ ਇਰਦੇ ਗਿਰਦੇ ਕੁਝ ਹੈਜਾ ਹੈ ? *lahaur de irde girde kujh haijā hai ?*
21. No, but some people are suffering from small-pox	ਨਹੀਂ, ਪਰ ਕੁਝ ਮਨੁਖ ਮਾਤਾ ਨਾਲ ਪਏ ਹਨ। *nahīṅ par kujh manukh mātā nāl pae han.*
22. What medicine do your doctors administer in the case of fever ?	ਤੁਹਾਡਾ ਡਾਕਦਾਰ ਤਪ ਵਾਸਤੇ ਕੀ ਦੁਆ ਦੇਂਦਾ ਹੈ। *tuhāḍā ḍākdār tap wāste kī duā deṅdā hai.*
23. I suffered from fever during the whole of my leave, and, therefore could not rejoin my regiment.	ਮੈਨੂੰ ਸਾਰੀਆਂ ਛੁਟੀਆਂ ਤੇ ਤਪ ਚੜ੍ਹਦਾ ਰਿਹਾ ਇਸ ਕਰਕੇ ਆਪਨੀ ਪਲਟਨ ਨਾਲ ਨਾਂ ਰਲ ਸਕਿਆ *maiṅ nūṅ sāriāṅ chhuṭṭiāṅ te tap chaṛhdā rihā is karke āpṇ palṭaṇ nāl nā ral sakiā.*

24. There has been a great deal of cholera this year.

ਐਤਕੀਂ (ਐਸ ਵਰਹੇ) ਵਡਾ ਹੈਜ਼ੇ ਦਾ ਜ਼ੋਰ ਰਿਹਾ ਹੈ ॥ *aitkī (ais warhe) waddā haije dā jor rihā hai.*

25. The men should be warned to drink the river water, which is cleaner than that of the wells.

ਸਪਾਹੀਆਂ ਨੂੰ ਆਗਿਆ ਮਿਲਨੀ ਚਾਹੀਦੀ ਹੈ ਕਿ ਦਰਿਆ ਦਾ ਪਾਨੀ ਪੀਣ ਕਿਉਂ ਜੋ ਓਹ ਖੂਹ ਨਾਲੋਂ (ਨਿਰਮਲ) ਸਾਫ ਹੈ। *sipāhiān nūn āgiyā milnī chāhīdī hai ki dariyā dā pānī pīṇ kion jo oh khūh nālon (nirmal) sāf hai.*

26. The doctor says the man will not recover, and that he has only a few more hours to live.

ਡਾਕਦਾਰ ਸਾਹਿਬ ਆਖਦਾ ਹੈ ਕਿ ਇਹ ਮਨੁਖ ਰਾਜੀ ਨਹੀਂ ਹੋਵੇਗਾ ਤੇ ਇਸ ਦੀ ਜ਼ਿੰਦਗੀ ਥੋੜੇ ਘੰਟੇ ਹੋਰ ਹੈ। *dākdār sāhib ākhdā hai ki ih manukh rājī nahīn howegā te is dī jindgī thoṛe ghanṭe hor hai.*

27. You were ill, certainly; but could you not have sent some one to tell me!

ਠੀਕ ਤੂੰ ਮਾਂਦਾ ਸਾ ਪਰ ਕਿਸੇ ਨੂੰ ਘਲ ਕੇ ਮੈਨੂੰ ਖਬਰ ਬੀ ਨਾ ਦੇ ਸਕਿਆ। *ṭhīk tūn māṇdā sā par kise nūn ghal ke main nūn khabar wī nā de sakiā.*

28. That man was bitten by a mad dog last night, therefore if we do not cut off his leg at once he may die.

ਉਸ ਮਨੁਖ ਨੂੰ ਕਲ ਰਾਤ ਹਲਕਾਏ ਕੁਤੇ ਨੇ ਵਢਿਆ ਇਸ ਲਈ ਜੇ ਅਸੀ ਤਾਬੜਤੋੜ ਉਸਦੀ ਲੱਤ ਨਾ ਵਢ ਸਿਟੀਏ ਤਾਂ ਮਰ ਜਾਊਗਾ। *us manukh nūn kal rāt halkāe kutte ne waḍhiā is laī je asī tābaṛ toṛ us dī latt nā waḍh siṭṭīe tān mar jāūgā.*

29. He told me that you were attacked by cholera.

ਉਨ ਮੈਨੂੰ ਕਿਹਾ ਕਿ ਤੈਨੂੰ ਹੈਜ਼ਾ ਹੋਗਿਆ ਹੈ *un main nūn kihā ki tai nūn haijā hogiā hai.*

30. Was there any plague case in your village last year, if so how many

ਪਿਛਲੇ ਵਰਹੇ ਤੁਹਾਡੇ ਪਿੰਡ ਵਿਚ ਮਹਾਂ ਮਾਰੀ ਦੀ ਬਮਾਰੀ ਹੋਈ ਸੀ ਤਾਂ ਕਿੰਨੇ

men died ?	ਮਨੁਖ ਮੋਏ ਸੇ? *pichhle warhe tuhāḍe pinḍ wich mahāṅmārī dī bamārī hoī sī tāṅ kinne manukh moe se.*
31. Can you breathe without pain ?	ਸਾਹ ਲਿਆਂ ਕੁਛ ਪੀੜ ਤਾਂ ਨਹੀਂ ਹੁੰਦੀ? *sāh liāṅ kujh pīṛ tāṅ nahīṅ huṅ ?*
32. Can you lie on your right or left side with most ease ?	ਤੂੰ ਸੱਜੇ ਯਾ ਖਬੇ ਪਾਸੇ ਅਰਾਮ ਨਾਲ ਲੇਟ ਸਕਨਾ ਹੈਂ । *tūṅ sajje jāṅ khabbe pāse arām nāl leṭ saknā haiṅ.*
33. Have you any pain in your back ?	ਤੇਰੀ ਪਿਠ ਵਿਚ ਕੁਝ ਪੀੜ ਹੁੰਦੀ ਹੈ ? *terī piṭh wich kujh pīṛ huṅdī hai.*
34. Sir, I am suffering from rheumatism and all my joints are aching.	ਹਜ਼ੂਰ ਮੈਨੂੰ ਬਾਈ ਦੀ ਬਮਾਰੀ ਹੈ ਤੇ ਸਾਰੇ ਜੋੜਾਂ ਵਿਚ ਪੀੜ ਹੁੰਦੀ ਹੈ । *hajūr maiṅ nūṅ bāī dī bimārī hai te sāre joṛāṅ wich pīṛ huṅdī hai.*
35. Does your heart beat much after meals ?	ਤੇਰਾ ਦਿਲ ਖਾਨ ਦੇ ਪਿਛੇ ਬਹੁਤ ਧੜਕ-ਦਾ ਹੈ । *terā dil khān de pichhe bahut dhaṛakdā hai.*
36. Did he break his arm by falling ?	ਡਿੱਗਨ ਨਾਲ ਉਸਦੀ ਬਾਂਹ ਟੁਟ ਗਈ । *ḍigan nāl usdī bāṅh ṭuṭ gaī.*
37. You always complain of toothache shall I extract your tooth ?	ਤੂੰ ਸਦਾ ਦੰਦ ਦੀ ਪੀੜ ਦਸਦਾ ਰਹਿੰਦਾ ਹੈਂ ਕੀ ਮੈ ਤੇਰਾ ਦੰਦ ਕਢ ਸੁਟਾਂ ? *tūṅ sadā daṅd dī pīṛ das dā rahiṅdā haiṅ kī maiṅ terā daṅd kadh suṭāṅ ?*
38. Let two dozen leeches be applied to his thigh.	ਉਸਦੇ ਪਟ ਤੇ ਦੋ ਦਰਜਨ ਜੋਕਾਂ ਲਾਦੇ । *us de paṭ te do darjaṇ jokāṅ lā de.*
39. Have you applied the mustard poultice on his stomach as I told you ?	ਤੂੰ ਉਸ ਦੇ ਢਿਡ ਉਤੇ ਰਾਈ ਦਾ ਲੇਪ ਕੀਤਾ ਸੀ ਜਿਸਤਰਾਂ ਮੈਂ ਤੈਨੂੰ ਦਸਿਆ ਸੀ? *tūṅ us de ḍhiḍ utte rāī dā lep kītā sī jistrāṅ maiṅ tai nūṅ dasiā sī.*

39. You must be careful what you eat; never eat anything hard.
ਤੈਨੂੰ ਖਾਨ ਪੀਨ ਦਾ ਪਰਹੇਜ਼ ਰਖਿਆ ਲੋੜੀਦਾ ਹੈ ਕੋਈ ਕਰੜੀ ਚੀਜ਼ ਨਾ ਖਾਵੀਂ।
tuiṅ nūṅ khān pīn dā parhej rakhiā loṛīdā hai koi karṛī chīj nāṅ khāwiṅ.

40. Last time when you fell from your horse did you injure your collar bone?
ਪਿਛਲੀ ਵਾਰੀ ਜਦ ਤੂੰ ਘੋੜੇ ਤੋਂ ਡਿਗਾ ਸੀ ਤਾਂ ਤੇਰੇ ਹੱਸ ਦੀ ਹੱਡੀ ਨੂੰ ਸਟ ਲਗੀ ਸੀ॥ *pichhlī wārī jad tūṅ ghoṛe toṅ diggā sī tāṅ tere hass dī haḍḍī nūṅ saṭ laggī sī.*

SECTION IX.—Miscellaneous.

1. Have you seen any one going in that direction?
ਤੁਸੀ ਕਿਸੇ ਮਨੁਖ ਨੂੰ ਉਸ ਬਨੀਂ ਜਾਂਦੇ ਵੇਖਿਆ ਹੈ। *tusīn kise manukh nūṅ us banīṅ jāṅde wekhiā hai?*

2. Were they walking or riding?
ਉਹ ਪੈਦਲ ਜਾਂਦੇ ਸਨ ਜਾਂ ਸਵਾਰ। *oh paidal jāṅde san jāṅ sawār.*

3. Some were walking and one was in a doolee.
ਕੁਝ ਟੁਰਦੇ ਸੇ ਅਤੇ ਇਕ ਡੋਲੀ ਵਿਚ ਸੀ *kujh turde se te ikk ḍolī wich sī.*

4. Were they soldiers or villagers?
ਓਹ ਸਪਾਹੀ ਸੇ ਕਿ ਪਿੰਡ ਵਾਲੇ। *oh sapāhī se ki piṅḍ wāle?*

5. They were soldiers and workmen.
ਓਹ ਸਪਾਹੀ ਤੇ ਮਜੂਰ ਸਨ। *oh sapāhī te majūr san.*

6. How long is it since they went out of your sight?
ਕਦਕੁ ਤੇ ਓਹ ਤੁਹਾਥੋਂ ਦਿਸਣੋਂ ਰਹੇ। *kadku te oh tuhāthoṅ disnoṅ rahe?*

7. They passed here about an hour ago.
ਘੰਟਾਕੁ ਹੋਇਆ ਹੈ ਜੋ ਓਹ ਏਥੋਂ ਦੀ ਲੰਘੇ। *ghaṅṭāku hoiā hai jo oh ethoṅ dī laṅghe.*

8. Is that a city, a town, or a village?
ਓਹ ਸ਼ਹਿਰ ਹੈ ਕਿ ਨਗਰ ਜਾਂ ਕੋਈ ਪਿੰਡ। *oh shahir hai ki nagar jāṅ koī piṅḍ?*

9. What is behind that tree ?	ਉਸ ਰੁਖ (ਬਿਰਛ) ਦੇ ਪਿਛੇ ਕੀ ਹੈ ? *us rukh (birchh) de pichhe kī hai ?*
10. Are there boats here in the rains ?	ਬਰਸਾਤ ਵਿਚ ਇਥੇ ਬੇੜੀਆਂ ਰਹਿੰਦੀਆਂ ਹਨ ? । *barsāt wich ithe beṛīāṅ rahindīāṅ haṇ.*
11. Do the hill men bring wood from the forest ?	ਪਹਾੜੀਏ ਜੰਗਲ ਵਿਚੋਂ ਬਾਲਨ ਲਿਆਉਂਦੇ ਹਨ ? । *pahāṛīe jaṅgal wichoṅ bālan liāuṅde han ?*
12. Is that ground sound or full of holes ?	ਓਹ ਭੋਂ ਪੱਕੀ ਹੈ ਕਿ ਖੁਡਾਂ ਵਾਲੀ ? । *oh bhoṅ pakkī hai ki khuḍāṅ wālī ?*
13. Who is the head man of that village ?	ਉਸ ਪਿੰਡ ਦਾ ਲੰਬਰਦਾਰ ਕੌਣ ਹੈ ? । *us piṅḍ dā lambardār kaun hai ?*
14. Is there any one who speaks Persian here ?	ਇਥੇ ਕੋਈ ਫਾਰਸੀ ਬੋਲਨ ਵਾਲਾ ਮਨੁਖ ਹੈ । *ethe koī phārsī bolanwālā maṇukh hai ?*
15. He speaks very slowly.	ਓਹ ਬਹੁਤ ਹੌਲੀ ਬੋਲਦਾ ਹੈ । *oh bahut haulī boldā hai.*
16. Speak very distinctly.	ਬਹੁਤ ਚੰਗੀ ਤਰਾਂ ਬੋਲ । *bahut changī tarāṅ bol.*
17. Do you understand me ?	ਤੂੰ ਮੇਰੀ ਗਲ ਸਮਝਦਾ ਹੈਂ । *tūṅ merī gal samjhdā hain ?*
18. No, I don't understand you.	ਨਹੀਂ ਮੈ ਤੇਰੀ ਗਲ ਨਹੀਂ ਸਮਝਦਾ । *nahīṅ maiṅ terī gal nahīṅ samjhdā.*
19. Send a man with me to show the way.	ਮੇਰੇ ਨਾਲ ਇਕ ਮਨੁਖ ਰਾਹ ਦਸਣ ਲਈ ਘਲ । *mere nāl ikk maṇukh rāh dasan laī ghal.*
20. Which is the shortest way to Pindi ?	ਪਿੰਡੀ ਨੂੰ ਕੇਹੜਾ ਰਾਹ ਨੇੜੇ ਹੈ? *piṅḍī nūṅ kehṛā rāh neṛe hai ?*

21. Is the road metalled or unmetalled?	ਸੜਕ ਪੱਕੀ ਹੈ ਜਾਂ ਕੱਚੀ ? *sarak pakkī hai jāṇ kachchī?*
22. Is it a good road for walking or for riding?	ਪੈਰੀਂ ਤੁਰਨ ਦੇ ਲਈ ਚੰਗੀ ਹੈ ਜਾਂ ਸਵਾਰੀ ਦੇ ਲਈ ? । *pairīṅ turaṇ de laī chaṅgī hai jāṅ sawārī de laī?*
23. How many heads of families lives in this village, and who is the chief?	ਇਸ ਪਿੰਡ ਵਿਚ ਕਿਨੇ ਸਰਦਾਰ ਰਹਿੰਦੇ ਹਨ ਤੇ ਸਭਤੋਂ ਵਡਾ ਕੌਣ ਹੈ ? । *is piṅd wich kiṅe sardār rahiṅde haṇ te sabh toṅ waddā kaun hai?*
24. There are 2,500 inhabitants in that village.	ਉਸ ਪਿੰਡ ਵਿਚ ਦੋ ਹਜਾਰ ਪੰਜ ਸੌ ਵਸਕੀਨ ਹਨ । *us piṅd wich do hajār paṅj sau waskīṇ haṇ.*
25. How many cattle have they?	ਓਹਨਾਂ ਕੋਲ ਕਿੰਨੇ ਪਸ਼ੂ ਹਨ । *ohṇāṅ kol kiṇṇe pasū han.*
26. What supplies can be obtained in this country?	ਇਸ ਦੇਸ ਵਿਚ ਕੀ ਰਸਤ ਮਿਲ ਸਕਦੀ ਹੈ । *is des wich kī rasat mil sakdī hai?*
27. There is wheat, Indian corn, barley and fruit.	ਕਣਕ ਜੁਵਾਰ ਜੌਂ ਤੇ ਫਲ ਮਿਲ ਸਕਦੇ ਹਨ । *kaṇak juār jauṅ te phal mil sakde han.*
28. The barley is green but the* rice is nearly ripe.	ਜੌਂ ਹਰੇ ਹਨ ਪਰ ਝੋਨਾ ਪਕਣ ਉਤੇ ਹੈ । *jauṅ hare han par jhoṇā pakan utte hai.*
29 All the men are ploughing.	ਸਭ ਲੋਕ ਹਲ ਵਾਹੁੰਦੇ ਹਨ । *sabh lok hal wāhuṅde haṇ.*
30. Is there a well in this village?	ਇਸ ਪਿੰਡ ਵਿਚ ਕੋਈ ਖੂਹ ਹੈ ? । *is piṅd wich koī khūh hai?*
31. How deep is the water?	ਪਾਣੀ ਕਿਨਾ ਡੂੰਘਾ ਹੈ ? । *pānī kiṅṅā dūṅghā hai.*

* Rice with husk is called ਝੋਨਾ *jhoṇā* otherwise ਚੌਲ *chaul.*

32. Where is the spring ?	ਸੁੰਬ ਕਿਥੇ ਹੈ ? । *sumb kithe hai ?*
33. What kind of trees are there in the forest ?	ਜੰਗਲ ਵਿਚ ਕਿਹੇ ਜੇਹੇ ਰੁਖ ਹਨ। *jaṅgal wich kihe jihe rukh han ?*
34. Are there thorns in those bushes ?	ਓਨਾਂ ਝਾੜੀਆਂ ਵਿਚ ਕੰਡੇ ਹਨ ? । *unhāṅ jhāṛīāṅ wich kaṅḍe haṇ ?*
35. Go along the foot path.	ਡੰਡੀ ਡੰਡੀ ਚਲਿਆ ਜਾ । *daṅḍī daṅḍī chaliā jā.*
36. Is there any danger at night on this road ?	ਰਾਤ ਨੂੰ ਇਸ ਸੜਕ ਉਤੇ ਕੁਝ ਭੈ ਹੈ ? *rāt nūṅ is saṛak utte kujh bhai hai ?*
37. If a man is armed there is no danger.	ਜੇਕਰ ਮਨੁਖ ਦੇ ਕੋਲ ਹਥਿਆਰ ਹੋਣ ਤਾਂ ਕੁਝ ਭੈ ਨਹੀਂ । *jekar manukh de kol hathyār hoṅ tāṅ kujh bhai nahīṅ.*
38. Shall I go to the right of left ?	ਮੈਂ ਸੱਜੇ ਹਥ ਜਾਵਾਂ ਕਿ ਖੱਬੇ ਹੱਥ ? *main sajje hath jāwāṅ ki khabbe hath ?*
46. Will the horse sink in the mud here ?	ਇਸ ਖੋਭੇ ਵਿਚ ਘੋੜਾ ਖੁਬ ਜਾਊ। *is khobhe wich ghoṛā khub jāū?*
40. Call another man.	ਦੂਜੇ ਮਨੁਖ ਨੂੰ ਸਦ । *dūje manukh nūṅ sad.*
41. There has been a great deal of rain in the hills.	ਪਹਾੜ ਵਿਚ ਬੜਾ ਮੀਂਹ ਪਿਆ ਹੈ । *pahāṛ wichch baṛā mīṅh piā hai.*
42. There is a flood in the river.	ਦਰਿਆ ਵਿਚ ਹੜ ਆਇਆ ਹੈ । *daryā wich haṛ āyā hai.*
43. That day I made a great mistake.	ਉਸ ਦਿਨ ਮੈਥੋਂ ਬੜੀ ਭੁਲ ਹੋਈ। *us din maithoṅ baṛī bhul hoī.*
44. There has been a great slaughter there.	ਉਥੇ ਬੜੀ ਵਢ ਕਟ ਹੋਈ । *uthe baṛī waḍh kaṭṭ hoī.*
45. Stand near the heap of stones.	ਪਥਰਾਂ ਦੇ ਢੇਰ ਕੋਲ ਖਲੋ । *pathrāṅ de ḍher kol khalo.*

46. Move a little to the right.
ਜ਼ਰਾਕੁ ਸਜੇ ਹਥ ਵਲ ਸਰਕ ਜਾ । *jarākū sajje hath wal sarak jā.*

47. Can you see the man who went forward with the flag ?
ਤੁਸੀ ਉਸ ਮਨੁਖ ਨੂੰ ਵੇਖ ਸਕਦੇ ਹੋ ਜੇਹੜਾ ਝੰਡੀ ਲੈਕੇ ਅਗੇ ਗਿਆ । *tusīṅ us manukh nūṅ wekh sakde ho jehṛā jhaṇḍī lai ke agge giā?*

48. Have you received your pay in full ?
ਤੈਨੂੰ ਪੂਰੀ ਤਲਬ ਮਿਲ ਗਈ । *taiṅ nūṅ pūrī talab mil gaī ?*

49. I shall not pay you unless you finish the work before night.
ਰਾਤ ਦੇ ਅਗੇ ਜੇਕਰ ਤੂੰ ਇਹ ਕੰਮ ਨਹੀਂ ਕਰ ਲਵੇਂਗਾ ਤਾਂ ਤੈਨੂੰ ਕੁਝ ਨਹੀਂ ਮਿਲੇਗਾ । *rāt de agge jekar tūṅ ih kaṅm nahīṅ kar lawengā tāṅ tainūṅ kujh nahīṅ milegā.*

50. Mix some hemp with the lime for the plaster.
ਲੇਂਬੀ ਲਈ ਚੂਨੇ ਵਿਚ ਕੁਝ ਸਨ ਰਲਾ । *lembī laī chūne wich kujh san ralā.*

51. This mortar is too thick it wants more water.
ਇਹ ਗਾਰਾ ਬਹੁਤ ਗਾੜ੍ਹਾ ਹੈ ਪਾਣੀ ਹੋਰ ਪਾ । *ih gārā bahut gāṛhā hai pāṇī hor pā.*

52. Dig a little deeper.
ਜ਼ਰਾ ਹੋਰ ਡੂੰਘਾ ਪੁਟ । *jara hor dūnghā puṭ.*

53. How many men went on the first work?
ਪਹਿਲੇ ਕੰਮ ਤੇ ਕਿਨੇਂ ਮਨੁਖ ਗਏ ਹਨ । *pahile kaṅm te kinne manukh gae haṇ ?*

54. This is only sand.
ਇਹ ਨਿਰੀ ਰੇਤ ਹੈ । *ih nirī ret hai.*

55. Collect all the tools.
ਸਾਰੇ ਹਥਿਆਰ ਕਠੇ ਕਰ । *sāre hathiār kaṭhe kar.*

56. A good deal of damage has been done to that bridge by the flood.
ਹੜ ਨਾਲ ਉਸ ਪੁਲ ਦਾ ਬਹੁਤ ਨੁਕਸਾਨ ਹੋਇਆ ਹੈ । *haṛ nāl us pul dā bahut nuksāṇ hoiā hai.*

57. There is a crack in the walls of that hospital.

ਉਸ ਹਸਪਤਾਲ ਦੀਆਂ ਕੰਧਾਂ ਵਿਚ ਇਕ ਤੇੜ ਹੈ । *us haspatāl dīān kandhān wich ikk teṛ hai.*

58. This case cannot be settled to-day, tell them to come to-morrow.

ਇਹ ਮੁਕਦਮਾ ਅਜ ਨਹੀਂ ਹੋ ਸਕਦਾ ਉਨਾਂ ਨੂੰ ਆਖ ਜੋ ਕਲ ਆਉਣ । *ih mukadmā aj nahīn ho sakdā unhān nūn ākh jo kal āun.*

59. He has been imprisoned for 10 years.

ਉਹ ਨੂੰ ਦਸਾਂ ਵਰਿਆਂ ਦੀ ਕੈਦ ਹੋਈ ਹੈ । *oh nūn dasāṇ warihān dī kaid hoī hai.*

50. The man has been warned to appear in the tahsildar's court.

ਓਸ ਆਦਮੀ ਨੂੰ ਹੁਕਮ ਗਿਆ ਹੈ ਜੋ ਤਹਸੀਲਦਾਰ ਦੀ ਕਚਹਿਰੀ ਵਿਚ ਹਾਜ਼ਰ ਹੋਵੇ । *os ādmī nūn hukam giā hai jo tahsīldār dī kachahrī wich hājar howe.*

Section X.—Shooting.

HUNTING.

1. Is there any danger in shooting on those hills?

ਓਨਾਂ ਪਹਾੜਾਂ ਤੇ ਸ਼ਕਾਰ ਕਰਨ ਦਾ ਕੁਝ ਭੈ ਹੈ ।*unhān pahāṛān te shakār karaṇ dā kujh bhai hai?*

2. Am I likely to find water fowl on the river side?

ਮੈਨੂੰ ਦਰਿਆ ਦੀ ਵਲ ਮੁਰਗਾਬੀਆਂ ਲਭਨ ਗੀਆਂ । *main nūn dryā dī wal murgābīān labhaṇ giān.*

3. What game is there in this part of the country?

ਇਸ ਪਾਸੇ ਵਲ ਕਿਹੋ ਜਿਹਾ ਸ਼ਿਕਾਰ ਮਿਲਦਾ ਹੈ । *is pāse wal kiho jihā shikār mildā hai?*

4. Snipe and duck, but they all go away

ਚਾਹੇ ਤੇ ਬਤਕਾਂ ਮਿਲ ਸਕਦੀਆਂ ਹਨ ਪਰ ਏਹ ਸਭ ਬਹਾਰ ਦੀ ਰੁਤ ਵਿਚ ਚਲੀ

during the spring. — ਆਂ ਜਾਂਦੀਆਂ ਹਨ। *chāhe te batkān mil sakdīān han' par ih sabh bahār dī rut wich chaltān jāndīān han.*

5. You must get up early to be able to shoot them. — ਤੁਹਾਨੂੰ ਓਨਾਂ ਦਾ ਸ਼ਕਾਰ ਕਰਨ ਲਈ ਤੜਕੇ ਉਠਨਾ ਚਾਹੀਦਾ ਹੈ। *tuhāṇūṅ unhāṅ dā shakār karan laī tarke uṭhnā chāhī dā hai.*

6. I went yesterday to a Jhil near Jagadhri. It was very dry, and full of high grass. I shot only 5 snipe. — ਕਲ ਮੈਂ ਜਗਾਧਰੀ ਦੇ ਨੇੜੇ ਇਕ ਝੀਲ ਨੂੰ ਗਿਆ ਓਹ ਬਹੁਤ ਸੁਕੀ ਹੋਈ ਤੇ ਲਮੇ ਘਾਹ ਨਾਲ ਭਰੀ ਹੋਈ ਸੀ ਤੇ ਮੈਂ ਨਿਰੇ ਪੰਜ ਚਾਹੇ ਮਾਰੇ। *kal main jagādhrī de nere ikk jhīl nūṅ giā oh bahut sukkī hoī te bahut lamme ghāh nāl bharī hoī sī te main nire panj chāhe māre.*

7. Deer have entirely disappeared. — ਹਰਨ ਤਾਂ ਦਿਸਨੋਂ ਹੀ ਰਹਿ ਗਏ ਹਨ। *haraṅ tāṇ disṇoṇ hī rah gae haṅ.*

8. Yesterday I went out shooting. I came to the river but could not find a ford. — ਕਲ ਮੈਂ ਸ਼ਿਕਾਰ ਨੂੰ ਗਿਆ ਮੈਂ ਦਰਿਆ ਤੇ ਅਪੜਿਆ ਪਰ ਥਾਹ (ਗਾਹਨ) ਨਾ ਲਭੀ। *kal main shikār nūṅ giā main dryā te apṛiā par (gāhan) thāh nā labhī.*

9. Luckily there was a boat, but only one oar and the rudder was broken. — ਕਿਸਮਤ ਨਾਲ ਓਥੇ ਇਕ ਬੇੜੀ ਸੀ ਪਰ ਕੇਵਲ ਇਕਹੀ ਸੀ ਜਿਸਦਾ ਚਪਾ ਤੇ ਪਤਵਾੜ ਟੁਟੇ ਹੋਏ ਸਨ। *kismat nāl othe ikk beṛī sī par kewal ikk hī sī jisdā chappā te patwār tutte hoe san.*

10. I shot a duck which rose on the right bank, but missed two snipe on the left. — ਮੈਂ ਇਕ ਬਤਕ ਮਾਰੀ ਜੋ ਸੱਜੇ ਪਾਸਿਓਂ ਉਡੀ ਸੀ ਪਰ ਖਬੇ ਪਾਸੇ ਦੇ ਚਾਹੇ ਨਾ ਮਾਰੇ। *main ikk battak mārī jo sajje pāsioṅ uḍḍī sī par khabe pāse de chāhe nā māre.*

11. I saw a flock of geese but it was too far away.

ਮੈਂ ਵਡੀਆਂ ਬਤਕਾਂ ਦੀ ਡਾਰ ਵੇਖੀ ਪਰ ਓਹ ਵਡੀ ਦੂਰ ਸੀ ।। *maiṅ waddīāṅ batkāṅ dī dār wekhī par oh waddī dūr sī.*

12. Owing to bad luck I secured only four birds.

ਮੰਦੇ ਭਾਗਾਂ ਦੇ ਕਾਰਨ ਮੈਂ ਨਿਰੇ ਚਾਰ ਪੰਛੀ ਮਾਰੇ । *maṅde bhāgāṅ de kāran maiṅ niṛe chār paṅchhī māre.*

13. Why is sport so bad this year ?

ਐਤਕੀ (ਐਸ ਵਰਹੇ) ਸ਼ਕਾਰ ਅਜਿਹਾ ਹਲਕਾ ਕਿਉਂ ਹੈ । *aitkī (ais warhe) shakār ajihā halkā kyoṅ hai.*

14. The rains are now over, all the jhils are dry, and the birds are returning towards the hills.

ਹੁਨ ਮੀਂਹ ਪੈ ਹਟਿਆ ਹੈ ਤੇ ਝੀਲਾਂ ਸੁਕ ਗਈਆਂ ਹਨ ਤੇ ਪੰਛੀ ਪਹਾੜਾਂ ਦੀ ਵਲ ਮੁੜੇ ਜਾਂਦੇ ਹਨ । *huṇ mīṅh pai haṭiā hai te jhīlāṅ suk gaīāṅ han te paṅchhī pahāṛāṅ dī wal muṛe jāṅde haṇ.*

15. Some cattle were in the jhils they frightened the birds.

ਕਈ ਡੰਗਰ ਝੀਲਾਂ ਵਿਚ ਸਨ ਤੇ ਉਨ੍ਹਾਂ ਨੇ ਪੰਛੀਆਂ ਨੂੰ ਡਰਾ ਦਿਤਾ । *kaī dṅgar jhīlāṅ wich san te uhnāṅ ne panchhīāṅ nūṅ darā dittā.*

16. There is little sport in my country because the hills are very steep and roads bad.

ਮੇਰੇ ਦੇਸ ਵਲ ਥੋੜਾ ਜਿਹਾ ਸ਼ਕਾਰ ਹੈ ਕਿਉਂ ਜੋ ਪਹਾੜ ਸਿਰ ਤਲਵਾਏ ਹਨ ਤੇ ਰਸਤੇ ਖ਼ਰਾਬ ਹਨ । *mere des wal thoṛā jihā shikār hai kyoṅ jo pahāṛ sir talwāe haṇ te raste kharāb han.*

* SECTION XI.—Colloquial.

੧ ਤੁਹਾਨੂੰ ਹਾੜ੍ਹੀ ਦੇ ਕਿੱਨੇ ਦਾਣੇ ਹੋਏ ਹਨ।
੨ ਪੰਦਰਾਂ ਮਾਣੀਆਂ ਬਾਰਾਂ ਵਟੀਆਂ ਤੇ ਛੀ ਸੇਰ।
੩ ਤੁਹਾਡੀ ਭਿਆਲੀ ਕਿਸ ਦੇ ਨਾਲ ਸੀ ?।
੪ ਮੈਂ ਕਦੀ ਕਿਸੇ ਨਾਲ ਭਿਆਲੀ ਨਹੀਂ ਕੀਤੀ।
੫ ਵਾਹੀ ਕਿਨੀਆਂ ਜੋਗਾਂ ਦੀ ਸੀ ?
੬ ਬਰਾਨੀ ਹੀ ਵਾਹੀ ਸੀ ਜਾਂ ਖੂਹ ਦੀ ਵੀ ਸੀ ?
੭ ਕੁਝ ਬਰਾਨੀ ਤੇ ਕੁਝ ਖੂਹ ਦੀ।
੮ ਖੂਹ ਉੱਤੇ ਕਿਨੇ ਵਿਗੇ ਸੇ ਤੇ ਬਰਾਨੀ ਕਿਨੇ ?
੯ ਖੂਹ ਵਿੱਚ ਤੁਹਾਡਾ ਕਿਤਨਵਾਂ ਹਿੱਸਾ ਹੈ ?
੧੦ ਮੈਂ ਤੀਸਰੇ ਹਿੱਸੇ ਦਾ ਮਾਲਕ ਹਾਂ।
੧੧ ਕਿਨਿਆਂ ਦਿਨਾਂ ਪਿੱਛੋਂ ਤੁਹਾਨੂੰ ਖੂਹ ਦੀ ਵਾਰੀ ਆਉਂਦੀ ਹੈ।
੧੨ ਇੱਕ ਅਠਵਾਰੇ ਵਿੱਚ ਦੋ ਵਾਰੀ।
੧੩ ਇੱਕ ਦਿਨ ਵਿੱਚ ਕਿੱਨੀ ਪੈਲੀ ਸਿੰਜ ਸਕਦੇ ਹੋ ?
੧੪ ਜੇਕਰ ਬੈਲ ਤਕੜੇ ਹੋਣ ਤਾਂ ਇਕ ਦਿਨ ਵਿੱਚ ਤਿੰਨ ਚਾਰ ਵਿਘੇ ਪੈਲੀ ਸਿੰਜੀ ਜਾ ਸਕਦੀ ਹੈ।
੧੫ ਇੱਕ ਜੋਗ ਨੂੰ ਕਿਨੇ ਚਿਰ ਤਕ ਜੋਈ ਰੱਖਦੇ ਹੋ
੧੬ ਤਿੰਨ ਚਾਰ ਘੰਟੇ ਜੋਕੇ ਫੇਰ ਉਸਨੂੰ ਖੋਲਕੇ ਪੱਠਾ ਦੱਥਾ ਪਾ ਦੇਂਦੇ ਹਾਂ ਅਤੇ ਦੂਜੀ ਜੋੜੀ ਨੂੰ ਜੋ ਦੇਂਦੇ ਹਾਂ।
੧੭ ਜੇਕਰ ਤੁਹਾਡੀ ਵਾਰੀ ਵਿੱਚ ਖੂਹ ਵਿਗੜ ਜਾਵੇ ਤਾਂ ਤੁਹਾਨੂੰ ਬਨਾਉਣਾ ਪੈਂਦਾ ਹੈ ਕਿ ਸਾਰੇ ਭਿਆਲਾਂ ਨੂੰ ?
੧੮ ਜਿਸਦੀ ਵਾਰੀ ਵਿੱਚ ਖੂਹ ਵਿਗੜੇ ਉਸੇ ਨੂੰ ਬਨਾਉਣਾ ਪੈਂਦਾ ਹੈ।
੧੯ ਮਾਲ੍ਹ ਕਿਨਿਆਂ ਚਿਰਾਂ ਪਿਛੋਂ ਪਾਉਂਦੇ ਹੋ ?
੨੦ ਮਾਲ੍ਹ ਅਸਕਰ (ਅਕਸਰ) ਤਿੰਨੀ ਚੌਂ ਮਹੀਨੀ ਪਾਉਂਦੇ ਹੁੰਦੇ ਹਾਂ ਪਰ ਜੇਕਰ ਛੇਤੀ ਘਸ ਜਾਏ ਤਾਂ ਨਵੀਂ ਪਾ ਦਿੰਦੇ ਹੋਂਦੇ ਹਾਂ।
੨੧ ਤੁਸੀਂ ਦੋਵੇਂ ਭਿਆਲ ਹੀ ਕੰਮ ਕਰਦੇ ਹੋ ?
੨੨ ਨਹੀਂ ਇੱਕ ਸੇਪੀ ਨਾਲ ਰਲਾਇਆ ਹੋਇਆ ਹੈ।
੨੩ ਓਹ ਸੇਪੀ ਕੌਣ ਹੈ ?
੨੪ ਓਹ ਆਪਣੇ ਘਰ ਦਾ ਚੂਹੜਾ ਹੈ।
੨੫ ਓਹ ਤੁਹਾਨੂੰ ਕੀ ਕੰਮ ਦਿੰਦਾ ਹੈ ?
੨੬ ਸਾਰਾ ਵਾਹੀ ਦਾ ਕੰਮ ਉਸੇ ਦੇ ਸਿਰ ਤੇ ਹੈ ਪਰ ਵੱਡਾ ਕਠਨ ਕੰਮ ਇਹ ਕਰਦਾ ਹੈ ਜੋ ਸਿਆਲ ਨੂੰ ਜਦ ਖੂਹ ਵਗਦਾ ਹੈ ਤਾਂ ਰਾਤ ਦੇ ਵੇਲੇ ਪਾਣੀ ਅੱਗੇ ਹੁੰਦਾ ਹੈ ਤੇ ਕਿਆਰਾ ਮੋੜਦਾ ਹੈ।

---

* For hard words consult the vocabulary at the end.

੨੭ ਉਸਨੂੰ ਰਾਤ ਪਾਣੀ ਅਗੇ ਪਾਲਾ ਨਹੀਂ ਲਗਦਾ?

੨੮ ਨਹੀਂ ਓਹ ਉਥੇ ਇਕ ਧੂੰਆਂ ਪਾ ਲੈਂਦਾ ਹੈ ਅਤੇ ਉਸਉਤੇ ਬੈਠਕੇ ਅੱਗ ਸੇਕਦਾ ਰਹਿੰਦਾ ਹੈ।

੨੯ ਮੈਂ ਜਾਣਦਾ ਹਾਂ ਜੋ ਉਹ ਰਾਤ ਸੌਂਦਾ ਤਾਂ ਨਹੀਂ ਹੋਣਾ?

੩੦ ਨਹੀਂ ਜੇ ਸਵੇਂ ਤਾਂ ਪਾਣੀ ਵਰਾਨ ਹੋਜਾਵੇ।

੩੧ ਇੱਕ ਵੇਰ ਦੀ ਪੈਲੀ ਸਿੰਜੀ ਹੋਈ ਕਿਨੇ ਦਿਨਾਂ ਤੀਕ ਰਹ ਸਕਦੀ ਹੈ?

੩੨ ਜੇ ਚੰਗੀ ਤਰਾਂ ਸਿੰਜੀ ਜਾਵੇ ਤਾਂ ਪੰਦਰਾ ਵੀਹਾਂ ਦਿਨਾਂ ਤੱਕ ਉਸਦਾ ਕੁਝ ਨਹੀਂ ਵਿਗੜਦਾ।

੩੩ ਜੇ ਸੋਕਾ ਪੈ ਜਾਵੇ ਤਾਂ ਕੀ ਕਰਦੇ ਹੋ?

੩੪ ਦੂਜੇ ਖੂਹ ਦੇ ਖ਼ਿਆਲ ਤੋਂ ਵਾਰੀ ਮੰਗਦੇ ਹਾਂ ਜੇ ਓਹ ਦੇਵੇ ਤਾਂ ਬਚ ਜਾਂਦੀ ਹੈ ਨਹੀਂ ਤਾਂ ਕੁਝ ਵਾਹ ਨਹੀਂ।

੩੫ ਖੂਹ ਦਾ ਤੁਹਾਡੇ ਹਿੱਸੇ ਵਰਹੇ ਵਿਚ ਕੀ ਆਉਂਦਾ ਹੈ?

੩੬ ਅਸੀ ਚੁਹਾਰਮ ਦੇ ਮਾਲਕ ਹਾਂ ਅਤੇ ਦਸ ਰੁਪਜੇ ਦੇਣੇ ਪੈਂਦੇ ਹਨ।

੩੭ ਜੇ ਖੂਹ ਵਿਗੜ ਜਾਵੇ ਤਾਂ ਕੌਣ ਬਣਾਉਂਦਾ ਹੈ?

੩੮ ਜੇ ਵਿਗੜੇ ਸੇਪ ਵਾਲਾ ਤਰਖਾਣ ਬਣਾਉਂਦਾ ਹੈ।

੩੯ ਉਸਨੂੰ ਕੀ ਦੇਂਦੇ ਹੁੰਦੇ ਹੋ?

੪੦ ਵਿਆਹ ਸ਼ਾਦੀ ਉਤੇ ਰੁਪਈਆ ਅਤੇ ਸਾਰੇ ਟਬਰ ਦੀ ਰੋਟੀ ਅਰ ਫੇਰ ਫਸਲ ਉਤੇ ਦਾਣੇ।

੪੧ ਓਹ ਲੁਹਾਰਾ ਤਰਖਾਣਾ ਦੋਵੇਂ ਕੰਮ ਕਰ ਲੈਂਦਾ ਹੈ?

੪੨ ਨਹੀਂ ਲੁਹਾਰ ਅਡ ਹੁੰਦਾ ਹੈ ਅਤੇ ਉਸਨੂੰ ਵੀ ਤਰਖਾਣ ਵਾਂਗੂੰ ਦਿੰਦੇ ਹਾਂ।

੪੩ ਸੇਪ ਵਾਲੇ ਚੂਹੜੇ ਨੂੰ ਕੀ ਦਿੰਦੇ ਹੁੰਦੇ ਹੋ?

੪੪ ਫਸਲ ਵਿਚੋਂ ਵੀਹਵਾਂ ਹਿਸਾ।

੪੫ ਖੂਹ ਦੇ ਲਈ ਟਿੰਡਾਂ ਕਿਥੋਂ ਲੈਂਦੇ ਹੋ?

੪੬ ਆਪਣੇ ਘੁਮਿਆਰ ਕੋਲੋਂ।

੪੭ ਉਸਨੂੰ ਮੁਲ ਦੇਂਦੇ ਹੋ?

੪੮ ਨਹੀਂ ਉਸਨੂੰ ਵੀ ਤਰਖਾਣ ਵਾਂਙੂ ਦਾਣਾ ਫਕਾ ਦਿੰਦੇਹਾਂ।

੪੯ ਸਾਰੇ ਹਾੜੀ ਦੇ ਫਸਲ ਦੀ ਤੁਹਾਡੀ ਕਿਨੀ ਕਣਕ ਹੁੰਦੀ ਹੈ?

੫੦ ਸਾਹੀ ਬਰਾਨੀ ਅਤੇ ਖੂਹ ਦੀ ਪਾਕੇ ਚਾਰਸੌ ਭਰੀ ਹੁੰਦੀਹੈ।

੫੧ ਇਕ ਭਰੀ ਵਿਚ ਕਿਨੇ ਪੂਲੇ ਹੁੰਦੇ ਹਨ ਤੇ ਦਾਣੇ ਕਿਨੇ ਨਿਕਲਦੇਹਨ?

੫੨ ਇਕ ਭਰੀ ਵਿਚ ੧੫ ਪੂਲੇ ਹੁੰਦੇ ਹਨ ਤੇ ਦਾਣੇ ਮਣ ਜਾ ਸਵਾ ਮਣ ਨਿਕਲਦੇ ਹਨ।

੫੩ ਭਰੀਆਂ ਵਿਚੋਂ ਕਣਕ ਕਿਸ ਤਰਾਂ ਕਢਦੇ ਹੋ?

੫੪ ਪਹਿਲਾਂ ਤਾਂ ਸਾਰੀਆਂ ਭਰੀਆਂ ਪਿੜ ਵਿਚ ਲੈ ਆਉਂਦੇ ਹਾਂ ਫੇਰ ਉਸ ਨੂੰ ਫਲੇ ਨਾਲ ਗਾਹ ਸੁਟ ਦੇ ਹਾਂ।

੫੫ ਜੇ ਥੋੜੀ ਹੋਵੇ ਤਾਂ ਮੇਹੜ ਪਾਉਂਦੇ ਹਾਂ।

੫੬ ਇਕ ਦਿਨ ਵਿਚ ਕਿਨੀਆਂ ਭਰੀਆਂ ਗਾਹੁੰਦੇ ਹੋ ?

੫੭ ਜੇ ਸਾਰਾ ਦਿਨ ਲਗੇ ਰਹੀਏ ਤਾਂ ਪੰਜਾਹਕੁ ਭਰੀਆਂ ਦਾ ਸੈਂਡ ਹੋ ਜਾਂਦਾ ਹੈ।

੫੮ ਤੁਹਾਨੂੰ ਹਾੜੀ ਦੀ ਕਣਕ ਕਿਨੀ ਆਈ।

੫੯ ਸਾਢੇ ਚਾਰ ਸੌ ਮਣ ਜਿਸ ਵਿਚੋਂ ਪੰਜਾਹ ਮਣ ਕਮੀਨਾਂ ਨੂੰ ਦੇ ਦਿੱਤੀ।

੬੦ ਤੁਹਾਨੂੰ ਤੂੜੀ ਕਿਨੀ ਆਈ ?

੬੧ ਤੂੜੀ ਪੰਜ ਸੌ ਪੰਡਾਂ ਨਿਕਲੀ ਸੀ ।

੬੨ ਉਸਨੂੰ ਪਿੰਡ ਲੈ ਆਂਦਾ ਹੈ ਕਿ ਬਾਹਰ ਹੀ ਰਹਿਣ ਦਿਤਾ ਹੈ ?

੬੩ ਚਾਲੀਕ ਪੰਡਾਂ ਘਰ ਲੈ ਆਂਦੀਆਂ ਹਨ ਅਰ ਰਹਿੰਦੀ ਦੇ ਖੂਹ ਉਤੇ ਮੂਸਲ ਬਨ੍ਹ ਦਿਤੇ ਹਨ।

੬੪ ਤੁਹਾਡੇ ਕੋਲ ਕਿਨੇ ਪਸੂ ਹਨ ?

੬੫ ਮੇਰੇ ਕੋਲ ਤੀਹ ਢਗੇ ਅਤੇ ਪੰਜ ਮਹੀਆਂ ਅਰ ਪੰਜ ਸਤ ਗਊਆਂ ਹਨ।

੬੬ ਤੁਹਾਡੇ ਪਿੰਡ ਦੇ ਕੋਲ ਕੋਈ ਨਹਿਰ ਹੈ ?

੬੭ ਨਹਿਰ ਤਾਂ ਨਹੀਂ ਪਰ ਇਕ ਸੂਆ ਹੈ।

੬੮ ਕੀ ਉਸ ਸੂਏ ਦਾ ਪਾਣੀ ਸਾਰੇ ਪਿੰਡ ਦੀ ਜ਼ਮੀਨ ਵਿਚ ਪੈਂਦਾ ਹੈ ?

੬੯ ਨਹੀਂ ਅਧੇ ਪਿੰਡ ਨੂੰ ਆਉਂਦਾ ਹੈ ਤੇ ਅਧੇ ਉਤੇ ਨਹੀਂ ਚੜ ਸਕਦਾ।

੭੦ ਨਹਿਰ ਦੀ ਜ਼ਮੀਨ ਦਾ ਬਰਾਨੀ ਨਾਲੋਂ ਕਿਨਾ ਜ਼ਾਦਾ ਮਾਮਲਾ ਦਿੰਦੇ ਹੋ

੭੧ ਬਰਾਨੀ ਨਾਲੋਂ ਨਹਿਰ ਉਤੇ ਦੂਣਾ ਲਗਦਾ ਹੈ ।

੭੨ ਜੇ ਨਹਿਰ ਦਾ ਪਾਣੀ ਉਚੇ ਥਾਂ ਚੜ੍ਹਾਉਣਾ ਹੋਵੇ ਤਾਂ ਕੀ ਕਰਦੇ ?

੭੩ ਜਾਂ ਤਾਂ ਝੁਟੇ ਨਾਲ ਚੜ੍ਹਾਉਂਦੇ ਹਾਂ ਜਾਂ ਝਲਾਰ ਨਾਲ ।

੭੪ ਢੀਂਗੁਲੀ ਤੁਹਾਡੇ ਨਹੀਂ ਲਾਉਂਦੇ ?

੭੫ ਨਹੀਂ ਮਾਝੇ ਵਿਚ ਢੀਂਗੁਲੀ ਘਟ ਵਰਤਦੇ ਹਨ।

੭੬ ਨਹਿਰ ਵਿਚੋਂ ਪੈਲੀ ਵਿਚ ਪਾਣੀ ਕੀਕੂ ਪਾਉਂਦੇ ਹੋ ?

੭੭ ਨਹਿਰ ਵਿਚੋਂ ਇਕ ਖਾਲ ਕਢ ਦੇ ਹਾਂ ਅਤੇ ਉਸ ਖਾਲ ਵਿਚੋਂ ਪਾਣੀ ਪੈਲੀ ਵਿਚ ਆਉਂਦਾ ਹੈ ।

੭੮ ਜੇ ਤੁਸੀਂ ਪਾਣੀ ਲੈਣਾ ਹੋਵੇ ਤਾਂ ਕਿਸ ਪਾਸੋਂ ਲੈਂਦੇ ਹੋ ?

੭੯ ਜੇ ਪਾਣੀ ਦੀ ਲੋੜ ਹੋਵੇ ਤਾਂ ਜਿਲੇਦਾਰ ਨੂੰ ਆਖਦੇ ਹਾਂ।

੮੦ ਉਸਦੇ ਹੇਠਾਂ ਹੋਰ ਕੌਣ ਕੰਮ ਕਰਦਾ ਹੈ ?

੮੧ ਇਕ ਚਪੜਾਸੀ ਹੁੰਦਾ ਹੈ।

੮੨ ਓਹ ਕੀ ਕੰਮ ਕਰਦਾ ਹੈ ?

੮੩ ਓਹ ਵੇਖਦਾ ਹੈ ਜੋ ਕਿਤੇ ਪਾਣੀ ਖਰਾਬ ਨਾ ਹੋਵੇ ਅਤੇ ਕੋਈ ਚੋਰੀ ਪਾਣੀ ਨਾ ਲੈ ਲਵੇ।

੮੪ ਜੇ ਕੋਈ ਚੋਰੀ ਪਾਣੀ ਲੈ ਲਵੇ ਤਾਂ ਕੀ ਹੁੰਦਾ ਹੈ ?

੮੫ ਜੇ ਚਪੜਾਸੀ ਵੇਖ ਲਵੇ ਤਾਂ ਜਰਮਾਨਾ ਹੁੰਦਾ ਹੈ।

੮੬ ਓਹ ਜਰਮਾਨਾ ਕੌਣ ਕਰਦਾ ਹੈ ?

੮੭ ਨਹਿਰ ਵਾਲਾ ਸਾਹਿਬ।

੮੮ ਤੁਸੀ ਇਕ ਵਿਗੇ ਦਾ ਕੀ ਮਾਮਲਾ ਦਿੰਦੇ ਹੋ ?

੮੯ ਸਰਕਾਰੇ ਛੇ ਆਨੇ ਵਿਗਾ ਭਰਦੇ ਹਾਂ।

੯੦ ਜੇਕਰ ਕੋਈ ਤੁਹਾਡੀ ਭੋਂ ਬੀਜੇ ਓਸਥੋਂ ਕੀ ਲੈਂਦੇ ਹ ?

੯੧ ਕਦੀ ਰੁਪਈਆ ਵਿਗਾ ਕਦੀ ਸਵਾ ਰੁਪਈਆ।

੯੨ ਤੁਸੀਂ ਮਾਮਲਾ ਸਰਕਾਰੇ ਕੀਕਰ ਤਾਰਦੇ ਹੋ ?

੯੩ ਅਸੀਂ ਤਾਂ ਨੰਬਰਦਾਰ ਨੂੰ ਦੇਂਦੇ ਹਾਂ।

੯੪ ਤੁਸਾਡੇ ਪਿੰਡ ਵਿਚ ਕਿੱਨੇ ਨੰਬਰਦਾਰ ਹਨ ?

੯੫ ਤਿਨ ਨੰਬਰਦਾਰ ਤੇ ਦੋ ਆਲਾ ਨੰਬਰਦਾਰ।

੯੬ ਓਹਨਾ ਦੇ ਉਤੇ ਵਡਾ ਕੌਣ ਹੈ ?

੯੭ ਉਸ ਨੂੰ ਜੈਲਦਾਰ ਆਖਦੇ ਹਨ।

੯੮ ਲੰਬਰਦਾਰ ਕੀ ਕੰਮ ਕਰਦਾ ਹੈ ?

੯੯ ਓਹ ਆਪਣੀਆਂ ਸਾਮੀਆਂ ਦਾ ਮਾਮਲਾ ਕਠਾ ਕਰਦਾ ਹੈ।

੧੦੦ ਓਹ ਕਠਾ ਕਰਕੇ ਕਿਸ ਨੂੰ ਦੇਂਦਾ ਹੈ ?

੧੦੧ ਸਾਰੇ ਨੰਬਰਦਾਰ ਆਪਣਾ ਆਪਣਾ ਰੁਪਈਆ ਕੱਠਾ ਕਰਕੇ ਪਟਵਾਰੀ ਨੂੰ ਦੇਂਦੇ ਹਨ।

੧੦੨ ਪਟਵਾਰੀ ਕੌਣ ਹੁੰਦਾ ਹੈ ?

੧੦੩ ਪਟਵਾਰੀ ਜਮੀਨ ਕਛਦਾ ਹੈ ਅਤੇ ਜਿਤਨਾ ਮਾਮਲਾ ਕਿਸੇ ਦੇ ਜਿਮੇਂ ਹੋਵੰ ਓਹ ਦਸਦਾ ਹੈ ਅਤੇ ਮਾਮਲਾ ਤਸੀਲ ਵਿਚ ਤਾਰ ਦੇਂਦਾ ਹੈ।

੧੦੪ ਇਕ ਵਰਹੇ ਵਿਚ ਕਿਨੀ ਵਾਰ ਮਾਮਲਾ ਦੇਂਦੇ ਹੋ ?

੧੦੫ ਇਕ ਵਰਹੇ ਵਿਚ ਦੋ ਕਿਸਤਾਂ ਤਾਰਦੇ ਹਾਂ ਹਾੜੀ ਅਤੇ ਸੌਣੀ।

੧੦੬ ਮਾਮਲਾ ਸਦਾ ਇਕੋ ਰਹਿੰਦਾ ਹੈ ?

੧੦੭ ਹਾਂ ਜਦ ਤੀਕਰ ਬੰਦੋਬਸਤ ਨਾ ਹੋਵੇ ਇਕੋ ਰਹਿੰਦਾ ਹੈ।

੧੦੮ ਜੇ ਕੋਈ ਜਟ ਮਾਮਲਾ ਨਾ ਦੇਵੇ ਤਾਂ ਕੀ ਹੁੰਦਾ ਹੈ ?

੧੦੯ ਨੰਬਰਦਾਰ ਉਸਦੇ ਨਾਂਓਂ ਬਰੰਟ ਜਾਰੀ ਕਰਦਾਹੈ ਅਤੇ ਓਹ ਤਸੀਲੇ ਬੁਲਾਇਆ ਜਾਂਦਾ ਹੈ ਅਰ ਜਦ ਤਕ ਮਾਮਲਾ ਨਾ ਤਾਰੇ ਹਵਾਲਾਟ ਵਿਚ ਬੰਦ ਰਹਿੰਦਾ ਹੈ।

੧੧੦ ਹਛਾ ਹੁਣ ਬਸ ਇਨੀ ਗਲ ਬਾਤ ਬਤੇਰੀ ਹੈ।

IDIOMS.

1. A mortal wound. — ਕਾਰੀ ਘਾਓ। *kāri ghāo*

2. To mount a Battery. — ਤੋਪਖਾਨਾ ਬੀੜਨਾ। *top khānā bīṛnā.*

3. Now-a-days. — ਅਜ ਕਲ। *aj kal.*

4. Both sides claimed the victory. — ਦੋਹਾਂ ਆਪੋ ਆਪਨੀ ਫਤੇ ਦਸੀ। *dohāṅ āpo āpnī fatte dassī.*

5. To fall ill (with fever). — * ਤਪ ਚੜ੍ਹਨਾ। *tap chaṛhnā.*

6. To fight hard. — ਭਾਰੀ ਲੜਾਈ ਕਰਨੀ। *bhārī laṛāī karnī.*

7. Beyond one's power. — ਬਲ ਤੋਂ ਬਾਹਰ। *bal toṅ bāhar.*

8. What is the matter with him? — ਓਸਨੂੰ ਕੀ ਹੋਇਆ ਹੈ। *us nūṅ kī hoiyā hai?*

9. As a matter of fact. — ਜੇ ਸਚ ਪੁਛੋ ਤਾਂ। *je sach puchho tāṅ.* / ਅਸਲ ਵਿਚ। *asal wich.*

10. On enquiry we learned. — ਪੁਛਨ ਤੇ ਸਾਨੂੰ ਮਲੂਮ ਹੋਇਆ। *puchhan te sāṇūṅ malūm hoiā.*

11. According to one's means. — ਜਿਨੀਕੁ ਸਮਰਥ ਹੋਵੇ। *jinīku samrath howe.* / ਜਿਨੀਕੁ ਪਹੁੰਚ ਹੋਵੇ। *jinīku pahuṅch howe*

12. Along the road. — ਰਸਤੇ ਦੇ ਕਨਾਰੇ ਕਨਾਰੇ। *raste de kanāre kanāre.*

13. One of them. — ਓਨ੍ਹਾਂ ਵਿਚੋਂ ਇਕ। *unhāṅ wichoṅ ikk.*

14. Just then. — ਉੱਸੇ ਵੇਲੇ। *usse wele.*

15. Soon after this. — ਇਸਤੋਂ ਥੋੜਾ ਚਿਰ ਪਿਛੇ। *is toṅ thoṛā chir pichhe.*

---

*Note the idiom ਤਪ (*tap*) fever takes ਚੜ੍ਹਨਾ (*chaṛhnā*

16	Said to the man who was with him.	ਆਪਣੇ ਨਾਲ ਦੇ ਮਨੁਖ ਨੂੰ ਕਿਹਾ। āpṇe nāl de maṇukh nūṅ kihā.
17.	From beginning to end.	ਆਦ ਤੇ ਅੰਤ ਤੀਕ। ād te aṅt tīk.
18.	During his life time.	ਉਸਦੇ ਜੀਉਂਦੇ ਜੀ। us de jīonde jī.
19.	I feel very hungry.	*ਮੈਨੂੰ ਵੱਡੀ ਭੁਖ ਲਗੀ ਹੋਈ ਹੈ। maiṅ nūṅ waḍḍī bhukh laggī hoī hai.
20.	Outwardly.	ਉਪਰੋਂ ਤਾਂ upron tāṅ ਉਪਰਲੇ ਮਨੋਂ। uparle manoṅ.
21.	Inwardly.	ਅੰਦਰਲੇ ਮਨੋਂ ਜਾਂ ਖਾਨਿਓ andarle maṇoṅ jāṅ khānion.
22.	There is no hurry	ਕੁਝ ਕਾਹਲ ਨਹੀਂ। kujh kāhal nahīṅ.
23.	To put a thing under ones arm.	ਕਛ ਵਿੱਚ ਮਾਰਨਾ। kachh wichch mārnā.
24.	To levy a fine.	ਜਰਮਾਨਾ ਕਰਨਾ। jarmāṇā karṇā.
25.	A forced march.	ਡਬਲ ਕੂਚ। dabbal kūch.
26.	I have been waiting for a long time.	ਮੈਂ ਚਰੋਕਨਾ ਉਡੀਕਦਾ ਹਾਂ। maiṅ charokṇā uḍīkdā hān.
27.	To seize (take possession of a place).	ਲੈ ਲੈਣਾ or ਖੋਹ ਲੈਣਾ। lai lainā or khoh lainā.
28.	To drive of the enemy.	ਵੈਰੀ ਨੂੰ ਭਾਜੜ ਪਾਉਣਾ wairī nūṅ bhājaṛ pāoṇā.
29.	All were subject to his authority.	ਸਾਰੇ ਉਸਦੇ ਅਧੀਨ ਸੀ। sāre usde adhīn sī.
30.	The rain fell in torrents.	ਮੀਂਹ ਮੋਹਲੇ ਧਾਰ ਪਿਆ। mīṅh mohle dhār piā.
31.	Periodical rain.	ਮੌਸਮੀ ਬਰਸਾਤ। mosmī barsāt.
32.	For the most part.	ਬਹੁਤ ਕਰਕੇ। bahut karke.

* Note the construction ਭੁਖ (bhukh) hunger and ਤੇਹ (teh) thirst takes ਲਗਨਾ

33. They were sound sleep. — ਓਹ ਬੇਸੁਧ ਸੁਤੇ ਪਏ ਸੇ। *oh besudh sutte pae se.*

34. To scratch one's head. — ਸਿਰ ਖੁਰਕਨਾ। *sir khurkanna.*

35. He fell down like a bag of bones. — ਓਹ ਚਕਨਾਚੂਰ ਹੋਕੇ ਡਿਗ ਪਿਆ। *oh chaknā chūr hoke dig piā.*

36. Our artillery shewed such skill that the enemy retired. — ਸਾਡੇ ਤੋਪਖਾਨੇ ਨੇ ਅਜੇਹੀ ਸੂਰ ਬੀਰਤਾ ਦਿਖਾਈ ਜੋ ਵੈਰੀ ਦਾ ਮੂੰਹ ਮੋੜ ਦਿਤਾ *sāḍe topkhāne ne ajehī sūr bīrtā dikhāī jo wairī dā mūṅh moṛ dittā.*

37. We could not help. — ਸਾਡੀ ਕੁਝ ਵਾਹ ਨਾ ਚਲੀ। *sāḍī kujh wāh nā chalī.*

38. To make a night attack. — ਛਾਪਾ ਮਾਰਨਾ। *chhāpā mārṇā.*

39. He was severely but not dangerously wounded. — ਘਾ ਤਾਂ ਓਹਦੇ ਕਾਰੀ ਲਗਿਆ ਪਰ ਮਰਨ ਦਾ ਧੋਖਾ ਨਾਸੀ। *ghā tāṅ ohde kārī lagiā par marṇ dā dhokhā nā sī.*

40. It does not matter. — ਕੁਝ ਚਿੰਤਾ ਨਹੀਂ। *kujh chintā nahīṅ.*

41. Restore order. — ਤਹਿਤ ਬਠਾਓਨਾ। *tahat baṭhāonā.*

42. To give no answer. — ਚੁਪ ਵਟਨਾ। *chup waṭnā.*

43. To enjoy (happily). — ਮੌਜਾਂ ਉਡਾਉਨਾ। *maujāṅ uḍāoṇā.*

44. Round-about. — ਦੁਵਾਲੇ। *duwāle.*

45. A rumour. — ਉਡਦੀ ਖਬਰ। *uḍḍī khabar.*

46. Through and through. — ਵਾਰ ਪਾਰ। *wār pār.*

47. For God's sake. — ਰਬ ਦੇ ਵਾਸਤੇ। *rub de wāste.*

48. This is beyond our power. — ਏਹ ਸਾਡੇ ਬਲ ਤੇ ਬਾਹਰਹੈ। *eh sāḍe bal te bāhar hai.*

49. In the evening. — ਸੰਧਿਆ ਵੇਲੇ। *sandhiā wele.*

50. With the first light of morning. ਦਿਨ ਚੜ੍ਹਦਿਆਂ ਹੀ । *din charhdiān hī*

51. Early in the morning. ਸਵੇਰੇ । *sawere.* ਤੜਕੇ *tarke.*

52. At two o'clock. ਦੋ ਵਜੇ । *do wajje*

53. In the afternoon. ਤੀਜੇ ਪਹਿਰ (ਲੌਡੇ ਵੇਲੇ) *tīje pahir (laudewele).*

54. In the evening. ਤਕਾਲਾਂ (ਸੰਧਿਆਂ) ਵੇਲੇ। *takālān (sandhiān) wele.*

55. Just before day break. ਦਿਨ ਚੜ੍ਹਨ ਤੋਂ ਰਤਾਕੁ ਅੱਗੇ । *din charahn ton ratāku agge.*

56. As the sun was setting. ਜਦ ਸੂਰਜ ਡੁਬਨ ਲਗਾ । *jad sūraj dubān laggā.*

57. About noon. ਦੁਪਹਿਰੇ(ਦੁਪਹਿਰਕੁਵੇਲੇ) *dupahre (dupaharku wele).*

58. Saw the camp in a state of confusion. ਸੈਨਾ ਦੀ ਹਾਲਤ ਉਲਟ ਪਲਟ (ਵਿਗੜੀ ਹੋਈ) ਵੇਖੀ । *sainā dī hālat ulaṭ pulaṭ (wigarī hoī) wekhī.*

59. He was one of the confederates. ਉਹ ਵੀ ਇਕ ਸਾਂਝੀਆਂ ਵਿਚੋਂ ਸੀ । *oh wī ikk sānjhīān wichchon sī.*

60. Whose name I have forgotten now. ਜਿਸਦਾ ਨਾਓਂ ਹੁਨ ਮੇਰੇ ਚੇਤੇ ਨਹੀਂ । *jis dā nāon hun mere chete nahīn.*

61, Some of the enemy's troops ਵੈਰੀ ਦੀਆਂ ਫੌਜਾਂ ਵਿਚੋਂ ਕੁਝ। *wairī dīān faujān wichhon kujh.*

62. One of the two. ਦੋਹਾਂ ਵਿਚੋਂ ਇੱਕ । *dohān wichchon ikk*

63. One of them. ਉਨ੍ਹਾਂ ਵਿਚੋਂ ਇੱਕ । *unahān wichchon ikk.*

64. As night began to fall. ਜਦ ਰਾਤ ਪੈਨ ਲਗੀ । *jad rāt pain laggī.*

65. To remain in prison. ਕੈਦ ਕਟਨਾ । *kaid kaṭnā.*

66. He has received no injury. ਉਸਨੂੰ ਕੋਈ ਜ਼ਰਬ ਨਹੀਂ ਆਈ। *usnūn koī jarb nahīn āī.*

67.	After a short time.	ਰਤਾਕੁ ਪਿਛੇ। *ratāku pichhe.*
68.	As much as you can.	ਜਿਨਾਂ ਤੈਥੋਂ ਹੋਸਕੇ *jiṇāṅ taithoṅ ho sakke.*
69	This year.	ਐਤਕੀਂ। *aitakīṅ.*
70.	God knows what would happen.	ਕੀ ਜਾਨੀਏ ਕੀ ਹੋਵੇ। *kī jānīe kī howe.*
71.	To look after the house.	ਘਰ ਦੀ ਤਕੜਾਈ ਰਖਨਾ। *ghar dī takṛāī rakhnā.*
72.	The crops are the height of a man	ਖੇਤੀਆਂ ਮਰਦ ਮਰਦ ਖਲੋਤੀਆਂ ਹਨ। *khetīāṅ marad marad khalotīāṅ han.*
73.	According to one's means.	ਜਿਨੀਕੁ ਪਹੁੰਚ ਹੋਵੇ। *jinīku pahuṅch howe.*
74.	To serve with great distinction.	ਵੱਡੀ ਪਤ ਨਾਲ ਨੌਕਰੀ ਕਰਨਾ। *waḍḍī pat nāl naukrī karṇā.*
75.	To turn out of the caste !	ਛੇਕ ਦੇਨਾ। *chhek denā.*
76.	Down the stream.	ਲਹਿੰਦੀ ਤੁਲ (ਵਲ) *laiṅhdī tul (wal).*
77.	Up the stream.	ਚੜ੍ਹਦੀ ਤੁਲ (ਵਲ) *chaṛhdī tul (wal).*
78.	Not long ago.	ਥੋੜਾ ਚਿਰ ਹੋਇਆ ਹੈ। *thoṛā chir hoiā hai.*
79	Took council with Karam Singh.	ਕਰਮ ਸਿੰਘ ਨੂੰ ਮਿਲਕੇ ਸਲਾਹ ਕੀਤੀ। *karam singh nūṇ mil ke salāh kītī.*
80.	What plan shall we adopt.	ਕੀ ਡੌਲ ਕਰਨੀ ਚਾਹੀਦੀ ਹੈ। *kī ḍaul karnī chāhīdī hai.*
81.	To oppose the enemy.	ਵੈਰੀ ਦਾ ਸਾਹਮਨਾ ਕਰਨ ਲਈ। *wairī dā sāhmnā karn laī.*
82.	With the assistance of that army	ਉਸੇ ਫੌਜ ਦੀ ਕੁਮਕ ਨਾਲ। *use fauj dī kumak nāl.*
83.	Took possession of the fort.	ਕਿਲੇ ਵਿੱਚ ਦਬਾਓ ਕਰ ਲਿਆ। *kile wichch dabāo kar liā.*
84.	He sent aword.	ਓਸਨੇ ਕਹਾ ਭੇਜਿਆ। *usne kahā bhejiā.*

85. The force has gone and joined Bhagwan Singh. ਸੈਨਾ ਭਗਵਾਨ ਸਿੰਘ ਦੇ ਨਾਲ ਜਾ ਰਲੀ ਹੈ । *sainān Bhagwān Singh de nāl jā ralī hai.*

86. To defeat the enemy is difficult. ਵੈਰੀ ਦਾ ਜਿੱਤਨਾ ਕਠਨ ਹੈ । *wairī dā jitnā kathaṇ hai.*

87. Contrary to his expectation. ਉਸ ਦੇ ਭਰੋਸੇ ਤੇ ਉਲਟਾ । *usde bharose te ulaṭā.*

88. He came and attacked the fort. ਕਿਲ੍ਹਾ ਮਾਰਨ ਆਨ ਪਿਆ । *kilā māraṇ ān piā.*

89. Do not allow Ram Singh to take possession of the fort. ਰਾਮ ਸਿੰਘ ਨੂੰ ਕਿਲ੍ਹੇ ਵਿਚ ਦਬਾਉ ਨਾ ਕਰਨ ਦੇਨਾ । *Rām Singh nūṅ kile wich dabāo nā karan denā*

90. Having come by way of the Delhi Gate. ਦਿਲੀ ਦਰਵਾਜ਼ੇ ਦੇ ਰਸਤੇ ਹੋਕੇ । *dilli darwāje de raste hoke.*

91. He entered into the city. ਸ਼ਹਿਰ ਦੇ ਅੰਦਰ ਆਨ ਵੜਿਆ । *shahar de andar ān waṛiā.*

92. The army made straight for the fort. ਫੌਜ ਕਿਲੇ ਵਲ ਸਿਧੀ ਹੋ ਪਈ । *fauj kile wal sidhhī ho paī.*

93. Having suffered many hardships. ਕਈ ਤਰਾਂ ਦੇ ਦੁਖ ਉਠਾਕੇ । *kaī tarāṅ de dukh uṭhāke.*

94. A panic arose in the fort. ਕਿਲ੍ਹੇ ਵਿਚ ਥਰਥਲਾ ਮਚ ਗਿਆ । *kile wich tharthalā mach giā.*

95. The guns ceased to fire. ਗੋਲੇ ਚਲਣੋਂ ਹਟ ਗਏ । *gole chalṇoṅ haṭ gae.*

96. The noise which had been. ਜੋ ਰੌਲਾ ਪੈ ਗਿਆ ਸਾ । *jo raulā pai giā sā.*

97. With the force of their blows ਉਨ੍ਹਾਂ ਦੀ ਸੱਟ ਨਾਲ । *unhāṅ dī saṭṭ nāl.*

98. The gate was knocked down. ਦਰਵਾਜ਼ਾ ਢੈ ਪਿਆ । *darwājā ḍhai piā.*

99. Came and made a charge. ਹਲਾ ਕਰਕੇ ਆਨ ਪਿਆ । *hallā karke ān piā.*

100. Several guns were destroyed. — ਕਈ ਤੋਪਾਂ ਵਰਾਨ ਹੋਗਈਆਂ । *kaī topāṅ warāṇ ho gaīāṅ.*

101. Turned them out of the fort. — ਉਨ੍ਹਾਂ ਨੂੰ ਕਿਲੇ ਵਿਚੋਂ ਕਢ ਦਿਤਾ *unhāṅ nūṅ kile wichoṅ kaḍh dittā.*

102. The volley of the artillery men. — ਗੋਲਮਦਾਜ਼ਾਂ ਦੀਆਂ ਸ਼ਲਕਾਂ । *golamdājāṅ dīāṅ shalkāṅ.*

103. Caused them to retire. — ਓਨਾਂ ਦਾ ਮੂੰਹ ਫੇਰ ਦਿਤਾ । *uṇhāṅ dā mūṅh pher dittā*

104. The walls were thrown down. — ਕੰਧਾਂ ਢਹਾ ਸੁਟੀਆਂ । *kaṅdhāṅ dhahā suṭīāṅ*

105. Having created a disturbance in the fort. — ਕਿਲੇ ਵਿਚ ਰੌਲਾ ਮਚਾ ਕੇ । *kile wich raulā machāke.*

106. Not to advance a step. — ਇਕ ਪੈਰ ਵੀ ਅਗੇ ਨਹੀਂ ਪਟਨਾ । *ikk pair wī agge nahīṅ piṭnā.*

107. At random. — ਅਟਕਲ ਪਚੂ । *aṭkal pachū.*

108. We became pale. — ਸਾਡੇ ਮੂੰਹ ਪੀਲੇ ਫਟਕ ਹੋ ਗਏ । *sāḍe mūṅh pīle phaṭak hogae.*

109. Have you got any money. — ਤੇਰੇ ਕੋਲ ਕੁਝ ਰੁਪੈ ਹਨ । *tere kol kujh rupai haṇ.*

110. To fall on the face. — ਮੂੰਹ ਦੇ ਭਾਰ ਡਿਗਣਾ । *mūṅh de bhār ḍignā.*

111. I whispered to him. — ਮੈਂ ਉਸਦੇ ਕੰਨ ਵਿੱਚ ਆਖਿਆ । *main us de kaṇṇ wichch ākhiā.*

112. To be ready to cry. — ਅਖਾਂ ਭਰਨਾ । *akhāṅ bharṇā.*

PROVERBS.

1. Friends are plenty when the purse is full. ਬਣੀ ਭਣੀ ਦਾ ਸਭ ਕੋਈ ਸਾਥੀ *banī tanī dā sabh koī sāthī.*

2. What a pack of fools is here. ਇਥੇ ਮੂਰਖਾਂ ਦੀ ਕਿੱਨੀ ਭੀੜ ਹੈ *ithe mūrakhāṅ dī kinnī bhīṛ hai.*

3. To make game of. ਠੱਠੇ ਵਿਚ ਉਡਾਉਣਾ *ṭhaṭhe wichoh udāonā.*

4. A friend in need is a friend indeed. ਯਾਰ ਓਹ ਜੇਹੜਾ ਲੋੜਦੇ ਵੇਲੇ ਕੰਮ ਆਵੇ *yār oh jehṛā loṛ de wele kaṅm āwe.*

5. I abandoned all hope of recovery. ਮੈਂ ਜ਼ਿੰਦਗੀ ਤੋਂ ਹਥ ਧੋ ਬੈਠਾ ਹਾਂ *main jindgī toṅ hath dho baiṭhā hān.*

6. Adversity flatters no man. ਬਿਪਤਾ ਦਾ ਕੋਈ ਸਾਥੀ ਨਹੀਂ *biptā dā koī sāthī nahīṅ.*

7. Fall not out with a friend for a trifle. ਪੰਜੀਂ ਮਿਤ ਪੰਜਾਹੀਂ ਠਾਕੁਰ *paṅjīṅ mit paṅjāhīṅ ṭhākur.*

8. If you wish for good advice consult an old man. ਹਛੀ ਮਤ ਚਾਹੋ ਤਾਂ ਬੁਢੇ ਨੂੰ ਪੁਛਨ ਜਾਓ *hachhī mat chāho tāṅ budhe nūṅ puchhaṇ jāo.*

9. Two of a trade never agree. ਇਕ ਮਿਆਨ ਵਿਚ ਦੋ ਤਲਵਾਰਾਂ ਨਹੀਂ ਸਮਾਉਂਦੀਆਂ *ikk miāṇ wich do talwārāṅ nahīṅ samāoṅdīāṅ.*

10. Charity begins at home. ਪਹਲੇ ਆਪਨਾ ਫੇਰ ਪਰਾਯਾਂ *pahle āpnā pher parāiā.*

11. We shall be all alike in our grave. ਕਬਰ ਵਿਚ ਸਭ ਇਕੋ ਜਿਹੇ *kabar wich sabh ikko jihe.*

12. To kill two birds with one stone. ਇਕ ਕੰਮ ਦੋ ਕਾਜ *ikk kaṅm do kāj.*

13. No living man all things can. ਦੁਨੀਆਂ ਦੇ ਕੰਮ ਕਦੀ ਪੂਰੇ ਨਹੀਂ ਹੁੰਦੇ *duniāṅ de kaṅm kadī pūre nahīn huṅde.*

14. All is well that ends well. ਅੰਤ ਭਲਾ ਸੋ ਭਲਾ *aṅt bhalā so bhalā.*

15. Discover not a secret to another. ਅਪਨਾ ਭੇਦ ਕਿਸੇ ਨੂੰ ਨਾ ਦੱਸੋ *apnā bhed kise nūṅ nāṅ dasso.*

16. Grief is the canker of the breast. ਸੋਗ ਦਿਲ ਦਾ ਰੋਗ । *sog dil dā rog.*

17. Man is a bundle of habits. ਆਦਮੀ ਆਦਤਾਂ ਦਾ ਪੁਤਲਾ ਹੈ । *ādmī ādtāṅ dā putlā hai.*

18. How long will he halt between the opinions. ਦੁਬਧਾ ਵਿਚ ਕਦ ਤਕ ਝੂਲੋਗੇ । *dubdhā wich kad tak jhūlo ge.*

19. Hold no grudge against another. ਇੱਕ ਦੂਜੇ ਨਾਲ ਈਰਖਾ ਨਾ ਰਖੋ । *ikk dūje nāl īrkkā nā rakho.*

20. Handsome is that handsome does. ਕੰਮ ਪਿਆਰਾ ਹੈ ਚੰਮ ਪਿਆਰਾ ਨਹੀਂ । *kaṅm piārā hai chanm piārā nahīṅ.*

21. No evil happens to the just. ਸਚ ਨੂੰ ਆਂਚ ਨਹੀਂ । *sach nūṅ āṅch nahīṅ.*

22. Health is above wealth. ਅਰੋਗਤਾ ਧਨ ਨਾਲੋਂ ਵਧੀਕ ਹੈ । *arogtā dhan nāloṅ wadhīk hai.*

23 God helps those who help themselves. ਉਦਮ ਅਗੇ ਲਛਮੀ ।*udam agge luchhmīṅ*

24. Thou didst hide thy face and I was troubled. ਸਾਂਈ ਅਖੀਂ ਫੇਰੀਆਂ ਵੈਰੀ ਜਗ ਜਹਾਨ । *sāīṅ akhīṅ pherīān wairī jag jahān.*

25. Honor thy father and thy mother. ਅਪਨੇ ਮਾਂ ਪਿਓ ਦਾ ਆਦਰ ਕਰੋ । *āpṇe māṅ pio dā ādar karo.*

26. A friend should bear with a friend's infirmities. ਮਿਤਰਾਂ ਦੇ ਔਗੁਨ ਨਹੀਂ ਚਤਾਰੇ ਜਾਂਦੇ। *mitrāṇ de augāṅ nahīṅ chitāre jāṅde.*

27 Hours of pleasure are short. ਖੁਸ਼ੀ ਦੀਆਂ ਘੜੀਆਂ ਛੋਟੀਆਂ ਹੁੰਦੀਆਂ ਹਨ । *khushī diāṅ ghaṛīān chhoṭīāṅ hundīāṅ haṇ.*

28. He that has many irons in the fire will find some of them cool.
ਕੰਮ ਕਰਨ ਵਾਲੇ ਪਾਸੋਂ ਭੁੱਲ ਹੋਵੇਗੀ । *kanm karaṅ wāle pāson bhul howegī.*

29. Good jack makes good jill. ਜਿਹਾ ਗਭਰੂ ਤਿਹੀ ਵਹੁਟੀ । *jihā gabhrū tih wahuṭī.*

30. No joy without money. ਧਨ ਬਿਨਾ ਮੰਗਲ ਕਿਥੇ। *dhan bināṅ maṅgal kithe.*

31. All covet all loss. ਅਧੀ ਛੱਡ ਸਾਰੀ ਨੂੰ ਧਾਇ ਐਸਾ ਡੁੱਬੇ ਥਾਹ ਨ ਪਾਇ *adhi chhaḍ sārī nūṅ dhāe aisā ḍube thāh nā pāe.*

32. He that is angry is seldom at ease. ਕ੍ਰੋਧੀ ਨੂੰ ਚੈਨ ਕਿਥੇ *karodhī nūṅ chain kithhe*

33. Alms giving never makes any man poor. ਦਾਨ ਦੀਏ ਧਨ ਨਾ ਘਟੇ *dān die dhan nā ghaṭe.*

34. Let another praise thee and not thy own mouth. ਆਪਨੇ ਮੂਹੋਂ ਮੀਯਾਂ ਮਿਠੂ ਨਾ ਬਨੋ
Dont blow your own trumpet. *āpne mūṅhoṅ mīāṅ mithū nāṅ bano.*

35. Blows will answer blows. ਮੋਰੀ ਵਿੱਚ ਇੱਟ ਮਾਰੇ ਛਿਟਾਂ ਪੈਂਦੀਆਂ ਹਨ *more wichch iṭṭ māre chhiṭān paiṅdīāṅ haṇ.*

36. He who sows reaps. ਜੋਤੇ ਹਲ ਤਾਂ ਪਾਵੇ ਫਲ *jote hal tāṅ pāwe phal.*

37. As the country só the garb. ਜੈਸਾ ਦੇਸ ਵੈਸਾ ਭੇਸ *jaisā des waisā bhes.*

38. Tit for tat. ਜੈਸੇ ਕੋ ਤੈਸਾ *jaise ko taisā.*

39. Know the bone which has fallen to thy lot. ਭਾਗਾਂ ਵਿੱਚ ਜੋ ਲਿਖਿਆ ਹੈ ਸੋ ਭੋਗਨਾ ਪਵੇਗਾ *bhāgāṅ wichch jo likhiā hai so bhognā pawegā.*

40. Good swimmers are often drowned. ਅਕਸਰ ਤਾਰੂ ਹੀ ਡੁਬਦਾ ਹੈ *aksar tārū hī ḍubdā hai.*

41. Mocking is catching. ਮੂੰਹ ਝਗਾਉਂਨ ਨਾਲ ਮੂੰਹ ਵਿੰਗਾ ਹੋ ਜਾਂਦਾ ਹੈ। *mūṅh jhagāon ṇāl mūṅh wingā ho jāṅdā hai.*

42. What is more miserable than discontent. ਹੌਕੇ ਨਾਲੋਂ ਬੁਰਾ ਕੀ ਹੈ *hauke nāloṅ burā kī hai.*

43. A good name is better than precious ointment. ਅਮੀਰੀ ਨਾਲੋਂ ਸੋਭਾ ਚੰਗੀ ਹੈ *amīrī nāloṅ sobhā changī hai.*

44. Use good means and God will bless the end. ਹਥ ਪੈਰ ਹਲਾਓ ਰਬ ਬਰਕਤ ਦੇਵੇਗਾ *hath pair halāo rab barkat dewegā.*

45. As some times even poisons turn medical· ਕਦੀ ਜਹਿਰ ਵੀ ਦੁਆ ਹੋਕੇ ਲਗਦੀ ਹੈ
One mans meat is another man poison. *kadī jaihar wī duā ho ke lagdī hai.*

46. Grey hairs are death blossoms. ਚਿਟੇ ਵਾਲ ਮੌਤ ਦਾ ਸਨੇਹਾ *chiṭṭe wāl maut dā sanehā.*

47. A pebble and a diamond are alike to the blind. ਅੰਨ੍ਹੇ ਨੂੰ ਹੀਰਾ ਤੇ ਕੰਕਰ ਇਕੋ ਜੇਹਾ ਹੈ *annhe nūṅ hīrā te kaṅkar ikko jehā hai.*

48. Pleasant blowes fly fast. ਖੁਸ਼ੀ ਦੇ ਦਿਹਾੜੇ ਛੇਤੀ ਬੀਤ ਜਾਂਦੇ ਹਨ *khushī de dihāṛe chhetī bīt jāṅde haṇ.*

49. Policy goes beyond strength. ਜੋਰ ਓਹ ਕੰਮ ਨਹੀਂ ਦੇਂਦਾ ਜੋ ਤਤਬੀਰ ਦੇਂਦੀ ਹੈ *jor oh kaṅm nahīṅ dendā jo tatbīr deṅdī hai.*

50. Great designs require great brains. ਵਡਿਆਂ ਕੰਮਾਂ ਨੂੰ ਵਡੀ ਅਕਲ ਲੋੜੀਦੀ ਹੈ । *wadiāṅ kaṅmāṅ nūṅ waddī akal loṛīdī hai*

51. Practice what you preach. ਜੋ ਨਸੀਹਤ ਕਰੋ ਉਸ ਉਤੇ ਆਪ ਅਮਲ ਕਰੋ *jo nasīhat karo us utte āp amal karo.*

52. Might is right. ਜੋਰਾਵਰ ਦੀ ਜੁਤੀ ਸਿਰ ਤੇ *jorāwar dī juttī sir te.*

53. Love laughs at locksmiths. ਪ੍ਰੇਮ ਸਭ ਜੰਦਰੇ ਤੋੜ ਸੁਟਦਾ ਹੈ *parem sabh jaṅdre toṛ suṭdā hai.*

54. Many a mickle makes a muckle. ਫੂਈ ਫੂਈ ਕਰਕੇ ਤਲਾ ਭਰਦਾ ਹੈ *phūī phūī karke talā bhardā hai.*

55. Poverty breeds strife. When poverty comes in at the door love flies out at the window. ਗਰੀਬੀ ਦੰਗੇ ਦੀ ਜੜ ਹੈ *garībi daṅge dī jaṛ hai.*

56. Money begets money. ਪੈਸੇ ਨੂੰ ਪੈਸਾ ਕਮਾਂਦਾ ਹੈ *paise nūṅ paisā kamāṅdā hai.*

57. Kick not against the pricks.
Puff not against the wind. ਉਤਾਂ ਥੁਕਿਆਂ ਅਪਣੇ ਮੂੰਹ ਤੇ ਪੈਂਦਾ ਹੈ । *utāṅ thukiāṅ āpṇe mūṅh te paiṅdā hai.*

58. There is something black in the pulse. ਦਾਲ ਵਿੱਚ ਕੁਝ ਕਾਲਾ ਹੈ । *dāl wichch kujh kālā hai.*

59. Might over comes right. ਜਿਸਦੀ ਤੇਗ ਉਸਦੀ ਦੇਗ *jis dī teg us dī deg.*

60. A little leaven leavens the whole lump. ਇਕ ਮਛੀ ਸਾਰੇ ਪਾਣੀ ਨੂੰ ਗੰਧਲਾ ਕਰ ਦੇਂਦੀ ਹੈ *ikk machhī sāre pāṇī nūṅ gaṅdhlā kar deṅdī hai.*

PART VI.

PUNJABI CHITS.

No. 1.

(5) (1)੧ੳ (2)ਸਤਿ(3)ਗੁਰ(4)ਪ੍ਰਸਾਦਿ

(6)ਲਿਖਤਮ ਕਰਮਸਿੰਘ(7)ਜੋਗ ਭਾਈਪਰਮਸਿੰਘ (8)ਸ੍ਰੀ ਵਾਹਿਗੁਰੂਜੀਕੀ ਫਤੇ(9)ਵਾਚਣੀ

(10)ਹੋਰ (11)ਭਾਈਜੀ ਬਹੁਤਦਿਨਹੋਏਹਨ ਤੁਸਾਂਨੀ ਕਦੀਕੋਈ ਚਿਠੀਨਹੀਂ ਆਈ ਮਲੂਮ

ਨਹੀਂ ਇਸਦਾਕੀ(12)ਕਾਰਣਹੈ (13)ਭਾਭੁਤਾ ਮਾਲਦਾਲਿਖਣਾਏਥੇਇਸਵੇਲੇਇਹਭਾਅਹੈ

(14)ਕਣਕ ੧੫ ਸੇਰ (15)ਛੋਲੇ ੨੧ ਸੇਰ (16)ਜੌਂ ੨੭ ਸੇਰ (17)ਸਰੋਂ ੧੦ ਸੇਰ (18)ਕਪਾਹ ੩ ਸੇਰ॥

ਹੋਰਜੋ ਕੰਮ ਟਹਲ ਸਾਡੇਲੈਕ ਹੋਵੇ ਲਿਖਣਾ॥

ਮਿਤੀ ਲਿਖੀ ਕੱਤਕ ਵੀ ੧੯ (19)ਦਸਖਤ ਕਰਮਸਿੰਘ ਲਾਹੌਰ ਵਿਚੋਂ

1 ੧ੳ ਇਕ ਓਅੰਕਾਰ there is one God. 2 ਸਤਿ true. 3 ਗੁਰ spiritual guide. 4 ਪ੍ਰਸਾਦਿ by the faveour of. 5 ੧ ਓ ਸਤਿਗੁਰ ਪ੍ਰਸਾਦਿ there is one God (you can see him) by the favour of true spiritual guide. 6 ਲਿਖਤਮ written by. 7 ਜੋਗ to. 8 ਸ੍ਰੀ ਵਾਹਿਗੁਰੂ ਜੀ ਕੀ ਫਤੇ (victory of *Divine* God that is a Sikh complement 9 ਵਾਚਣੀ read. 10 ਹੋਰ further. 11 ਭਾਈ ਜੀ lit the (brother) comm on term applied to every Sikh. 12 ਕਾਰਨ reason 13 ਭਾ current price. 14 ਕਨਕ wheat. 15 ਛੋਲੇ gram 16 ਜੌਂ barley. 17 ਸਰੋਂ oil seed. 18 ਕਪਾਹ cotton. 19 ਦਸਖਤ signed.

---

* In Punjábi language some words are generally spoken in the following manner as ਪਾਣੀ ਧਾਂਣੀ water. ਰੋਟੀ ਊਟੀ bread. ਲਗਾਮ ਊਮ bridle. ਆਟਾ ਕੋਟਾ flour. ਭਾ ਭੁਤਾ current rate where the latter part has no meaning it is only added for intensifying.

* All proper names will be under lined.

No. 2.

(1) ੧ਓ ਸਤਿਗੁਰ ਪ੍ਰਸਾਦਿ

(1) ਲਿਖਤੰਮ ਗੰਡਾਸਿੰਘ ਜੋਗ ਭਾਈ ਸੋਣਾਸਿੰਘ ਸ੍ਰੀ ਵਾਹਿਗੁਰੂ ਜੀ ਕੀ ਫਤੇ ਬੁਲਾਈ
ਵਾਰਣੀ। ਹੋਰ ਮਾਈ ਨੂੰ ਮੇਰਾ (2) ਮਥਾ ਟੇਕਣਾ ਜੀ। (3) ਇਥੇ ਸੁਖ ਅਨੰਦ ਹੈ ਤੁਹਾ
ਡੀ ਸੁਖ ਸ੍ਰੀ (4) ਗੁਰੂ ਰਾਮਦਾਸ ਪਾਸੋਂ ਮੰਗਦੇ ਹਾਂ। ਚਿਠੀ ਤੁਹਾਡੀ ਪਹੁੰਚੀ (5) ਹਵਾ
ਲ ਮਲੂਮ ਕੀਤਾ। ਹੋਰ ਜੀ ਤੁਸਾਂ ਜੋ ਲਿਖਿਆ ਹੈ ਕਿ ਚਾਰ (6) ਪਸੂ ਮਰ ਗਏ ਹਨ
ਸੋ ਭਾਈ ਜੀ ਏਹ ਤਾਂ ਪਰਮੇਸੁਰ ਦੀ (7) ਮਰਜੀ ਹੈ ਜੋ ਰਾਹੇ ਸੋ ਕਰੇ। ਜਦ (8) ਮਾੜੇ ਦਿਨ
ਆਉਂਦੇ ਹਨ ਤਾਂ ਏਸੇ ਤਰਾਂ ਹੁੰਦਾ ਹੈ। ਸਾਨੂੰ ਸੁਣਕੇ ਬੜਾ (9) ਹਮਸੋਸ ਲਗਾ ਹੈ।
ਹੱਛਾ ਜੇ ਕਰਤਾਰ ਦਾ (10) ਭਾਣਾ। ਹੋਰ ਜੀ ਤੁਹਾਡੀ ਵਲ ਮੀਂਹ ਪਾਣੀ ਪਿਆ ਹੈ ਕਿ
ਨਹੀਂ। (11) ਖੇਤੀ ਪਤੀ ਦਾ ਕੀ ਹਾਲ ਹੈ। ਹੋਰ ਜੀ ਮੈਂ ਲਹਿਣਾ ਸਿੰਘ ਦੇ ਹਥ ੮ ਰੁਪ
ਯੇ ਭੇਜੇ ਹਨ ਮੈਨੂੰ ਕੁਝ ਕਪੜਾ ਤੇ ਇਕ ਪਗ ਮਲ ਦੇਣੀ ਜੀ।

ਚਿਠੀ ਲਿਖੀ ਮਾਘ ਵਦੀ ੧੩

ਦਸਖਤ ਗੰਡਾਸਿੰਘ

ਲਿਖਤਮ see letter No. 1. 2 ਮਥਾ ਟੇਕਣਾ to bow down forehead (used for respect). 3 ਇਥੇ ਸੁਖ ਅਨੰਦ ਹੈ here all is well. 4 ਗੁਰੂ ਰਾਮਦਾਸ name of fourth Guru. 5 ਹਵਾਲ circumstance 6 ਪਸੂ cattle, (beast.) 7 ਮਰਜੀ (f) will. 8 ਮਾੜਾ (ਭੈੜਾ) bad. 9 ਹਮਸੋਸ sorrow. 10 ਭਾਣਾ only used for will of God. 11 ਖੇਤੀ (f) Cultivation here ਪੱਤੀ has no meaning but they generally use ਖੇਤੀ ਪੱਤੀ vide note on page 1.

No. 3.

੧ੴ ਸਤਿਗੁਰ ਪ੍ਰਸਾਦਿ॥

ਲਿਖਤਮ ਗੁਪਾਲ ਸਿੰਘ ਜੋਗ ਬਾਪੂ[1] ਹੋਰਾਂ[2] ਸ੍ਰੀ ਵਾਹਿਗੁਰੂ ਜੀ ਕੀ ਫਤੇ ਵਾਰਣੀ ਹੋਰ ਭਾਈ[1]
ਆਜੀ ਮੈਂ ਰਾਜ਼ੀ ਬਾਜ਼ੀ ਹਾਂ ਤੁਹਾਡੀ ਸੁਖ ਸਦਾ ਗੁਰਾਂ[3] ਜੀ ਕੋਲੋਂ ਮੰਗਦਾ ਹਾਂ। ਤੁਸਾਂ ਮੈਨੂੰ ਆ-
ਗਿਆ[4] ਦਿਤੀ ਸੀ ਜੋ ਚਾਚੇ[5] ਹੋਰੀ[2] ਤੈਨੂੰ ਸਦ ਦੇਣਗੇ ਅਰਥਾਤ ਤੈਨੂੰ ਖੇਤੀ ਪਤੀ ਦਾ ਕੰਮ ਵੀ ਸਿਖਾ
ਉਣਗੇ ਤੇ ਨਾਲੇ ਆਪਣੇ ਪਾਸ ਰਖਣਗੇ ਸੋ ਪਿਤਾ[1] ਜੀ ਤੁਹਾਡੀ ਆਗਿਆ ਅਨੁਸਾਰ ਮੈਂ
ਚਾਚੇ ਹੋਰਾਂ ਕੋਲ ਗਿਆ। — ਉਨਾਂ ਜਾਂਦਿਆਂ[6] ਹੀ ਦੋ ਪੈਲੀਆਂ ਮੇਰੇ ਸਪੁਰਦ ਕਰ ਦਿਤੀਆਂ
ਅਤੇ ਆਖਣ ਲਗੇ ਬੀਬਾ ਪੈਹਲਾਂ ਏਹ ਦੋ ਪੈਲੀਆਂ ਵਾਹ[7] ਲੈ ਫੇਰ ਹੋਰ ਕੰਮ ਦਸਾਂਗੇ ਸੋ
ਭਾਈ ਆਜੀ ਮੈਂ ਏਦਾਂ ਹੀ ਕੀਤਾ ਹੈ। ਜਦ ਮੈਂ ਪੈਲੀ ਨੂੰ ਵਾਹੁਣ ਦੇ ਲਈ ਜਾਂਦਾ ਹੁੰਦਾ ਸੀ ਤਾਂ
ਇਕ ਦੋ ਦਿਨ ਮੈਨੂੰ ਕਹਿੰਦੇ ਰਹੇ ਬੀਬਾ ਟੁੱਕ[8] ਖਾ ਕੇ ਤੇ ਲੱਸੀ[9] ਦਾ ਛੰਨਾ[10] ਪੀ ਕੇ ਜਾਯਾ ਕਰ।
ਕਿਉਂ ਜੋ ਧੁਪ ਬੜੀ ਪੈਂਦੀ ਹੈ। ਪਰ ਜਾਂ ਪੰਜ ਸਤ ਦਿਨ ਬੀਤ ਗਏ ਤਾਂ ਨਾ ਕਿਨੇ ਮੈਨੂੰ ਟੁਕ[11]
ਟਕ ਦਾ ਹੀ ਪੁਛਿਆ ਤੇ ਨਾਂ ਲੱਸੀ ਲੁੱਸੀ[12] ਹੀ ਪਿਲਾਈ ਤੇ ਹੁਣ ਜਦ ਮੈਂ ਪੈਲੀ ਤੋਂ ਆਉਂਦਾ ਹਾਂ
ਤਾਂ ਬਗੀ[13] ਰੋਟੀ ਮੈਨੂੰ ਦੇਛਣ ਦੇਂਹਨਾ। ਸੋ ਭਾਈ ਆਜੀ ਮੈਂ ਔਖਾ ਹਾਂ ਮੈਨੂੰ ਆਪਣੇ ਕੋਲ
ਸਦਵਾ ਲਓ।

ਲਿਖੀ ਛਨਿਛਰਵਾਰ ਮਿਤੀ[14] ਪੋਹ ਦਿਨ ੧੩

1 ਬਾਪੂ ਪਿਤਾ, ਭਾਈਆ fathek 2 ਹੋਰਾਂ, ਹੋਰੀ is a term of respect as ਚਾਚੇ ਹੋਰਾਂ ਮੈਨੂੰ ਆਖਿਆ Respective uncle told me, the first one is used with the oblique case and the 2nd with the nominative. 3 ਗੁਰਾਂ is the agent case of ਗੁਰੂ spiritual guide. 4 ਆਗਯਾ permission, order. 5 ਚਾਚੇ inflected form of ਚਾਚਾ uncle. 6 ਜਾਂਦਿਆਂ ਹੀ at the instant of arrival. 7 ਵਾਹ ਲੈ finish ploughing. 8 ਟੁਕ peice of bread 9 ਲਸੀ butter milk. 10 ਛੰਨਾ metal cup.

ਟੁਕ ਟਕ peice of bread 11 and ਲਸੀ ਲੁੱਸੀ butter milk 12 double words as in chit No. 1 and 2. 13 ਬਗੀ stale 14 ਮਿਤੀ dated.

No. 4.

ੴ ਸਤਿਗੁਰ ਪ੍ਰਸਾਦਿ॥

ਲਿਖਤਮ ਕੇਸਰਾਸਿੰਘ ਜੋਗ ਭਾਈ ਨਰਿੰਦਰਸਿੰਘ ਵਾਹਿਗੁਰੂ ਜੀ ਕੀ ਫਤੇ ਵਾਚਣੀ। ਹੋਰ ਏਥੇ ਸੁਖ ਹੈ ਤੁਸਾਡੀ ਸੁਖ ਸਦਾ ਕਰਤਾਰ[1] ਜੀ ਪਾਸੋਂ ਮੰਗਦੇ ਹਾਂ ਹੋਰ ਭਾਈ ਜੀ ਅਸੀ ਕੁਇਟੇ ਤੋਂ ਪਰੇ ਇਕ ਜਗਾ ਦੇ ਵਿਚ ਸਰਕਾਰ ਦੇ ਹੁਕਮ ਨਾਲ ਭੇਜੇ ਗਏ ਹਾਂ ਅਤੇ ਓਥੇ ਇਕ ਸੁਰੰਗ[2] ਪੁਟਦੇ[3] ਹਾਂ ਉਸ ਕੰਮ ਦੇ ਕਰਨ ਦੇ ਲਈ[4] ਸਾਨੂੰ ਤਲਬ ਥੋਂ ਬਿਨਾਂ[5] ਰਸਤ ਤੇ ਬਾਰਾਂ ਆਨੇ ਰੋਜ ਸਰਕਾਰੋਂ ਮਿਲਦੇ ਹਨ ਜੇਕਰ[6] ਅਸੀ ਛੀ ਕੁ[7] ਮਹੀਨੇ ਏਥੇ ਕੰਮ ਕਰਦੇ ਰਹੇ ਤਾਂ ਸਾਡੇ ਕੋਲ ਬਥੇਰੇ[8] ਰੁਪੈ ਹੋ ਜਾਣਗੇ ਤਦ ਅਸੀ ਆਪਣਾ ਘਰ ਵੀ ਉਸਾਰਾਂਗੇ[9] ਹੋਰ ਏਥੇ ਸਾਨੂੰ ਕਿਸੇ ਤਰਾਂ ਦਾ ਔਖ[10] ਨਹੀ ਸਭ ਤਰਾਂ ਦਾ ਸੌਖ[11] ਸਰਕਾਰ ਨੇ ਸਾਡੇ ਰਹਿਣ ਦੇ ਲਈ ਬਣਾ ਛਡਿਆ ਹੈ ਹੋਰ ਇਸ ਵੇਲੇ ਕੰਮ ਦੇ ਕਰਕੇ ਘਟ[12] ਵੇਹਲ[13] ਹੈ ਫੇਰ ਕਿਸੇ[14] ਵੇਲੇ[14] ਇਕ ਹੋਰ ਚਿਠੀ ਲਿਖਾਂਗਾ ਜਿਸ ਦੇ ਵਿਚ ਏਥੋਂ ਦਾ ਸਾਰਾ ਹਾਲ ਹੋਵੇਗਾ॥

ਚਿਠੀ ਲਿਖੀ ਐਤਵਾਰ ਮਾਘ ਪਰੀ ੧੫

ਦਸਖਤ ਕੇਸਰਾਸਿੰਘ

1 ਕਰਤਾਰ creator (God). 2 ਸੁਰੰਗ (f) a mine. 3 ਪਟਣਾ to dig. 4 ਲਈ for. 5 ਬਿਨਾਂ besides. 6 ਜੇਕਰ or ਜੇ if. 7 ਛੀਕੁ about six see at the end of numerals. 8 ਬਥੇਰੇ very many, sufficient. 9 ਉਸਾਰਨਾ to build. 10 ਔਖ trouble. 11 ਸੌਖ comfort ease. 12 ਘਟ less. 13 ਵੇਹਲ leisure 14 ਕਿਸੇ ਵੇਲੇ some time.

No. 5.

ੴ ਸਤਿਗੁਰਪ੍ਰਸਾਦਿ।

ਲਿਖਤਮ ਨਥਾ ਸਿੰਘ ਪਾਸੋਂ ਭਗਤ ਸਿੰਘ ਜੋਗ ਸ੍ਰੀ ਵਾਹਿਗੁਰੂ ਜੀ ਕੀ ਫਤੇ
ਵਾਚਣੀ। ਹੋਰ ਏਥੇ ਸਰਬ ਸੁਖ ਹੈ ਤੁਸਾਡੀ ਸੁਖ ਸ੍ਰੀ ਵਾਹਿਗੁਰੂ ਜੀ ਪਾਸੋਂ
ਮੰਗਦੇ ਹਾਂ। ਹੋਰ ਭਾਈ ਜੀ ਤੁਸਾਡਾ ਵਿਆਹ ਸਾਵਣ ਦੀ ਤੀਸਰੀ ਦਾ ਗਿਣਿ
ਆਗਿਆ ਹੈ ਸੋ ਤੁਸਾਨੂੰ ਬਹੁਤ ਛੇਤੀ ਆਵਣਾ ਚਾਹੀਦਾ ਹੈ। ਕਈ ਚੀਜਾਂ
ਬਣਵਾਣੀਆਂ ਹਨ। ਤੁਸਾਂ ਜੋ ੫੦੦) ਪੰਜ ਸੌ ਰੁਪੈ ਦੇ ਹੁੰਡੀ ਭੇਜੀ ਸੀ ਸੋ ਪਹੁੰ
ਚ ਗਈ ਹੈ ੩੫੦) ਸਾਢੇ ਤਿਨ ਸੌ ਰੁਪਈਆ ਹੋਰ ਲਗੇਗਾ। ਹੋ ਸਕੇ ਤਾਂ
ਪਹਿਲਾਂ ਭਿਜਵਾ ਦੇਣਾ ਨਹੀਂ ਤਾਂ ਆਪਣੇ ਨਾਲ (5) ਲਈ ਆਵਣਾ। ਤੁਸਾਡੇ
ਸਾਕ (6) ਚਾਚਾ (7) ਚਾਚੀ (8) ਭੂਆ (9) ਤੇ ਮਾਸੀ (10) ਮਾਮਾ (11) ਮਾਮੀ (12) ਸਭ ਆ ਗਏ ਹਨ ਪਰ ਇਕ
ਤੁਹਾਡਾ ਭਣਵਈਆ (13) ਨਹੀਂ ਆਇਆ। ਉਸ ਨੂੰ ਤੁਸੀ ਆਪ ਆ ਕੇ ਲਿਆਵੋਗੇ
। ਅਸੀ ਤੁਹਾਨੂੰ ਫੇਰ ਵੀ ਤਗੀਦ (14) ਕਰਦੇ ਹਾਂ ਜੋ ਚਿਠੀ ਪਹੁੰਚਣ ਸਾਰ ਚਲੇ ਆਓ

ਚਿਠੀ ਲਿਖੀ ਸੋਮਵਾਰ ਮਿਤੀ ਫਗਣ ਸੁਦੀ (15) ੧੦

1 ਪਾਸੋਂ from. 2 ਵਿਆਹ marriage. 3 ਗਿਣਿਆ ਜਾਣਾ to be counted fixed. 4 ਹੁੰਡੀ (f) money order. 5 ਨਾਲ with. 6 ਸਾਕ relation. 7 8 9 10 11 12 13 see among relation page. 36. 14 ਤਗੀਦ ਕਰਨਾ to urge. 15 ਸੁਦੀ light half of the month.

No. 6.

ੴ ਸਤਿਗੁਰ ਪ੍ਰਸਾਦਿ॥

ਲਿਖਤਮ ਨਥਾਸਿੰਘ ਜੋਗ ਭਾਈ ਸੁਖਾਸਿੰਘ ਸ੍ਰੀ ਵਾਹਿਗੁਰੂ ਜੀ ਕੀ ਫਤੇ ਵਾਚਣੀ
ਹੋਰ ਸੁਖ ਵਾਚਣੀ। ਭਾਈ ਜੀ ਚਿਠੀ ਤੁਸਾਡੀ ਪਹੁੰਚੀ ਸਮਾਚਾਰ[1] ਮਲੂਮ ਕੀਤਾ
ਤੁਸਾਂ ਲਿਖਿਆ ਹੈ ਜੋ ਸਾਡੀ ਵਲ[2] ਮੀਂਹ ਪਾਣੀ ਕੋਈ ਨਹੀਂ ਪਿਆ ਅਤੇ ਫਸਲ ਦਾ
ਕੁਝ ਹਾਲ ਨਹੀਂ ਖੇਤੀ ਪੱਤੀ ਸੁਕ ਗਈ ਹੈ ਭਾਈ ਜੀ ਸਾਡੀ ਵਲ ਤਾਂ ਬਹੁਤ ਮੀਂਹ
ਪਿਆ ਹੈ ਐਨਾ[3] ਮੀਂਹ ਹੋਇਆ ਹੈ ਜੋ ਪਕਣ ਤੀਕ ਰ ਕੋਈ ਪਾਣੀ ਦੇਣ ਦੀ ਲੋੜ
ਨਹੀਂ ਰਹੀ॥ ਐਤਕੀ ਅਸਾਂ ਕਥਾਸਿੰਘ ਦਾ ਖੇਤ[4] ਵੀ ਲੈ ਲਿਆ ਸੀ। ਉਸ
ਵਿਚ ਅਸਾਂ ਸਰੋਂ[5] ਬੀਜ ਦਿਤੀ ਹੈ। ਹੋਰ ਆਪਣੇ ਖੇਤਾਂ ਵਿਚ ਕਮਾਦ[6] ਬੀਜ ਦਿਤਾ
ਹੈ। ਹੋਰ ਹਾਲ ਏਹ ਹੈ ਜੋ ਸਾਡੇ ਦੋ ਕੋਠੇ[7] ਕਣਕ ਦੇ ਭਰੇ ਹੋਏ ਹਨ ਜੇ ਕਰ ਤੁਸਾਡੀ
ਵਲ ਕਣਕ ਮਹਿੰਗੀ[8] ਹੋਵੇ ਤਾਂ ਖਬਰ ਦੇਣੀ ਤਾਂ ਅਸੀ ਆਪਣੀ ਕਣਕ
ਗਡਿਆਂ[9] ਵਿਚ ਭਰ ਕੇ[10] ਤੁਸਾਡੀ ਵਲ[11] ਭੇਜ ਦੇਈਏ ਅਤੇ ਤੁਸਾਂ ਉਸਨੂੰ ਭਾ
ਸਾਰ[12] ਵੇਚ ਦੇਣਾ। ਏਥੇ ਤਾਂ ਐਤਕੀ ਸਭ ਦਾਣਾ ਫਕਾ[13] ਸਸਤਾ[14] ਹੈ। ਹੋਰ ਸਭ
ਸੁਖ ਸਾਂਦ ਹੈ ਪਰ ਧਨੀ ਨੂੰ ਦੋ ਤਿੰਨਾਂ ਦਿਨਾਂ ਤੋਂ ਕਸ[15] ਆਉਂਦੀ ਹੈ। ਚਿਠੀ ਦਾ ਉਤਰ
ਛੇਤੀ ਭੇਜਣਾ॥

ਚਿਠੀ ਲਿਖੀ ਮੰਗਲਵਾਰ ਚੇਤ੍ਰ ਦਿਨ ੧੧

1 ਸਮਾਚਾਰ circumstance. 2 ਸਾਡੀ ਵਲ towards us. 3 ਐਨਾ so much 4 ਖੇਤ field. 5. ਸਰੋਂ (f) oil seed 6 ਕਮਾਦ sugar cane. 7 ਕੋਠਾ store house 8 ਮਹਿੰਗਾ dear (expensive.) 9 ਗਡਾ bullock cart. 10 ਭਰਨਾ to fill, to load. 11 ਵਲ towards 12 ਭਾ ਸਾਰ according to the current rate. 13 ਦਾਣਾਫਕਾ corn grass in this case. ਫਕਾ has no meaning. 14 ਸਸਤਾ cheap. 15 ਕਸ (f) fever.

No. 7.

ੴ ਸਤਿਗੁਰ ਪ੍ਰਸਾਦਿ॥

ਲਿਖਤੁਮ ਲਾਲ ਸਿੰਘ ਅਗੇ ਜੋਗ ਚਾਚਾ(1) ਅਮਰ ਸਿੰਘ ਫਤੇ ਬੁਲਾਈ ਵਾਚਣੀ ਹੋਰ ਸੁਖ ਵਾਚਣੀ ਜੀ॥ ਚਿਠੀ ਤੁਹਾਡੀ ਮਿਲੀ ਹਾਲ ਮਲੂਮ ਕੀਤਾ॥ ਜੇਹੜੀ ਤੁਸਾਂ ਤਾਰ ਖਬਰ(2) ਘਲੀ ਸੀ ਕਿ ਸਾਨੂੰ ਤੁਹਾਡੇ ਬਿਮਾਰ ਹੋਣ ਦੀ ਖਬਰ ਹੀਰਾ ਸਿੰਘ ਫਗਵਾੜੇ ਵਾਲੇ ਨੇ ਦਿਤੀ ਹੈ ਅਤੇ ਇਸ ਕਰਕੇ ਤੁਹਾਡੀ ਖਬਰ ਮੰਗਾਉਣ ਦੇ ਲਈ ਅਸਾਂ ਤਾਰ ਘਲਣੀ ਹੈ ਸੋ ਭਾਈ ਜੀ ਆਖਣ ਵਾਲੇ ਨੇ ਤੁਹਾਨੂੰ ਕੂੜ ਆਣ ਕੇ ਦਸਿਆ ਹੈ॥ ਜਦ ਦਾ ਮੈਂ ਮੁਲਤਾਨ ਵਿਚ ਆਨ ਕੇ ਨੌਕਰ ਹੋਇਆ ਹਾਂ ਇਕ ਦਿਨ ਵੀ ਬਿਮਾਰ ਨਹੀ ਹੋਇਆ। ਤੁਸਾਂ ਕਿਸੇ ਗਲ ਦਾ ਫਿਕਰ ਨਾ ਕਰਨਾ॥ ਹੋਰ ਆਪਣੀ ਰਾਜੀ ਬਾਜੀ ਦੀ ਖਬਰ ਘਲਦੇ ਰਿਹਾ ਕਰੋ॥ ਹੋਰ ਇਸ ਗਲ ਦਾ ਭੀ ਉਤਰ ਘਲਣਾ ਕਿ ਪੈਲੀ(3) ਜੇਹੜੀ ਨਾਈਆਂ ਨੂੰ ਅਧ ਉਤੇ(4) ਦਿਤੀ ਹੋਈ ਸੀ ਉਨਾਂ ਤੁਹਾਨੂੰ ਹਿਸਾ(5) ਵੰਡ ਕੇ ਦੇ ਦਿਤਾ ਹੈ ਕਿ ਨਹੀ॥ ਉਸ ਕੋਲੋਂ ਸਾਰੀਆਂ ਚੀਜਾਂ ਦਾ ਹਿਸਾ ਵੰਡਾ ਲੈਣਾ ਅਤੇ ਫੇਰ ਉਨਾਂ ਨੂੰ ਜਮੀਨ ਨਾ ਦੇਣੀ ਕਿਉਂਜੋ ਉਹ ਕੁਪੱਤੇ(6) ਆਦਮੀ ਹਨ॥ ਹੋਰ ਮੈਂ ਸੌਣ ਦੇ ਮਹੀਨੇ ਵਿਚ ਛੁਟੀ ਲੈਕੇ ਆਵਾਂਗਾ॥ ਮੁੰਡੇ ਕੁੜੀਆਂ ਨੂੰ ਰਾਜੀ ਰਖਣਾ ਕਿਸੇ ਗਲੋਂ ਤੰਗ(7) ਨਹੀ ਰਖਣਾ॥ ਚਿਠੀ ਦਾ ਉਤਰ ਆਸਾ ਸਿੰਘ ਦੇ ਹਥ ਘਲਣਾ॥

ਚਿਠੀ ਲਿਖੀ ਬੁਧਵਾਰ ਵਸਾਖ ਵਦੀ(8) ੧੪

1 ਚਾਚਾ uncle. 2 ਤਾਰ ਖਬਰ (f) telegram 3 ਪੈਲੀ (f) field. 4 ਅਧ ਉਤੇ (to give land for cultivation on half income). 5 ਹਿਸਾ part, share. 6 ਕੁਪੱਤਾ wicked. 7 ਤੰਗ troubled (narrow.) 8 ਬਦੀ (f) dark ha

No. 8.

੧ ਓ ਸਤਿਗੁਰਪ੍ਰਸਾਦਿ।

ਲਿਖਤੁਮ ਨਿਹਾਲਸਿੰਘ ਜੋਗ ਭਾਈ ਗੁਪਾਲਸਿੰਘ ਸ੍ਰੀ ਵਾਹਿਗੁਰੂ ਜੀ ਕੀ ਫਤੇ ਵਾਚਣੀ। ਹੋਰ ਸੁਖ ਵਾਚਣੀ। ਭਾਈ ਜੀ ਜੇਹੜੀ(1) ਗਊ(2) ਤੁਸੀ ਸਾਡੇ ਕੋਲ ਛਡ ਗਏ ਸਾਓ ਗੱਭਣ(3) ਹੋ ਗਈ ਹੈ ਅਤੇ ਸਾਡੇ ਵਾਲੀ ਗਊ ਸੂ ਪਈ(4) ਹੈ ਵਛੀ(5) ਦਿਤੀ ਸੂ। ਜੇ ਕਰ ਤੁਹਾਡੀ ਗਊ ਦੁਧ ਨਾ ਦਿੰਦੀ ਹੋਵੇ ਤਾ ਅਸੀ ਤੁਸਾਨੂੰ ਆਪਣੀ ਗਊ ਭੇਜ ਦੇਈਏ। ਇਸ ਵੇਲੇ ਉਹ ਪੰਜਾਂ ਸੇਰ ਕੱਚਾ(6) ਦੁਧ ਦੇਂਦੀ ਹੈ। ਹੋਰ ਮੈਂ ਤੁਹਾਂ ਨੂੰ ਇਕ ਬੜੀ ਖੁਸ਼ੀ ਦੀ ਖਬਰ ਸੁਨਾਉਨਿਆਂ ਮੇਰਾ ਵਡਾ ਪੁਤ ਨਥਾਸਿੰਘ ਬਾਰਵੇਂ ਰਸਾਲੇ ਵਿਚ ਭਰਤੀ ਹੋ ਗਿਆ ਹੈ। ਏਹ ਸਰਦਾਰ ਜੀਵਨਸਿੰਘ ਰਸਾਈਦਾਰ(7) ਦੀ ਮੇਹਰਬਾਨੀ ਕਰਕੇ ਬੰਦੋਬਸਤ ਹੋ ਗਇਆ ਹੈ। ਹੋਰ ਜਗੂਸਿੰਘ ਨੂੰ ਸਾਡੀ ਵਾਹਗੁਰੂ ਜੀ ਕੀ ਫਤੇ ਆਖਣੀ।

ਚਿਠੀ ਲਿਖੀ ਵੀਰਵਾਰ ਜੇਠ ਵਦੀ ੧੪

ਦਸਖਤ ਨਿਹਾਲਸਿੰਘ ਲੰਬਰਦਾਰ(8)

1 ਜੇੜ੍ਹੀ (f) the one which. 2 ਗਊ (f) cow. 3 ਗਭਣ pregnant (applied to animals.) 4 ਸੂਣਾ to bring forth (used for animals only.) 5 ਵਛੀ (f) calf. 6 ਕੱਚਾ ਸੇਰ 2½ kachha seers are equal to one pakka seer (only used by the villagers). 7 ਰਸਾਈਦਾਰ Capt. 8 ਲੰਬਰਦਾਰ *head*man of the village.

No. 9.

੧ ਓ ਸਤਿਗੁਰਪ੍ਰਸਾਦਿ।

ਲਿਖਤੁਮ ਮਜਾਣਸਿੰਘ ਪਾਸੇ[1] ਭਾਈ ਧਨਈਆਸਿੰਘ ਜੋਗ ਸ੍ਰੀ ਵਾਹਿਗੁਰੂ
ਜੀ ਕੀ ਫਤਹ ਵਾਚਣੀ। ਹੋਰ ਭਾਈ ਜੀ ਏਥੇ ਸਰਬ[2] ਸੁਖ ਹੈ ਤੁਸਾਡੀ ਸੁਖ ਸ੍ਰੀ ਵਾਹਿਗੁ[3]
ਰੂ ਜੀ ਪਾਸੋਂ ਮੰਗਦੇ ਹਾਂ। ਚਿਠੀ ਤੁਸਾਡੀ ਪਹੁੰਚੀ ਹਾਲ ਜਾਣਿਆ ਤੁਸਾਂ ਲਿਖਿਆ ਹੈ
ਜੋ ਸਾਨੂੰ ਨੌਕਰ ਹੋਏ ਦੀ ਖਬਰ ਨਹੀਂ ਦਿਤੀ ਸੋ ਭਾਈ ਜੀ ਨੌਕਰੀ ਵਿਚੋਂ ਕੰਨ ਖੁਰਕ[4]ਣ
ਦਾ ਤਾਂ ਵੇਹਲ[5] ਨਹੀਂ ਲਗਦਾ ਖਬਰ ਕੀ ਕਿਸੇ ਨੂੰ ਦੇਂਦੇ। ਸਵੇਰੇ ਛੀ ਬਜੇ ਉਠੀਦਾ
ਏ[6] ਬਾਹਰ ਜੰਗਲ[7] ਪਾਣੀ ਜਾ ਕੇ ਅਜੇ ਆ ਕੇ ਬੈਠੀਦਾ ਵੀ ਨਹੀਂ ਜੋ ਹੁਕਮ ਆਉਂਦਾ
ਹੈ ਰੰਗਰੂਟੀ[8] ਵਾਸਤੇ ਚਲੋ ਸੋ ਅੱਠ ਵਜੇ ਉਥੋਂ ਆਈਦਾ ਏ ਫੇਰ ਘੋੜਾ ਮਲੀਦਾ[9]
ਹੈ ਜੀਨ ਲਗਾਮ ਝੂਮ[10] ਸਾਫ ਕਰਦਿਆਂ ਦਸ ਵਜ ਜਾਂਦੇ ਹਨ ਫੇਰ ਪ੍ਰਸਾਦ[11] ਤਿ
ਆਰ ਕਰੀਦਾ ਹੈ ਖਾਂਦਿਆਂ ਪੀਂਦਿਆਂ ਬਾਰਾਂ ਵਜ ਜਾਂਦੇ ਹਨ ਫੇਰ ਕਦੀ ਕੁਝ ਨੌਕਰੀ
ਬੋਲ ਗਈ ਕਦੀ ਕੁਝ ਕੰਮ ਹੋ ਗਿਆ ਵੇਹਲ ਲਗੇ ਤੇ ਚਿਠੀ ਲਿਖੀਏ। ਹੁਣ ਆਸਾ
ਹੈ ਜੋ ਦੂਜੇ ਮਹੀਨੇ ਤੀਕਰ ਕੰਮ ਕੁਝ ਸਿਖ ਜਾਂਦਾ ਗੋ ਫੇਰ ਭਾਵੇਂ ਇਕ ਚਿਠੀ ਰੋਜ ਪਾ
ਦਿਤਾ ਕਰਾਂਗੇ। ਹੋਰ ਜੋ ਕੰਮ ਟਹਲ ਹੋਵੇ ਲਿਖਣਾ।

ਚਿਠੀ ਏਸ ਪਤੇ[12] ਤੇ ਪਾਉਣੀ। ਚਿਠੀ ਪਹੁੰਚੇ ਰਾਵਲਪਿੰਡੀ ਛੌਣੀ ਰਸਾਲਾ ਨੰ: ੧੩
ਤੁਰਪ ਛੀਵਾਂ ਮਜਾਣਸਿੰਘ ਸਵਾਰ ਨੂੰ ਮਿਲੇ।

ਚਿਠੀ ਲਿਖੀ ਛਨਿਛਰਵਾਰ ਮਿਤੀ ਫਗਣ ਦਿਨ ੧੬ ਸੰਮਤ ੧੯੫੦

ਮਈਆਸਿੰਘ ਸਵਾਰ

1 ਪਾਸੇ from. 2 ਸਭ all. 3 ਵਾਹਿ ਗੁਰੂ God. 4 ਕੰਨ ਖੁਰਕਣਾ to scratch the ear (although it itches.) 5 ਵੇਹਲ leisure. 6 ਏ ਹੈ is. 7 ਜੰਗਲ ਪਾਣੀ ਜਾਣਾ to go for call of nature. 8 ਰੰਗ ਰੂਟੀ (f) recruiting. 9 ਮਲਨਾ to groom (rub.) 10 ਲਗਾਮ ਝੂਮ bridle. ਝੂਮ is used for intensifying. 11 ਪ੍ਰਸਾਦ food. 12 ਪਤਾ address.

No. 10.

੧ ਓ ਸਤਿਗੁਰਪ੍ਰਸਾਦਿ।

ਲਿਖਤੁਮ ਨਰੈਨਸਿੰਘ ਅਗੇ ਜੋਗ ਭਾਈ ਈਸਰਸਿੰਘ ਨੂੰ (1) ਹਥਜੋੜਕੇ
ਸ੍ਰੀ ਵਾਹਿਗੁਰੂਜੀਕੀ ਫਤੇ ਵਾਚਣੀ ਹੋਰ ਜੀ ਸਮਾਚਾਰ ਇਹ ਹੈ ਜੋ (2) ਹਾੜ੍ਹੀ
ਐਤਕੀਦੀ ਐਡੀ ਲਗੀਸੀ ਜੋ ਕੁਛ (3) ਓੜਕ ਨਹੀਸਾ ਪਰ ਪਰਮੇਸੁਰ ਦਾ
ਭਾਣਾ ਵੇਖੋ ਜਦ ਪਕਕੇ (4) ਵਾਢੀ ਦੇ ਰੰਗ ਉਤੇ ਹੋਈ ਤਾਂ (5) ਚਾਣਚਕ ਮੀਂਹ ਲੈਹ
ਪਿਆ ਜੋ (6) ਛਪੜ ਟੋਭਾ ਇਕ ਹੋਗਿਆ ਮੀਂਹ ਤੇ ਤਾਂ ਕੁਛ ਬਹੁ (7) ਜਾਨ ਨਹੀ ਹੋਈ
ਆ ਪਰ (8) ਗੜੇ ਜੋ ਮੀਂਹ ਦੇ ਨਾਲ ਪਏ (9) ਛਟਾਂਕ ਛਟਾਂਕ ਪਕੇ ਦੇ ਸਨ ਅਰ ਜਿਥੇ
ਜਿਥੇ ਪਏ (10) ਕਖ ਨਹੀ ਛਡਿਆ ਸਾਨੂੰ (11) ਆਸ ਸੀ ਜੋ ਦੋ ਸੌ ਮਣ ਕਣਕ ਆਊ ਪਰ
ਹੁਣ ਪੰਜਾਹ ਮਣ ਆਜਾਵੇ ਤਾਂ ਵੀ ਬੜੇ ਭਾਗ ਹਨ ਸੋ ਤੂੰ ਐਤਕੀ ਦੀ (12) ਕਿਸਤ
ਲਈ (13) ਮਾਮਲੇ ਜੋਗੇ ਰੁਪੈ ਘਲਾ ਦਿਤੀ ਤਗੀਦ ਜਾਣਨੀ ਹੋਰ ਸਬ ਸੁਖ
ਹੈ॥

ਲਿਖੀ ਨਰੈਣਸਿੰਘ ਜਟ ਵੀਰਪਾਲਾਂ ਵਿਚੋਂ
ਮਿਤੀ ਚੇਤਰ ਦੀ ੧੮

1 ਹਥਜੋੜਕੇ with hands folded (respects.) 2 ਹਾੜ੍ਹੀ winter crops. 3 ਓੜ (ਓੜਕ) end. 4 ਵਾਢੀ cutting. 5 ਚਾਣਚਕ suddenly. 6 ਛਪੜ ਟੋਭਾ ਇਕ ਹੋਗਿਆ ponds and tanks have all become full 7 ਜਾਨ loss. 8 ਗੜੇ hail. 9 ਛਟਾਂਕ one-sixteenth of a seer. 10 ਕਖ ਨਹੀਂ ਛਡਿਆ left nothing (not even grass was left) 11 ਆਸ (f) hope. 12 ਕਿਸਤ (f) instalment. 13 ਮਾਮਲਾ revenue.

No. 11.

ੴ ਸਤਿਗੁਰਪ੍ਰਸਾਦਿ।

ਲਿਖਤਮ ਨੰਦ ਸਿੰਘ ਅਗੇ ਜੋਗ ਲਾਲਾ ਭਗਤ ਰਾਮ ਨੂੰ ਬਹੁਤ ਕਰਕੇ ਮਥਾ ਟੇਕਣਾ (1) ਜੀ। ਹੋਰ ਜੀ ਤੁਹਾਨੂੰ ਮਲੂਮ ਹੈ ਜੋ ਤੁਸੀ ਮੁੱਢ ਤੇ (2) ਲਾਕੇ ਸਾਡੇ ਸ਼ਾਹ (3) ਹੋ ਅਤੇ ਸਾਡੇ ਵਡੇ ਤੁਹਾਡੇ ਵਡਿਆਂ ਕੋਲੋਂ ਹੁਦਾਰ (4) ਲੈਂਦੇ ਰਹੇ ਅਰ ਕਿਸੇ ਤਰਾਂ ਕਦੇ ਨਾ ਵਿਗੜੀ। ਹੁਣ ਸੁਣਿਆ ਹੈ ਕਿ ਤੁਸੀ ੧੫੦) ਰੁਪਯਾ ਬਦਲੇ ਸਾਡੇ ਉਤੇ ਅਰਜ਼ੀ ਪਾਉਣ ਲਗੇ ਹੋ। ਅਸੀ ਤੁਹਾਨੂੰ ਮੂੰਹੋਂ ਮੂੰਹ (5) ਆਖਨੇ ਹਾਂ ਜੋ ਸੌਣੀ (6) ਦਾ ਦਾਣਾ ਫਕਾ ਆਲ ਦੇ ਅਸੀਂ ਤੁਹਾਡੀ ਕੌਡੀ ਕੌਡੀ (7) ਨਬੇੜ ਦੇਵਾਂਗੇ। ਤੁਸੀਂ ਆਪਣਾ ਹਠ (8) ਕਰਦੇ ਹੋ ਅਰ ਆਖਦੇ ਹੋ ਜੋ ਅਰਜ਼ੀ ਪਾਕੇ ਹੀ ਰੁਪਏ ਲੈਣੇ ਹਨ ਸੋ ਜੀ ਕਿਰਪਾ ਕਰਕੇ ਜਿਥੇ ਦੋ ਵਰ੍ਹੇ ਲੰਘਾਏ ਜੇ ਦੋ ਮਹੀਨੇ ਹੋਰ ਠੈਹਰ ਜਾਓ ਅਰ ਹਾਕਮਾਂ ਤਾਈਂ ਨਾ ਅਪੜੋ (9) ਅਸੀ ਪਰ ਬੈਠਿਆਂ ਨੂੰ ਟਕੋਰ ਕੇ ਤੁਹਾਡਾ ਹਸਾਬ ਨਿਬੇੜ (10) ਜਾਵਾਂਗੇ। ਹੋਰ ਭੁਲ ਕੇ ਪਰਸੋਂ ਮੈਂ ਆਪ ਭੀ ਤੁਹਾਡੀ ਸੇਵਾ ਵਿਚ ਹਾਜ਼ਰ ਹੋਵਾਂਗਾ।

ਲਿਖੀ ਵੀਰਵਾਰ ਨੰਦ ਸਿੰਘ

1 ਮਥਾ ਟੇਕਣਾ to bow-down (respects) 2 ਮੁਢਤੇ from beginng. 3 ਸ਼ਾਹ banker 4 ਹੁਦਾਰ ਲੈਣਾ to borrow (money) 5 ਮੂੰਹੋਂ ਮੂੰਹ again and again (month to, month.) 6 ਸੌਣੀ summer crops. 7 ਕੌਡੀ ਕੌਡੀ every farthing: (ਕੌਡੀ a small shell used as a coin) 8 ਹਠ ਕਰਨਾ to persist. 9 ਅਪੜਨਾ to reach (to go.) 10 ਨਬੇੜਨਾ to settle

No. 12.

੧ੴ

ਲਿਖਤਮ ਕੇਸਰ ਸਿੰਘ ਅਗੇ ਜੋਗ ਭਾਈ ਗੁਪਾਲ ਸਿੰਘ ਨੂੰ ਹਥ ਜੋੜ ਕੇ ਫਤੇ
ਬੁਲਾਈ ਵਾਹਗੁਰੂ ਜੀ। ਹੋਰ ਜੀ ਹਕੀਕਤ ਏਹ ਹੈ ਜੋ ਜੇਠ ਦੀ ੧੦ ਦੇ ਦਿਨ ਤੁਸਾਂ
ਦੇ ਘਰ ਨੂੰ ਸੰਨ੍ਹ (1) ਲਗੀ ਪਹਿਲਾਂ ਤਾਂ ਚੋਰਾਂ ਨੇ ਅੰਦਰ ਵੜ ਕੇ ਕਪੜਿਆਂ
ਦੀਆਂ ਸੰਦੂਕਾਂ ਭੰਨੀਆਂ (2) ਅਤੇ ਸਾਰੇ ਰੇਸ਼ਮੀ ਅਰ ਕੀਮਤੀ ਬਸਤ੍ਰ (3) ਕਢ ਲੈ ਗਏ
ਅਰ ਫੇਰ ਗਹਿਣਾ (4) ਵੀ ਉਨਾਂ ਦੇ ਹਥ ਆ ਗਿਆ ਅਤੇ ੫੦੦) ਰੁਪਈਆ ਮਾ
ਮਲੇ ਦਾ ਜੋ ਤੁਸਾਂ ਉਗਰਾਹਿਆ (5) ਸੀ ਅਰ ਤੁਸੀਂ ਲੈ ਤਾਰਨ (6) ਜਾਣਾ ਸੀ ਉਹ ਭੀ ਲੈ ਗਏ
। ਗੱਲ ਕਾਹਦੀ (7) ਦੋ ਹਜਾਰ ਦੇ ਲਗ ਭਗ (8) ਨੁਕਸਾਨ ਹੋ ਗਿਆ ਹੈ ਅਤੇ ਜਦ ਚੋ
ਰ ਨਿਕਲੇ ਤਾਂ ਜਾਂਦੇ ਹੋਏ ਸਬਜੀ (9) ਘੋੜੀ ਜੇਹੜੀ ਅਸਾਂ ਦਵਾਲੀ ਦੀ ਮੰਡੀ (10) ਤੋਂ ੧੬੦)
ਰੁਪੈ ਨੂੰ ਖਰੀਦੀ ਸੀ ਉਹ ਭੀ ਕਢ ਲੈ ਗਏ। ਠਾਣੇਦਾਰ ਪਿੰਡ ਵਿਚ ਆਇਆ ਹੋ
ਇਆ ਹੈ ਅਰ ਦੋ ਤਿਨ ਬਦਮਾਸ਼ ਪਕੜੇ ਹੋਏ ਹਨ ਪਰ ਅਜੇ ਤਾਈਂ ਮਾ
ਲ ਦਾ ਕੁਝ ਪਤਾ ਨਹੀਂ ਲਗਾ ਜੇ ਭਾਗਾਂ ਵਿਚ ਹੋਊ ਤਾਂ ਮਿਲ ਜਾਊ।

1 ਸਨ੍ਹ burglary, house breaking. 2 ਭੰਨਣਾ to break. 3 ਕੀਮਤੀ ਬਸਤ੍ਰ valuable cloths. 4 ਗਹਿਣਾ jewellary. 5 ਉਗਰਾਹੁਣਾ to collect (from other people.) 6 ਤਾਰਨਾ to settle, to pay.) 7 ਗਲ ਕਾਹਦੀ in short. 8 ਲਗ ਭਗ nearly. 9 ਸਬਜੀ (f) grey. 10 ਮੰਡੀ (f) market (house or cattle fair.)

No. 18.

੧ੳ

ਲਿਖਤਮ ਬੀਰਸਿੰਘ ਜੋਗ ਕਿਰਪਾਲਸਿੰਘ ਨੂੰ ਮਲੂਮ ਹੋਵੇ ਜੋ ਤੇਰੇ ਸੌਰਿਆਂ[1]
ਨੇ ਵਿਆਹ ਦੇ ਦਿਤਾ ਹੈ ਅਰ ਭਾਦ੍ਰੋਂ ਦਾ ਅਠਾਰਵਾਂ ਸਾਹਾ[2] ਹੈ ਅਸਾਂ ੬੦) ਰੁਪੈ
ਦਾ ਘਿਉ ੪੦) ਦੀ ਖੰਡ[3] ੨੦) ਦੀ ਸਕਰ[4] ੩੦) ਦੀ ਕਣਕ ੧੦) ਦੇ
ਮਾਂਹ[5] ਲੈ ਲਏ ਹਨ ਅਰ ਕੋਈ ੨੦੦) ਰੁਪਏ ਦੀ ਵਰੀ[6] ਅਤੇ ਹਿਕਮੁਕ[7] ਉਤੇ
ਲਗੇ ਹਨ ਸੋ ਤੇਰੀ ਮਾਤਾ ਆਖਦੀ ਹੈ ਤੂੰ ਭੀ ਆਪਣੇ ਕਮਾਨ ਅਫਸਰ[8] ਕੋਲੋਂ ਦੋ ਮਹੀ
ਨਿਆਂ ਦੀ ਛੁਟੀ ਲੈਕੇ ਛੇਤੀ ਨਾਲ ਆ ਜਾਵੇਂ ਜੇ ਉਹ ਕੁਝ ਰੋਕ ਟੋਕ[9] ਕਰੇ ਤਾਂ ਏਹੋ[10]
ਅਰਦਾਸ ਵਖਾਲ ਦੇਵੀਂ ਅਰ ਜੇ ਫੇਰ ਵੀ ਨਾ ਮੰਨੇ ਤਾਂ ਅਸੀਂ ਏਥੋਂ ਨੰਬਰਦਾਰਾਂ
ਦੀਆਂ ਮੋਹਰਾਂ[11] ਲੁਆਕੇ ਅਰਜੀ ਘਲਾਂਗੇ ਛੁਟੀ ਤਾਂ ਤੈਨੂੰ ਜਰੂਰ ਮਿਲ ਜਾਊ
ਤੇ ਧੀਆਂ ਸਹੁਰਿਆਂ ਆਖ ਘਲਿਆ[12] ਹੈ ਜੋ ਅਸਾਂ ਮੁਕਲਾਵਾ[13] ਭੀ ਵਿਆਹ
ਦੇ ਨਾਲ ਹੀ ਦੇਵਣਾ ਹੈ।

ਲਿਖੀ ਐਤਵਾਰ ਪੋਹ ਦੀ ੧੯

ਦਸਖਤ ਬੀਰਸਿੰਘ ਰਾਣੀਪਿੰਡ ਵਿਚੋਂ

1 ਸੌਰੇ father in laws people. 2 ਸਾਹਾ marriage date. 3 ਖੰਡ (f) sugar. 4 ਸ਼ਕਰ raw sugar. 5 ਮਾਂਹ (f) a kind of Dhal. 6 ਵਰੀ (f) brides clothes. 7 ਹਿਕੱਮੁਕ other things 8 ਕਮਾਨ ਅਫਸਰ Commanding Officer. 9 ਰੋਕ ਟੋਕ (f) hesitation, objection. 10 ਏਹੋ this very. 11 ਮੋਹਰ (f) seal. 12 ਆਖ ਘਲਣਾ to send a word 13 ਮੁਕਲਾਵਾ bringing home a wife after marriage.

No. 14.

੧ੴ

ਲਿਖਤਮ ਕਰਮ ਸਿੰਘ ਜੋਗ ਭਾਈ ਸਾਧੂ ਸਿੰਘ ਹੋਰਾਂ ਨੂੰ ਹਥ ਜੋੜ ਕੇ ਫਤੇ ਬੁਲਾਈ ਵਾਰ
ਵੀਹਾਂ ਹੋਰ ਜੀ ਸਾਡੀ ਪੜਤਲ(1) ਨੂੰ ਕਾਬਲ ਵੱਲ ਲਾਮ(2) ਵਿਚ ਜਾਣ ਦਾ ਹੁਕਮ ਆ ਗਿਆ ਹੈ
ਅਤੇ ਏਸ ਮਹੀਨੇ ਦੀ ੨੨ ਤਰੀਕ ਸਾਡਾ ਕੂਚ(3) ਹੈ ਛੁਟੀ ਇਕ ਦਿਹਾੜੇ ਦੀ ਵੀ ਨਹੀਂ ਮਿਲ
ਦੀ ਜੇ ਕਰ ਹੋ ਸਕੇ ਤਾਂ ਤੁਸੀਂ ਛੇਤੀ ਮੇਰੇ ਕੋਲ ਕੂਚ ਹੋਣ ਤੋਂ ਪਹਿਲਾਂ ਪਸ਼ੌਰ ਅਪੜ(4) ਕੇ ਮੇਰੀ
ਵਹੁਟੀ ਤੇ ਮੇਰੇ ਮੁੰਡੇ ਕੁੜੀਆਂ ਨੂੰ ਲੈ ਜਾਓ ਸਰਕਾਰ ਆਖਦੀ ਹੈ ਜੋ ਟਬਰ(5) ਟੋਰ ਨੂੰ ਡੀਪੋ
ਵਿਚ ਛਡ ਜਾਓ ਮੈਂ ਜੀ ਏਥੇ ਛਡਣ ਦੇ ਵਿਚ ਕੁਝ ਇਜ਼ਤ(6) ਨਹੀਂ ਜੀ ਕੁਰ ਜਾਣੋ ਆ ਕੇ
ਲੈ ਜਾਓ।

ਲਿਖੀ ਕਰਮ ਸਿੰਘ ਪਸ਼ੌਰ ਵਿਚੋਂ

1 ਪੜਤਲ (f) Regiment. 2 ਲਾਮ (f) field. 3 ਕੂਚ march. 4 ਅਪੜਨਾ to arrive. 5 ਟਬਰ famillly here ਟੋਰ has no meaning *vide* Chit No. 1. 6 ਇਜ਼ਤ respect.

No. 15.

੧ੴ

ਲਿਖਤਮ ਜਵਿੰਦਾ ਸਿੰਘ ਜੋਗ ਭਾਈ ਦੇਵਾ ਸਿੰਘ ਫਤੇ ਬੁਲਾਈ ਵਾਚਣੀ ਹੋਰ
ਜੀ ਅਸੀਂ ਐਤਕੀ ਨਥਾ ਸਿੰਘ ਤਰਖਾਣ ਨਾਲ ਭਿਆਲੀ(1) ਕੀਤੀ ਹੈ ਇਕ ਜੋਗ(2)
ਸਾਡੀ ਤੇ ਇਕ ਢੱਗਾ(3) ਉਸ ਦਾ ਹੈ ਦਸਾਂ ਵਿਘੇ ਸੌਣੀ ਬੀਜ ਦਿਤੀ ਹੈ ਪੰਦ੍ਰਾਂ ਵਿਘੇ
ਹਾੜੀ ਲਈ ਰਖੀ ਹੈ ਮੀਂਹ ਵੇਲੇ ਸਿਰ(4) ਪੈ ਗਿਆ ਸੀ ਸੌਣੀ ਚੰਗੀ ਹੈ ਅਤੇ ਹਾੜੀ
ਲਈ ਵਾਹਣ(5) ਕਰ ਛਡੇ ਹਨ ਮਕਈ(6) ਗਡੀ ਹੈ ਆਸ ਹੈ ਜੋ ਪੰਜਾਹ ਜਾਂ ਸਠ ਮਣ
ਛਲੀ(7) ਆ ਜਾਣਗੀਆਂ ਤਿਲ(8) ਅਸਾਂ ਐਤਕੀ ਨਹੀਂ ਬੀਜੇ ਚਰੀ ਡੰਗਰਾਂ ਜੋਗੀ
ਬੀਜੀ ਹੈ ਪਠੇ ਦਾ ਤੋੜਾ ਨਹੀਂ ਆਵੇਗਾ ਗੋਰੀ ਗਾਂ ਸੂ ਪਈ ਹੈ ਪੰਜ ਸੇਰ ਪਕਾ ਦੁਧ
ਦੇਂਦੀ ਹੈ ਅਤੇ ਮੁੰਡੇ ਕੁੜੀਆਂ ਸਭ ਰਾਜ਼ੀ ਹਨ।

1 ਭਿਆਲੀ (f) partnership. 2 ਜੋਗ (f) pair of bullocks 3 ਢਗਾ bullock. ਵੇਲੇ ਸਿਰ at the proper time. 5 ਵਾਹਣ ploughed field. 6 ਮਕਈ (f) Indian 7 ਛਲੀ (f) ear of Indian corn. 8 ਤਿਲ oil seed.

No. 16.

੧੬

[1] ਸ੍ਰੀ [2] ਸਰਬ ਉਪਮਾ ਜੋਗ ਭਾਈ ਗਿਆਨ ਸਿੰਘ ਜੀ ਜੋਗ ਦਾਸ ਨਥਾ ਸਿੰਘ ਦੀ ਸ੍ਰੀ ਵਾਹਗੁਰੂ ਜੀ ਕੀ ਫਤੇ ਵਾਚਣੀ ਹੋਰ ਭਾਈ ਜੀ ਏਥੇ ਸਰਬ ਸੁਖ ਹੈ ਤੁਹਾਡੀ ਸੁਖ ਗੁਰੂ ਰਾਮਦਾਸ ਜੀ ਪਾਸੋਂ ਮੰਗਦੇ ਹਾਂ ਚਿਠੀ ਤੁਹਾਡੀ ਪਹੁੰਚੀ ਹਾਲ ਮਲੂਮ ਕੀਤਾ ਤੁਸਾਂ ਜੋ ਲਿਖਿਆ ਹੈ ਕਿ ਸਾਡੀ ਵਲ ਅਜੇ ਤੀਕ ਕੁਝ ਮੀਂਹ ਪਾਣੀ ਨਹੀ ਪਿਆ ਤੇ ਅਸੀ ਅਜੇ ਤੀਕ ਕੁਝ ਨਹੀ [3] ਬੀਜਿਆ ਹਲ ਵਾਹ ਕੇ ਜਮੀਨ ਛਡ ਛਡੀ ਹੈ। ਭਾਈ ਜੀ ਏਥੇ ਤਾਂ [4] ਚਰੋਕਣੇ ਮੀਂਹ ਪੈ ਰਹੇ ਹਨ ਤੇ ਸਾਨੂੰ [5] ਮਕਈ ਤੇ ਇਖ ਬੀਜਿਆ ਪੰਦ੍ਰਾਂ ਦਿਨ ਹੋ ਗਏ ਹਨ ਤੇ ਪੈਲੀ ਵੀ [6] ਗਿਠ ਗਿਠ ਉਚੀ ਹੋ ਗਈ ਹੈ ਪਰਸੋਂ ਮਾਤੇ ਭਰਾ ਤਾਰਾ ਸਿੰਘ ਦੀ ਚਿਠੀ ਚਤ੍ਰਾਲ ਵਿਚੋਂ ਆਈ ਸੀ ਓਹ ਲਿਖਦਾ ਹੈ ਕਿ ਸਾਡੀ ਫੌਜ ਸਭ ਤੋਂ ਅਗੇ ਵੈਰੀਆਂ ਦੇ ਨਾਲ ਲੜ ਰਹੀ ਹੈ ਅਤੇ ਉਸ ਨੂੰ ਅਜੇਹੇ [7] ਹਥ ਵਿਖਾਲੇ ਜੋ ਆਸਾ ਹੈ ਕਿ ਉਹ ਫੇਰ ਕਦੀ ਸਿਖਾਂ ਦੇ ਸਾਹਮਣੇ ਨਹੀ ਹੋਣਗੇ। ਹੋਰ ਪਿਛਲੇ ਮਹੀਨੇ ਦੀ ੧੨ ਨਿਹਾਲ ਸਿੰਘ ਦਾ ਵਿਆਹ [8] ਚੋਰੀ ਹੋ ਗਿਆ ਹੈ ਹੋਰ ਮੇਰੇ ਜੋਟੇ ਦੇ ਛੋਟੇ ਵਛੇ ਤੁਹਾਡੇ ਪਾਸ ਹਨ ਉਨਾਂ ਨੂੰ [9] ਪਠਾ ਦਥਾ ਚੰਗਾ ਪਾਉਂਦੇ ਰਹਿਣਾ ਜੋ [10] ਮਾੜੇ ਨਾ ਹੋ ਜਾਣ ਬਾਲ ਬਚਿਆਂ ਦੇ ਸਿਰ ਪਰ ਪਿਆਰ ਦੇਣਾ।

ਚਿਠੀ ਲਿਖੀ ਐਤਵਾਰ ਹਾੜ ਦੀ ੧੨

ਦਸਖਤ ਨਥਾ ਸਿੰਘ ਖਮਾਣੋਂ ਵਿਚੋਂ

1 ਸ੍ਰੀ respect (Divine.) 2 ਸ੍ਰਬ ਉਪਮਾ ਜੋਗ fit for all praises. 3 ਬੀਜਣ to sow. 4 ਚਰੋਕਣਾਂ for a long time. 5 ਮਕਈ f) Indian corn. 6 ਗਿਠ (f a span from the thumb to the little fingure. 7 ਹਥ ਵਖਾਲਣਾ to show bravery (t show hands) 8 ਚੋਰੀ ਵਿਆਹ marriage performed (secretly.) 9 ਪੱਠਾ ਦੱਥਾ fodder. 10 ਮਾੜਾ thin (bad.)

No. 17.

ੴ

ਲਿਖਤਮ ਕਾਨ੍ਹਸਿੰਘ ਜੋਗ ਕਰਮਾਅੰਸਰ ਹਥਜੋੜਕੇ ਮਥਾਟੇਕਿਆ
ਵਾਰਣਾ ਹੋਰਜੀਏਥੇਸੁਖਹੈ ਤੁਹਾਡੀਸੁਖਸਤਿਗੁਰੂ(1)ਤੇਮੰਗਦੇਹਾਂ ਹੋਰ
ਜੀਚਿਠੀਆਪਦੀਪੁਜੀ(2) ਹਕੀਕਤਮਲੂਮਹੋਈ ਤੁਸਾਂਜੋਸਾਹਾ(3) ਲਿਖਿਆ
ਹੈਸੋਬਹੁਤਨੇੜੇਹੈ ਸਾਨੂੰਰਜਾਨਹੀਮਿਲਦੀਕੋਈਦਿਨਲੈਣਦਾਸਾਹਾਕਢੋ
ਤੇਤਸੀ ਮੀਰਪੁਰ ਲਿਖਭੇਜਣਾ ਕਿਨੀਂਗਰਦੀਪਤ੍ਰੀ(4)ਭੇਜਦੇਣਾ ਪਾਂਧਾਜੀ
ਸਾਨੂੰਕਿਸੇਜੱਨ(5)ਪਾਇਤਾਹੈ ਕਿਮੁੰਡਾਇਕ ਅਖੋਂਲਾਆਹੇਤੇਟੀਰਾ(6)ਹੈ ਤੁਸਾਂਜਾ
ਕੇਆਪਦੇਖਣਾ ਅਸਾਂਏਥੇਂਗੁਲਬਦਨਤੇਤਿਲਾ(7)ਤੇਗੋਟਾ(8) ਖਰੀਦਲਿਆਹੈ
ਕਪੜੇਸੀਪੀਦੇਹਨਾ ਕਾਕੀਨੂੰਧਸਲ(9) ਨਿਕਲਆਈਸੀ ਪਰਹੁਣਰਾਜੀਹੈ।
ਇਸਖਤਦਾ ਉਤ੍ਰ ਛੇਤੀਭੇਜਣਾ ਅਸਾਂਅਜੇਚੌਂਕ(10) ਡੰਡੀਆਂ(11)ਬਨਾਉਣੀਆਂ
ਹਨ।

ਲਿਖੀਹਾੜ੍ਹ ਦਿਨ ੩੧

1 ਸਤਗੁਰੂ true God. 2 ਪੁਜਣਾ to arrive. 3 ਸਾਹਾ day appointed for marriage 4 ਪਤ੍ਰੀ (f) horoscope. 5 ਜੱਨ doubt. 6 ਟੀਰਾ squint eyed. 7 ਤਿੱਲਾ gold thread. 8 ਗੋਟਾ gold lace. 9 ਧਸਲ (f). measles. 10 ਚੌਂਕ head ornament. 11 ਡੰਡੀ (f) earing.

No. 18.

੧ ਓ ਸਤਿਗੁਰਪ੍ਰਸਾਦਿ।

(1) ਸ੍ਰੀ ਸਰਬ ਉਪਮਾ ਜੋਗ ਸ੍ਰੀ ਸਰਬ (2) ਗੁਨ ਨਧਾਨ ਉਜਲ ਦੀਦਾਰ ਭਾਈਆ
ਰਾਮ ਸਿੰਘ ਜੀ ਜੋਗ ਲਿਖਤਮ ਦਾਸ ਚੰਦਾ ਸਿੰਘ ਦੀ ਵਾਹਿਗੁਰੂ ਜੀ ਕੀ ਫਤੇ ਬਾ
ਚਣੀ। ਹਕੀਕਤ ਏਹ ਹੈ ਜੋ ਜੀ ਖਤ ਤੁਸਾਡਾ ਪਹੁੰਚਾ ਬਹੁਤ ਅਨੰਦ ਹੋਇਆ॥ ਤੁਸਾਡੇ
ਲਿਖੇ ਮੂਜਬ ਭਾਗੂ ਸਾਹ ਬਾਣੀਏ ਨਾਲ ਹਸਾਬ ਕੀਤਾ ਸੀ ਜਿਸਦੀ (3) ਬਹੀ ਉਤੇ
ਸੱਠ ਰੁਪਏ ਨਿਕਲੇ ਸੀ। ਬੀਹ ਰੁਪੈ (4) ਬਿਆਜ ਨਿਕਲੀ ਸੀ ਜੀ। ਸੋ ਚਾਲੀ ਮਣ
ਦਾਣੇ ਦੇਕੇ (5) ਲੇਖਾ ਚੁਕਾ ਦਿਤਾ ਸੀ ਜੀ
ਬਾਕੀ ਸਾਡੇ ਕੋਲ ਖਾਣ ਜੋਗੇ ਦਾਣੇ ਰਹਿ ਗਏ ਜੀ ਪਰ ਇੱਕ ਬੜਾ ਨੁਕਸਾਨ ਹੋਇ
ਆ ਜੀ (6) ਲਾਖਾ ਬਲਦ (7) ਅਫਾਰੇ ਨਾਲ ਮਰ ਗਿਆ ਜੀ ਸੋ ਜੀ ਜੇ ਚਾਲੀ ਰੁਪੈ ਹੋਰ
ਭੇਜੋ ਹੋਰ ਬਲਦ ਲਈਏ ਜੀ। ਇੱਕ (8) ਵੈੜਕਾ ਹੈਗਾ ਪਰ ਅਜੇ ਕੰਮ ਨਹੀਂ ਦੇਣ ਵਾਲਾ
ਹੈ ਜੀ ਮੀਂਹ ਅਜੇ ਤਕ ਨਹੀ ਪਿਆ ਜੀ ਮੀਂਹ ਦੀ ਬੜੀ ਲੋੜ ਹੈ ਜੀ॥ ਸਾਰੇ
ਲੋਕ ਮੂੰਹ ਚੱਕ ਚੱਕ ਵੇਖ ਰਹੇ ਹਨ ਜੀ ਕਦ ਮੀਂਹ ਪੈਂਦਾ ਹੈ। (9) ਬਾਹੀ (ਵਾਹੀ) ਦੇ
ਦਿਨ ਲੰਘਦੇ ਜਾਂਦੇ ਹਨ ਜੀ ਜੇ ਮੀਂਹ ਨਾ ਪਿਆ ਬੜਾ ਜ਼ੋਰ ਲਗਾਂਗੇ ਜੀ॥ ਮੈਨੂੰ ਚਾਰ
ਦਿਨ (10) ਕਸ ਆਈ ਸੀ ਹੁਣ ਮੈਂ ਰਾਜੀ ਹਾਂ ਜੀ ਖਤ ਭੇਜਦੇ ਰਿਹਾ ਕਰੋ ਜੀ।

ਚਿਠੀ ਲਿਖੀ ਹਾੜ ਦਿਨ ੧੫ ਸੰਮਤ ੧੯੫੨

1 ਸ੍ਰੀ ਸ੍ਰਬ ਉਪਮਾ ਜੋਗ fit for all praizes. 2 ਸ੍ਰਬ ਗੁਣ ਨਧਾਨ full of all qualities. 3 ਬਹੀ ledger. 4 ਬਿਆਜ interest. 5 ਲੇਖਾ ਚੁਕਾਉਣਾ to settle account. 6 ਲਾਖਾ black. 7 ਅਫਾਰਾ swelling of the belly. 8 ਵੈੜਕਾ young bull. 9 ਬਾਹੀ (f) ploughing. 10 ਕਸ (f) fever.

No. 19.

੧ ਓ ਸਤਿਗੁਰ ਪ੍ਰਸਾਦਿ॥

ਲਿਖਤਮ ਆਲਾਸਿੰਘ ਅਗੇ ਜੋਗ ਰਾਜਾ ਜੁਵਲਾਸਿੰਘ ਵਾਹਿਗੁਰੂ ਜੀ
ਕੀ ਫਤੇ ਬੁਲਾਈ ਵਾਚਣੀ ਜੀ॥ ਏਥੇ ਸੁਖ ਹੈ ਤੇ ਤੁਹਾਡੀ ਸੁਖ ਸਾਂਦ ਵਾਹਿਗੁਰੂ
ਜੀ ਪਾਸੋਂ ਮੰਗਦੇ ਹਾਂ ਜੀ ਹਕੀਕਤ ਏਹੁ ਹੈ ਕਿ ਸਾਡੇ ਪਿੰਡ ਇਕ ਏਹ ਵਡਾ ਹਨੇਰ ਹੋ
ਇਆ ਹੈ ਜੀ ਪਿਛਲੇ ਹੀ ਮੰਗਲਵਾਰ ਵਡੀ ਹਨੇਰੀ ਵਗਦੀ ਸੀ ਤੇ ਉਸ ਦਿਨ ਦੂਜੀ
ਰਸਿੰਘ ਹੋਰਾਂ ਦਾ ਵੇਲਣਾ (1) ਵਗਦਾ ਸੀ ਅਤੇ ਧੂਏਂ ਦੇ ਕੋਲ ਖੋਰੀ (2) ਦਾ ਢੇਰ ਲਗ
ਰਹਿਆ ਸੀ ਅਤੇ ਹਨੇਰੀ ਨਾਲ ਉਸ ਢੇਰ ਨੂੰ ਅੱਗ ਲਗ ਪਈ ਅਤੇ ਫੇਰ ਗੁੜ੍ਹ- (3)
ਹਾਲ ਨੂੰ ਲਗ ਗਈ ਅੰਦਰ ਜੋ ਨੌ ਆਦਮੀ ਸਨ ਸਭ ਸੜ ਕੇ ਮਰ ਗਏ ਸਨ ਪਰ
ਦੂਜੀ ਸਿੰਘ ਪਤੇ ਜੀ ਓਥੋਂ ਦਾਗੀ ਨਿਕਲ ਆਇਆ ਸੀ ਜੀ ਪਰ ਉਹਦੀ ਪੀ ਭੂਪੇ
ਪਿਆਰ ਦੀ ਪੀ ਨਾਲ ਗੁਰੁ ਪਾਵ ਲਈ ਗਈ ਹੈਈ ਸੀ ਤਿੰਨਾਂ ਨੂੰ ਕਢ ਵਦੇ
ਲਈ ਫੇਰ ਅੰਦਰ ਜਾ ਵੜਿਆ ਸੀ ਕੁੜੀਆਂ ਨੂੰ ਤੇ ਕੱਢ ਲਿਆ ਸੀ ਪਰ ਉਹਦਾ
ਮੂੰਹ ਸਿਰ ਸੜ ਗਿਆ ਸੀ ਇਸ ਕਰਕੇ ਉਹ ਤਿੰਨ ਚਾਰ ਦਿਨ ਪਿਛੋਂ ਮਰ ਗਿਆ
ਅਤੇ ਹੋਰ ਦੀ ਪੰਜ ਛੀ ਆਦਮੀ ਮਰ ਗਏ ਹਨ॥

ਚਿੱਠੀ ਲਿਖੀ ਮੰਗਲਵਾਰ ਮਿਤੀ ਅਖਾੜੀ ੭
ਸੰਮਤ ੧੯੪੬ ਦਸਖਤ ਆਲਾਸਿੰਘ
ਤਲਵੰਡੀ ਦਿਓਂ

1 ਵੇਲਨਾ sugar mill. 2 ਖੋਰੀ the dry leaves of sugar cane. 3 ਗੁੜ੍ਹ ਹਾਲ a place where they make sugar &c.

No. 20.

੧ ੴ ਸਤਿਗੁਰਪ੍ਰਸਾਦਿ।

ਲਿਖਤਮ ਜੁਵਾਲਾਸਿੰਘ ਜੋਗ ਭਾਈ ਆਲਾਸਿੰਘ ਫਤੇ ਬੁਲਾਈ ਵਾਚਣੀ ਜੀ। ਹੋਰ
ਜੀ ਹਾਲ ਏਹੁ ਹੈ ਕਿ ਚਿਠੀ ਤੁਸਾਡੀ ਪਹੁੰਚੀ ਹਾਲ ਮਲੂਮ ਕੀਤਾ ਤੁਸਾਂ ਜੋ ਲਿਖਿਆ ਹੈ ਕਿ
ਸਾਡੇ ਪਿੰਡ ਵਿੱਚ ਬਹੁਤ ਆਦਮੀ ਗੁਜ਼ਰੇ ਹਾਲਾਂ ਵਿੱਚ ਸੜਕੇ ਮਰ ਗਏ ਹਨ ਤੇ ਭਾਈ ਵ
ਜੀਰਸਿੰਘ ਦੀ ਮੂੰਹ ਸਿਰ ਸੜਨ ਨਾਲ ਮਰ ਗਿਆ ਹੈ ਮੈਨੂੰ ਏਹ ਗਲ ਸੁਣ ਕੇ ਵਡਾ
ਅਫਸੋਸ ਲਗਦਾ ਹੈ ਕਰਤਾਰ ਦਾ ਭਾਣਾ ਐਵੇਂ ਹੀ ਹੋਵੇਗਾ ਹੁਣ ਤੁਸੀ ਆਪਣਾ
ਕੰਮ ਸੋਚ ਸੰਭਲ ਕੇ (1) ਕਰਿਆ ਕਰੋ ਅਤੇ ਜੇਕਰ ਤੁਹਾਨੂੰ ਪੈਸੇ ਧੇਲੇ (2) ਦੀ ਲੋੜ ਹੋਵੇ
ਤਾਂ ਲਿਖਣਾ ਮੈਂ ਘਲ ਦੇਵਾਂਗਾ ਨਹੀਂ ਤਾਂ ਰਾਮਸਹਾਇ ਕੋਲੋਂ ਹੁਦਾਰ ਲੈ ਲੈਣੇ
ਜੀ ਮੈਂ ਆਪੇ ਉਸਨੂੰ ਮਹੀਨੇ ਕੁ ਤੀਕ ਘਲ ਦੇਵਾਂਗਾ ਅਤੇ ਹੋਰ ਫਸਲ ਦਾ ਹੀ
ਦਾ ਹਾਲ ਲਿਖਣਾ ਪੈਲੀ ਨੂੰ ਹਫਤਿਆਂ ਨਾਲ ਵਾਹ ਸਿੰਜ (3) ਕੇ ਬੀਜਿਆ ਕਰੋ ਕਿਉਂ
ਜੋ ਜਦ ਤੇ ਮੈਂ ਨੌਕਰ ਹੋਇਆ ਹਾਂ ਦਾਣਾ ਫਕ ਸਦਾ ਤੁਹਾਡੀ ਪੈਲੀ ਦੇ ਚੋਖਾ ਹੁੰਦਾ
ਹੈ ਅਤੇ ਜੇਕਰ ਹੋਰ ਜੋਗ (4) ਦੀ ਲੋੜ ਹੋਵੇ ਤਾਂ ਮੁਲ ਲੈ ਲੈਣੀ। ਹੋਰ ਕੋਠੇ ਕਾਠੇ ਸਭ
ਲਿਬ ਛਣੇ ਲੇ ਕਿਉਂ ਜੋ ਬਰਸਾਤ ਵਿਚ ਢਠ (5) ਨਾ ਜਾਣ। ਹੋਰ ਖੋਲੇ (6) ਵਾਲੇ ਕੋਠੇ ਨੂੰ ਛਤ
ਛਡਣਾ ਓਥੇ ਹੀ ਚੋਰ ਉਚੱਕੇ ਦਾ ਬਹੁਤ ਡਰ ਰਹਿੰਦਾ ਹੈ। ਹੋਰ ਜੇਕਰ ਮੈਨੂੰ
ਛੁਟੀ ਮਿਲ ਗਈ ਤਾਂ ਦਸਾਂ ਪੰਦਰਾਂ ਦਿਨਾਂ ਤੀਕ ਆਵਾਂਗਾ। ਚਿਠੀ ਦਾ
ਉਤ੍ਰ ਛੇਤੀ ਘਲਣਾ।।

ਚਿਠੀ ਲਿਖੀ ਮਾਘ ਵਦੀ ੧੫

ਦਸਖਤ ਜੁਵਾਲਾਸਿੰਘ ਪਸੌਰ ਵਿਚੋਂ

---

1 ਸੋਚ ਸੰਭਲਕੇ carefully. 2 ਪੈਸਾ ਧੇਲਾ lit. pice or half a pice.
3 ਸਿੰਜਨਾ to irrigate. 4 ਜੋਗ pair of bullocks. 5 ਢਠਜਾਣਾ to fall down
6 ਖੋਲਾ ruin, a house without any roof.

No. 21.

੧ੳ ਸਤਿਗੁਰਪ੍ਰਸਾਦਿ॥

ਜੋਗ ਭਾਈਆ ਹਾਕਮਾ ਸਿੰਘ ਲਿਖੀ ਕੇਸਰ ਸਿੰਘ ਕੀ ਵਾਹਿਗੁਰੂ ਜੀ ਕੀ ਫਤੇ ਬੁਲਾਈ ਵਾਚਣੀ ਹੋਰ ਜੀ ਏਥੇ ਸੁਖ ਹੈ ਤੁਸਾਡੀ ਸੁਖ ਸਾਂਦ ਵਾਹਿਗੁਰੂ ਪਾਸੋ ਮੰਗਦੇ ਹਾਂ ਹੋਰ ਜੀ ਮੈਂ ਪਿਛੇ ਦੁਨਾਲ ਵਿਚ ਬੜਾ ਮਾਂਦਾ ਰਿਹਾ ਹੁਣ ਅਰ ਮਾਨੋਂ ਨੇਤਕੀ ਤਪ (1) ਆਉਂਦਾ ਰਿਹਾ ਸਵਾ ਮਹੀਨਾ ਹਸਪਤਾਲ ਵਿੱਚ ਪਿਆ ਰਿਹਾ ਸਾਡਾ ਡਾਕਦਾਰ ਸਾਹਿਬ ਬੜਾ ਚੰਗਾ ਹੈ ਰੋਜ ਦੇਖਲੈ ਖਬਰ ਰਖਦਾ ਹੈ ਕਿਸੀ ਗੁਲੋਂ ਔਖ ਨਹੀ ਸੀ ਕਸ ਹਟੀ ਤਾਂ ਮਰੋੜ (2) ਲਪਏ ਦਸ ਕੁ ਦਿਨ ਔਖਾ ਰਿਹਾ ਪਰ ਹੁਣ ਨੌ ਬਰਨੌ (3) ਹਾਂ ਫਿਕਰ ਨਹੀਂ ਕਰਨਾ ਵਤੁਰਪ (4) ਜੋ ਨੌਕਰੀ ਤੇ ਗਏ ਸੇ ਸੋ ਆਗਏ ਹੁਨ ਸਾਡਾ ਤੁਰਪ ਜਾਵੇਗਾ ਨੌਕਰੀ ਵਿੱਚ ਕਛ ਭਤਾ ਮਿਲੇਗਾ ਰਾਸ਼ਨ (5) ਸਰਕਾਰੀ ਮਿਲੇਗਾ ਮੇਰੀ ਹੁਣ ਦਫੇਦਾਰੀ ਦੀ ਰੌਲ (6) ਹੈ ਮੇਰੇ ਦਹਨੇ ਵਾਲਾ ਮਿਲ ਜਨ ਪਾਗੀਆ ਹੈ ਦੇਖੀਏ ਕਦ ਜਗਾ ਮਿਲਦੀ ਹੈ ਕੰਮ ਮੈਂ ਹੌਲਦਾਰੀ ਦਾ ਕਰਦਾ ਹਾਂ

ਦਸਤਖਤ ਕੇਸਰ ਸਿੰਘ ਲੌਸ ਨੇਕ

ਪਲਟਨ ਨੰਬ੍ਰ ੩੫ ਨੌਸ਼ੈਹਰਾ

---

1 ਨੇਤਕੀ ਤਪ daily fever. 2 ਮਰੋੜ dysentery 3 ਨੌ ਬਰਨੌ quite well. 4 ਤੁਰਪ errnption of English Troops. 5 ਰਾਸ਼ਨ "Rations." 6 ਰੌਲ turn.

No. 22.

ੴ ਸਤਿਗੁਰਪ੍ਰਸਾਦਿ॥

ਲਿਖਤੁਮ ਜ਼ਾਮ ਸਿੰਘ ਜੋਗ ਜਮਾਦਾਰ ਰਤਨ ਸਿੰਘ ਵੀਰਾਂ ਹੇ ਗੁਰੂ
ਜੀ ਕੀ ਫਤੇ ਪਹੁੰਚੇ।

ਤੁਸੀ ਜਦ ਤੇ ਰਜ਼ਾ[1] ਕਟ ਕੇ ਗਏ ਹੋ ਕੋਈ ਖਤ ਪਤ੍ਰ ਨਹੀ ਭੇਜਿਆ ਦੇਵਾ ਸਿੰਘ
ਦਾ ਮੁਕਦਮਾ ਫਤੇ ਹੋ ਗਿਆ ਅਧੀ ਜ਼ਮੀਨ ਮਿਲ ਗਈ ਚੀਫਕੋਟ[2] ਤੋਂ ਜਾਂਦੂਣਾ
ਖਰਚ ਦੀ ਬੜਾ ਹੋਇਆ ਕਰਮ ਚੰਦ ਸ਼ਾਹ ਨੇ ਬੜੀ ਮਦਦ ਦਿਤੀ ਆਖਦੇ ਹਨ
ਸਤ ਸੈ ਰੁਪਏ ਲਗਾ[3] ਕਲ ਦੇਵਾ ਸਿੰਘ ਤੇ ਸਾਮ ਸਿੰਘ ਸਥ ਵਿਚ ਲੜ
ਪਏ ਸਾਮ ਸਿੰਘ ਮੁਕਦਮਾ ਹਾਰਨ ਕਰਕੇ ਗੁਸੇ ਵਿੱਚ ਬੋਲਿਆ ਦੇਵਾ ਸਿੰਘ
ਨੂੰ ਗਾਲ਼ ਗਲੋਚ ਕਢਨ ਲਗਾ ਦੋਨੋ ਗੁਥਮ ਗੁਥਾ ਹੋ ਪਏ ਨਿਹਾਲ ਸਿੰਘ
ਲੰਬਰਦਾਰ ਛੁਡਾਇ ਲੜਾਈ ਨ ਕਮੀ ਗਲ ਤੋਂ ਹੋ ਪਈ ਦੇਵਾ ਸਿੰਘ ਦਾ
ਪੁਤ੍ਰ ਧਰਮ ਸਿੰਘ ਗੋਡੀ[4] ਕਰਦਾ ਸੀ ਜਦ ਨੂੰ ਸਾਮ ਸਿੰਘ ਦਾ ਪੁਤ੍ਰ ਰਤਨ ਸਿੰਘ
ਉਸ ਤੋਂ ਸਵੇਰੇ ਪਠੇ ਵਢਨ ਲਗਾ ਜੋ ਹਨੀ ਦੇਵਾ ਸਿੰਘ ਨੂੰ ਮਿਲ ਗਈ ਧਰਮ
ਸਿੰਘ ਹਟਕਿਆ ਰਤਨ ਸਿੰਘ ਆਪ ਲੋਪ ਉਹਨੂੰ ਦਸਿਆ ਇਸ ਤੇ ਗਲ
ਵਧ ਗਈ। ਹੋਰ ਜੀ ਮੈਂ ਇਕ ਮਹਿੰ ਖਰੀਦੀ ਹੈ ਦਸ ਸੇਰ ਪਕਾ ਦੁਧ ਦੇਂਦੀ ਹੈ
ਮਗਰ ਕਟੀ ਹੈ ਹੋਰ ਸਭ ਸੁਖ ਹੈ

---

1 ਰਜਾ furlough. 2 ਚੀਫ ਕੋਟ Chief Court. 3 ਲਗਨਾ to cos
4 ਗੋਡੀ ਕਰਨਾ to hoe.

No. 23.

੧ ੴ ਸਤਿਗੁਰਪ੍ਰਸਾਦਿ।

ਦਾਦਾ ਬੂਟਾ ਸਿੰਘ ਜੋਗ ਲਿਖਤੁਮ ਨੈਣ ਸਿੰਘ ਕੀ ਹੱਥ ਜੋੜ ਕੇ ਸ੍ਰੀ
ਵਾਹਿਗੁਰੂ ਜੀ ਕੀ ਫਤੇ ਬੁਲਾਈ ਪਹੁੰਚੇ।
ਹੋਰ ਜੀ ਅਸੀ ਰਾਜੀ ਖੁਸੀ ਹਾਂ ਤੁਹਾਡੀ ਸੁਖ ਸਾਂਦ ਗੁਰਾਂ ਪਾਸੋਂ ਮੰਗਦੇ ਹਾਂ
ਦਾਦਾ ਜੀ ਸਾਡੀ ਛਾਉਣੀ ਬਦਲ ਗਈ ਹੈ ਹੁਣ ਸਾਨੂੰ ਐਬਟਾਬਾਦ ਦੀ ਛਾਉਣੀ
ਮਿਲੂ ਸਾਡਾ ਕੂਚ ਹੋਣ ਵਾਲਾ ਹੈ ਤੁਸੀ ਜਦਿਵਾ ਸਿੰਘ ਨੂੰ ਭੇਜੋ ਮੈਂ ਉਸ ਨਾਲ
(1)
ਕਾਕੇ ਨੂੰ ਨਾਲੇ ਉਸ ਦੀ ਮਾਂ ਨੂੰ ਘਰ ਭੇਜਾਂਦਿਆਂ ਇੱਕ ਸਿੰਡਾ ਲੈ ਕੇ ਪਾਲਿਆ ਸੀ ਇੱਕ
(2)
ਬੈਲ ਲਿਆ ਸੀ ਇਹਨਾਂ ਨੂੰ ਘਰ ਲੈ ਜਾਊ ਹੁਣ ਤਲਬ ਮਿਲਣੀ ਹੈ ਚਾਰ ਕੌਡਾਂ
(3)
ਬਰੀਆਂ ਦੀ ਘਰ ਭੇਜਾਂਦਿਆਂ ਗੇ ਤੁਸਾਂ ਨਾਲ ਹੋਕੇ ਬਰਾਂਡਾ ਬਣਵਾ ਦੇਣਾ ਤੇ ਖੂਹ
(4)
ਦੀ ਮਣ੍ਹ ਢੱਠੀ ਹੋਈ ਹੈ ਸੋ ਬਣਵਾ ਦੇਣੀ ਪਤਾ ਛੇਤੀ ਭੇਜਣਾ ਅਸੀ ਤੁਰਨ ਵਾਲੇ
ਹਾਂ ਲਿਖੀ ਮੰਗਲਵਾਰ

1 ਸਿੰਡਾ buffalo 2 ਬਰਾਂਡਾ verandh. 3 ਚਾਰ ਕੌਡਾਂ (4 kauris) some money. 4 ਮਣ੍ਹ a pakka work at the top of well.

No 24.

੧ ਓ ਸਤਿਗੁਰਪ੍ਰਸਾਦਿ॥

(1)
ਬਰਖਰਦਾਰ ਚੰਦਾ ਸਿੰਘ ਜੋਗ ਲਿਖਤੁਮ ਚੰਚਲ ਸਿੰਘ ਦੀ ਬਰਖਰਦਾਰੀ
ਪਹੁੰਚੇ। ਅਸੀ ਸਿਵੀ ਓਥੰ ਮੁੜ ਪਏ ਹਾਂ ਤੁਸਾਂ ਕੁਛ ਫਿਕਰ ਨਾ ਕਰਨਾ ਰਾਜੀ ਬਾ
ਜੀਹਾਂ ਦੇ ਮਣੀ ਨੇ ਪਹਾੜਾਂ ਵਿੱਚ ਕੂਚ ਮੁਕਾਮ ਹੁੰਦਾ ਰਿਹਾ — ਏਥੇ ਬਰਫ ਜ਼ੋਰ ਦੀ ਪਈ ਪੈਂਦੀ
ਹੈ ਕਦੇ ਕਦੇ ਧੁਪ ਨਿਕਲਦੀ ਪੈਂਦੀ ਹੈ ਸਰਕਾਰ ਦੇ ਲੋਕ ਪਹਾੜੀ ਮੁਲਕ ਹੋਏ ਹਨ ਰਾਸ਼ਨ ਭੀ
(2) (3)
ਚੰਗਾ ਮਿਲਦਾ ਹੈ ਪਰ ਤਦ ਭੀ ਬਿਖੜਾ ਬਿਖਨਾ ਮੁਲਕ ਹੈ ਏਥੇ ਆਕੀ ਲੋਕ ਰਹਿੰ
ਦੇ ਹੈਨ ਮਰਨ ਮਾਰਨੇ ਨੂੰ ਨਹੀਂ ਡਰਦੇ ਆਖਦੇ ਹਨ ਗਾਜ਼ੀ ਬਣੀਦੇ ਹਾਂ ਪਰ ਤੈਂ ਤਲਵਾਰ ਲੈ
ਕੇ ਗਭੀ ਮੈਂਦੀ ਲਾ ਕੇ ਔਲੀ ਔਲੀ ਕਰਕੇ ਚੋਰੀਆਂ ਪੈਂਦੇ ਹਨ ਬੁਰੇ ਬੰਦੇ ਤਰਸ ਹਨ
(4)
ਨੇ ਜਮਾਦਾਰ ਦਾ ਟਟੂ ਚੁਰਾ ਲੈ ਗਏ ਮਸੀਂ ਹੱਥ ਲਗਾ ਦਸਾਂ ਦਿਹਾਂ ਦਿਨਾਂ ਤੋਂ ਰੀਖ
ਰ ਚਪਣਾ ਤੁਸੇ ਜਾਂਦੇ ਹੋਰ ਘਰ ਦਾ ਸਾਰਾ ਹਾਲ ਲਿਖਣਾ ਸਾਡਾ ਏਥੇ ਰਗੀਸਿਆਂ ਨੂੰ

1 ਬਰਖਰ ਦਾਰ happy, enjoying long life male children are so called. 2 ਬਿਖੜਾ impassable, difficult. 3 ਆਕੀ rebellious, disobedient. 4 ਮਸੀ hardly, with great difficulty.

No. 25.

੧ੴ ਸਤਿਗੁਰਪ੍ਰਸਾਦਿ।

ਲਿਖਤੁਮ ਗੀਤਾ ਪਰੋਹਤ ਜੋਗ ਆਸਾ ਸਿੰਘ ਅਸੀਰਬਾਦ ਬਾਚਣਾ ਹੋਰ ਏਥੇ ਸੁਖ ਹੈ ਤੁਹਾਡੀ ਸੁਖ ਸ੍ਰੀ ਨਾਰਾਇਨ ਤੇ ਮੰਗਾਂਵੇ ਹਾਂ। ਹੋਰ ਸਮਾਚਾਰ ਏਹੁ ਹੈ ਕਿ ਪਰਸੋਂ ਬੀਬੀ ਦੇ ਸਹੁਰਿਆਂ ਤੇ ਨਾਈ ਆਇਆ ਸੀ ਆਖਦੇ ਹੈਨ ਵਿਆਹੁ ਦੇਣ ਦੇ ਏਸ ਅਗਲੇ ਪਖ (1) ਵਿਚ ਆਖਦੇ ਹਨ ਸਾਹਾ (2) ਭੀ ਸੋਧਿਆ ਸੀ ਰਾਹੂ ਦਾ ਪਿਛਲਾ ਬਨਦਾ ਹੈ ਪਰ ਤੁਸੀ ਛੁਟੀ ਲੈਕੇ ਤੁਰਤ ਦਰਕਮ ਬਨੇਗਾ ਜਜਮਾ (3) ਨੀ ਬਾਰ ਬਾਰ ਤਕੀਦ ਕਰਦੀ ਹੈ ਕੇ ਛੁਟੀ ਲੈਕੇ ਆ ਜਾਓ ਬੀਬੀ ਬੂਹਿਓਂ ਉਠਾਈ ਜਾਏ ਹੁਣ ਵਿਆਹੁਣ ਜੋਗੀ (4) ਹੈ ਤੇ ਇਸ ਦੇ ਸਾਹੁਰੇ ਭੀ ਅਗਾਰ ਪਏ ਹੋਏ ਹੈਨ ਪਰ ਸਭ ਚੀਜਾਂ ਤਿਆਰ ਹੈ ਦੋ ਚਾਰ ਬੇਓਰ (5) ਬਨਾਉਣ ਵਾਲੇ ਹਨ ਨਥ (6) ਬਨਾ ਲਈ ਹੈ ਚੌਂਕ (7) ਹਸ (8) ਭੀ ਤਿਆਰ ਹਨ ਹੋਰ ਬਾਕੀ ਚੀਜਾਂ ਤੁਹਾਡੇ ਆਏ ਬਨ ਜਾਣਗੀਆਂ ਜਰੂਰ ਆ ਜਾਓ ਥੋੜਾ ਲਿਖਿਆ ਬਹੁਤ ਜਾਨਨਾ।

1 ਪਖ corrupted from the sanskrit word ਪਖਯ a period of 15 days, half a lunar month. 2 ਸਾਹਾ the dav appoint for wedding. 3 ਜਜਮਾਨ cliant of a brahman. ਜਜਮਾਨਨੀ his wife. 4 ਵਿਆਹੁਨ ਜੋਗੀ marriagable. 5 ਬੇਓਰ suit of 2 clothes. ਤੇਓਰ of 3 clothes 6 ਨਥ nose-ring. 7 ਚੌਂਕ head ornament worn by woman and children. 8 ਹਸ a silver or gold collar.

No 26

੧ ਓ ਸਤਿਗੁਰ ਪ੍ਰਸਾਦਿ॥

ਸ੍ਰੀ ਸਰਬ ਗੁਣ ਨਿਧਾਨ ਨਿਰਮਲ ਬੁਧ ਬਾਪੂ ਹੋਰਾਂ ਜੋਗ ਦਾਸ ਬਰਿਆਮ ਸਿੰਘ
ਦੀ ਹਥ ਜੋੜ ਕੇ ਫਤੇ ਬੁਲਾਵਣੀ ਹੋਰ ਜੀ ਐਤਕੀ ਪੈਲੀ ਬੀਜਣੇ ਦਾ ਬੁਰਾ ਹਾਲ
ਹੈ ਮੀਂਹ ਪਿਆ ਨਹੀ ਨਹਰ ਬੀ ਦਰਕਾਰੀ ਤੇ ਖੂਹ ਦਾ ਭੂਆ ਕਲਮ ਤੇ ਬੈਲ ਕੁਰੇ
ਪਏ ਹੈਨ ਰੋਗਾਂ ਨਾਲ ਵੀ ਜੀ ਕਾੜੀ ਨਹੀ ਸਭ ਦਾ ਆਪਾਂ ਕਰੇ ਔਖੀ ਤਾਂ ਰਹੀ
ਨਹੀਂ ਦੇਖੀ ਦਰਖਤ ਫਲ ਫੁਲ ਪਾਣੀ ਦੇ ਹੈਨ ਤੇ ਦਾਣੇ ਦਾ ਭਾਅ ਦਿਨੋ ਦਿਨ ਚੜ੍ਹ
ਨੂੰ ਤੁਰਿਆ ਜਾਂਦਾ ਹੈ ਹਾਲੀ ਦੇ ਦਾਣੇ ਬੀਜਣ ਲਈ ਸੇ ਸਾਊ ਲੀਦੀ ਜੁਆਰ ਖਾਣ
ਜੋਗੀ ਰਹੀ ਹੈ ਅਠੋ ਚੀ ਪਾਊ ਵੇਚੇ ਤਾਂ ਤੁਸਾਂ ਖਰਚ ਨਹੀ ਭੇਜਿਆ ਅਸੀਂ ਬਣੇ ਤੰਗ
ਹਾਂ ਕੁਛ ਖਰਚ ਭੇਜੋ ਤਾਂ ਤੁਸਾਡਾ ਗੁਜਾਰਾ ਚਲੂ ਬੀ ਹਰ ਪਏ ਦੇਵਣੇ ਕਹਿੰਦੇ ਹਨ

No 27

੧ ਓ ਸਤਿਗੁਰ ਪ੍ਰਸਾਦਿ॥

ਸ੍ਰੀ ਸਰਬ ਗੁਣ ਨਿਧਾਨ ਉਜਲ ਦੀਦਾਰ ਨਿਰਮਲ ਬੁਧ ਸ੍ਰੀ ਮਾਨ ਸਰਦਾਰ ਸਾ
ਹਿਬ ਰਸਾਲਦਾਰ ਮੇਜਰ ਸਰਦਾਰ ਤਾਰਾ ਸਿੰਘ ਜੀ ਸਰਦਾਰ ਬਹਾਦੁਰ ਜੋਗ
ਦਾਸ ਧਰਮ ਸਿੰਘ ਦੀ ਸ੍ਰੀ ਵਾਹਿਗੁਰੂ ਜੀ ਕੀ ਫਤੇ ਬੁਲਾਵਣੀ ਹੋਰ
ਸਮਾਚਾਰ ਇਹ ਕਿ ਵਾਚਣਾ ਹੋਰ ਜੀ ਏਥੇ ਸੁਖ ਹੈ ਆਪ ਦੀ ਆਪਦੇ ਪਰਵਾਰ ਸਹਿ
ਤ ਸਰਬਦੀ ਸੁਖ ਸ੍ਰੀ ਵਾਹਿਗੁਰੂ ਤੇ ਮੰਗਦੇ ਹਾਂ
ਅਗੇ ਜੀ ਮੈਂ ਆਪ ਦੇ ਚਰਨਾਂ ਤੋਂ ਜੁਦਾ ਹੋ ਕੇ ਕੱਲ ਘਰ ਪਹੁੰਚਾਂ ਜਾਂ ਤੁਰਨ ਲਗਿਆਂ

* For all the hard words consult the vocabulary at the end.

ਧਰਮਸਾਲਾਦੀਕੁੰਜੀਜਮਾਦਾਰਹਰੀਸਿੰਘਨੂੰਦੇਆਇਆਸਾਂਹੋਰਜੀ
ਜਮਾਦਾਰਹਰੀਸਿੰਘਜੀਨੂੰਆਪਣਾਧਰਮਸਾਲਦੀਖਬਰਰਖੇਮਤਾਂ
ਕਿਤੇਕੋਈਨੁਕਸਾਨਹੋਜਾਂਦਾਹੋਵੇ ਹੋਰਜੀਅਸਵਾਰੇਸਾਹਿਬਦੇਨੋਅਲ
ਮਾਰੀਵਿਚਹਨਸੰਥਪਾਨਿਆਂਨਾਲ ਹੋਰਸਭਰੀਆਂਪਾਸਰੀਹਨਪੰਜਗ੍ਰੰ
ਥੀਪੋਥੀਜਨਮਸਾਖੀਗੁਰਬਿਲਾਸਆਦਿਕਪੁਸਤਕਅਲਮਾਰੀਵਿਚ
ਪਏਹਨ ਹੋਰਜੀਰੁਖਸਤਮੁਕੀਤੇਮਗਰੋਂਛੇਤੀਹਾਜਰਹੋਜਾਮਾਂਗਾ
ਸਭਨੂੰਫਤੇਪਹੁੰਚੇ

No 28

੧ਓ ਸਤਿਗੁਰਪ੍ਰਸਾਦਿ।

ਲਿਖਤੁਮਚੰਦਾਸਿੰਘਜੋਗਭਾਈਭਾਗਸਿੰਘਜੀਵਾਹਿਗੁਰੂਜੀਦੀ
ਫਤੇਵਾਚਣੀ।ਆਗੇਚਿਠੀਪਹੁੰਚੀਬੜੀਖੁਸੀਹੋਈਹੋਰਜੀਤੁਸਾਂਜੋਸਭੇਦਾ
ਹਾਲਪੁਛਿਆਸੀਸੋਜੀਸਭਾਚੰਗਾਅਰਦਾਸਾਂਕੀਤਾਰਿਹਾਹੈਜੀਇਕਕਲੀ
ਨਹੀਪਈ ਕਣਕਛੋਟੋਮੇਂਹੋਗਈਐਥਾਈਏਨੀਆਂਨਾਲਗੀਕਦੇਵੇਖਣ
ਵਿਚਨਾਆਈਸੁਣਨਵਿੱਚਆਇਆਨਬੇਦਾਏਦਾਕਾਲਪਿਆਸਮਾਰ
ਸਾਰੀਸੁਰਤਵਿਚਏਹੋਜੇਹਾਸਮਾਨਹੀਬੀਤਿਆ।

ਅਨਾਜਬਹਲੇਰਜੀਹਨਛੇਸੱਤੋਂਏਪੇਪਲੇਵਿੱਚਪਤਵੇਹਨਗਰੀਬਜਾਦੇ
ਲੈਂਦੇਹਨਸੁਣਮਾਹਪਵੇਤਾਂਕਾਲਜਾਏਦੁਖਦੇਦੁਖਬਹੁਤਲੋਕਸਕਾਰੇ
ਹਨਪਰਪੇਸ਼ਕੁਝਨਹੀਜਾਂਦੀਵਾਹੇਚਬਕੋਵਿਹਾਰੀਲਿਆਈਦੀਹੈਸਾਂਈ
ਖੈਰਕਰੇਤਦਹੀਬਚਾਹੈਹੋਰਜੀਕਣਕਛਨੀਬਦਲਹੁੰਦੇਹਨਜੇਕਦੇਮੇਂਹ

ਰਕਰਦੇਦੇ॥ No 29

੧ ੴ ਸਤਿਗੁਰਪ੍ਰਸਾਦਿ।

ਸ੍ਰੀਮਤੁਮਾਤਾਸਾਹਿਬਦੇਵਾਂ ਜੋਗ ਕਰਮਸਿੰਘ ਵਾਹਿਗੁਰੂਜੀਕੀਫਤੇਦਾ
ਨੀ ਹੋਰ ਜੀ ਏਥੇ ਸੁਖ ਸੁਖਾਲੇ ਤੁਹਾਡੀ ਸੁਖ ਸਾਂਦ ਸਤਿਗੁਰੂ ਪਾਸੋਂ ਚਾ
ਹੀਦੇ ਹਾਂ ਜੀ ਹੋਰ ਜੀ ਤੁਸਾਂ ਸਾਡੇ ਪਾਸ ਸੁਖ ਸਾਂਦ ਦੀ ਖਬਰ ਦੇਦੇ ਨੀ ਸੁਣ
ਕੇ ਖੁਸੀ ਆਵਦੇ ਨਾਲ ਤੇ ਆਪ ਦਾ ਤੇਰਾ ਸਾਪੂਲੇ ਹਜੀ ਨੂੰ ਆਂਦੇ ਗਾ ਤੇ ਰੋਲ ਦੀ
ਪੋਨੇ ਕੀਨੇ ਲਿਆਂਦੇ ਸਾ ਅਗੇ ਜੀ ਮੈਂ ਦਚਾਲੇ ਲਈ ਹੈ ਹੋਰ ਜੀ ਹੁਣ ਤੂ ਰਨ
ਦੀਤਿਆ ਗੀ ਹੈ ਇਕ ਦੋ ਕਪੜੇ ਬਨਾਉ ਨੇ ਹਨ ਜਦ ਬਨ ਜਾ ਦੇਗਨ ਤਾਂ ਲੈ ਕੇ ਤੂ
ਪਦਾਗੇ ਏਪਰ ਦੇ ਲੈ ਹਗੇ ਜੋ ਹਨੇ ਹੁਏ ਹਨ ਅਰਕਾ ਕੇਦੀ ਮਾਂ ਨੇਕ ਸੀ ਦੇਹ ਕਹਿ
ਭੇਜਿਆ ਲੈ ਹਗਾ ਲੈ ਕੇ ਆਉਨਾ ਹੋਰ ਜੀ ਹੋਰ ਦੀ ਜਾਂ ਭੀ ਲੈ ਆਉਦਾ ਪਰ
ਫਾਉਨੀ ੴ ਰੋਲ ਤਾਈ ਪੈਤੀ ਕੋ ਰਤੁਰਨਾ ਪੈਂਦਾ ਹੈ ਰਸਤਾ ਬਨ੍ਹਾ ਵਿਖਲਾਵੇ
ਅਸਵਾਰੀ ਨਗੀ ਲਭਦੀ ਹੋਰ ਜੀ ਰਤਨਸਿੰਘ ਦੇ ਪਾਸ ਖਬਰ ਦੇਣੀ ਕਿ
ਹੁਰ ਜੀ ਖੁਸੀ ਪਹੁੰਚੀਆ ਹੈ

ਲਿਖੀ ਦੁਤ ਮਘਰ ਸੰ: ੧੮੫੧

No 30

੧ ੴ ਸਤਿਗੁਰਪ੍ਰਸਾਦਿ

ਸ੍ਰੀ ਸਰਬ ਗੁਣ ਨਿਧਾਨ ਮਾਤਾ ਰਾਜਸਿੰਘ ਜੀ ਜੋਗ ਦਾਸ ਹਰਸਿੰਘ.
ਦੀ ਫਤੇ ਵਾਹਗੁਰੂ ਜੀ ਮਾਤਾ ਜੀ ਏਥੇ ਸਭ ਰਾਜੀ ਬਾਜੀ ਹਨ ਤੁਸਾਡੀ ਸੁਖ ਰਾਮ

ਜੋ ਪਾਸੋਂ ਮੰਗਾਏ ਤਾਂ।

ਸਾਮਾ ਜੀ ਜਦ ਦੇ ਆਪ ਗਏ ਕੋਈ ਹਰਿ ਨੀਪ ੜੀਨ ਗੰਡੇ ਜੀ ਤੁਸੀਂ ਆਖ ਗਏ
ਸੀ ਅਸੀਂ ਜਾਂਦੇ ਤੈਨੂੰ ਸਦਾਂਗੇ ਸੋ ਦੋ ਮਹੀਨੇ ਹੋਏ ਤੁਸਾਂ ਨਹੀ ਸਦਿਆ ਸੋ ਤਾਂ
ਵਾਹੀ ਪਤੀ ਦਾ ਕੰਮ ਤੀ ਛਡ ਬੈਠਾ ਹਾਂ ਨਹੀਂ ਨਿਟਾ ਕਰੇ ਸਨ ਕਦੇ ਨੌਕਰੀ ਮੋ
ਗਾ ਸੋ ਮੈਨੂੰ ਛੇਤੀ ਸਦ ਲੌ ਸ੍ਰੀ ਗੁਰੂ ਸੰਪਦਾ ਪੂਤ ਸਾਹੁ ਸਿੰਘ ਘਰ ਮਾਦੀ ਤ
ਰਤੀ ਵਿੱਚ ਗਿਆ ਮੈਨੂੰ ਨਾਲ ਸਦ ਵਾਸੀ ਪਰ ਸੈਨ ਹੀ ਗਿਆ ਹੋਰ ਜੀ ਇਕ
ਤੁਹਾਡਾ ਮੋਰ ਕਾ ਹੁਗਦਾ ਹੁਗਦਾ ਮੋਘੇ ਵਿਚ ਕ੍ਰਿਗਾ ਪਰ ਕੁਝ ਨੁਕਸਾਨ ਨਹੀ
ਹੋਇਆ ਨੌਕਰ ਨੇ ਹੈ ਹੋਰ ਸਭ ਖਰਾ ਜੀ ਹਨ ਉਤਰ ਛੇਤੀ ਭੇਜਣਾ ਥੋੜੇ ਲਿਖੇ ਨੂੰ
ਬਹੁਤ ਜਾਨਣਾ

No 31

੧ ਓ ਸਤਿਗੁਰਪ੍ਰਸਾਦਿ॥

ਸ੍ਰੀ ਸਰਬ ਉਪਮਾ ਜੋਗ ਬਾਪੂ ਜੀ ਦਾਸ ਰਤਨ ਸਿੰਘ ਦੀ ਗੁਰ ਫਤਹਿ ਸ੍ਰੀ
ਲਈ ਬਾਚਣੀ ਜੀ ਅਸੀ ਜੋ ਦੇ ਦੇ ਮੁਰਗੀ ਆਏ ਹਾਂ ਤੇ ਦੇ ਦਾ ਤੁਸਾਂ ਖਤ ਨ
ਹੀਂ ਪਾਇਆ ਤੁਹਾਡੇ ਖਤ ਨਾ ਆਉਣੇ ਤੇ ਸਾਡੇ ਦਿੱਲ ਗਦਾ ਅਨਭੁਟ ਕਦਾ ਹੈ
ਅਸਾਂ ਸਾਉਣੀ ਸਾਂਭ ਲਈ ਹੈ ੧੫ ਪੰਡਾਂ ਦਿਹਾੜਿਆਂ ਵਿਚ ਸੋਰ ਦਾ ਅਤੇ
੨੨ ਵਿਚੋਂ ਛੋਲੇ ਗਡਾ ਦਿਤੇ ਹਨ ੧੫ ਪੰਡਾਂ ਦਿਹਾੜਿਆਂ ਵਿੱਚ ਰੌਣੀ ਕਰਾ
ਛੱਡੀ ਹੈ ਜੋ ਦੋ ਦਰਆ ਦੇਗਾ ਕਨਕ ਕੇਰ ਦਿਆਂਗੇ ਕਮਾਦ ਲਈ ਤੇ ਕਮ

ਛੱਡੀਹੈਖੂਹਦੀਪੈਲੀਲੋਕਹਿਸੇਤੇਮੰਗਦੇਹਨਪੰਜਵੂਅੰਜੀਆਖਦੇਹਨ
ਅਸਾਂਅਧਆਖਿਆਹੈਓਹੁਨਹੀਮੰਨਦੇਔਤਕੀਦਿਆਂਭੀਗੱਲਖੂਹਦਾਵ
ਤੇਤੇਨਾਂਗਲਕੀਤਾਹੈਚੀਨੇਵੈਗਏਹਨਕਾਵੰਨਤੋਤੇਪਈਹੈਸਾਰੀਸੇਉਕਨੇ
ਖਾਲਈਹੈਫਲਟੁੱਟਕੇਸਾਰੇਬੈਨਤੇਪਨਨੇਸਮੇਤਖੂਹਦਿਰਜਾਪਈਹੈ
ਅਸੀਂਅਕਲਾਪੇਕਿਤਲਾਕਿਤਲੋਹੈਦੀਏਤੁਸੀਂਸਿੱਧੀਨਹੀਂਵਾਹਦੇਨੂੰਗ
ਸਾਰੀਆਂਤੁਹਾਨੂੰਮਥਾਟੇਕਦੀਆਂਹਨਅਰਕਾਕੇਗਸ਼ੋਜੇਨੂੰਕੇਫਤਹਕਹਿੰਦੇ
ਹਨਚਨੂੰਚੂਹੜਾਸਲਾਮਆਖਦਾਹੈ

ਆਪਦਾਦਾਸਚਨਨਤਸਿੰਘਚਕਨੰਬਰ੪੫

੧ਓ ਸਤਿਗੁਰਪ੍ਰਸਾਦਿ॥

ਸ੍ਰੀਸਰਬਉਪਮਾਜੋਗਭਾਈਨੌਧਸਿੰਘਜੀਦਾਸਨਦਾਸਦਲਸਿੰਘਦੀ
ਸ੍ਰੀਵਾਹਿਗੁਰੂਜੀਦੀਫਤੇਵਾਚਣੀਜੀਹੋਰਸੁਖਵਾਚਣੀਏਥੇਔਤਕੀਐ
ਤਾਂਭੀਹਾਲਹੋਇਆਹੈਪਾਣੀਛਿਆਪਾਣੀਨਹੀਚਲਿਆਵਣਾਂਉਣਾਂਸਭਤੁੱਟਗ
ਈਆਂਹਨਅਰਦੂਜਾਕਾਂਗਆਈਹੈਜੋਪੈਲੀਆਂਦਾਫਕਾਨਹੀਛਡ
ਗਈਸਰਕਈਆਂਬਾਜਰੇਆਂਹਰਦਾਹਸਭਮਾਰਗਈਹੈਕੋਈਆਂਦੇਚੋਖੂਰ
ਤੀਰਤੀਬਾਹਿਕੇਰੁੜਗਏਹਨਜੋਪਿੰਡਨੂੰਵੱਟਨਾਂਮਾਰਦੇਤਾਂਪਿੰਡਦੇਬੀਕੰਧਾਂ
ਕੋਠੇਸਭਬਹਿਜਾਣੇਸਨਪਰਇਹੁਗੁਰੂਦੀਹੀਕਿਰਪਾਹੋਈਹੈਜੋਉਸਨੇ

ਗਭਰੂਆਂ ਦੇ ਮਨ ਵਿਚ ਉਦਾਸ ਮਦੇ ਦਿਤਾ ਅਬ ਜੋ ਕੁਛ ਗੁਰਮੁਖ ਪੁਰਖਾਂ ਨੇ ਗੁਰਮਤ ਆਖਿਆ ਉਸ ਨੇ ਉਸੇ ਤਰਾਂ ਕੀਤਾ ਹੋਰ ਸਾਡੇ ਮਾਲ [illegible] ਦੀ ਅਰ ਮਨੁਖਾਂ ਦੀ ਸੁਖ ਹੈ।

ਆਪਦਾ ਦਾਸ ਦਲਸਿੰਘ ਲਖੋਤਾਹਿਰੋ।

No 32

ੴ ਸਤਿਗੁਰਪ੍ਰਸਾਦਿ।

ਭਾਈ ਆ ਜੀ ਵਾਹਿਗੁਰੂ ਜੀ ਕੀ ਫਤੇ। ਐਥੇ ਸੁਖ ਹੈ ਤੇ ਤੁਹਾਡੀ ਸੁਖ ਆਨੰਦ ਸਤਿਗੁਰਾਂ ਪਾਸੋਂ ਚਾਹੁੰਦੇ ਹਾਂ ਜੀ। ਹੋਰ ਹਾਲ ਏਹ ਹੈ ਜੋ ਮੈਂ ਨਿਤ ਹੀ ਸਿਆਣਾ ਸਿੰਘ ਨੂੰ ਤਗੀਦ ਕਰਦਾ ਹੁੰਦਾ ਸੀ ਜੋ ਦਿਗ ਬਾਂਦਾ [illegible] ਨੇ ਦੀ ਚੋਰੀ ਨੀਤ ਰਾਤ ਕਰਾਈ ਰਖਿਆ ਕਰੋ ਪਰ ਉਹ ਮੇਰੀ ਗਲ ਸੁਣਦਾ ਭੀ ਨਹੀਂ ਸੀ ਤੇ ਆਖਦਾ ਹੁੰਦਾ ਸੀ ਜੋ ਐਥੇ ਕੇਹੜੇ ਚੋਰ ਆਉਂਦੇ ਹਨ। ਜੋ ਅਸੀਂ ਵਾੜੇ ਦੀ ਰਾਖੀ ਕਰੀਏ ਸੋ ਉਹੋ ਜੀ ਗਲ ਹੋਈ ਜੇਹੜੀ ਮੈਂ ਕਿਹਾ ਕਰਦਾ ਹੁੰਦਾ ਸੀ ਅਜ ਰਾਤ ਨੂੰ ਨਾਤਾਂ ਮੈਂ ਵੇਖੇ ਸੀ ਨਾ ਕੋਈ ਕਾਮਾ ਹੀ ਆਯਾ ਤੇ ਵਾੜਾ ਸੁੰਨਾ ਤਕ ਕੇ ਕੋਈ ਸਾਰੇ ਪਸੂ ਹਕ ਲੈ ਗਿਆ ਹੁਣ ਉਹ ਪਿਆ ਰੋਂਦਾ ਹੈ ਤੇ ਐਨਾ ਚਿਰ ਲਾਹੈ ਜੋ ਥਾਣੇ ਜਾਕੇ ਤਲਾਸ਼ ਭੀ ਨਹੀਂ ਦਿਤੀ।

No 34

੧ ਓ ਸਤਿਗੁਰਪ੍ਰਸਾਦਿ॥

ਭਾਈ ਚੰਦਾ ਸਿੰਘ ਜੀ ਤੁਹਾਡੇ ਆਖੇ ਤੇ ਫਲ ਤਾਂ ਮੀਂਹ ਬਥੇਰਾ ਸੀ
ਪਰ ਸਾਵੇਂ ਫਲ ਤਾਂ ਇਕ ਭੀ ਬਣੀ ਨਹੀਂ ਪਈ ਸੀ ਏਸ ਕਰਕੇ ਅਸੀਂ
ਬੁਰਕ ਨਹੀਂ ਬੀਜਿਆ ਸੀ ਪਰ ਹੁਣ ਸਾਨੂੰ ਕੁਝ ਸਹਾਰਾ ਹੋ ਗਿਆ ਹੈ ਕਿ
ਉਨ੍ਹੇਂ ਨੈਹਰ ਜੋ ਹਮੀ ਸਾਡੇ ਪਿੰਡ ਨੂੰ ਨਹੀਂ ਲਗਦੀ ਸੀ ਟੁਰ ਗਈ ਹੈ ਤੇ ਉਹ
ਦੇ ਪਾਣੀ ਨਾਲ ਸਾਡੇ ਸਾਰੇ ਖੇਤ ਭਰ ਗਏ ਹਨ ਤੇ ਅਜੇ ਤਾਈਂ ਓਹ ਨਹਿਰ
ਬੰਦ ਨਹੀਂ ਹੋਈ ਜਿਸ ਕਰਕੇ ਅਸੀਂ ਆਸ ਰਖਦੇ ਹਾਂ ਜੋ ਸਾਡੇ ਪਿੰਡ ਦੇ
ਦੋ ਭੋਂ ਸਾਰੇ ਹੀ ਭਰ ਜਾਣਗੇ ਤੇ ਡੰਗਰਾਂ ਨੂੰ ਪਾਣੀ ਦਾ ਬੜਾ ਆਰਾਮ ਹੋ
ਜਾਊਗਾ।

No 35

੧ ਓ ਲਿਖਤਮ ਨਿਹਾਲ ਸਿੰਘ ਜੋਗ ਭਾਈ ਦਿਲਬਾਗ ਸਿੰਘ
ਵਾਹਿਗੁਰੂ ਜੀ ਕੀ ਫਤੇ ਪ੍ਰਸ਼ਾਈ ਦਾ ਫਤੇ। ਚਿਠੀ ਲਿਖੀ ਹਰਸਾ ਪੁਰੋਂ
ਕਤਕ ਵਦੀ ੨੦ ਭੀ ਕੇ ਭਾਈ ਜੀ ਇਥੇ ਸੁਖ ਸਾਂਦ ਹੈ ਤੇ ਤੁਹਾਡੀ ਸੁਖ ਸਦਾ
ਸ੍ਰੀ ਵਾਹਿਗੁਰੂ ਜੀ ਪਾਸੋਂ ਮੰਗਦਾ ਹਾਂ ਤੁਸਾਂ ਪੁਛਿਆ ਹੈ ਉਤ੍ਰੋ ਐਤਕੀ ਮੈਂ
ਪਾਨੋਂ ਲੇਕੂ ਰਦਾਨਾ ਫਕਾ ਖਰੀਦ ਲਈ ਰਾਮ ਸਿੰਘ ਸਾਮ ਸਿੰਘ ਦੇ
ਨਾਲ ਤੇ ਗਾਂਦੀ ਗਾਂ ਭੁਪ ਜਾਲੈ ਕੇ ਗਿਆ ਤੇ ਇਕ ਗਡੇ ਛੋਲਿਆਂ ਦਾ
ਤੇ ਨਿਕ ਗਡੀ ਫਟ ਜਿਹਦੀ ਫਤਣ ਕਦਾ ਖਰੀਦਿਆ ਅਸਪੰਦਰਾਂ

ਮਣ ਦਾ ਉਸ ਭੀ ਖਰੀਦ ਕੇ ਬੈਲ ਦ ਉਪਰ ਲਦੀ ਆਸੀ ਤਿਨੇ ਤੁਰੀਆ
ਉਦੇਸਾਂ ਕੀ ਹੋ ਹੋਇ ਆਜੋ ਅਗੋਂ ਸਾਨੂੰ ਕੋਈ ਪੰਦਰਾਂ ਦੀਹ ਸੀਹੰਦਰ
ਗੇ ਮੁਸਣ ਤੋਂ ਠੇ ਕਿ ਜਿਨਾਂ ਦੇ ਹਥਾਂ ਵਿਚ ਕਣੀ ਕਣੀ ਤ੍ਰਿ ਠੀਆਂ ਤਾਂ ਗਾਂ ਸਨ
ਨਜਰੀ ਆਏ ਭਾਈ ਸੀ ਰਬ ਹੀ ਜਾਣਦਾ ਹੈ ਉਨਾਂ ਨੂੰ ਦੇਖ ਕਿ ਆਂਹੀ ਅ
ਜੇਹੀ ਘਣਕਣ ਛਿੜੀ ਜੋ ਕੈਹਣ ਦੀ ਗਲ ਹੀ ਨਹੀ ਆਸੀ ਸਭੋ ਤਿਨੇ ਜਣੇ
ਤੇ ਓਹ ਪੰਦਰਾਂ ਦੀਹ ਬੁਰਛੇ ਕਿਥੇ ਰਾਮ ਰਾਮ ਤੇ ਕਿਥੇ ਟੈਂ ਟੈਂ ਅਸੀ
ਉਨਾਂ ਦਾ ਸਾਹਮਣਾ ਤਾ ਕਰਨ ਜੋਗੇ ਹੀ ਨਹੀ ਸਾ ਤੇ ਨਾਹੀ ਸਾਡੇ ਕੋਲ
ਕੋਈ ਡਾਂਗ ਸੋਟਾ ਹੀ ਸੀ ਰਾਮ ਸਿੰਹ ਸਾਮ ਸਿੰਹ ਦਾ ਮੂੰਹ ਪੀਲਾ ਤੇ ਹੋਠ
ਸੁਕ ਗਏ ਤੇ ਲਤਾਂ ਕੇਲੇ ਦੇ ਪੱਤਿਆਂ ਵਾਂਗੂ ਕੰਬਣ ਮੂੰਹ ਗਲ ਨਾ ਨਿਕਲੇ ਅ
ਏਨਾਂ ਦਾ ਏਹ ਹਾਲ ਦੇਖ ਕੇ ਮੈਂ ਵੀ ਪੇਰੇਸ਼ਾਨ ਹੋਇਆ ਪਰ ਉਨਾਂ ਗਭਰੂ
ਦੀਦਿਆਂ ਨੇ ਆਉਂਦਿਆਂ ਹੀ ਕਿਹਾ ਸਿੰਘੋ ਕੁਝ ਤੁਹਾਡੇ ਪਾਸ ਹੈ ਤਾਂ ਤੁਸ
ਕਰੀ ਤੇ ਰਖ ਦਿਓ ਨਹੀ ਤਾਂ ਡਾਂਗਾਂ ਨਾਲ ਹਕਨਾ ਹੂਰ ਕ ਕਰਿਆਂਗੇ ਸੋ
ਓਹ ਸਾਡੇ ਸਿਰ ਪਰ ਡਾਂਗਾਂ ਲੈਈ ਖੜੇ ਤੇ ਅਸਾਂ ਤਿਨਾਂ ਨੇ ਕਪੜੇ ਲਾਹ
ਲੀਤੇ ਦੇ ਦਿਨੀ ਸਭ ਕੁਝ ਓਨਾਂ ਦੇ ਹਵਾਲੇ ਕੀਤਾ ਤੇ ਜਾਨ ਬਚਾਈ ਘਰ
ਆ ਕੇ ਸਦੇ ਦਾ ਗੁਰੂ ਦਾ ਕੜਾਹ ਕੀਤਾ ਤ ਸੁਖ ਮਨਾਈ ਏਹੋ ਜੇਹਾ ਅਜ
ਕਲ ਹਾਲ ਹੈ ਸਾਡੇ ਨਾਲ ਏਹ ਹੋ ਬੀਤੀ ਹੈ ਇਆ ਤਾਂ ਵਿਚਾਰੇ ਖਤ੍ਰੀਆਂ ਦੇ
ਬਾਬ ਕੀ ਹੁੰਦੀ ਹੈ ਉ ਸੋ ਅਕਲੇ ਦੁਕਲੇ ਤੁਸਾਂ ਨਾ ਨਿਕਲਨਾ ਹੋਰ ਸਭ
ਸੁਖ ਹੈ।

No 36

੧ ਓ ਸ੍ਰੀਯੁਤ ਕ੍ਰਿਪਾਸਾਗਰ ਭਾਈ ਰਤਨ ਸਿੰਘ ਜੀ

ਜੋਗ ਦਾਸ ਬਿਸਨ ਸਿੰਘ ਦੀ ਅੰਮ੍ਰਿਤਸਰੋਂ ਵਾਹਿਗੁਰੂ ਜੀ ਕੀ ਫਤਹ ਬੁਲਾਈ ਪਹੁੰਚੇ। ਭਾਈ ਜੀ ਇਥੇ ਸੁਖ ਹੈ ਅਤੇ ਤੁਹਾਡੀ ਸੁਖ ਸਦਾ ਹੀ ਅਕਾਲ ਪੁਰਖ ਦੇ ਹਜ਼ੂਰੋਂ ਮੰਗਦਾ ਹਾਂ ਜੀ। ਭਾਵੇਂ ਦਿਲ ਨਹੀਂ ਕਰਦਾ ਕਿ ਤੁਹਾਨੂੰ ਮੈਂ ਇਸ ਤਰਾਂ ਦੀ ਭਿਆਨਕ ਖਬਰ ਲਿਖਾਂ ਤੇ ਫਿਕਰ ਲਾਵਾਂ ਪਰ ਕੀ ਕਰਾਂ ਲਾਚਾਰੀ ਨੂੰ ਲਿਖਦਾ ਹਾਂ ਬਰਖਾ ਦੀ ਤੋਟ ਹੋਣ ਦੇ ਕਾਰਨ ਇਥੇ ਗਰਮੀ ਤਾਂ ਵਡਾ ਦੁਖ ਦੇ ਰਹੀ ਸੀ ਪਰ ਹੁਣ ਤਾਪ, ਹੈਜਾ, ਤੇ ਮਹਾਮਾਰੀ ਭੀ ਇਥੋਂ ਦੇ ਵਸਨੀਕਾਂ ਨੂੰ ਜਮੇਟ ਨਾਲ ਲਈ ਜਾਂਦੀ ਹੈ। ਡਾਕਦਾਰ ਲੋਕ ਇਸ ਦੇ ਰੋਕਣ ਲਈ ਬਥੇਰੇ ਉਪਰਾਲੇ ਤਾਂ ਕਰ ਰਹੇ ਹਨ ਪਰ ਅੱਗੇ ਜੋ ਗੁਰੂ ਕੀ ਮਰਜ਼ੀ। ਆਪਣੇ ਜਤਨਾਂ ਨਾਲ ਕੋਈ ਵਾਹੁ ਨਹੀਂ ਚਲਦੀ ਰੋਜ਼ ੩੦, ੪੦, ਪੁਰਸ਼ ਮਰ ਰਹੇ ਹਨ ਆਦਮੀ ਵਿਚਾਰੇ ਤਾਂ ਪਾਣੀ ਦੇ ਬੁਲਬੁਲੇ ਵਾਂਗ ਖਿਨ ਵਿਚ ਭਸਮ ਨਾਬੂਦ ਹੁੰਦੇ ਜਾਂਦੇ ਹਨ ਸੋ ਜੇ ਹੋਰ ਦੱਸ ਪੰਜ ਦਿਨਾਂ ਤੋਂ ਮੀਂਹ ਨਾ ਪਿਆ ਅਰ ਠੰਢ ਨਾ ਹੋਈ ਤਾਂ ਪਰਲੋ ਦਾ ਸਮਾ ਆ ਦਿਖਾਈ ਦੇਵੇਗਾ। ਇਸ ਕਰਕੇ ਭਾਈ ਜੀ ਮੇਰੀ ਮਰਜ਼ੀ ਹੈ ਜੋ ਤੁਸੀ ਆਪਣੀ ਘਰ ਵਾਲੀ ਤੇ ਬਾਲ ਬੱਚੇ ਨੂੰ ਉਥੇ ਆਪਣੇ ਪਾਸ ਅੰਬਾਲੇ ਮੰਗਵਾ ਲਵੋ ਤਾਂ ਚੰਗਾ ਹੋਵੇਗਾ ਅਗੇ ਜੋ ਸਤਗੁਰਾਂ ਤੁਹਾਡੀ ਮਰਜ਼ੀ ਹੋਵੇ ਕਰੋ ਇਹ ਨਾ ਸਮਝਣਾ ਜੋ ਇਹੁ ਕਦ ਲਾਂਭੇ ਚਾਹੁੰਦੇ ਹਨ ਸਾਡੇ ਸਿਰ ਮਥੇ ਤੇ ਰਹਿਣ ਸਾਡੇ ਪਾਸ ਤਾਂ ਰੌਣਕ ਲਗੀ ਹੋਈ ਹੈ ਖੁਰਾਕਾਂ ਮੰਨਣਾ ਤੇ ਉਤਰ ਛੇਤੀ ਭੇਜਣਾਂ

ਤੁਹਾਡਾ ਸ਼ੁਭ ਚਿੰਤਕ ਬਿਸਨ ਸਿੰਘ ਅੰਮ੍ਰਿਤਸਰੋਂ

No 37

੧ ੴ ਸਤਿਗੁਰ ਪ੍ਰਸਾਦਿ॥

ਸ੍ਰੀ ਸਰਬ ਉਪਮਾਂ ਜੋਗ ਭਾਈ ਮੂਲਾ ਮੱਲ ਜੀ ਬੀਰ ਸਿੰਘ ਦੀ ਫਤਹਿ ਵਾਚਣੀ ਹੋਰ
ਸੁਖ ਵਰਤਣੀ ਹੋਰ ਭਾਈ ਜੀ ਅੰਮ੍ਰਿਤਸਰ ਜੀ ਦੇ ਦਾਣੇ ਫੱਕੇ ਦਾ ਭਾ ਭੁੱਤਾ ਸਾਰਾ ਵੇਰਵੇ
ਨਾਲ ਲਿਖ ਕੇ ਘੱਲਣਾ ਅਸਾਂ ਤੁਸਾਡੀ ਗੱਡੀ ਤੇ ਪੰਜ ਗੱਡੇ ਕਣਕ ਦੇ ਘੱਲੇ ਹਨ ਆਪ
ਨੇ ਸੋਚ ਸਮਝ ਕੇ ਵੇਚ ਕੇ ਰਕਮ ਵਣ੍ਹੇ ਮੁੰਡੇ ਜੇਠਾ ਸਿੰਘ ਦੀ ਕੰਨੀ ਪਾ ਦੇਣੀ ਕੋਈ ਫ਼ੇ
ਖਨ ਵਿਚ ਫਰਕ ਨਾਂ ਹੋਵੇ ਸਾਡੀ ਕਣਕ ਤੋਲੀ ਹੋਈ ਹੈ ਅਰਦਾਸੀਆ ਮੁੰਡਿਆ
ਨੂੰ ਸ਼ਰਾਬ ਜੋਗਾ ਕੋਈ ਰੁਪਿਆ ਨਾ ਦੇਣਾਂ ੧੦ ਦਸਾ ਰੁਪਿਆ ਦਾ ਖਰਾ ਗੁੜ ੭ ਪੰਜਾ
ਦੀ ਸ਼ਕਰ ਅਤੇ ਦੂਹ ਰੁਪਿਆ ਦਾ ਤਲੈਚਾ ਲੈ ਕੇ ਘੱਲ ਦੇਣਾ ੧੫ ਗਜ ਖੱਦਰ ਦਾ
ਕਪੜਾ ਅਤੇ ਇੱਕ ਬੂਰਾ ਲੈ ਕੇ ਘੱਲ ਦੇਣਾ ਦੋ ਪੜੇ ਰਜਾਈਆਂ ਦੇ ਚਾਰ ਗਜ ਲੱਠਾ
ਫਤਹਿ ਦੇ ਉਛਾੜ ਜੋਗਾ ਬੀ ਲੈ ਕੇ ਘੱਲਣਾ ਇਹੁ ਸਾਰੀਆਂ ਵਸਤਾ ਆਪਣੀ ਹਥੀਂ
ਲੈ ਕੇ ਦੇਣੀਆ ਮਤੇ ਕੋਈ ਮੁੰਡਿਆਂ ਨੂੰ ਠੱਗ ਲਏ ਹੋਰ ਸਾਡੇ ਲੈਕ ਜੋ ਟਹਿਲ ਹੋਵੇ
ਸਾਨੂੰ ਲਿਖ ਕੇ ਘੱਲਣੀ

ਆਪਦਾ ਭਲਾ ਚਾਹੁਣਵਾਲਾ ਬੀਰ ਸਿੰਘ ਬੁਰਜੋਂ

No 38

੧ ੴ ਸਤਿਗੁਰ ਪ੍ਰਸਾਦਿ।

ਹਜ਼ੂਰ ਤੁਸੀਂ ਜੋ ਮੈਨੂੰ ਚਿੱਠੀ ਲਿਖੀ ਸੀ ਭਈ ਜੇਕਰ ਤੁਹਾਡੇ ਪਿੰਡਾਂ ਦੇ ਨੇੜੇ ਤੇੜੇ ਕੁਝ
ਸ਼ਿਕਾਰ ਹੋਵੇ ਤਾਂ ਅਸੀਂ ਇੱਕ ਮਹੀਨੇ ਦੀ ਛੁੱਟੀ ਲੈ ਕੇ ਆ ਜਾਈਏ. ਸੋ ਹਜ਼ੂਰ ਤੁਸੀ

ਨਪਨਕਾ ਚਲੇਆਓ ਮੈਂ ਸਭ ਬੰਦੋਬਸਤ ਕਰ ਛਡਿਆ ਜੋ ਸੂਰਾਂ ਦੀਆਂ ਡਾਰਾਂ ਦੀਆਂ ਡਾਰਾਂ ਸਾਡੇ ਖੇਤਾਂ ਵਿਚ ਫਿਰਦੀਆਂ ਹਨ ਜੋ ਹਰੀਆਂ ਸਾਡੀ ਪੈਲੀ ਦਾ ਇਕ ਦਾਣਾ ਭੀ ਨਹੀ ਹਰਾਂ ਹੋਣ ਦੇਂਦੀਆਂ ਜੇ ਤੁਸੀ ਆਕੇ ਇਹਨਾਂ ਨੂੰ ਖਪਾਓ ਤਾਂ ਅਸੀ ਤੁਹਾਡਾ ਹੀ ਜਸ ਗਾਮੀਏ ਤੇ ਹੋਰ ਏਥੇ ਸਹੇ, ਤਿੱਤਰ, ਬਟੇਰੇ ਬਹੁਤ ਹਨ ਪਰ ਮੁਰਗਾਬੀਆਂ ਅਜੇ ਤਾਈਂ ਨਹੀ ਆਈਆਂ ਹੋਰ ਮਿਰਗਾਂ ਦੇ ਸ਼ਿਕਾਰ ਲਈ ਜੇ ਤੁਸੀ ਆਖੋ ਤਾਂ ਸਾਡੇ ਪਿੰਡ ਤੋਂ ਪੰਜ ਕੋਹ ਦੀ ਵਿਥ ਪਰ ਇਕ ਢਾਬ ਹੈ ਉਥੇ ਮੈਂ ਤੁਹਾਨੂੰ ਲੈ ਚਲਾਂਗਾ ਨਾਲੇ ਰੇਲ ਦਾ ਟੇਸ਼ਣ ਭੀ ਉਹਦੇ ਕੋਲ ਹੀ ਹੈ।

No 39

ੴ ਸਤਗੁਰਪ੍ਰਸਾਦਿ।

ਲਿਖਤੁਮ ਭੂਰਾ ਸਿੰਘ ਅਗੇ ਜੋਗ ਚਾਚਾ ਬਘੇਲ ਸਿੰਘ ਦੇ ਫਤੇ ਵਾਹਿਗੁਰੂ ਜੀ ਕੀ ਬੁਲਾਈ ਵਾਚਣੀ ਐਥੇ ਸੁਖ ਹੈ ਤੁਸਾਂ ਦੀ ਸੁਖ ਸਤਗੁਰਾਂ ਪਾਸੋਂ ਚਾਹੁੰਦੇ ਹਾਂ ਜੀ। ਚਿਠੀ ਤੁਸਾਡੀ ਪਹੁੰਚੀ ਜਿਸ ਨੂੰ ਪੜ੍ਹਕੇ ਅਸੀ ਰਾਜ਼ੀ ਹੋਏ ਹਾਂ ਜੀ ਵਡਿਆਂ ਦਾ ਏਹੋ ਧਰਮ ਹੈ ਜੋ ਆਪਣੇ ਪਰਵਾਰ ਦਾ ਭਲਾ ਚਾਹੁੰਦੇ ਹਨ ਜੀ ਤੁਸਾਂ ਜੋ ਲਿਖਿਆ ਹੈ ਕਿ ਬਰਖਾ ਪੈਣ ਵਾਲੀ ਹੈ ਅਰ ਪੈਲੀ ਬੀਜ ਲੈਣੀ ਜਿਸ ਤੇ ਖਾਣ ਜੋਗੇ ਦਾਣੇ ਘਰ ਆ ਜਾਣ। ਚਾਚਾ ਜੀ ਅਸੀ ਕੀ ਦਸੀਏ ਜੋ ਰਬ ਨੇ ਤਾਂ ਉਪਰੋਂ ਲੋਹੇ ਦੀ ਲਾਉ ਖਿਚ ਲੀਤੀ ਅਜੇ ਤਾਈਂ ਇਕ ਬੂੰਦ ਭੀ ਪਾਣੀ ਦੀ ਨਹੀ ਪਾਈ ਪਰਜਾ ਤ੍ਰਾਹ ਤ੍ਰਾਹ ਕਰਦੀ ਹੈ ਕਈ ਘਰਾਂ ਨੇ ਖੂਹੇ ਜੋਤ ਕੇ ਪੈਲੀ-

ਆਂ ਕੀਤੀਆ ਹਨ। ਜਿਨਾਂ ਵਿਚ ਰਹੀਆ ਅਰ ਗਵਾਰਾਂ ਵਾਢਿਆਂ ਦੇ ਖਾਣ ਲਈ ਬੀਜੀਆਂ ਹਨ ਪਸੂਆਂ ਦੀ ਭੁਖ ਦਾ ਦੁਖ ਦੇਖਿਆ ਨਹੀ ਜਾਂਦਾ ਸਰਕਾਰ ਗਾਏ ਸੇਰ ਕੁ ਧਾਰ ਦਿੰਦੀ ਸੀ ਪਰ ਨੀਰੇ ਦੇ ਦੁਖ ਤੇ ਭੁਖੀ ਰਹੀ ਜਿਸ ਦੇ ਥਣ ਵਿਚ ਹੁਣ ਦੁਧ ਦੀ ਲਸ ਭੀ ਨਹੀ ਰਹੀ ਬਾਲ ਲਸੀ ਖੁਣੋਂ ਤਰਸਦੇ ਹਨ। ਬਲਦਾਂ ਦੀਆਂ ਦੋਵੇਂ ਜੋਗਾ ਮਾੜੀਆ ਹੋਗਈਆਂ ਹਨ ਖੂਹੇ ਦਾ ਕੰਮ ਔਖਾ ਹੀ ਕਰਨਗੇ ਜੇ ਰਬ ਮੀਂਹ ਪਾਇ ਦੇਂਦਾ ਤਾਂ ਅਸੀ ਹਲ ਦਾ ਮੁੰਨਾ ਪਕੜ ਲੈਂਦੇ ਚਾਰ ਬਿਗੇ ਜਮੀਨ ਬੀਜ ਕੇ ਖਾਣ ਜੋਗੇ ਦਾਣੇ ਘਰ ਪਾਇ ਲੈਂਦੇ॥ ਨਿਆਈ ਵਾਲੇ ਖੇਤ ਦੀ ਕਿਕਰ ਵਢ ਕੇ ਸੁਹਾਗਾ ਬਣਾ ਲੀਤਾ ਹੈ ਦਾਦੀ ਦਾ ਮਨ ਤੁਹਾਂ ਨੂੰ ਮਿਲਨੇ ਲਈ ਚਾਹੁੰਦਾ ਹੈ ਸੋ ਤੁਸੀ ਜਰੂਰ ਆ ਕੇ ਮਿਲ ਜਾਣਾ। ਸਭਨਾਂ ਭਰਾਵਾਂ ਦੀ ਫਤੇ ਬੁਲਾਈ ਵਾਚਣੀ ਜੀ।

ਚਿਠੀ ਲਿਖੀ ਹਾੜ ਵਦੀ ਸਤ ਦਿਨ ਮੰਗਲਵਾਰ

ਰਾਮਪੁਰੇ ਬਘੇਲ ਸਿੰਘ ਨੂੰ ਰੂੜ ਸਿੰਘ ਨੇ।

No. 40

੧ੴ ਸਤਿਗੁਰ ਪ੍ਰਸਾਦਿ।

ਲਿਖਤੁਮ ਗੁਪਾਲ ਸਿੰਘ ਦਾਸ ਜੋਗ ਭਾਈ ਬੁਢਾ ਸਿੰਘ ਜੀ ਫਤੇ ਵਾਗੁਰੂ ਜੀ ਦੀ ਵਾਚਣੀ ਜੀ। ਹੋਰ ਜੀ ਐਥੇ ਸੁਖ ਹੈ ਜੀ ਤੇਰਾ ਹੀ ਸੁਖ ਸਾਂਦ ਚਾਹੁੰਦੇ ਹਾਂ ਜੀ ਹੋਰ ਹਾਲ ਏਹ ਹੈ ਜੀ ਮੈਨੂੰ ਛੁਟੀ ਹੋਵੇਗੀ ਤਾਂ ਆਵਾਂਗਾ। ਹੋਰ ਰੁਪੈ ਭੇਜੇ ਸਨ ਕਿ ਨਹੀ ਹਾਲ ਲਿਖੋ।

No 41

੧ਓ ਸਤਿਗੁਰਪ੍ਰਸਾਦਿ।

ਸ੍ਰੀ ਸਰਬ ਉਪਮਾ ਜੋਗ ਬਾਪੂ ਜੀ ਦਾਸਨਦਾਸ ਮਤਾਬ ਸਿੰਘ ਜੀ ਅਰ
ਵਰਯਾਮ ਸਿੰਘ ਦੀ ਚਰਨ ਬੰਦਨਾ ਵਾਚਣੀ ਅਸੀਂ ਆਪ ਦਿਆਂ ਚਰਨਾਂ ਤੇ
ਟੁਰਕੇ ਗਤ ਪ੍ਰਿਪਲੀ ਆ ਗਏ ਸਾਂ ਜਦੋਂ ਤਰੂ ਕੇ ਟੁਰਕੇ ਅਜੇ ਅਸੀਂ ਦੋ ਤ੍ਰ-
ਕੋਹਾਂ ਤੇ ਆਏ ਸਾਂ ਤਾਂ ਸਾਨੂੰ ਪੰਦ੍ਰਾਂ ਕੁ ਆਦਮੀ ਡਾਕੇ ਵਾਲੇ ਮਿਲੇ ਉਹਨਾ ਆਉਂ
ਦਿਆਂ ਨਾਲ ਹੀ ਸਾਡੇ ਗਡੇ ਰੋਕ ਲਏ ਆਖਨ ਲਗੇ ਜੋ ਕੁਛ ਤੁਹਾਡੇ ਕੋਲ ਹੈ
ਰਖ ਦਿਓ ਨਹੀ ਤਾਂ ਔਖੇ ਪਏ ਹੋਵੋਗੇ ਅਸਾਂ ਪੌਹਲਾਂ ਤਾਂ ਆਖਿਆ ਜਾਨ ਦੇਓ
ਅਸੀਂ ਭੀ ਤੁਹਾਡੇ ਜੱਟ ਭਰਾ ਹੀ ਹਾਂ ਕੋਈ ਕਿਰਾੜ ਨਹੀ ਉਹਨਾਂ ਨੇ ਇਕਨਾ ਸੀਂ
ਛਵੀ ਕਢਕੇ ਆਖਨ ਲਗੇ ਆਓ ਜਟ ਬੱਨੇ ਇਹ ਗਲ ਸੁਣਦਿਆਂ ਸਾਰ
ਸਾਡੇ ਵਸਾਊ ਬੀ ਲਕੜੀਆਂ ਪਾੜਨ ਵਾਲਾ ਕੁਹਾੜਾ ਕਢ ਲਿਆ ਅਰ
ਛਵੀ ਵਾਲੇ ਨੂੰ ਆਖਿਆ ਜੇ ਪਿਉ ਦਾ ਪੁਤ੍ਰ ਹੈਂ ਤਾਂ ਜਾਈਂ ਨਾ ਅਸਾਂ ਬੀ ਦੰਦ੍ਰਾ
ਨਹੀ ਪਾਈਆਂ ਹੋਈਆਂ ਇਹ ਸੁਣਦਿਆਂ ਸਾਰ ਛਵੀ ਵਾਲਾ ਕੁਝ ਢਿਲਾ
ਹੋ ਗਿਆ ਅਰ ਉਹ ਪਿਛਾਂ ਹਟ ਗਿਆ ਏਹ ਹਟਦੇ ਵੇਖ ਅਸਾਂ
ਫਿਰ ਗੇਹਕ ਦਿਤੇ ਅਜੇ ਅਸੀ ਥੋੜੀ ਹੀ ਦੂਰ ਗਏ ਸਾਂ ਤਾਂ ਉਹਨਾਂ ਨੇ ਪਿਛਲੇ
ਗਡੇ ਵਾਲੇ ਨੂੰ ਆ ਫੜਿਆ ਉਹਨੂੰ ਡਾਂਗਾਂ ਨਾਲ ਆਉਂਦਿਆਂ ਹੀ ਭਨ ਸੁਟਿ
ਓਨੇ ਅਰ ਸਾਡਾ ਬਲਦ ਖੋਲਕੇ ਲੁਟਦੇ ਇਕ ਸੌ ਰੁਪਏ ਖਸਕਾ ਦਿਤੇ ਨੇ ਇਹ
ਰੌਲਾ ਸੁਣ ਅਸੀਂ ਗਡੇ ਖਲਵਾਕੇ ਪਿਛੇ ਭਜਕੇ ਆਏ ਤਾਂ ਦੂਜੀ ਪਾਸੀ ਬਹੁਤੀ

ਤਾਂਗ ਵੜੀ ਸਾਡੇ ਮਨਾ ਸਿੰਘ ਦਾ ਸਿਰ ਖੁਲ੍ਹ ਗਿਆ ਉਹਨਾਂ ਦੇ ਬੀ ਅਸਾਂ ਚਾਰ ਪੰਜ ਜ਼ਖਮੀ ਕੀਤੇ ਅਰ ਦੋਹਾਂ ਦੇ ਗੋਰੇ ਕਢ ਦਿਤੇ ਉਹਨਾਂ ਨੂੰ ਬਹੁਤ ਦਬਾ ਕੇ ਆਪਣਾ ਬਲਦ ਮੁੜਾਇਆ ਮਨਾ ਸਿੰਘ ਨੂੰ ਗਡੇ ਵਿਚ ਪਾ ਲਿਆ ਅਰ ਉਰਲੇ ਪਿੰਡ ਆ ਕੇ ਉਹਨੂੰ ਦੁਧ ਘਿਓ ਦਿਤਾ ਅਰ ਜਖਮ ਵਿਚ ਚੰਗੀ ਤਰਾਂ ਲੀਰਾਂ ਸਾੜ ਕੇ ਦਿਤੀਆਂ ਹੁਣ ਆਸੀਂ ਮੁਲਿਆਣੀ ਆਪਣੇ ਗਏ ਹਾਂ ਮਨਾ ਸਿੰਘ ਨੂੰ ਅਰਾਮ ਹੈ ਕਿਸੇ ਤਰਾਂ ਦਾ ਫਿਕਰ ਨਾ ਕਰਨਾ ਅਸੀ ਅਨੰਦ ਪਰਸੰਨ ਹਾਂ।

ਆਪਦਾ ਦਾਸ ਅਤਾਬਾ ਸਿੰਘ ਅਰ ਵਰਯਾਮ ਸਿੰਘ ਮੁਲਿਆਣੀ ਤੇ॥

No 42

ੴ ਸਤਗੁਰ ਪਰਸਾਦਿ।

ਭਾਈ ਨਿਹਾਲ ਸਿੰਘ ਜੀ ਵਾਹਿਗੁਰੂ ਜੀ ਕੀ ਫਤੇ ਅਸੀ ਤੁਹਾਨੂੰ ਪਹਿਲਾਂ ਭੀ ਲਿਖਿਆ ਸੀ ਜੋ ਅਸਾਡੇ ਲਈ ਕੋਈ ਬਲਦ ਮੁਲ ਲੈ ਰਖਣਾ ਤੇ ਹੁਣ ਫੇਰ ਤੁਹਾਨੂੰ ਤਗੀਦ ਕਰਦੇ ਹਾਂ ਜੋ ਕਿਸੇ ਆਹਰੋਂ ਸਸਤੇ ਭਾਂ ਫੇਰੀ ਟੋਲ ਰਖਣੀ ਕਿਉਂ ਜੋ ਸਾਡਾ ਕੰਮ ਚਾਰ ਬਲਦਾਂ ਬਿਨਾ ਨਹੀਂ ਚਲਦਾ ਨਾਲੇ ਸਾਡੀ ਸੰਜੀ ਪਹੁੰਚ ਨਾਲੋਂ ਔਤਕੀ ਵਧ ਗਈ ਹੈ ਹੁਣ ਸਾਡੇ ਕੋਲ ਅਗੇ ਨਾਲੋਂ ਦੂਣੀ ਭੋਂ ਹੈ ਨਾਲੇ ਜੋ ਮੱਕੀ ਨੂੰ ਅਠਮੇ ਦਿਨ ਮਗਰੋਂ ਨਾ ਸਿੰਜੀਏ ਤਾਂ ਅਗਲੇ ਦਿਨ ਨੂੰ ਸੁਕ ਜਾਂਦੀ ਹੈ ਹੋਰ ਅਸੀ ਕੁਛ ਭਾਜੀਆਂ ਭੀ ਬੀਜੀਆਂ ਹੋਈਆਂ ਹਨ ਜਿਹਾ ਕੁ ਗੰਢੇ, ਗੋਂਗਲੂ ਮੂਲੀਆਂ, ਗਾਜਰਾਂ ਬਤਾਊ ਆਦਿਕ ਉਹਨਾਂ ਨੂੰ ਭੀ ਦੂਜੇ ਚੌਥੇ ਦਿਨ ਪਾਣੀ ਦੇਣਾ ਪੈਂਦਾ ਹੈ ਭਲਾ ਜੇ ਬਲਦ ਹੀ ਨਾ ਹੋਣਗੇ ਤਾ ਕਾਹਦੇ ਨਾਲ ਸਿੰਜਾਂਗੇ ਕਿਉਂ ਜੋ ਸਾਡੀ ਤਾਂ ਸਾਰੀ ਭੋਂ ਹੀ ਖੂਹ ਉਤੇ ਹੀ ਹੈ।

ਦਸਖਤ ਕਰਮ ਸਿੰਘ ਰਾਹੋਂ ਵਿਚੋਂ॥

੫੮ No 43

ਅਜ ਮੈਂ ਇਕ ਨਗਰ ਦੇ ਵਿਚ ਗਸ਼ਤ ਕਰਦਾ ਕਰਦਾ ਗਿਆ ਤਾਂ ਮੈਨੂੰ ਉਸ ਪਿੰਡ
ਵਿਚ ਕੋਈ ਬੰਦਾ ਨਾ ਦਿਸਿਆ ਓੜਕ ਨੂੰ ਮੈਂ ਭੌਂਦਾ ਭੌਂਦਾ ਇਕ ਪਿੰਡ ਵਿਚ ਗਿਆ ਤਾਂ ਉਥੇ
ਇਕ ਸਾਧੂ ਧੂਆਂ ਲਾਈ ਬੈਠਾ ਸਾ ਮੈਂ ਉਦੀ ਵਲ ਗਿਆ ਤਾਂ ਉਨ ਮੈਨੂੰ ਆਖਿਆ ਆ ਬੈਠ ਜਾ
ਤਾਂ ਮੈਂ ਬੈਠ ਗਿਆ ਫੇਰ ਪਲਕ ਪਿਛੋਂ ਉਨੇ ਮੈਨੂੰ ਰੋਟੀ ਖੁਵਾਈ ਫੇਰ ਗਲਾਂ ਕਥਾਂ ਕਰਦੇ
ਆਂ ਉਸਨੇ ਏਹ ਆਖਿਆ ਕਿ ਇਸ ਪਿੰਡ ਦੇ ਰੈਣ ਵਾਲੇ ਬੰਦੇ ਫੌਜ ਦੇਖ ਕੇ ਤੇ ਰੰਨਾਂ
ਮੁੰਡੇ ਕੁੜੀਆਂ ਟਟੂ ਟੈਰੇ ਉਠ ਮਝੀਂ ਗਾਈਂ ਢਗੇ ਸੰਢੇ ਖਚਰਾਂ ਘੋੜੇ ਲੈਕੇ ਭਾਜ ਨ
ਕਰ ਗਏ ਨੇ ਮੈਂ ਇਹ ਸਾਰੀ ਕਥਾ ਸੁਨ ਕੇ ਉਦੀ ਸਚੀ ਸਮਝੀ ਤੇ ਫੇਰ ਮੈਂ ਸਾਧੂ ਨੂੰ ਮਥਾ
ਟੇਕਿਆ ਤੇ ਆਪਣੇ ਕਮਾਨ ਅਫਸਰ ਵਲ ਏਹ ਸਾਰੀਆਂ ਗਲਾਂ ਦਸਨ ਲਈ
ਟੁਰ ਪਿਆ ਮੈਨੂੰ ਉਦੇ ਰਾਹੇ ਪਾਸੇ ਆਪਨੇ ਵੈਰੀਆਂ ਦਾ ਮਸਾਲਾ ਦਿਸਿਆ ਅਰ
ਬੰਦੂਕਾਂ ਦੀਆਂ ਗੋਲੀਆਂ ਬੇਓੜਕ ਕੀਆਂ ਨਸਾਨੇ ਦੇ ਨਾਲ ਮਾਰਦੇ ਸਨ ਦੁਸਮਨ
ਦੀ ਫੌਜ ਮੇਰੀ ਫੌਜ ਨਾਲੋਂ ਢੇਰ ਸੀ ਮੇਰੀ ਫੌਜ ਥੋੜ ਸੀ।

੧੮ No 44

ਲਿਖਤਮ ਨਰਿੰਦ੍ਰ ਸਿੰਘ ਜੋਗ ਭਾਈ ਜਗੀਦਰ ਸਿੰਘ ਵਾਹਗੁਰੂ ਜੀ ਕੀ ਫਤੇ ਵਾ
ਚਣੀ ਹੋਰ ਭਾਈ ਜੀ ਦੁਨੀਆ ਉਤੇ ਕੇਹੇ ਕਠਨ ਦਿਨ ਆਏ ਹੋਏ ਹਨ ਇਕ ਪਾਸੇ
ਅਫਰੀਕਾ ਵਲ ਲੜਾਈ ਲਗੀ ਹੋਈ ਸੀ ਹੁਣ ਦੂਜੇ ਪਾਸੇ ਚੀਨ ਵਲ ਲਗ
ਪਈ ਹਜਾਰਾਂ ਲਖਾਂ ਆਦਮੀ ਮਾਰੇ ਜਾਨਗੇ। ਕਿਧਰੇ ਕਾਲ ਪੈ ਰਿਹਾ ਹੈ ਗਰੀਬ
ਗੁਰਬੇ ਦਾ ਟਬਰ ਨਾਲ ਰੋਟੀ ਦਾ ਗੁਜਾਰਾ ਵਡਾ ਔਖਾ ਚਲਦਾ ਹੈ ਜੇਕਰ ਕਿਸੇ
ਦੇ ਘਰ ਦਿਨ ਦਾ ਪਕਦਾ ਹੈ ਤਾਂ ਰਾਤ ਦਾ ਨਹੀਂ ਪਕਦਾ ਭੁਖ ਦੇ ਦੁਖ ਲੋਕ ਵਡੇ ਤੰਗ
ਆ ਗਏ ਹਨ ਓਹ ਗਰੀਬ ਇਸ ਜੀਉਨ ਤੋਂ ਮਰਨ ਨੂੰ ਚੰਗਾ ਸਮਝਦੇ ਹਨ। ਕਿਧਰੇ
ਮਹਾਮਾਰੀ ਬਿਮਾਰੀ ਨਾਲ ਸੈਕੜੇ ਮਨੁਖ ਰੋਜ ਮਰ ਰਹੇ ਹਨ ਜਿਹਾ ਕ ਬੰਬਈ ਤੇ

ਕਰਾਚੀ ਵਿਚ ਤਾਊਨ ਦਾ ਜੋਰ ਤਾਂ ਪਹਿਲਾਂ ਸੀ ਹੁਣ ਸੁਣਿਆ ਹੈ ਉਹ ਰਤਾ ਕੁ ਘਟ
ਗਿਆ ਹੈ ਹੈਜੇ ਨੇ ਹੁਣ ਕਿਰਪਾ ਕੀਤੀ ਹੈ ਜਿਸ ਨਾਲ ਕਈ ਮਨੁਖ ਰੋਜ ਮਰ ਜਾਂਦੇ
ਹਨ ਪਰਮੇਸਰ ਹੁਣ ਕਿਰਪਾ ਕਰੇ ਤਾਂ ਚੰਗੀ ਗਲ ਹੈ ਨਹੀਂ ਤਾਂ ਲੋਕਾਂ ਦੇ ਬਚਣ ਦੀ
ਕੋਈ ਵਾਹ ਨਹੀਂ ਕਈ ਵਰਿਹਾਂ ਤੋਂ ਵੇਲੇ ਸਿਰ ਮੀਂਹ ਨਹੀਂ ਪੈਂਦਾ ਜਿਸ ਕਰਕੇ ਫਸ
ਲਾ ਕੁਝ ਹੁੰਦੀਆਂ ਹੀ ਨਹੀਂ।

ਲਿਖੀ ਸਾਵਣ ਦੀ ੧੨ ਨਰਿੰਦਰ ਸਿੰਘ ਲਿਖਾਰਦਾਰ

No 45

ੴ ਸਤਿਗੁਰਪ੍ਰਸਾਦਿ।

ਲਿਖਤੁਮ ਨਿਹਾਲ ਸਿੰਘ ਜੋਗ ਗੀਰਾ ਸਿੰਘ ਫਤੇ ਸ੍ਰੀ ਵਾਹਿਗੁਰੂ ਜੀ ਕੀ ਬੁਲਾਈ
ਵਾਚਣੀ ਜੀ ਚਿਠੀ ਲਿਖੀ ਹਰਨਾਮ ਪੁਰ ਤੋਂ ਸਮਾਚਾਰ ਇਹ ਹੈ ਕਿ ੮ ਵੀਂ
ਕਤਕ ਨੂੰ ਅਸੀਂ ਲਾਹੌਰ ਦੀ ਮੰਡੀ ਵਿਚੋਂ ਦੋ ਗਡੇ ਛੋਲਿਆਂ ਦੇ ਵੇਚ ਕੇ ਆਪਣੇ
ਪਿੰਡ ਨੂੰ ਆਉਂਦੇ ਸੇ। ਰਾਹ ਵਿਚ ਸਾਨੂੰ ਸੋਹਣੇ ਸੋਹਣੇ ਛੇ ਗਭਰੂ ਮਿਲੇ। ਜਿਨ੍ਹਾਂ
ਦੇ ਹੱਥਾਂ ਵਿਚ ਛਵੀਆਂ ਸੀਆਂ ਉਹ ਲਲਕਾਰ ਕੇ ਸਾਡੇ ਕੋਲ ਆ ਖੜੋਤੇ
ਅਰ ਉਨ੍ਹਾਂ ਨੇ ਸਾਨੂੰ ਖੜੇ ਹੋਣ ਲਈ ਆਖਿਆ ਅਸੀਂ ਤਿੰਨ ਜਣੇ ਸੇ ਜਿਨ੍ਹਾਂ
ਵਿਚੋਂ ੧ ਮਾਂਦਾ ਸਾ ਤੇ ੧ ਕੁੜਾ ਸਾ। ਅਸੀਂ ਉਨ੍ਹਾਂ ਦਾ ਸਾਹਮਣਾ ਤਾਂ ਕਰ ਨਹੀਂ ਸਕ
ਦੇ ਸੇ ਇਸ ਕਰਕੇ ਅਸਾਂ ਆਪਣੇ ਗਡੇ ਖੜੇ ਕਰ ਲੀਤੇ। ਫੇਰ ਡਾਕੂਆਂ ਨੇ ਸਾਡੇ
ਉਤੇ ਹਲਾ ਕੀਤਾ ਤੇ ਸਭ ਕੁਝ ਲੁਟ ਲੀਤਾ ਸਾਡਾ ਰੁ ੨੫) ਦਾ ਘਾਟਾ ਹੋਇਆ
ਜਿਨ੍ਹਾਂ ਵਿਚੋਂ ੨੦੦) ਨਕਦ ਸੇ ਤੇ ਬਾਕੀ ੨ ਸੋਟੀਆਂ ਉਹ ਗਡੇ ਵਿਚੋਂ ਬੌਲਦ
ਕਢਣ ਲਗੇ ਤਾਂ ਗਡੇ ਵਾਲਿਆਂ ਪੁਛਿਆ ਕਿ ਤੁਸੀਂ ਇਹ ਕੀ ਕਰਦੇ ਹੋ ਤਾਂ
ਇਕ ਨੇ ਮੇਰੇ ਸਿਰ ਵਿਚ ਗੰਡਾਸਾ ਮਾਰਿਆ ਜਿਸ ਦੇ ਕਾਰਨ ਮੈਂ ਗਸ਼ ਖਾ ਕੇ
ਡਿਗ ਪਿਆ। ਦੂਜੇ ਦਿਨ ਜਦ ਮੈਨੂੰ ਸੁਰਤ ਆਈ ਤਦ ਮੈਂ ਆਪਣੇ ਆਪ ਨੂੰ
ਥਾਣੇ ਵਿਚ ਦੇਖਿਆ। ਇਸ ਤੇ ਬਿਨਾ ਇਹ ਪਰਗਟ ਹੋਇਆ ਕਿ ਦੋ ਖਬੀਆਂ
ਪਾਸੀਆਂ ਮੇਰੀਆਂ ਟੁਟ ਗਈਆਂ ਸੀਆਂ ਨਾਲੇ ਸਜੇ ਗੋਡੇ ਦੀ ਚਪਣੀ
ਮੂਲੋਂ ਹੀ ਚੂਰਾ ਚੂਰਾ ਹੋ ਗਈ ਸੀ।

No 46

ੴ ਸਤਿਗੁਰਪ੍ਰਸਾਦਿ ।

ਲਿਖਤਮ ਸੈਣਾਸਿੰਘ ਜੋਗ ਭਾਈ ਦਰਿਆਮਸਿੰਘ ਸ੍ਰੀ ਵਾਹਿਗੁਰੂ ਜੀ ਕੀ ਫਤੇ ਵਾਚਣੀ
ਹੋਰ ਇਥੇ ਸੁਖ ਹੈ ਤੇ ਤੁਹਾਡੀ ਸੁਖ ਸਦਾ ਕਰਤਾਰ ਪਾਸੋਂ ਮੰਗਵਾਦੇ ਹਾਂ ਹੋਰ ਭਾਈ ਜੀ ਰੀਨਦੀ
ਵੰਲ ੨੦, ੩੪, ਤੇ ੧੪ ਅਤੇ ਹੋਰ ਕਈ ਦੇਸੀ ਪਨ੍ਤਲਾਂ ਨੂੰ ਜਾਨ ਦਾ ਹੁਕਮ ਹੋਇਆ ਹੈ ਜੇਕਰ
ਸਾਡੀ ਪਲਟਨ ਨੂੰ ਵੀ ਉਥੇ ਜਾਨ ਦਾ ਹੁਕਮ ਆ ਜਾਵੇ ਤਾਂ ਅਸੀ ਵੀ ਕੁਝ ਸਰਕਾਰ ਦਾ ਲੂਣ
ਖਾਧਾ ਹੋਇਆ ਹਲਾਲ ਕਰ ਵਿਖਾਈਏ ਤੇ ਵੈਰੀ ਨਾਲ ਦੋ ਚਾਰ ਹੱਥ ਕਰ ਵੇਖੀਏ ਸੁਣਿਆ
ਹੈ ਜੋ ਸਾਡੇ ਕਰਨੈਲ ਸਾਹਿਬ ਨੇ ਆਪ ਵੀ ਪਲਟਨ ਦਾ ਨਾਂ ਭੇਜਿਆ ਹੈ ਪਰ ਸਾਨੂੰ ਮਲੂਮ ਨ੍ਹੀ
ਏਹੁ ਕਿੱਥੋਂ ਤੀਕ ਸੱਚ ਹੈ ਵਾਹਿਗੁਰੂ ਕਰੇ ਜੋ ਸਾਨੂੰ ਵੀ ਲੜਾਈ ਤੇ ਜਾਨ ਦਾ ਹੁਕਮ ਆਵੇ ।
ਸਾਡੀ ਪਲਟਨ ਸਰਧਰ ਤਿਆਰ ਹੈ ਪਰ ਕੀ ਕਰੀਏ ਆਪੇ ਨਹੀਂ ਜਾ ਸਕਦੇ ਨਹੀ ਤਾਂ ਲੜ
ਨਦੀ ਤੇ ਲੜਾਈ ਵੇਖਣ ਦੀ ਸਾਨੂੰ ਵਡੀ ਚਾਹ ਹੈ ਤੁਹਾਨੂੰ ਜਾਦ ਹੋਵੇਗਾ ਫੋਰਟ ਲਾਕਹਰ
ਟਦੇ ਕਿਲੇ ਵਿੱਚ ਅਸੀ ਪਿਛਲੀ ਲੜਾਈ ਵਿਚ ਪਠਾਨਾਂ ਨਾਲ ਕਿਹਾ ਕੁ ਜੱਫਾ ਮਾਰਿਆ
ਸੀ ਭਾਵੇਂ ਸਾਡਾ ਵੀ ਕੁਝ ਜਾਨ ਹੋਇਆ ਸੀ ਕੁਝ ਸਪਾਹੀ ਘਾਇਲ ਹੋਏ ਤੇ ਕੁਝ ਮਾਰੇ ਗਏ
ਪਰ ਅਸੀ ਵੀ ਜੋ ਪਠਾਨ ਹੱਥ ਲਗੇ ਉਸ ਦੇ ਨਾਲ ਆਜੇਹੀ ਕੀਤੀ ਜੋ ਵੇਖਣ ਵਾਲੇ ਪਠਾਨ
ਵਡੇ ਹਰਾਨ ਹੁੰਦੇ ਸੀ

ਸੈਣਾਸਿੰਘ ਜਮਾਦਾਰ ਪਲਟਨ ੪੫

No 47

ੴ ਸਤਿਗੁਰਪ੍ਰਸਾਦਿ ।

ਲਿਖਤੁਮ ਕਰਮਾਸਿੰਘ ਜੋਗ ਸੂਬੇਦਾਰ ਚੰਦਾਸਿੰਘ ਹੱਥ ਜੋੜ ਕੇ ਸ੍ਰੀ ਵਾਹਿਗੁਰੂ ਜੀ ਦੀ

ਫਤੇ ਬੁਲਾਈ ਬਾਚਣੀ। ਹੋਰ ਜੀ ਏਥੇ ਪਿੰਡ ਸਭ ਰਾਜੀ ਖੁਸ਼ੀ ਹਨ ਤੁਹਾਡੀ ਸੁਖ ਸਾਂਦ ਸ੍ਰੀ
ਗੁਰੂ ਤੇ ਹਮੇਸ਼ ਮੰਗਦੇ ਹਾਂ ਜੀ। ਤੁਸਾਂ ਜੋ ਸਮੇਂ ਦਾ ਹਾਲ ਪੁਛਿਆ ਸੀ ਸੋ ਜੀ ਸਮੇਂ ਦਾ ਇਹੁ ਹਾਲ
ਹੈ ਕਿ ਪਿਛੇ ਦਸਕੁ ਦਿਨਾਂ ਤੋਂ ਬੱਦਲੀਆਂ ਕਿਣੀਆਂ ਪਈਆਂ ਮਾੜੀਆਂ ਜੇਹੀਆਂ॥ ਓਥੇ ਗਿੱਲ
ਕਰ ਗਈਆਂ ਬਾਹਰ ਭੀ ਨਹੀਂ ਭਿਜੇ। ਪਰ ਸਾਥੋਂ ਚੜਨ ਦੀ ਵਲ ਪੰਜੀ ਸਤੀ ਕੋਹੀ ਹਠਾਂ ਮੀਂ
ਹ ਪੈ ਗਿਆ॥ ਨਮੀ ਖਿਆਈ ਕ ਰਾਂਗੀ ਆ॥ ਹੁਣ ਹਲ ਚਲਦੇ ਹਨ ਕਈ ਜਗਾ ਚੰਦਰਾ
ਬੀ ਪਿਆ ਕਮਾਦ ਕਪਾਹ ਦਾ ਤਾਂ ਨਾਸ ਕਰ ਗਿਆ॥ ਤੁਸਾਈਆਂ ਜੀ ਬਰਖਾ ਖੂਹੋਂ ਡੰਗਰਾਂ
ਦਾ ਬੁਰਾ ਹਾਲ ਹੈ। ਅਕਿਤੇ ਪੱਠਾ ਨਿਗਾ ਨਹੀਂ ਆਉਂਦਾ ਜੀਕਰ ਤਾਂ ਰਿਹਾ ਹੀ ਨਹੀਂ। ਦਰਖਤਾਂ ਦੇ
ਛਿਲ ਬਦ ਬਢਕੇ ਪਾਈਦੇ ਹਨ। ਰਬ ਬਰਖਾ ਕਰ ਦੇਵੇ ਤਾਂ ਹੀ ਬਚਾਉ ਹੈ ਨਹੀਂ ਕੋਈ ਠਕਾ
ਣਾ ਨਹੀਂ। ਹੋਰ ਜੀ ਤੁਸਾਂ ਰਜ਼ਾ ਲੈ ਕੇ ਕਦ ਆਉਣਾ ਹੈ। ਜਦ ਆਓ ਮੇਰੇ ਲਈ ਦਸ
ਬਾਰਾਂ ਗਜ ਖੱਦਰ ਹੰਡਨ ਸਾਰ ਲੈ ਆਉਣਾ॥ ਓਸ ਪਾਸੇ ਦਾ ਕਪੜਾ ਚੰਗਾ ਸੁਣੀਦਾ
ਹੈ॥ ਹੋਰ ਜੀ ਆਪਣੀ ਸੁਖ ਸਾਂਦ ਦੀ ਚਿੱਠੀ ਪਤ੍ਰੀ ਭੇਜਦੇ ਰਿਹਾ ਕਰੋ। ਭਾਈ ਨੂੰ ਮਥਾ ਟੇ
ਕਿਆ ਪਹੁੰਚੇ। ਕਾਕੇ ਨੂੰ ਪਿਆਰ ਦੇਣਾ॥ ਲਿਖੀ ਮਘਰ ਦਿਨ ੧੮ ਸੰਮਤ ੧੯੫੩

No. 48

੧ਓ ਸਤਿਗੁਰ ਪ੍ਰਸਾਦਿ॥

ਲਿਖਤੁਮ ਕਰਮ ਸਿੰਘ ਜੋਗ ਭਾਈਆ ਚੇਤਾ ਸਿੰਘ ਜੀ ਹੱਥ ਜੋੜ ਕੇ ਸ੍ਰੀ ਵਾਹਿਗੁਰੂ ਜੀ ਕੀ
ਫਤੇ ਬੁਲਾਈ ਬਾਚਣੀ॥ ਹੋਰ ਜੀ ਏਥੇ ਸਭ ਸੁਖ ਹੈ ਤੁਹਾਡੀ ਸੁਖ ਸਾਂਦ ਸ੍ਰੀ ਗੁਰੂ ਜੀ ਤੇ
ਮੰਗਦੇ ਹਾਂ ਜੀ॥ ਹੋਰ ਜੀ ਕਲ ਸੁਬਾ ਸਿੰਘ ਮਿਲਿਆ ਸੀ। ਆਖਦਾ ਸੀ ਤੁਹਾਡੀ ਵਲ
ਮੀਂਹ ਦੀ ਇੱਕ ਕਣੀ ਨਹੀਂ ਡਿਗੀ ਜੀ ਡੰਗਰ ਪਸੂ ਘਾ ਖੂਣੋਂ ਬੜੇ ਔਖੇ ਹੋ ਰਹੇ ਹਨ ਟੋ
ਬਿਆਂ ਵਿੱਚ ਕਿਤੇ ਪਾਣੀ ਦੀ ਬੂੰਦ ਨਹੀਂ ਦਿਸਦੀ॥ ਏਧਰ ਸਾਡੀ ਵਲ ਭੀ ਏਹੋ ਜੇਹਾ ਹਾ
ਲ ਹੈ। ਨੈਹਰ ਕਦੇ ਪਾਣੀ ਦੇਂਦੀ ਹੈ ਕਦੇ ਨਹੀਂ ਦੇਂਦੀ ਜੀ। ਕਈਆਂ ਦੀ ਸਾਉਣੀ ਸੁੱਕ
ਗਈ ਹੈ ਜੀ॥ ਜਿਨਾਂ ਦੇ ਖੇਤਾਂ ਨੂੰ ਵੇਲੇ ਸਿਰ ਪਾਣੀ ਮਿਲ ਜਾਂਦਾ ਹੈ ਓਹਨਾਂ ਦੇ ਪਉਂਆਂ ਬਾਰਾਂ
ਹੋ ਜਾਂਦੇ ਹਨ॥ ਜਮੀਨ ਤਾਂ ਰਾਂਢੀ ਹੋ ਗਈ ਹੈ॥ ਇੱਕ ਇੱਕ ਚੱਕ ਵਿੱਚੋਂ ਹਜਾਰਾਂ ਮਣ ਦਾਣਾ
ਪੈਦਾ ਹੁੰਦਾ ਹੈ॥ ਕਪਾਹ ਢੇਰਾਂ ਦੇ ਢੇਰ ਉਤਰਦੀ ਹੈ॥ ਪਰ ਸਾਨੂੰ ਭੀ ਮੀਂਹ ਦੀ ਲੋੜ

ਤੈ ਹਵੀ ਹੈ। ਰਬ ਦੇ ਹੱਥ ਡੋਰੀ ਹੈ। ਚਾਹੇ ਇੱਕ ਪਲਕ ਵਿੱਚ ਜਲ ਥਲ ਕਰ ਦੇਵੇ। ਸਾਡਾ ਮੋਗਾ ਸਾਡੀ ਪੈਲੀ ਤੋਂ ਬਹੁਤ ਦੂਰ ਹੈ। ਇਸ ਕਰਕੇ ਸਾਨੂੰ ਪਾਣੀ ਦੀ ਲੋੜ ਰੈਂਹਦੀ ਹੈ। ਹੋਰ ਜੀ ਆਪਣੀ ਸੁਖ ਸਾਂਦ ਦੀ ਖਬਰ ਭੇਜਦੇ ਰਿਹਾ ਕਰੋ। ਸਾਡਾ ਧਿਆਨ ਤੁਹਾਡੀ ਵਲ ਰੈਂਹਦਾ ਹੈ ਚਿੱਠੀ ਲਿਖੀ ਹਾੜ੍ਹ ਦਿਨ ੧੧

No 49

ੴ ਸਤਿਗੁਰਪ੍ਰਸਾਦਿ।

ਲਿਖਤੁਮ ਭਾਊ ਮਲ ਅਗੇ ਜੋਗ ਕੁੰਦਨ ਲਾਲ ਲਾਲਾ ਜੀ। ਰਾਮ ਰਾਮ ਵਾਚਣੀ ਸਮਾਚਾਰ ਏਹੁ ਹੈ ਜੋ ਐਤਵਾਰ ਦੀ ਤਕਾਲਾਂ ਨੂੰ ਰਾਮ ਲਾਲ ਦਾ ਕੋੜਮਾ ਬੜੇ ਚਾਉ ਨਾਲ ਉਹਦੇ ਮੁੰਡੇ ਨੂੰ ਵਿਆਹੁਣ ਗਇਆ ਜਿਸ ਨੇ ਮੈਨੂੰ ਤਾਂ ਮਲੋ ਮਲੀ ਨਾਲ ਤੋਰ ਲਿਆ ਜਾਂ ਅਸੀਂ ਆਪਣੇ ਪਿੰਡ ਦੇ ਸਿਵਿਆਂ ਨੂੰ ਲੰਘ ਕੇ ਨਹਿਰ ਦੇ ਪੁਲ ਉੱਤੇ ਪਹੁੰਚੇ ਤਾਂ ਸਾਨੂੰ ਅਜੇਹੀ ਹਨੇਰੀ ਆਈ ਜੋ ਹੱਥ ਪਸਾਰਿਆਂ ਭੀ ਕੁਛ ਨਹੀਂ ਦਿਸਦਾ ਸੀ ਤੇ ਕੋਈ ਕੋਈ ਕਣੀ ਭੀ ਪੈਂਦੀ ਸੀ। ਅਸੀਂ ਵਿਆਹ ਦੇ ਚਾਉ ਵਿੱਚ ਗੱਡੀਆਂ ਨੂੰ ਉਸੇ ਤਰਾਂ ਲਈ ਗਏ ਤੇ ਨਾਂ ਰੋਕਿਆ ਪੁਲ ਤੋਂ ਅਗਾਂਹ ਕੋਈ ਦੂਰ ਕੋਹ ਹੀ ਗਏ ਹੋਸਾਂਗੇ ਜੋ ਸਾਨੂੰ ਡਾਕੂਆਂ ਨੇ ਆ ਘੇਰਿਆ ਓਹਨਾਂ ਦੇ ਹੱਥਾਂ ਵਿੱਚ ਨੰਗੀਆਂ ਤਲਵਾਰਾਂ ਤੇ ਭਰੀਆਂ ਹੋਈਆਂ ਬੰਦੂਕਾਂ ਅਤੇ ਚਮਕਦੀਆਂ ਛਵੀਆਂ ਦੇਖ ਕੇ ਸਭਨਾਂ ਦੇ ਮੂੰਹ ਪੀਲੇ ਫਟਕ ਹੋ ਗਏ ਸਾਡਾ ਆਪਣਾ ਅੱਲੇ ਬਕਰੀ ਜੋ ਚਾਹੇ ਸੋ ਕਰੇ ਲਾਲਾ ਜੀ ਭਲਾ ਫੇਰ ਕੀ ਬਣਦਾ ਸੀ ਸਭ ਡਰ ਕੇ ਡਕਾ ਲੁੱਟ ਪੁੱਟ ਕੇ ਲੈ ਗਏ ਲਾਲਾ ਜੀ ਮੂਰਖਤਾਈ ਤਾਂ ਸਾਰੀ ਸਾਡੀ ਹੀ ਹੈ ਕਿਉਂ ਜੇ ਪੁਲ ਉੱਤੇ ਅਸੀਂ ਪਲ ਕੁ ਅਟਕ ਜਾਂਦੇ ਤਾਂ ਕਾਹਨੂੰ ਐਹ ਹਾਲ ਹੁੰਦੇ ਅਛਾ

ਹੋਰ ਐਥੇ ਸਭ ਰਾਜ਼ੀ ਖੁਸ਼ੀ ਹੈ

ਭਾਊ ਮਲ ਦਿਲੀ ਤੋਂ

No 50

੧ੴ

ਲਿਖਤੁਮ ਸ਼ਾਮ ਸਿੰਘ ਜੋਗ ਭਾਈ ਰਾਮ ਸਿੰਘ ਵਾਹਿਗੁਰੂ ਜੀ ਕੀ ਫਤੇ ਵਾਚਣੀ ॥ ਹੋਰ ਸੁਖ ਵਾਚਣਾ ਹੋਰ ਭਾਈ ਜੀ ਹਿੰਦੁਸਤਾਨ ਨੇ ਇਸ ਲੜਾਈ ਵਿੱਚ ਆਦਮੀਆਂ ਘੋੜਿਆਂ ਤੇ ਬਲੇਦੇ ਦਾਗੀ ਦੇ ਜਾਨਵਰਾਂ ਤੇ ਬਦੂਕਾਂ ਤੋਪਾਂ ਤੇ ਲੜਾਈ ਦੇ ਅਸਬਾਬ ਦੀ ਸਹਾਇਤਾ ਅਫਰੀਕਾ ਤੇ ਚੀਨ ਦੀ ਲੜਾਈ ਦੇ ਲਈ ਦਿਤੀ ਤੇ ਸੁਣਿਆ ਹੈ ਜੋ ੧੫੦੦ ਜਾਂ ੨੦੦੦ ਸਿਖੇ ਹੋਏ ਬੋਲ ਦੀ ਚਾਗੀ ਦੇਹਨ ਤੇ ਜਿਨਾਂ ਦੇ ਲਈ ਪੱਠਾ ਦੱਥਾ ਵੀ ਨਾਲ ਜਾਣਾ ਚਾਹੀਦਾ ਹੈ ਤੇ ਔਖੀ ਗਲ ਏਹੁ ਹੈ ਜੋ ਮੀਂਹ ਨਾਂ ਪੈਣ ਨਾਲ ਘਾ ਤਾਂ ਇਕ ਵਲ ਰਿਹਾ ਅੰਨ ਦੇ ਭਾ ਤੂੜੀ ਹੋ ਗਈ ਹੈ ਸੋ ਵੀ ਮਿੱਟੀ ਵਲੀ ਹੱਥ ਆਉਂਦੀ ਹੈ ਸਰਕਾਰ ਨੇ ਮੈਨੂੰ ਠੇਕਾ ਦੇ ਦਿੱਤਾ ਹੈ ਤੇ ਮੈਂ ਲਾਇਲਪੁਰ ਦੇ ਅਲਾਕੇ ਵਿੱਚ ਤੂੜੀ ਖਰੀਦਣ ਲਈ ਚਲਿਆ ਹਾਂ ਤੁਸੀਂ ਪਿਛੇ ਮੇਰੇ ਬਾਲ ਬਚੇ ਨੂੰ ਖਰਚ ਪੱਠਾ ਦੇ ਛੱਡਣਾ

ਚਿੱਠੀ ਲਿਖੀ ਵੀਰਵਾਰ ਕਤਕ ਦੀ ੧੩

ਸ਼ਾਮ ਸਿੰਘ

VOCABULARY.

ੴ ਸਤਿਗੁਰਪ੍ਰਸਾਦਿ ।

ਅ

ਅਸਵਾਰੀ *aswārī, s. f.* riding, the state of being mounted.

ਅਸੀਰਬਾਦ *asīrbād, s. f.* Benediction, salutation.

ਅੱਸੂ *assū, s. m.* The name of the 7th month of the civil year.

ਅਸਵਾਰਾ ਸਾਹਿਬ *aswārāsāhib, s. m.* Sikh's religious Granth.

ਅਕਸਰ *aksar, adv.* Generlly.

ਅਕਲ *akl, s. f.* Understanding sense, reason, wisdom.

ਅਕਲਾਪਾ *aklāpā, adv.* Alone.

ਅਕਾਸ *akās, s. m.* Heaven, the firmament.

ਅਕਾਲ ਪੁਰਖ *akāl purukh, s. m.* The immortal One (God).

ਅਕਾਲੀ *akālī, s. m.* An immortal, one (the name of a class of Sikh devotees.)

ਅਖਸਰ *akhsar, adj.* Many *adv.* mostly often, Generally.

ਅਖਰ *akkhar, s. m.* A letter of the alphabet.

ਅੱਗ *agg, s. f.* Fire ਅਗ ਲਾਉਣਾ *agg lāonā, v. a.* To set fire.

ਅਗਾਹਾਂ *agāhāṇ adv,* Before, forward, ahead infront, also ਗਾਹਾਂ *gahāṅ.*

ਅੱਗੇ *agge, prep.* Before (both in time and place.)

ਅਜ *ajj adv.* To-day.

ਅੱਜ ਕਲ *ajj kal, adj.* Now a days.

ਅਜੇ *aje, adv.* yet, hitherto.

ਅਟਕਣਾ *ataknā, v. n.* To be stopped, to be prevented, to adhere, to stop

ਅਠਵਾਰਾ *aṭhwārā, s. m.* week.

ਅਡ *add,* separate.

ਅੰਤ *ant, s. m.* End.

ਅੰਦਰ *andar prep,* Within, in.

ਅੰਦਰ *andar, s. m.* The inside.

ਅੰਦਰਲੀ *andarlī, adv. s. m.* Inner.

ਅੰਨ੍ਹਾ *annhā, s. m.* A blind, a blindman.

ਅਨਾਮ *anām, s. m.* Prize, reward.

ਅਮਨ *aman, s. m* Ease, peace.

ਅਰਮਾਨ *armān, s. m.* Inclination, ease.

ਅਰਮਾਨ *armān inter.* Alas.

ਅਲਮਾਰੀ *almārī, s. f.* Almarah.

ਅਲਾਕਾ *alākā, s. m.* Dependence.

ਅਵੱਸ *awass, adv.* By chance.

ਅਵਾਜ਼ *awāz, s. f.* Voice, noise sound.

ਆਉਂਦੜ *āondaṛ, s. f* Income.

ਆਕੀ *ākī, adj.* Rebellious, disobedient.

ਆਕੀ ਹੋਣਾ *ākī honā,* to rebel.

ਆਖਣਾ *ākhṇā, v. a.* To say, to command to tell.

ਆਗਿਆਕਾਰ *āgiākār adj.* Subject, obedient to orders.

ਆਦਕ *ādak, adv.* etcetra

ਆਦਰ *ādar, adj.* Respect, difference, honor

ਆਪਾਂ *pron*: We.

ਆਨੰਦ *ānand, adj.* Happy, glad.

ਆਪਸ *āpas, pron*: (oblique cases Plu: of ਆਪ *āp*) one another.

ਆਪਸਵਿਚ *āpas wich, pron*: Among themselves.

ਆਰੰਭ *ārambh, s. m.* Beginning.

ਐਤਕੀ *aitkī, adv* Now, this time, the present year.

ਐਨਾ *ainā, adv.* So much.

ਐਵੇਂ *aiwen, s. m.* Thus in this way, invain.

ਔਖ *aukh, s. m.* Difficulty.

ਔਖਾ *aukhā, adj.* Difficult, distressed.

ੲ

ਇਸ *is pron*, (oblique cases of ਇਹ this, he, she it.

ਇਸਕਰਕੇ *is karke adv.* For this reason.

ਇਨਾਮ *inām, s. m.* a present.

ਏਦਰ *edhar adv.* Here, on this side.

ਏਡੀ *eḍī, adv.* So much.

ਏਥੇ *ethe, adv.* Here

ੳ

ਉਹਦਾ *ohdā*, appointment.

ਉਗਰਾਨਾ *ugrānā, v. a.* To collect.

ਉਂਗੁਲ *unggul, s. f.* A finger.

ਉਂਗਲ ਭਰ *unggal bhar*, a finger's breadth, and sometimes though rarely, a finger length.

ਉਚੱਕਾ *uchakkā s. m.* A piek-pockect, a thief.

ਉਛਾੜ *uchhāṛ s. m.* Cover.

ਉੱਜਲ *ujjal, adj.* Bright, shining.

ਉਜਾੜ *ujāṛ s. f.* A desert.

ਊਠ *ūṭṭh s. m.* A camel.

ਉੱਤਰ *uttar s. m.* An answer, ; the north; ਉੱਤਰਦੇਸ *uttar des*, the northern country ਉਤਰਦੇਣਾ *uttar deṇā*, To answer.

ਉੱਦਮ *uddam s. m.* Industry, effort.

ਉਪਮਾ *upamā s. f.* Greatness, glory.

ਓਟ *ot s. f.* Protection, shelter.

ਓੜ ਪੋੜ *oṛ poṛ s. m.* Remedy.

ਸ

ਸਸਤਾ *sastā, adj.* cheap.

ਸਹਤ *siht, prep*, with.

ਸਹਾ *sahā s. m.* A rabbit, a hare, bird.

ਸਹਾਇਤਾ *sahāitā s. f.* Help.

ਸਹਾਰਾ *sahārā s. m.* Help, support, endurance, patience.

ਸ਼ਹਿਰ *shahir s. m.* A city.

ਸਹੀ *sahī s. f.* A signature, ਸਹੀਕਰਨੀ *sahīkarnī* or ਦੇਣੀ *deṇī* to sign.

ਸਹੁਰਾ *saharā* A father-in-law.

ਸਹੁਰਾ ਘਰ *sahurā ghar*, a father-in-law's house.

ਸੱਕਰ *sakkar, s. f.* Sugar in a course unpurified state.

ਸ਼ਕਾਰ *shakār, s. m.* Hunting, game.

ਸ਼ਕਾਰ ਕਰਨਾ *shakār karnā, v. a.* to hunt.

ਸ਼ਕਾਰ ਖੇਡਨਾ *shakār khednā, v. a.* to hunt, to sport.

ਸ਼ਕਾਰ ਮਾਰਨਾ *shakār mārnā, v. a.* to kill the game.

ਸੰਖ *sankh, s. m.* A conch blown by Hindus in their worship.

ਸਜਾ *sajā, s. f.* Punishment.

ਸੱਜਾ *sajjā, adj.* Right (not left).

ਸੱਟ *saṭṭ, s. f.* A blow, a stroke.

ਸੰਢਾ *sanḍhā, s. m.* a male buffalo.

ਸੱਤ *sat, adj.* seven.

ਸਤਿ *sati, adj.* True.

ਸਤਿਗੁਰ *satigur.* True spiritual guide.

ਸਥ *satth, s. f.* A place before the great of a town or village where men and cattle congregate in the morning.

ਸੱਥ *satth, s. f.* The council of five called pancháyat.

ਸੱਦਣਾ *saddnā, v. a.* To call.

ਸਦਾ *sadā, adv.* Always, ever.

ਸੰਢਾ *sandhā, s. m.* A male buffalo.

ਸਪਾਰਸ਼ *spārash, s. f.* recommendation,

ਸਪੁਰਦ ਕਰਨਾ *sapurd karnā. v. a.* hand over, to entrust.

ਸਮਤ *samat, s. m.* year.

ਸਮਝਣਾ *samjhnā, v. a.* know, understand.

ਸਭ ਤ੍ਰਿਹਕ *sub tirehak, s. m.* well wisher.

ਸਮਾਂ *samā, s. m.* Time period.

ਸਮਾਚਾਰ *samāchār, s. m.* news, information

ਸਮੇਟਣਾ *sameṭnā, v. a.* To constringe, to shrink.

ਸਰਹਾਣਾ *sarahāṇā, s. m.* a pillow.

ਸਰਕੜਾ *sarakṛā, s. m.* a reed.

ਸਰਕਾਰੀ *sarkārī, adv.* Belonging to the Government.

ਸ਼ਰਤ *shart, s. f.* a condition, an agreement.

ਸਰਦੀ *sardī, s. f.* a cold, coldness.

ਸਰਬ *sarab,* all.

ਸ਼ਰਾਬ *sharāb, s. f.* Wine.

ਸ਼ਰਾਬੀ *sharābī, s. m.* a drunkard.

ਸਰੋਂ *saroṅ s. f.* Oil seed.

ਸਲਾਹ *salāh, s. f.* advice.

ਸਵਾ *sawā,* a quarter more than the number immediately following, as ਸਵਾਤਿੰਨ 3¼ *sawā tinn.*

ਸਵਾਰ *sawār, s. m.* a rider.

ਸਵਾਰੀ *sawārī, s. f,* riding.

ਸੜਕ *saṛak, s. f.* a road.

ਸੜਕ ਸੜਕ ਜਾਣਾ *saṛk saṛk jānā, v. a.* To go forward on the high road.

ਸੜਨਾ *saṛnā, v. a.* To be burned.

ਸਾਇਤ *sāit* or ਸਾਇਦ *sāid ad.* Perhaps

ਸਾਂਈ *sāīn, s. m.* Lord, master.

ਸਾਉਣ *sāon, s. m.* The name of the 5th Hindu month beginning in July

ਸਾਉਣੀ *sāonī, s. f.* The summer crop.

ਸ਼ਾਹ *shāh, s. m.* one who lends money on interest, a banker.

ਸ਼ਾਹਜ਼ਾਦਾ *shāhjādā, s. m.* Prince.

ਸ਼ਾਹੀ *shāhī, s. f.* ink.

ਸਾਹਾ *sāhā, s. m.* The day appointed for a wedding

ਸਾਹਰੇ *sāhure, s. m. plu.* A father-in-law's family.

ਸਾਹ *sāh, s m.* Breath.

ਸਾਗਰ *sāgar, s. m.* The sea, the ocean.

ਸ਼ਾਦ *shād,* a glad.

ਸਾਧ *sādh, s. m.* A saint.

ਸਾਧੂ *sādhū, s. m.* Fakir.

ਸਾਫਾ *v. a.* A turban.

ਸਾਂਭਨਾ *v. a.* To support, to sustain, to stop to take care of.

ਸਾਰਾ *sārā, a.* All, every, the whole.

ਸਾਲ *sāl, s. m.* a year.

ਸਾਲਾਨਾ *sālānā,* yearly.

ਸਿਆਣਾਂ *siānā, s. m.* Knowing, wise.

ਸਿਆਲ *siāl, s. m.* winter.

ਸਿਖ ਮਤ *sikh mat, s. f.* advice, instruction.

ਸਿਖਿਆ ਹੋਇਆ *s. m.* Trained.

ਸਿਜਨਾਂ *sijjnā, v. a.* To be wet.

ਸਿਧਾ *siddhā,* a straight.

ਸਿਧਾ ਕਰਣਾ *sidhā karnā* or ਬਣਾਉਣਾ *jā banāonā, v. a.* to straighten.

ਸੀਂਹ *sīnh, s. m.* a lion

ਸੁਆਦ *suād, s. m.* Taste, relish, flavor.

ਸੁਹਾਗਾ *suhāgā, s. m.* Borax.

ਸੁਕਣਾ *sukknā, v. a.* To dry, to wither, to become to dry, to evaporate.

ਸੁਕਰਵਾਰ *sukkarwār, s. m.* Friday.

ਸੁਖ *sukh, s. m.* Ease, tranquillity, easy circumstances, contentment, happiness.

ਸੁਖ *sukkh, adv.* well, very well, no matter, no consequence

ਸੁਟਣਾ *suttanā. v. a.* To cast, to throw down.

ਸੁਣਨਾਂ *sunnā, v. a* To hear, to hearken, to listen, to mind.

ਸੁਦਾਗਰ *sudāgar, s. m.* A merchant, a trader.

ਸੁੰਨਾ *sunnā, adj* Empty.

ਸੁਭਾਉ *subhāu, s. m* Temperament. disposition, nature, habit.

ਸੂਆ *sūā, s. m.* small canal.

ਸੂਬਾ *sūbā, s. m.* A Province, the Governor of a province.

ਸੂਰ *sūr, s. m.* a hog.

ਸੂਬੇਦਾਰ *sūbedār, s. m.* The Chief of a province, a military officer whose rank correspond to that of Captain.

ਸੇਉਂਕ *seunk, s. f.* white ant.

ਸੇਕਨਾ *seknā, v. a.* to warm ones self.

ਸੇਂਜੀ *senjī, s. f.* The name of a weed which generally grows among wheat

ਸੇਪੀ *sepī, s. m,* a kind of servant who gets so much on cutting the crops.

ਸੇਰ *ser, s. m.* A seer weight.

ਸ਼ੇਰ *sher, s. m.* A lion.

ਸੈਂਕੜਾ *sainkrā,* one hundred.

ਸੈਂਡ *saind, s. m.* a mixture of wheat and chaff.

ਸੈਨਾ *sainā, s. f.* An army, a host.

ਸੋਹਣਾ *sohnā, adj.* pretty.

ਸੋਕਾ ਪੈਣਾ *sokā painā, v. a.* to get dry.

ਸੋਚ *soch s. f.* Meditation, consideration.

ਸੋਚ ਸੰਭਲਕੇ *soch sambhal ke, adv.* Carefully.

ਸੋਚਣਾਂ *sochnā, v. a.* To consider.

ਸੋਟਾ *soṭā, s. m.* A cane, a walking stick.

ਸੋਧਣਾਂ *sodhṇā, v. a.* To correct.

ਸੌ *sau,* one hundred.

ਸੌਣੀ *sauṇī, v. a* harvest, the crop of winter.

ਹ

ਹਸ *hass, s. m.* A silver or gold collar, worn as an ornament by women and children, the collar bone.

ਹਸਤਪਤਾਲ *hostpatāl, s. m.* Hospital.

ਹਵਾਲਾਟ *hawālāṭ, s f.* confinement.

ਹਕਣਾਂ *hakkṇā, v. a.* to drive.

ਹਕੀਕਤ *hakīkat, s. f.* Truth, fact circumstance.

ਹਜੂਰ *hajūr, s. f.* presence, a title of respect, Sir

ਹਟਾਉਣਾ *haṭāuṇā, v. a* To cause to be removed.

ਹਟੀ *haṭṭī, s. f.* A shop.

ਹੰਢਨਸਾਰ *hundan sār, adj.* Durable.

ਹਥ *hatth. s. m.* The hand.

ਹੱਥ ਜੋੜਨਾ *hatthjoṛnā, v. a.* To fold hands in a supplicating manner

ਹੱਦ *hadd, s. f.* Boundary, limit.

ਹਨੇਰਾ *hanerā, s. m.* Darkness.

ਹਨੇਰੀ *hanerī, s. f.* A dust, storm.

ਹਮਸੋਸ *hamsos, s. m.* Sorrow, concern lamentation.

ਹਮਲਾ *hamlā, s. m.* An assault, an invasion, an attack.

ਹਰਨ *harn, s. m.* A deer, a buck.

ਹਰਾਨ *harān, adj.* Astonished, amazed.

ਹੱਲਾ *hallā, s. m.* An attack, an invasion.

ਹਲਾਲ *halāl, adj.* Lawful.

ਹਲਾਲ ਕਰਨਾ *halāl karnā, v. a.* to slaughter in a lawful way.

ਹਵਾਲਾਟ *hawālāṭ, s f.* A prison.

ਹੜ੍ਹ *haṛh, s. m.* A mountain torrent, temporary rush of water.

ਹਾਣੀ *hāṇī, adj. s. f.* of the same age.

ਹਾਰ *hār, s f.* Defeat, discomfiture.

ਹਾਲ ਚਾਲ *hālchāl, s. m.* State, condition

ਹਾੜ *hāṛh, s. m.* The name of the fourth Hindu solar month which begins in the middle of June.

ਹਾੜੀ *hāṛī, s. f.* winter crops.

ਹਿੱਸਾ *hissā, s. m.* share.

ਹਿੱਕ *hikk adj.* One. i. q. ਇਕ

ਹਿੱਲਣਾ *hillṇā, v. n.* To shake, to be moved.

ਹੁਣ *huṇ, adv.* Now.

ਹੁਦਾ *huddā, s. m.* Commission, engagement. occupation, business.

ਹੁਦਾਰ ਲੈਣਾ *hudār laiṇā, v a.* To borrow

ਹੁਦੇਦਾਰ *huddedār, s. m.* An Officer, a Commissioner.

ਹੁਨਾਲ *hunāl, s. m.* The hot weather.

ਹੇਠ *heṭh, prep.* Under, below, beneath.

ਹੇਠਾਂ *heṭhān, adj.* Of inferior rank, or dignity.

ਹੈਜਾ *haijā, s. m.* Cholera.

ਹੋਂਠ *honṭh, s. m.* The lip.

ਹੌਲਦਾਰ *hauldāṛ, s. m.* An havaldar.

ਕ

ਕਸ *kas, s. f.* Fever.

ਕਚਹਿਰੀ *kachahirī, s. f.* A Court.

ਕੱਚਾ *kachchā, adj.* Raw, unripe, temporary.

ਕਛਣਾ *kachhnā, v a.* to meisure

ਕਟ *kat, s. m.* loin.

ਕੱਟਣਾ *kaṭṭṇa, v. a.* To pass (time) to cut (thing).

ਕਠਾ ਕਰਨਾ *kaṭhā karnā. v. a.* to collect.

ਕੱਢਣਾ *kaddhṇā, v. a.* To cast out, to exclude

ਕੰਢਾ *kanḍhā, s. m.* Shore, margin, bank,

ਕਣਕ *kaṇak, s. f.* Wheat.

ਕਣੀ *kaṇī, s f.* A drop of rain. The dust and refuse of rice when it is cleaned.

ਕੱਤਕ *kattak, s. m.* The name of the serventh Hindu month beginning in September.

ਕਥਾ *kathā, s. m.* A story, narrative.

ਕਦੀਂ *kadīṇ, adv* Ever, sometimes,

ਕੰਧ *kandh, s. f.* A wall.

ਕਨਕ *kanak, s. f.* Wheat

ਕਨਾਰਾ *kanārā, s. m.* Side, border, margin, boundary.

ਕੱਨੀ *knnnī, s. f.* Border.

ਕਪਤਾਨ *kpatān, s. m.* A Captain.

ਕੱਪੜ *kappaṛ, s. m.* Cloth.

ਕੁਪਾਹ *kupāh, s. f.* Raw cotton, also

ਕਪਾਹਾ *kapāhā,* The cotton plant.

ਕਬਜ਼ਾ ਕਰਨਾ *kabjā karnā, v. a.* To take possession of, to possess.

ਕੰਬਣਾ *kambṇā, v. n* To shake, to tremble.

ਕੱਮ *kamm, s. m.* Work, business.

ਕੱਮ ਕਾਜ *kamm kāj, s. m.* Work, business

ਕਮਾਦ *kamād, s. m.* A crop, a sugarcane.

ਕਮਾਨ ਅਫ਼ਸਰ *kamān afsār, s. m..* Commanding Officer.

ਕਮੀਜ਼ *kamīj, s. f.* A shirt.

ਕਮੀਨ *kamīn, s. m.* poor people.

ਕਰਤਾਰ *kartār, s. m.* A creator, (to title of God).

ਕੁਰਤੂਤ *kartūt, s. f.* Action, business, deed.

ਕਰੜਾ *karṛā, adj* hard, severe.

ਕਰਾਰ *karār, s. m.* Promise, agreement.

ਕਰੋਧੀ *karodhī, s. m.* Angry, enraged. wroth.

ਕੜ੍ਹੀ *kaṛhī s. f.* Cruel (prepared in a variety of ways).

ਕੜਾਹ *kaṛāh, s. m.* A kind of sweetmeat made of flour, sugar and *ghī.*

ਕਾਸਾ *kāsā, s. m.* A cup.

ਕਾਕਾ *kākā, s. m.* An elder brother, a little child.

ਕਾਂਗ *kāṇgg, s. f.* A pen, a wave, a billow.

ਕਾਂਜਨ *kāṇjan, s. f.* A beam which rests on the two pillars of a Persian wheel.

ਕਾਣਾ *kāṇā, adj.* One eyed.

ਕੱਾਮਾ *kāmmā, s. m.* A labourer, servant.

ਕਾਰਨ *kāran s. m.* Cause, account, reason

ਕਾਲ *kāl, s. m* Famine, dearth, drought.

ਕਿਆਰਾ ਮੋੜਨਾ *kiārā morṇā,* to give water from one field to another.

ਕਿਸ਼ਤ *kist, s. f.* instalment.

ਕਿਹੜਾ *kihṛā, pron.* Who? which? whom? what?

ਕਿੱਕਰ *kikkar, s. f.* The name of a tree the Babul, acacia tree.

ਕਿਣੀ *kiṇī, s. f.* A drop of rain.

ਕਿਤਲ *kital, s. m.* A very deadly snake probably from *qātil.*

ਕਿੱਨਾ *kinnā, adv.* How much.

ਕਿਨਾ ਚਿਰ *kinnā chir, adv.* How long.

ਕਿਰਾੜ *kirāṛ, s. f.* A. khatri, a shop-keeper.

ਕਿਲਾ *kilā, s. m.* A fort.

ਕੀ *kī, pron.* What ?

ਕੁਹਾੜਾ *kuhāṛā, s. m.* An axe.

ਕੁੰਜੀ *kunjī, s. f.* A key.

ਕੁਝ ਵਾਹ ਨਹੀਂ *kujh wāh nahīn,* cannot be helped.

ਕੁਪਾ *kuppā,* a large vessel made of raw hide.

ਕੁੱਬਾ *kubbā, adj.* Hunch backed.

ਕੁੜੀ *kuṛī, s. f.* A girl, a daughter, a virgin.

ਕੂਚ *kūch, s. m.* Marching.

ਕੂਚ ਕਰਨਾ *kūch karnā, v. a.* To march, to die.

ਕੇਰਨਾ *kernā, v. a.* To pour, to scatter.

ਕੈਦ *kaid, s f.* Imprisonment.

ਕੈਦ ਕਰਨਾ *kaid karnā, v. a* To imprison.

ਕੈਲਾ *kailā, adj.* Grey.

ਕੋਹ *koh, s. m.* The common *kachchā koh* is professedly 2040 yards less than 1¼ miles ; but in reality it seems in most places to be nearer a mile. and a half.

ਕੋਠਾ *koṭhā, s. m.* A house.

ਕੋਠੀ *koṭhī, s. f.* A house, a treasury.

ਕੋਰਾ *korā, s. m.* Snow, ice.

ਕੋਲ *kol, prop.* Near, by, with.

ਕੋੜਮਾ *koṛmā, s. m.* Family, tribe.

ਕੌਡੀ *kauḍī, s. f.* A small shell.

ਖ

ਖਚਰ *khachchar, s. m. f.* A mule.

ਖੰਡਰ *khaṇḍar, s. m* Ruins.

ਖੱਤਾ *khattā, s m.* A field small and low.

ਖਤਾਬ *khatāb, s. m.* Title, appelation.

ਖੱਦਰ *khaddar, s. m.* A very coarse kind of cotton cloth.

ਖਪਾਉਣਾ *khapāuṇā, v. a.* To destroy.

ਖਬਰ *khabar, s. f.* Report.

ਖੱਬਾ *khabbā, adj.* Left belonging to the left hand.

ਖਰਚਣਾ *kharchṇā, v. a.* To spend, also. ਖਰਚ ਕਰਨਾ *kharch karnā.*

ਖਰਾ *kharā, adj.* Pure, good.

ਖਰੀਦਗੀ *kharīdgī, s. f.* The price of a thing, buying.

ਖਲਵਾਨ *khalwān, s. m.* A farmyard.

ਖਲਵਾਨਾ *khaluāiā, v a.* To make st p.

ਖੜੋਣਾ *kharoṇā, v n.* To stand up, to stop.

ਖਾਣਾ *khāṇā, v. a.* To eat.

ਖਾਲ *khāl s. f.* a drain.

ਖਿਆਲ *khiāl, s. m.* Thought, imagination, fancy.

ਖਿਚਣਾ *khichchṇā, v a.* To draw, to stretch

ਖਿਨ *khin, s. m.* A minute.

ਖੁਆਉਣਾ *khuāuṇā, v. a.* To feed, to cause to eat.

ਖੁਸ਼ੀ *khusī, s. f.* Gladness, joy, delight.

ਖੁੱਲਣਾ *khullhṇā, v. n.* To open, to be opened.

ਖੁਲਮਖੁਲਾ *khullamkhullā, adv.* openly.

ਖੁਲਾ *khullā, adj.* open.

ਖੁਵਾਉਣਾ *khuwāuṇā, v. a.* To cause to eat

ਖੂਹ *khūh*, s. m. A well.

ਖੁਣੋਂ *khuṇoṇ*, prep. without, for want of.

ਖ਼ੂਨੀ *khūnī*, s. m. A murderer.

ਖੇਤ *khet*, s. m. A field under cultivation; a battle field.

ਖੇਤੀ *khetī*, s. f. Agriculture, cultivation.

ਖੇਤੀ ਪੱਤੀ *khetī pattī*, s. f. Cultivation agriculture, husbandry.

ਖੋਜ *khoj*, s. m. Search.

ਖੋਜਣਾ *khojṇā*, v. a. To seek, to search; also. ਖੋਜ ਕਢਣਾ *khoj kadhṇā*.

ਖੋਤਾ *k'oṭā*, s. m. An ass; also name of a large, red, and white worm.

ਖੋਪਰੀ *khoprī*, s. f. A skull.

ਖੋਰੀ *khorī*, s. f The dry leaves of the sugar cane.

ਖੋਲਾ *kholā*, adj. Old ruin.

ਗ

ਗਸ਼ *gash*, s. m. Fainting.

ਗਸ਼ ਖਾਣਾ *gash khāṇā*, to faint.

ਗਸਤ or ਗਛਤ *gast or gachhat*, s. f. going round.

ਗਹਣੇ ਧਰਨਾ *gahne dharnā*, v. a. To mortgage.

ਗਜ *gaj*, s. m. An elephant, a yard, a yard stick.

ਗੱਡਾ *gaḍḍā*, s. m. A large cart.

ਗਡਾਉਣਾ *gaḍāuṇā*, v. a. To drive in, buried.

ਗੰਡਾਸਾ *gaṇḍāsā*, s. m. A sort of axe, a pole axe.

ਗਦਰ *gadar*, s m. Revolt, rebellion.

ਗੱਦੀ *gaddī*, s. f. A cushion, a pad, a throne.

ਗੰਨਾ *gannā*, s. m. Sugar cane.

ਗਭਰੂ *gabhrū*, s. m. A young man, a young husband.

ਗਰਕ ਕਰਨਾ *gark karnā*, v. a. To be drowned.

ਗਰਮ *garm*, adj Warm, hot.

ਗਰਮੀ *garmī*, adj s. f. Heat, warmth.

ਗਰੀਬ *garīb*, adj. Poor, gentle.

ਗੱਲ *gall* s. f. Word, thing.

ਗੱਲ ਕਾਹਦੀ *gall kāhdī* or ਗੱਲ ਕੀ *gall kī*, in short.

ਗਵਾਰਾ *gawārā*, s. m. A kind of grain.

ਗਾਈਂ *gāīṇ*, s. f. A cow, also ਗਾਂ *gāṇ* and ਗਾਈਂ *gāīṇ*.

ਗਾਹਣਾਂ *gāhṇā*, v. a. to tred out.

ਗਾਜੀ *gājī*, s. m. A bravo man.

ਗਾਨਾ *gānā*, v. n. To sing.

ਗਾਲ *gāl*, s f. Abuse.

ਗਿੱਦੜ *giddaṛ*. s. m. A Jackal.

ਗਿਲ *gil*, s. f. Moisture, dampness.

ਗੁਆਉਣਾ *guāuṇā*, v. a. to lose.

ਗੁਸਾ *gussā*, s. m. Anger.

ਗੁਜਾਰਾ ਕਰਨਾ *gujārā karnā*, v. a. To live.

ਗੁਡਹਾਲ *guḍihāl*, s. m. A place where they make sugar.

ਗੁਣ *guṇ*, s. m. Virtue, quality.

ਗੁੰਦਣਾ *gundṇā*, v. a. To plait (hair). To work into a plot.

ਗੁਰਬਲਾਸ *gurblas* s. m. Name of a religious book of Sikhs.

ਗੁਰਮੰਤਾ gurmatā, s. m Consultation.

ਗੁਰਮੁਖ gurmukh, s. m. A good pious man.

ਗਲੋਚ gloch, s. m. Abuse.

ਗੁੜ guṛ, s. m. Inspissated juice of the sugar cane, coarse sugar.

ਗੋਡਾ goḍā, s. m. The knee.

ਗੋਡੀ goḍī, s. f. Effort, labour.

ਗੋਡੀ ਕਰਨਾ goḍī karnā or ਗੋਡਨਾ godnā, v. a. To labour hard.

ਗੋਰਾ gorā, adj. White man.

ਗੋੱਲਾ gollā, s. m. A slave.

ਗੋਲੀ golī, s. f. A small ball, a shot.

ਘ

ਘਸ ਜਾਣਾ ghas jānā, v. n. to be worn out.

ਘੱਟ ghaṭṭ, adj. Deficient, less.

ਘੱਟ ghaṭṭ, adv. In a small measure, seldom.

ਘਤਣਾ ghaṭṭṇā, v. a. To throw, to pour

ਘਰਵਾਲੀ gharwālī, s. f. Wife.

ਘਰਾਣਾ gharāṇā } s. m. A family or tribe.
ਘਰਾਨਾ gharāṇā }

ਘੱਲਣਾ ghallnā, v. a. To send.

ਘੜਿਆਲ ghaṛiāl, s. m. A gong, a time piece, a clock.

ਘਾਇਲ ghāil, adj. Wounded.

ਘੁੱਟਣਾ ghuṭannā, s. m. A trousers.

ਘੁਮਿਆਰ ghumiār, s. m. potter.

ਘਿਉ gheu, s. m. Clarified butter (ghi).

ਘੇਰਾ gherā, s. m. A circle, a siege.

ਘੇਰਾ ਪਾਉਣਾ gherā pāunā, v. a. To lay a siege, to besiege.

ਘੋੜਚੜ੍ਹਾ ghoṛchaṛhā, s. m. A mounted servant, horseman.

ਚ

ਚੱਕ chakk, s. m. A frame on which the wall of a well is built. A bite.

ਚਕਨਾਚੂਰ chaknāchūr, adj. In scraps, in pieces.

ਚੱਖਣਾ chakkhṇā, v. a. To taste.

ਚੰਗਾ changā, adj. Good, excellent.

ਚੱਦਰ chaddar, s. f. A shawl, sheet also ਚਾਦਰ

ਚੰਦਰਮਾ chandarmā, s. m. The moon.

ਚੰਦਰਾ chandrā, s. m. A whitelow, hailstorm.

ਚਣਾ chanā, s. m. Gram.

ਚਪਣੀ chappṇī, s. f. The cover of an earthen vessel ; the knee pan.

ਚਪੜਾਸੀ chaprāsī, s. f. Any one having a chapras, a messenger or other servant who is in the habit of wearing a chapras

ਚੱਬਣਾ chabbṇā, v. a To champ, to grind between the teeth, to chew.

ਚਰਨ charn s. m. A foot.

ਚੰਗ chang s. m. A trench.

ਚਲਾਕ chalāk, adj. Active, hardworking.

ਚੜ੍ਹਦੀ ਵਲ charḍī wal, adj. On the northside.

ਚੜ੍ਹਿਆਂ ਹੀ chaṛiāṇ hī, adj. In the very beginning.

ਚੜ੍ਹਨਾ chaṛhnā, v. a. To mount.

ਚਾਉ chāu, s. m. Desire. Pleasure.

ਚਾਉਲ chāul, s. m. Rice.

ਚਾਹ *chāh*, s. f. Desire, wish, appetite.

ਚਾਹਣਾ *chāhṇā*, v. a. To desire, to wish to like.

ਚਾਚਾ *chāchā*, s. m. A father's younger brother, uncle

ਚਾਤਰ *chātar*, adj clever, cunning.

ਚਾਨਣਾ *chāṇaṇā*, s.m. Moon-light, light

ਚਾਰਜ *chāraj*, s. m. charge.

ਚਿਠੀ *chiṭṭhī*, s. f. A letter, a note.

ਚਿਤਾਰਨਾ *chitārnā*, v. a. To remind, to warn

ਚਿੜੀ *chiṛī*, s f. A female sparrow.

ਚੀਤਾ *chītā*, s. m. Leopard.

ਚੀਪ ਕੋਰਟ *chip kort*, s. f. Chief Court.

ਚੁਹਾਰਮ *chuharam*, one forth.

ਚੁੱਕਣਾ *chukkṇā*, v. a To miss, to forget, to err.

ਚੁਗਣਾ *chugnā*, v a. To peck, to eat, to graze.

ਚੂਹੜਾ *chūhṛā*, s. m. sweeper.

ਚੂਰਾ *chūrā*. s. m. Crumbs, fragments.

ਚੂੜੀ *chūṛī*, s. f. A braclet.

ਚੇਤ *chet*, s m. The name of the first month in the civil year beginning about the middle of march.

ਚੋਰ *chor*, s. m. A thief.

ਚੋਰੀ *chorī*, s. f. A theft.

ਚੋਰੀ ਜਾਣਾ *chorī jānā*, v. n. To be stolen.

ਚੋਰੀ ਕਰਨਾ *chorī karnā*, v. a. To steal.

ਚੌਂਕ *chaunk*, s. m. An open square, in a city. An ornament which is commonly worn by women on the head.

ਚੌਂਕ *chauṇgk*, s. m. An head ornament.

ਚੌਕੜ *chaunkaṛ*, s. m. Four strings.

ਚੌਂਕੀ *chauṇkī*, s. f. A watch, in gaard a police station.

ਚੌਂਕੀ ਭਰਨੀ *chaunkī*, v a. also to keep watch.

ਚੌਂਕੀ ਪਹਿਰਾ ਦੇਣਾਂ *chaunkī pahirā denā*, v. a also to keep watch or guard.

ਛ

ਛਡਣਾਂ *chhaḍḍṇā*, v a To leave, to let alone, to forsake, to release, to liberate.

ਛਤ *chhatt*, s. f. A roof

ਛਤਣਾਂ *chhattnā*, v. a. To roof.

ਛਤਰੀ *chhatarī* or *chhattrī*, s. f. A small umbrella.

ਛਵੈਯਾ *chhawaiyā*, s. m. A thatcher.

ਛਵੀ *chhavi*, s. f. A concealed knife with wooden handle.

ਛਾਂ *chhāṅ*, s. f. A shadow, shade.

ਛਾਪਾ ਮਾਰਨਾ *chhāpā mārnā*, v. a To make a night attack.

ਛਿੜਨਾਂ *chhiṛnā*, v. a. To continue.

ਛੁਟੀ *chhuṭṭī*, s. f. Leave.

ਛੋਲਾ *chholā*, s. m. A kind of pulse gram.

ਜ

ਜਖਮ *jakham*, s m. A wound.

ਜੰਗਲ *janggal*, s. m. A jungle, a forest.

ਜਗੀਰ *jagīr*, s. f. Land given by Government as a reward for services.

ਜੰਜ *janjj*, s. f. A wedding party.

ਜੱਟ *jaṭṭ, s. m.* The name of a caste of farmers (both Hindu and Muhammadan)

ਜਤਨ *jatan, s. m.* Effort, endeavour, arrangement.

ਜਦ ਕਦੀਂ *jad kadiṇ, adv* Whenever.

ਜੰਦਰਾ *jandarā, s m* A padlock.

ਜਨਮਸਾਖੀ *janamsākhī, s. f.* A biography (particularly of Nának and the other Gurus

ਜਫਾ *japhā, s. m.* Opression, violence, hardship.

ਜੰਮਣਾ *jammnā, v. a.* to be born, to exist to grow.

ਜਮਾਦਾਰ *jamādār, s. m.* A military officer next to Subedar, a native officer at the head of an uncertain band.

ਜਮੀਨ *jamīn, s. f.* Cultivated land.

ਜਰਨੈਲ *jarnail, s. m.* General.

ਜ਼ਰੂਰ *jarūr,* necessary.

ਜਲ *jal, s. m.* Water.

ਜਲ ਥਲ *jal thal, s. m.* Ground covered with water, water over flowing dry land, marshy ground.

ਜੜ *jaṛ, s. f.* a root origin.

ਜਿਡੀਆਂ *jiddīaṅ,* as big.

ਜਿਤ *jitt, s. f.* victory.

ਜਿਲਾ *jillā, s. m* District.

ਜੀਵਣਾਂ *jīwnā, v. a.* To live.

ਜੁਆਈ *juāī, s. m.* A son-in-law.

ਜੁਆਨ *juān, s m* a youth..

ਜੁਆਰ *juār, s. f.* A kind of grain, a species of broom corn.

ਜੁਗਾਲੀ *jagālī, s f.* chewing the cud.

ਜਜਮਾਨ *jajmān, s. f.* for wedding (client to a Brahman.)

ਜੂੜਨਾ *jūṛnā, v. a.* To bind, to tie, to tie up.

ਜੇ,ਜੇਕਰ *je, jekar, conj* If to.

ਜੇਠ *jeṭh, s. m.* The name of the third month of the civil year beginning in the middle of May; a husband's elder brother.

ਜੋਗ *jog, s. f.* A yoke, of (oxen),

ਜੋਗ *jog, s. m.* junction faithing, a fortunate, opportunity, occasion; a kind of auster devotion intense meditation (practiced by a class of faqirs called jogis;)

ਜੋਗ ਕਮਾਉਣਾ to practice the devotions of jogis;

ਜੋਗ ਧਾਰਨਾਂ *v. a.* to assume the garb of a *jogī.*

ਜੋਗਾ *joggā, s. m.* Opportune, fit, proper able, capable, adequate.

ਜੋਤਨਾ *jotnā, v. a.* to yoke

ਜੋੜਨਾਂ *joṛnā, v. a.* To join, to mend, to add together, to reckon.

ਜੋੜੀ *joṛī, s. f.* pair of bullocks.

ਜੌਂ *jauṇ, s. m.* Barley; *i, q.* ਜਉ

ਜੰਦਰਾ *jandarā, s. m.* a lock.

ਜੰਗਾਲ *jangāl, s. m.* a rust.

ਜੰਗਾਲੀ *jangālī, adj.* Rusty.

ਝ

ਝੱਟਾ *jhaṭṭā, s. m.* watering with a sort o basket.

ਝਲਣ *jhallan, s. f.* A supporter, a prop a stick, suspended above to support a weaver's lay; a transverse beam over a persian wheel in which one of the gudgeons turns.

ਝਲਾਰ *jhālār, s. f.* an excavation by the side of a river for irrigation of water.

ਝੜਪਾ ਝੜਪੀ *jhaṛpā jhaṛpī*, s. f. sparring and fighting, (of birds.) to cause to spar or contends.

ਝੜਾਈ *jhaṛāī*, s. f. invasion ascent; the wages for shaking fruits from a tree, brushing clothes &c.

ਝਾੜਨਾ *jhāṛnā*, v. a. to sweep, to brush to shake, off, to reprove.

ਝਾੜੀ *jhāṛī*, s. f. A small thorn bush.

ਝੀਲ *jhīl*, s. f. A lake, a pond.

ਝੁਆਕਲ *jhoākal*, s. m. upper wheel of Persian wheel.

ਟ

ਟਹਿਲ *ṭahil*, s. f. service.

ਟਹਿਲਣ *ṭahilaṇ*, s f. A female servant.

ਟਕਾ *ṭakā*, s. m. Two pice, a coper coin equal to two pice, in the plural it means also money in general.

ਟੱਟੂ *ṭāṭṭū*, s. m. A pony.

ਟਮਟਮ *tamtam*, s. f. a trap.

ਟੱਬਰ *tabbar*, s. m. A family.

ਟਿੱਬਾ *ṭibbā*, s. m. A hillock, a small elevation, a heap of sand.

ਟਿੰਡ *tiṇḍ*, s. f. earthen well bucket.

ਟੁੱਟਣਾ *ṭuṭṭnā*, v. a. To break, to be broken, to fail, to burst, to brust forth or rush upon one.

ਟੁਰਨਾ *ṭuṛnā*, v. a. to start, to go, to move, to proceed, to go off, to pass.

ਟੂੰਬ *tūmb*, s. f a small peice of metal; a jewel, a piece of flesh (as heart' liver, head, and feet &c.)

ਟੇਸਨ *tesan*, s. m. station.

ਟੈਰਾ *ṭairā*, s. m. a pony.

ਟੈਂਕਾ *tainkā*, s. m. The name of the letter.

ਟੋਪਾ *toppā*. s. m. A grain measure containing about two seers, but in some place it differs.

ਟੋਪੀ *toppī*, s. f. A cap.

ਟੋਬ਼ਾ *tobā*, s. m. an unwalled tank, a pond

ਟੋਲ *ṭol*, s f. searching, search.

ਟੋਲ ਭਾਲ *ṭol bhāl*, s. f. feeting about, looking for, searching.

ਠ

ਠਗਣੀ *thagnā*, v. a. To cheat, to decieve, to inveigle, to steal (one's heart).

ਠਠਾ *ṭhaṭhā*, s. m. Fun, sport, ridicule, jesting, a joke.

ਠੰਡ *ṭhaṇḍ*, s. f. cool, cold.

ਠੰਢ *thaṇḍh*, s. f. cold, coldness; rest comfort, ; in the last sense.

ਠਾਣਾਂ *ṭhāṇā*, s. m. A police station a police office, a body of police men.

ਠੇਕਾ *thekā* s. m. hire, fare, fixed price, work done by contract, a job, a task. a particular mode of beating a drum.

ਡ

ਡਕੋ ਡਕਾ *ḍako ḍakā*, s. m. Every thing.

ਡੰਗਰ ਪਸੂ s. m. cattle, a stupid, simple man.

ਡਰ s m. fear, terror alarm.

ਡਾਕਾ ḍākā, s. m. robbery, plunder, an attack by robbers the collection of plunderers

ਡਾਢਾ ḍāḍhā s. m. strong firm, powerful.

ਡਾਰ ḍār, s f. the line of birds in flight; i. e. a flock.

ਡਿਗਣਾ ḍignā, v. a. To fall, to drop, to lie on the back in wrestling.

ਡੁਬਣਾ ḍubbnā v. a. to dive, to be dipped, to be immersed, to sink, to set, (the sun;) to be absorbed (in business;) to be ruined.

ਡੂਢ ḍūḍh, s. m. one and-a-half.

ਢ

ਢਗਾ ḍhaggā s. m. a small sized ox.

ਢਠ ਜਾਣਾ ḍhaṭh jānā. v. a. To fall down.

ਢਠਾ ḍhaṭṭhā, fallen.

ਢਾਡੀ ḍhāḍī, s. m a kind of good musician, a singer.

ਢਾਬ ḍhāb, s. f. an unwalled tank or pond, a natural pool, a lake, a deep depression in the earth.

ਢਾਲ ḍhāl, s. f. a shield, protection.

ਢਿਲ ḍhill, s. f. lateness, delay laziness, in attention, looseness, remissness.

ਢਿਲਾ ḍhillā, s. m loose, not tight, lazy, remiss, inattentive, late.

ਢੀਂਗਲੀ ḍhiṅgalī, a well bucket attached to pole.

ਢੇਰ ḍher, s. m. a heap, a pile, a quantity abundance, gratuity.

ਢੇਰੀ ਹੋਣਾ ḍherī honā, v. a. to fall down.

ਢੈ ਜਾਣਾ ḍhaij ānā. } v. a. to fall down.
ਢੈਣਾ ḍhainā, }

ਤ

ਤਕਣਾ takknā, v. a. to see, to look, to gaze, to expect to guess.

ਤਕਮਾਂ takmā. s. m. medal.

ਤਕੜਾਈ ਰਖਣਾ takrāi rakhnā. v. a. to take care to look after.

ਤਕਾਲਾਂ takālān, s. f. Evening.

ਤਕੀਦ takīd s. f. urgency, importunity Enjoining, to urge to enjoin.

ਤਕੁਲਾ takkulā. s. m. a spindle; the shaft of a wheel.

ਤਗੀਦ tagīd s. f. urgency. importunity enjoying ਤਗੀਦ ਕਰਨੀ to urge, to enjoin.

ਤਨ tan, s. m. The body.

ਤਬੇਲਾ tabelā, s. m. stable.

ਤਰਸ tars. s. m. pity, alarm, fear, terror.

ਤਰਸਣਾ tarasnā, v. a. to desire a thing anxiously, to long for, to thirst.

ਤਰਖਾਨ tarkhān, s. m. a carpenter.

ਤਰਨਾ tarnā, v. a. to swim to float.

ਤ੍ਰਾਹ ਤ੍ਰਾਹ tarāh tarāh int, mercy! mercy!

ਤ੍ਰਾਹ ਤ੍ਰਾਹ ਕਰਣਾ trāh trāh karnā, to call for mercy, to invoke protection.

ਤਰੀਕ tarik, s. f. Date.

ਤਲਬ talāb, s. f. pay salary wages.

ਤਲਾਹ talāh, s f. Information.

ਤਲਾਕ talāk, s. f. Divorce separation abstinence, prohibition.

ਤਲੌਂਚਾ *tulaunychā*, *s. m.* A coarse kind of sugar saturaled with molasses.

ਤੜਕੇ *tarṛke ad*, early in the morning

ਤਾਈ *tāī*, *s. f* Aunt, the wife of a father's elder brother.

ਤਾਂਈ *tāīn*, *s. f.* prep, to even to.

ਤਾਰਾ *tārā*, *s m.* A star.

ਤਾਰਨਾ *tārnā*, *v. a.* to pay up.

ਤਿਤਰ *tittar*, *s m.* a partridge.

ਤੁਸਾ *tusā* }
ਤੁਸਾਂ *tusāṇ* } *pron. obl. pl.* of ਤੂੰ you.

ਤੁਹਾਡੀ *tohādī*, yours.

ਤੁਰਤ ਫੁਰਤ *turt phurt ad.* immediately instantly, quickly.

ਤੁਰਨਾ *turnā*, *v. a.* to go, to despart to walk

ਤੁਰਪ cruption of the English word troops.

ਤੁਰ ਤੁਰਾ *tur turā* s. m nimble, active flippant.

ਤੂੜੀ *tūṛī*, *s. f.* The chaff of wheet.

ਤੇਜ *tej*, a sharp, hot, fiery, imputuous rapid, active.

ਤੇਜੀ *tejī*, *s. f.* sharpness, keenness, activity, rapidity, impetuousity dearness.

ਤੇਰਾਂ *terāṅ*, a thirteen.

ਤੋਟ *tot*, *s. f.* Difficiency.

ਤੋਪ *top*, *s.* a cannon, a gun.

ਤੋਬਰਾ *tabrā*, *s. m* A leather bag out of which a horse eats his grain.

ਤੋੜਨਾ *toṛnā*, *v. a.* to break to change, to pluck, (fruit.)

ਤੋੜਾ *toṛā*, *s. m.* The match of a gun, a bag one thousand rupeeps ; gold or silver card wound round the head as an ornamant ; a kind of helmet ; deficiency, scarcity want a peace of rope, a beam.

ਤੋੜੀ *toṛī*, *ad.* till, to, up.

ਥ

ਥਨ *than*, *s. m.* Teat.

ਥਾਨੇਦਾਰ *thānedār*, *s. m.* Deputy Inspector of Police.

ਥੀਣਾ *thīnā*, *v a.* to be.

ਥੋੜਾ *thoṛā*, a short, a little.

ਦ

ਦਸ *das*, Ten.

ਦਸਖਤ *daskhat*, sign, or signature.

ਦਹਨਾ *dahnā*, Right, before, above.

ਦਖਣ *dakkhan*, *s. m.* The south, the southern part of India.

ਦਥਾ *datthā* *s. m.* a bundle of grass or hemp a bundle of sugar cane (what is passed at once through the mill ; a pile of paper ; c. w. ਦੇਣਾ and ਲੈਣਾ

ਦਫਤਰ *daftar*, *s. m.* A book volume, a journal a record, a register, an office.

ਦਰਬਾਰ *darbār*, *s, m* A Court a hall, of audience, the holding of a Court the common appelation of the great Sikh. Temple at Amriatsr.

ਦਾਸ *dās*, *s. m.* A servant, aslave.

ਦਾਸਨ ਦਾਸ *dāsandās*, *s. m.* servant's servant.

ਦਾਗ *dāg*, *s m.* A spot a stain, a mark

c. w. ਲਗਣਾ a scar a mark made by burning with a hot iron cautery

ਦਾਗ ਦੇਣਾ to cauterize, to brand ;

ਦਾਗ ਲਾਉਣਾ to stain, to villofy.

ਦਾਣਾ *dānā*, *s. m.* a grain of corn

ਦਾਦੀ *dādi*, *s. f.* The wife of a *dādā*, *q. v.*

ਦਾਦੀ *dādi*, *s. f.* A paternal grand mother

ਦਿਸਣਾ *disnā*, *v. a.* To be seen, to be visible.

ਦਿਹਾੜਾ *dihāṛā*, *s. m* A day.

ਦਿਹਾੜੀ *dihāṛi*, *s. f.* A day, daily labor, wages.

ਦਿਖਾਈ *dikhāi*, *s. f.* showing, show appearance, display.

ਦਿਖਾਉਣਾ *dikhāunā*, *v. a.* to show, to point out, to exhibit.

ਦਿਨ ਡੁਬੇ *din dube*, at sunest.

ਦੀਦਾਰ *didār*, looking.

ਦੁਧ *duddh*, *s. m.* milk, the milky juice of certain plants.

ਦੁਪਹਿਰ *dopahir*, *s. f.* The termination of the second watch, noon ;

ਰਾਤਦੀ ਦੁਪਹਿਰ *rāt di dopahir*, midnight.

ਦੂਹਵਦੂਹ *dūhwadūh*, with one another

ਦੂਜਾ *dūjā*, second, othe another.

ਦੂਣੀ *dūni* *s. f.* a vally, the number two ; reduplication.

ਦੇਸ *des*, *s m* A country, (in the hills,) the plains in opposition to the mountains.

ਦੇਸੀ *desi*, *s f.* A country person, a citizen.

ਦੋ *do*, a two.

ਧ

ਧਮਕੀ *dhamki*, *s. f.* Threat, menace.

ਧਮੋੜੀ *dhamoṛi*, a yellow wasp.

ਧਰਮਸਾਲਾ *dharmsālā*, *s. f.* A College of *udāsi faqirs*, an alms house an inn where poor travellers are supplied gr tuitiously.

ਧਰੋਹ *dharoh*, *s. m* Fraud, deceit, dishonestly.

ਧਾਰਾ *dhārā*, *s. m.* A stream, a current.

ਧਾਵਾ *dhāwā*, *s. m.* invasion, attack assault

ਧਿਰ *dhir*, *s. f.* partiality, protection, defence, help party.

ਧੀ *dhi*, *s f.* A daughter.

ਧੇਲਾ *dhelā*, *s. f.* half pice.

ਧੁੰਦ *dhund*, *s. f.* a mist, a fog haziness, obscurity, fine dust, a disorder of the eyes.

ਧੁਪ *dhupp*, *s* f. sunshine.

ਧੁਪੇ ਰਖਣਾ or ਲਿਆਉਣਾ *dhuppe rakhnā jā liāunā*, *v. a.* To put inthe sun.

ਧੂਆਂ *dhūān*, *s. m.* smoke an ignited pile of chaff and rubbish around which people worm themselves in cold weather ; sitting obstinately before one's door to extort a favor or right.

ਧੂਆਂ ਪਾਉਣਾ *dnūān paunā*, *v. a.* to light a fiire.

ਧੂਆਂ ਲਾਉਣਾ To sit by a fire at one's door to extort a favor.

ਧੂਈਂ *dhūīn*, s. *f.* a small pile of burning wood, chaff &c. asound which muslmans sit while they listen to the praises of Pir Said Ahmad.

ਧੋਖਾ *dhokhā*, s. *m.* fraud, cheat deciet.

ਧੋਤੀ *dhotī* s *f* A cloth worn round the loins by Hindus

ਧੌਂਸਾ *dhaunsā*, s. *m.* a large cattle drum.

ਨ

ਨਸਣਾ *nassnā*, *v. a.* to flee. to run.

ਨਸਾਨਾ *nasānā*, s *m* A t rget a mark, a butt.

ਨਹਾਉਣਾ *nahāūnā* *v a.* to bathe to wash

ਨਹਿਰ *nahir*, s. *f.* A canal a stream.

ਨਹੀ ਤਾਂ *nāhīntān*, otherwise.

ਨਕ *nakk*, s. *m* The nose

ਨਕਲ *nakal*, s. *f.* A copy.

ਨਕਲ ਉਠਾਉਣੀ or ਕਰਨੀ *v a* to copy, to imitate.

ਨਗਰ *nagar*, s. *m* A city, a town.

ਨੰਗਾ *nanggā*, a naked.

ਨਥ *natth*, s *f* A nose ring; a rope in the nose of an ox.

ਨਦੀ *nadī*, s. *f.* A small stream, a creek a brook.

ਨਧੜਕ *nadharak*, a without fear.

ਨਧਾਨ *nadhān*, s. *m* The subject in which any quality in heres.

ਨਬੇ *nabbe*, a ninety 90.

ਨਾਰਾਇਣ *nārāin*. s. *m.* A name of Wishnu. but specially considered as the deity who was before all worlds.

ਨਾਲ *nāl* *prep* With, by.

ਨਾਲੇ *nāle*. *conj*. Both, and, also moreover.

ਨਿਆਈਂ *niāin* s *f* A place near a house a village filled with ordure and all sorts of filth; cultivation near a house or village.

ਨਿਰਮਲ *nirmal*, a clean pure, clear, transparent

ਨਿਰਾ *nirā*, *adv.* Only mearely.

ਨੀਰਾ *nīrā*, s. *m.* Fodder, a stake.

ਨੁਕਤਾ *nuktā*. s. *m.* A halter; a point a dot; a mystical signification Head collar.

ਨੁਖਸਾਨ *nukhsān* s. *m.* loss deficiency detriment, injury, damage, blemish, mischief.

ਨੂੰ *nūn*, *prep.* a son's wife (sign of dative and accusative.)

ਨੇਤਕੀ *netkī*, s. *m.* a daily fever.

ਨੇੜੇ *nere*. *prep*, near.

ਨੌਕਰੀ *naukarī*, s. *f.* a service attendance

ਨੌ ਬਰ ਨੌ *nau bar nau*, quite well.

ਨੰਬਰਦਾਰ *nambardār*, s. *m.* headman of the village.

ਪ

ਪੱਸਲੀ *passalī*, s. *f.* a rib the region of the ribs the side.

ਪਸਿੰਦ ਕਰਨਾ *pasind karnā*, *v. a.* to like.

ਪਸਾਰਨਾ *pasarnā*. *v. a.* To extend to stretch forth.

ਪਸ਼ੂ *pasū*, *s. m.* An irrational animal, a brute, a quadruped.

ਪਹਾੜ *pahāṛ*, *s. m.* A mountain.

ਪਹਿਨਣਾ *pahinnā*, *v. a.* to put on (cloths)

ਪਹਿਲਾਂ *pahilāṇ*, *adv.* First.

ਪਹੁੰਚਣਾ *pahunchnā*, *v a.* to arrive.

ਪਕਣਾ *paknā*, *v. a.* to ripen, to be cooked

ਪੰਘੂੜਾ *pangghūṛā*, *s. m.* a child's bed stead ; a board with one ends notched placed in a rope, swing for sitting or standing on.

ਪੰਛੀ *panchhī*, *s m.* a bird.

ਪੰਜਗਰੰਥੀ *panjgaranthī*, a name of a book of Sikh religion.

ਪਟੀ *pattī s. f.* A kind of coarse woollen cloth. a bandage, the side piece of a bedstead ; a wooden slate, a quarter or section of a place, raw or chusler of houses ; a breadth of cloth ; a portion of woman's hair when palated and combed towards each side ; a mass of molasses candy worked by confectionors of on a peg driven into a post ; the cricket bat ; a kind of coarse tape; a copper plate on which astromical calculation are engraved.

ਪੱਠਾ ਦਥਾ *pathā dathā*, *s. m* fodder.

ਪਠਾਣ *paṭhān*, *s. m.* A caste of musalmans being one of the four pri ncipal divisions ; (the same as, Afghan.)

ਪੰਡ *pand*, *s m.* a bundle.

ਪਤਨ *pattan*, *s. m.* A landing place, a quay, a ford, a pass, a bathing place on a river side, a place where the shore is smooth and hard, and the water fordable, any place where a river is crossed.

ਪਤ੍ਰ *pattar*, *s. m* a leaf.

ਪਤ੍ਰੀ *pattrī*, *s. f.* an almanac.

ਪਤਾ *patā*, *s. m.* a mark, a sign, a token a hint, address or place to which one is directed.

ਪਤੀ *patī*, *s. m.* A Lord, a master, a husband, an owner.

ਪਥਰ *patthar*, *s. m.* a stone.

ਪੰਦਰਾਂ *pandrān*, *a.* fifteen.

ਪਰਸਾਦ *parsād*, *s m.* food.

ਪਰਘਟ *parghaṭ* a apparent, manifest, *i. q*, ਪਰਗਟ *pargat.*

ਪਰਮੇਸੁਰ *paramesur*, *s. m.* God ; (appropriated by some to Shiv, but commonly used by the Sikhs to denote the Supreme being ;) (properly ਪਰਮਈਸ਼ਵਰ) *param iashwar.*

ਪਰਲੋ *parlo*, *s. f.* universal destruction, the consummation of all things the final conflagration, (properly speaking the parlo is the destruction of the world by water and fire ; and several such events are supposed to have occurred already between the different days of Brahma, and several more are yet expected the last which is to destroy the universe is called *mahā parlo*, (the great destruction ;) vexation oppression affliction, great calamity.

ਪਰਲੋਕ *parlok*, *s. m.* the next world including both heaven and hell, the future state.

ਪਰਵਾਰ *parwār*, *s. m.* A family embracing, progenitors, descendants, and dependents ; a halo round the moon.

ਪਰੂੰ *parūṇ*, *s. m.* last year, next year.

ਪਰੋਹਤ *parohat*, *s. m.* A family priest.

ਪਲਟਣ *palṭan*, *s. f.* A foot regiment.

ਪੜਤਲ *paṛtal*, *s. f.* Regiment.

ਪੜਾ *paṛā*, *s. m.* camp, rest camp.

ਪੜਾ *paṛā*, *s. m.* The upper part of *razāī*.

ਪੜਾਣਾ *paṛāṇā*, *s. m.* a place for bullocks for drawing water from a well.

ਪਾਸੋਂ *pāssoṅ*, *prep.* from, by, by means of.

ਪਾਟ *pāt*, *s. m.* breadth of a river.

ਪਾਟ *pāṭṭ*, *s. m.* Division branch.

ਪਾਟਣਾਂ *pāttanā*, *v. a.* to burst, to break to be torn.

ਪਾਰ *pār*, *ad.* on the other side (of a river &c.)

ਪਾਰ ਹੋਣਾ *pār honā*, *v. a.* to cross.

ਪਾਲਾ *pālā*, *s. m.* cold.

ਪਾੜਨਾ *pāṛnā*, *v. a.* to tear.

ਪਾੜ *pār*, a wooden in which water falls from the Persian wheel.

ਪਿਆਰ *piār*, *s. m.* love, affection.

ਪਿਛਲਾ *pichhlā*, later, last.

ਪਿਛੇ *pichchhe*, *ad. prep.* after, behind, in lieu of, on account of ; ਪਿਛੇ ਪੈਣਾ *pichhe painā*, to dance, to persecute.

ਪਿਛੋਂ *pichchhon*, after, behind, afterwards.

ਪਿਛੋਂ ਦੀ *pichkchhon dī*, from behind,

ਪਿਛੇ ਜਾਣਾ *pichchhe jānā*, *v. a.* to pursue.

ਪਿਟਣਾਂ *piṭṭnā*, *v. a.* To beat, (the face breast &c. ;) to mourn for the dead.

ਪਿੰਡ *pind*, *s m.* a village ; balls of rice &c., used by Hindus at the sradh of deceased relatives.

ਪਿਤਾ *pitā*, *s, m.* Father.

ਪਿਨਸਲ *pinsal*, *s. f.* pencil.

ਪਿਨਸਲ ਘੜਨਾ *pinsal gharnā*, *v. a.* to sharpen pencil.

ਪਿਨਸਨ *pinsan*, *s. f.* Pension.

ਪਿੜ *piṛ*, *s. m.* threshing floor.

ਪੀਲਾ *pīlā*, yellow.

ਪੁਸਤਕ *pustak*, *s. m.* A book.

ਪੁਠਾ *puṭhā*, *s. m.* the hip

ਪੁਤ੍ਰ *puttar*, *s m.* A son.

ਪੁਰਸ *puras*, *s. m.* A man.

ਪੁਰਖ *purakh*, *s. m.* A man, a male, human being.

ਪੁਰਜਾ *purjā*, *s. m.* a small piece of paper

ਪੁਰਾਣਾ *purāṇā*, *a.* old.

ਪੁਲ *pul*, *s. m* a bridge,

ਪੂਰਾ *pūrā*, *a.* full, complete, sufficient entire.

ਪੂਲਾ *pūlā*, *s. m.* small load of grass.

ਪੈਸਾ *paisā* *s. m.* a pice (the name of a copper coin,) money.

ਪੈਣਾ *paiṇā*, *v. a.* to fall, to lie, to lie down, to be situated, to go to bed, to be sick, to happen.

ਪੈਂਤੀ *paintī*, *a.* thirty-five.

ਪੈਲੀ *pailī*, *s. f.* field.

ਪੋਹ *poh*, *s. m.* The name of a month *viz.* from the middle of December to the middle of January.

ਪੋਨਾ *ponā*, *s. m.* a species of thick sugar cane.

ਫ

ਫਸਲ *fasal*, *s. f.* harvest.

ਫਕਾ *phakkā*, *s. m.* The quantity of grain, &c., thrown into the mouth at once the grain given periodically by farmers to the village carpenter, blacksmith, barber, &c.

ਫਕੀਰ *phakīr* or *fakīr*, *s. m.* a fakir (properly ਫਕੀਰ ਦੋਸਤ *fakīr dost*, a friend of fakir.

ਫਗਣ *phaggan*, *s. m.* The name of a month from the middle of February to the middle of March.

ਫਟਕ *phatak*, *s. m.* crystal.

ਫਤੇ *phate*, *s. f.* VictoriaL. L. ਹੋਣਾ *honā*, and ਕਰਨਾ ਬੁਲਾਉਣਾ *karnā bulāonā*, to give compliment.

ਫਲਹਾ *phalhā*, *s. m.* a wooden frame.

ਫਾਂਸੀ *phānsī*, *s. f.* A noose, a snare, a halter for hanging.

ਫਾਂਸੀ ਦੇਨਾ *phānsī denā*, *v. a.* to hang.

ਫਾਲੜੀ *phālṛī*, *s. f.* a diaper, a clout.

ਫਾਲਤੂ *fāltū* more.

ਫਿਸਲਨਾ *phisalnā*, *v. v* to slip, to slide; to fail of an agreement, to fly from a bargain.

ਫੀਤਾ *phītā*, *s. m.* tape.

ਫੁਟਣਾ *phuṭnā*, *v. a.* to burst, to break, to boil, to ooze out.

ਫੌਜ *fauj*, *s. f* an army.

ਬ

ਬਸਾਖ *basākh*, *s. m.* The name of the 2nd month in the civil year, beginning about the middle of April.

ਬਹਾਦਰ *bahādur*, *s. m.* a hero, a champion, a knight.

ਬਹਾਦਰੀ *bahādurī*, *s. f.* bravery, valor heroism.

ਬਹਿਜਾਣਾ *bahijānā*, *v a.* to float away, to be ready to sink.

ਬਕਰਾ *bakrā*, *s. m.* A he goat, (in composition pronounced *bakrā*; as ਬਕਰਾ ਈਦ

ਬਕਰੀ *bakkarī*, *s. f.* A she goat.

ਬਖਸ਼ਣਾ *bakhshnā*, *v. a.* to give to bestow, to for give.

ਬਖਸ਼ਾਉਣਾ *bakhshāunā*, *v. a.* to procure forgiveness for, (one ;) to procure the bestowal of (any thing.)

ਬਗੀਚਾ *bagīchā*, *s. m.* a small garden.

ਬਘਿਆੜ *baghiāṛ*, *s. m.* a wolf.

ਬਚਣਾ *bachanā*, *v. a* to be preserved, to be delivered, to be saved, to escape. to remain unexpended.

ਬਚਾਉਣਾ *bachāunā*, *v. a.* to save, to protect.

ਬਟੇਰਾ *baterā*, *s. m.* a small bird of the, partridge, species quils.

ਬਣਨਾ *bannā*, *v. a.* to be made.

ਬਤਕ *battak*, *s. j.* A duck, a goose.

ਬਥੇਰਾ *bather̄a*, *a.* much, many.

ਬੰਦ *band*, *s. m.* a joint, a knuckle.

ਬੰਦੂਕ *bandūk*, *s. f.* A musket, rifle, fowling piece &c.

ਬੰਦੋਬਸਤ *bandobast*, *s. m.* arrangement

ਬਧਨਾ *badhnā*, *s. m.* an earthen, water vessel with a spout like a teapot respect.

ਬਨਾ *bannā*, *s. m.* boundary.

ਬੰਬ *bamb*, *s. m.* a shaft.

ਬਮਾਰੀ *bamārī*, *s. f.* sickness, pestilence.

ਬਵਾ *bawā* or ਬਮਾਂ *bamāṅ*, *s. f.* Pestilence plague.

ਬਰਸ *baras*, *s. m.* a year.

ਬਰਸਾਤ *barsāt*, *s. f.* rain, the rainy season.

ਬਰਸਾਤੀ *barsātī*, *s. f.* belonging to the rainy season.

ਬਰਖਾ *barkhā*, *s. f.* Rain.

ਬਰਖਾ ਰੁਤ *barkhā rut*, *s. f.* the rainy season.

ਬਰਖੁਰਦਾਰ *barkhhurdār*, *s m.* Happy enjoying, long life, male children are so called.

ਬਰੰਟ *barant*, *s. m.* Warrant.

ਬਰਤਾਂਤ *bartānt*, *s. m.* circnmstance.

ਬਰਫ *barf*, *s. f.* snow.

ਬਰਬਰੀ *barabbarī*, *s. f.* equality, even ness.

ਬਰਬਾਦ ਕਰਨਾ *barbād karnā*, *v. v.* to destroy.

ਬਰਾਂਡੀ *brāndī*, *s. f.* great coat.

ਬਰਾਂਡਾ *brāndā*, *s. m.* outer room.

ਬਰਾਨੀ *barānī*, *s. f.* land depending on rain

ਬਰੂਦ *barūd*, *s. m.* ammunition.

ਬਲਦ *bald*, *s. m.* a bull, an ox.

ਬਲਵਾਨ *balwān*, *s. m.* a strong.

ਬਲੇਵਾ *balewā*, *s. m.* goods and chattles furniture baggage.

ਬਾਹਣ *bāhan*, *s. m.* a ploughed field.

ਬਾਹਲਾ *bāhalā*, *a* much, very much, many.

ਬਾਜਰਾਂ *bājrā*, *s. m.* a kind of grain resembling broom corn, the bread ot which is very coarse.

ਬਾਲਣਾ *bālnā*, *v. a.* to cause to burn, to, kindle, ਅੱਗ ਬਾਲਣੀ *agg bālnī* to kinde a fire.

ਦੀਵਾ ਬਾਲਣਾ *dīwā bālnā*, to light a lamp.

ਬਿਆਈ *biāī*, *s. f.* cracking of the heels from cold *&c.* sowing seed sowing time ; grain given by zamindars to carpenters and others at sowing time.

ਬਿਆਹਣਾ *biāhnā*, *v. a.* to marry (a wife) to get a son or daughter &c.) married ; *i. q.* ਵਿਆਹਣਾ

ਬਿਸਤਰਾ *bistarā*, *s. m.* bed, bedding.

ਬਿਜਲੀ *bijlī*, *s f.* Lightning.

ਬਿਨਾਂ *binā*, *prep.* Without.

ਬਿਰਛ *birchh*, *s. m.* a tree.

ਬਿਲ ਕੁਲ *bilkul*, at all.

ਬੀ *bī*, *s. m.* seed, a cutting of a plant, (as sugar cane,) for seed.

ਬੀ ਪਾਉਣਾ *bī pāonā*, *v. a.* to sow a seed.

ਬੀਜਨਾਂ bījnā, v. a. to sow. to plant.

ਬੀਤਨਾ bītnā, v. a. to elapse, to die

ਬੁਛਾੜ buchhāṛ, shower, to efface.

ਬੁਝਾਉਨਾ bujhāunā, v. a. to cause to understand, to extinguish.

ਬੁਢਾ buḍḍhā, s. m. old man.

ਬੁਢਾਪਾ budhāpā, s. m. old age.

ਬੁਢੀ buḍḍhī, s. f. an old woman a term applied to any woman, when addressing her, in a respectful way sometimes used instad of mother as ਹੇ ਬੁਢੀਏ he buddhie, O mother

ਬੂੰਦ bund, s. f. A drop, (of water &c.)

ਬੁਰਛਾ burchhā, s. m. Perverse, impolite, rude, unpolished, stupid.

ਬੁਲ ਬੁਲਾ bulbulā, s. m. a bubble.

ਬੂਹਾ būhā, s. m. a door, a window, a house.

ਬੇਉਰ beur, s. m. A woman's veil, and bodice.

ਬਗਾੜ bagāṛ, s. m. loss.

ਬੈਲ bail, s. m. a bull, an ox, a blockhead.

ਬੇੜ beṛ, s. m. a coarse rope, made of grass, straw, &c.

ਬੈੜ baiṛ, s. m. the wheel on which the well posts are strung.

ਬੈੜਕਾ baiṛkā, s. m. a young bull.

ਬੌਲਦ bauld, s. m. ox or bullock.

ਬੰਦੋਬਸਤ bandobast, s. m. settlement.

ਭ

ਭਸਨਾ ਭੂਸ bhasnā bhūs, 'entirely consumed.

ਭੰਗ bhang, s. f. Hemp confusion of hemp pride, self importance.

ਭੰਗੀ bhangyī, s. m. A drinker of bhang a man of the chuhra, caste, a mihtar.

ਭਜਨਾ bhajjnā, v. a. to be broken, to flee, to escape; (also ਭਜ ਜਾਣਾ

ਭਤਾ bhattā, s. m. Food taken to farmers and their workmen in the field allowance.

ਭਨਣਾਂ bhannā v. a. to break.

ਭਯਾਨਕ bhayānak, s. m. dreadful, terrible formidable, tremendous.

ਭਰੀ bharī, s. f. a load of grass.

ਭਰਤੀ bharti, a. enlisted.

ਭਰਨਾ bharnā, v. a. To be filled. to be-defiled (with mud, blood &c.)

ਭਲਮਣਸਊ bhalmansaū, s. m. goodness, worthiness, integrity a good act, an honorable peice of conduct.

ਭਾਈ bhāī, s. m a brother of friend, a man famous for learning and piety; a sect of Hindu faqirs, man of that sect

ਭਾਈਆ bhāīā, s. m. a father.

ਭਾਜੜ bhājaṛ, s. f. flight, rout, fleeing of the in habitants when war is at, hand; property carried away in flight.

ਭਾਣਾ bhānā, s. m. Desire, wish will view estimation; especially the will of God, fate, destiny.

ਭਾਦੋਂ bhāddon, s. m. The six month in the Hindu, year, being from the middle of August to the middle of September.

ਭਾਵੇਂ *bhāwen con*, thou mayest please, a although.

ਭੁਖ *bhukkh*, s. f. hunger, appetite, eagerness.

ਭੁਨਣਾ *bhunnā*, v. a. To parch, to roast to bake in ashes

ਭੁਲ *bhull*, s f. an error, a mistake, a fault, an amission.

ਭੂਰਾ *bhūrā*, s. m. a striped blanket, *viz.*, light brown with black stripes.

ਭੇਡ *bhed*, s. f. a sheep; the bud of the palah tree.

ਭੇਤ *bhet*, s m. a secret, a mistery, difference.

ਭੈ *bhai*, s. m. Fear, dread, alarm, terror.

ਭੈੜਾ *bhaiṛā*, s. m. Evil, bad, worthless wretched, wicked.

ਭੌਣਾਂ *bhaunā*, v. a. To turn around, to be dizzy, (the head;) to skim and circle in the air, (a kite or other bird to wander about.

ਮ

ਮਸਤ *mast*, s. m. Intoxicated, drunk; intoxicated with pride, proud, arrogant; lustful, heated with animal desire; full spirits, and energy, under a fanatical influence.

ਮਸੀਂ *masīn*, *ad.* hardly, with much difficulty; (commonly ਮਸੀ ਮਸੀ)

ਮਸੀਨ *masīn*, s. f. Gun.

ਮਹਾਂਮਾਰੀ *mahāṇ mārī*, s. f. A pestilence a plague.

ਮਹਾਂਰਾਜ *mahāṇ rāj*, s. m. A title of God a title given to kings, a term of respect applied to anyone.

ਮਹਿੰਗਾ *mahingā*, a. Dear, scarce, expensive, high priced.

ਮਹਿਰਾਬ *mihrāb*, s. m. an arch.

ਮਹੀਨਾਂ *mahīnā*, s. m. A month.

ਮਕਈ *makaī*, s. f. Indian corn, maize.

ਮੰਗਣਾ *mangnā*, v. a. To ask for, to demand, to beg, pray, to solicit to crave, to want, to desire, to want, to crave, to seek, betroth.

ਮਗਰੋਂ *magroṇ*, *ad.* From, afterwards afterwards.

ਮੰਗਲਵਾਰ *mangalwār*, s m. Tuesday.

ਮਘਰ *magghar*, s. m. the name of a month from the middle of November to the middle of December.

ਮਝੀ *majjhī*, s. f. A female buffalo.

ਮਠ *maṭhh*, s. f. Laziness.

ਮਠਾ *maṭṭhā*, s. m. Slow, Lazy (an ox, horse &c.)

ਮੰਡੀ *maṇḍī*, s. f. A market, a particular market for any one thing; the name of a city.

ਮਣ *man*, s, m. A weight equal to forty seers, a maunds, (kachcha man likewise contains forty seers kachcha, a seer kachcha being about thirty two tolas;)ਮਣਕੁ about a man.

ਮਣ *maṇ*, s. f. The pakka work at the top of a well; a kind of gem supposed to be found in the head of a snake.

ਮਤਲਬ *matlab, s. m.* meaning design' purpose object.

ਮਥਾ *matthā, s. m.* the forehead.

ਮਦਦ *madad, s. f.* help.

ਮਦਾਨ *madān, s. m.* A plain, an open field.

ਮਨ *man, s. m.* The mind, the heart. the soul; ਮਨ ਮਾਰਨਾਂ *man mārnā.* to deny one's self, to forbear, to subdue the desires.

ਮੰਨ *mann, s m* A thick cake of bread.

ਮੰਨਨਾ *mannā, v. a.* To mind, to obey, to observe. to acquiese in. to consent, to, to agree to, to believe, to suppose, a (cause ;) to vow, to pledge, one's self to, to agree to discharge, (another's debt.)

ਮਰਜੀ *marjī, s. f.* Will pleasure, purpose intention.

ਮਲਕੀਅਤ *malkiat, s f.* possession.

ਮਲਮ *mallham, s. f.* Ointment, material for plaster for a sore.

ਮਲੂਮਹੋਣਾਂ *malūm honā, v. a.* to look.

ਮਲੂਮ *malūm*, knowing.

ਮਲੂਕਣੀ *malūknī. s. f.* A beautiful woman, a belle.

ਮਲੋਮਲੀ *malomalī, s. f.* forcibly.

ਮਾਸ, *mās, s. m.* Flesh, a month.

ਮਾਂਹ *mānh, s. m.* a kind of dall *i. q.*, urd; a month.

ਮਾਘ *māgh, s. m* the name of month; (from the middle of January to the middle of february.)

ਮਾਂਢੀ *māndhī, s. f.* small, below, medium size, a dwarf.

ਮਾਂਦਾ *māndā, s. m.* sick, ill, tired, weary fatigued.

ਮਾਫ਼ੀ *māfī s. f.* Pardon, forgiveness, remission.

ਮਾਮਲਾ *māmlā, s. m.* an affair, negociation, a money transation, revenue.

ਮਾਮਾ *māmmā, s. m.* A mother's brother.

ਮਾਰਨਾ *mārnā. v a.* to strike, to beat, to kill.

ਮਾਲਸ਼ ਕਰਨਾ *mālish karnā, v. a.* to groom.

ਮਾਲ੍ਹ *mālh* the frame workof rope to which the earthen pots of Persian wheel attached

ਮਾੜਾ *mārā, s. m.* Lean, thin, emaciated enfeebled, weak; bad, worthless, scarce, ਮਾੜਾ ਸਮਾਂ *mārā sāmā* famine.

ਮਿਠਾ *mitthā*, a sweet; deficient, (salt;) scarce, dear time; as ਇਹ ਮਿਠਾ ਸਮਾਂ ਹੈ *ih mithā samā hai*, this is a time of scarcity.

ਮਿਤ੍ਰ *mittar, s. m.* A friend, a companion one beloved.

ਮਿਰਗ *mirg, s. m.* A deer, a wild animal.

ਮਿਲਨਾ *milnā, v a.* to meet, to associate,

ਮੀਂਹ ਪੈਣਾਂ *mīhn painā*, to rain.

ਮੀਂਹ *mīnh, s m.* Rain, a shower.

ਮੁਸਟੰਡਾ *mustandā, s. m.* stout and strong, but wanting in sense.

ਮਸੀਂ *masīn, adj.* hardly.

ਮੁਹਿਮ *muhimm, s. f.* a military expedition, any difficult or arduous undertaking.

ਮੁਕਦਮਾਂ *mukadmā, s. m.* Case.

ਮੁੰਡਾ *mundā, s. m.* A boy, a lad.

ਮੁਨਾਂ *munnā, s. m.* A post for supporting a spinning wheel, a similar post in a cotton gin, aplow handle,

ਮੁਰਗਾਬੀ *murgābī, s. f.* A waterfowl, a duck.

ਮੁਰੰਡੇ *murande, s. m. pl.* Wheat and gur mixed together.

ਮੁਰਦਾ *murdā, s. m.* dead.

ਮੁਲਲੈਣਾ *mull laiṅā, v. a.* to buy.

ਮੁਲ *mull, s. m.* Price, value, worth consideration.

ਮੁਲਕ *mulak, s. m.* Country, a region.

ਮੁੜਨਾ *muṛnā, v. a* To turn, to turn back to bring back, to return, to incline to make a repitition.

ਮੂਸਲ *mūsul, s. m.* stock of chaff.

ਮੂੰਹ *mūnh, s. m.* The mouth, the face; an aperture, an opening.

ਮੂਲੋਂ *mūlon, ad.* (lit from the root,) altogether, entirety, certainly, decidely; (used mostly in negative propositions.

ਮੇਹੜ *mehaṛ, s. m.* the oxen of threshing floor.

ਮੈਂਘਾ *maingghā a* Dear, costly, high priced, scarce.

ਮੈਂਘਾਈ *mainggkāī, s. f* dearness.

ਮੈਂਦੀ *maindī, s f.* cinnamon.

ਮੋਹੁਰ *mohur, s f.* a seal, a gold mohar; the front, the lead, the van, (of an army.)

ਮੋਹੁਰਲਾਉਣਾ *mohur lāonā, v a.* to seal

ਮੋਘਾ *moghā, s. m.* a wall roof or vessel.

ਮੋਰਚਾ *morchā, s. m.* Rust, an embrasure in the wall of a fort; a ditch, and embankment a trench.

ਯ

ਯਤਨ *yatan, s. m.* plan.

ਰ

ਰਸਾਲਾ *rasālā, s m.* A Cavalry, compa[illegible] consisting usually, of one hun[illegible] red man.

ਰਕਮ *raqam, s. m.* Money.

ਰਖਣਾ *rakhnā, v. ā.* to keep to put, to place to set, to lay down, to station, to have, to hold, to possess, to reserve, to save, to apply to ascribe to impute. to take into employ; to recieve, to accep[illegible] (also ਰਖਛਡਣਾ *rakhchhadnā* ਰਖਦੇਣਾ *rakhdenā* ਰੱਖਲੈਣਾ *rakhlainā* &c.)

ਰਖਵਯਾ *rakhwayyā, s. m.* One who keeps preserves. or takes care of; an employre.

ਰਜਾ *rajā, s. f.* The will of God, the Divine pleasure, fate, destiny, ਰਜਾ ਹੋਣਾ *rajāhonā* or ਹੋਜਾਣਾ *hojānā*, to die, furlough.

ਰਨ *rann, s. f.* A woman, a wife.

ਰਬ *rabb, s. m.* The Lord, God.

ਰਬੜ *rabaṛ, s. f.* going and coming in vain, failing of the object of a journe returning empty.

ਰਬੜ *rabaṛ, s. m.* India rubber.

ਰਲਨਾ *ralanā, v. a.* To meet, to be joined, agree to conspire, to be mixed.

ਰਲਾਉਣਾ *ralāonā, v a.* to mingle, to to join, to unite, to cause, agree.

ਰਵਾਂ *rawān, ad.* continuously, under way in motion, agoing (spoken commonly of work, business &c.)

ਰਾਸ਼ਨ *rāsan, s. m* Rations.

ਰਾਜ਼ੀਨਾਮਾ *rājīnāmā, s. m.* treaty.

ਰਾਤ *rāt, s. f.* night.

ਰੁਖਸਤ *rukhsat, s. f.* dismissed, having leave to go.

ਰੁਮਾਲ *rumāl, s. m.* a handkerchief.

ਰੁੜਨਾ *ruṛnā. v. a.* to get in motion, to get under way, to flow, to be swept away by a torrent.

ਰੇਸ਼ਮੀ *resmī,* silken.

ਰੇਲ *rel, s. f.* Rail.

ਰੈਜੀਡੈਂਟ *raisīdant, s. m.* Resident.

ਰੋਕ *rok, s m.* Cash, ready money.

ਰੋਕਣਾ *roknā, v. a.* to prevent, to restrain, to hinder, to detain, to stop to block up, to fend, to interrupt to prohibit, to check, to withhold to keep back, to obstruct.

ਰੋਟੀ *roṭī, s. f.* Bread, food, sustenance to feast.

ਰੋਣ *ron, s. f.* a hollowor, porous, portion in the earth, a marshy ground.

ਰੋਣਾ *ronā, v. a.* to cry, to weep, to lament, to mourn.

ਤੋਲ *rol, s. m.* a degree of fraud, a mixture of cheating, in conduct or language; (applied especially to games of chance or skill.)

ਰੌਣਕ *raunak s. f* pomp, splendor, show, glitter.

ਰੌਣੀ *rauni, s. f.* Water in a field previous to flowing.

ਲ

ਲਈ *laī, prep.* For, on account of, by reason of.

ਲਸ *las, s. m.* Gluton, any ਲੱਸ *lass* glutinous, substance viscosity; stickness

ਲਹਿਰ *lahir, s. f.* a wave.

ਲਕੜ *lakkaṛ, s. m.* Wood, a log, a stick

ਲਗਣਾ *laggnā, v. a.* to be applied, to come in contact, to be attached, to belong, cost.

ਲਗਭਗ, *lag bhag, a.* nearly, equal, about of the same size.

ਲੰਗੋਟਾ *langoṭā, s. m.* A strip of cloth between the legs attached to a string about the loins.

ਲੰਘਾਉਣਾ *langhāunā, v. a.* To cause to pass over, to spend, (time;) to kill.

ਲਠਾ *laṭṭhā s. m.* a beam, fine muslin, long cloth.

ਲਤ *latt, s f.* The leg, from the hip to the foot.

ਲਫਾਫਾ *s. m.* An envelope.

ਲਲਕਾਰਨਾ *lalkārnā, v. a.* to shout, to hallow, to set up the war whoop.

ਲੜਨਾ *laṛnā, v. a.* to fight, to contend, to war, to dispute, to quarrell.

ਲਾਉਂ *lāṇun, s. f.* A well rope drawn, by oxen; a long rope; a ceremony at Hindu weddings, in which the bride, and groom make four circuits about a fire the whole being called ਲਾਵਾਂ *lānwān.*

ਲਾਸ *lās*, s. *f*. The mark of a whip on the skin a dead body.

ਲਾਚਾਰੀ ਦੀ ਬਾਤ *lāchārī dī bāt*, forced matter.

ਲਾਟ *lāt*, s. m. Name of a rank.

ਲਾਭ *lābh*, s. m. Advantage, gain, profit, benefit.

ਲਾਮ *lām*, s. *f*. An assembled army, a large body of troops, a host arrayed far battle.

ਲਾਲਟੈਨ *lāltain*, s. *f*. a lantern.

ਲਾਲਾ *lalā*, s. m. A title given to a Hindu gentlemen, a father, an elder brother.

ਲਾਲਾ *lālā*, s. m. A father.

ਲਿਸਕਨਾ *lisknā*, v. a. to flash.

ਲਿਆਕਤ *liākat*, s. *f*. intelligence.

ਲਿਖਣ *likhan*, s. *f*. A pen.

ਲਿਖਣਾ *likhnā*, v. a. To write, to draw (picture &c.)

ਲਿਖਤ *likhat*, s. *f*. Writing, penmanship, a note.

ਲਿਖਤ ਪੜ੍ਹਤ *likhat parhat*, s. *f*. correspondence.

ਲਿਖਤਮ *likhtam*. A verbal form used in commencing a letter, is writing, writes.

ਲੀਰ *līr*, s. *f* A strip, a shred, (of cloth, paper &c.)

ਲੀਰਾਂ ਲੀਰਾਂ ਹੋਜਾਣਾ *līrān līrān ho jānā*, v. a to be torn to shreds.

ਲੁਹਾਰ *luhār* s. m. black smith.

ਲੁਕਣਾ *luknā*, v. a. To hide one's self, to be concealed.

ਲੁਟ *lutt*, s. *f*. Robbery rapine, violence plunder, pillage, spoil.

ਲੂਣ *lūn*, s. m. salt.

ਲੂੰਬੜੀ *lūmbarī*, s. *f*. A fox.

ਲੇਟਣਾ *letnā*, v. a. to lie, to lie down.

ਲੈਹਦਾ *laihndā*, s. m. Northside.

ਲੈਂਹਗਾ *lainhgī*, s, m. Petticoat.

ਲੋਹਾ *lohā*, s. m Iron.

ਲੋਹੜੀ *lohrī*, s. *f*. Name of a Hindu festival day.

ਲੋਟ *lot*, s. *f*. An earthern vessel with a very small mouth, used for holding money note.

ਲੋੜ *lor*, s. *f*. Necessity, need, want.

ਵ

ਵਸਤੁ *wastu*, s. *f*. A tning, matter.

ਵਸਨੀਕ *wasnīk*, s m. Inhabitant.

ਵਹੁਟੀ *wahutī*, s. *f*. wife.

ਵਖਰਾ *wakhrā*, s m. Part, portion.

ਵਗਣਾ *wagnā*, v. a. to flow.

ਵਟ *watt*, s. *f*. A boundary, line between fields.

ਵਟਾਉਣਾ *watāunā*, v. a. To cause to be twisted, to be changed, to exchange.

ਵਡਾਣਕ *wadānak*, s *f*. a kind of large grain wheat.

ਵਢਣਾ *waddhnā*, v. a. to cut, to reap.

ਵਧਣਾ *wadhnā*, v. a. To increase, to grow.

ਵਰਸਾਉਣਾ *warsāunā*, *v. a.* To cause to rain, to pour down.

ਵਰਤਣਾ *vartnā*, *v. a.* to use, to spend.

ਵਰਾਨ ਹੋਣਾ *varān honā*, *v a.* to be spoiled.

ਵਲ *val*, *s f.* side.

ਵੜਨਾ *varṇā*, *v. a* To go in to enter.

ਵਧ੍ਰਨਾ *varhnā*, *v. a.* to grow, sprout.

ਵਾ or ਵਾਉ *vā*, or *vāo*, *s. f.* wind.

ਵਾਹ *vāh*, *s. f.* Power, ability.

ਵਾਹ *vāh*, *s. m.* business, transaction.

ਵਾਹਗੁਰੂ *wāh gurū*, *s. m.* Name of God.

ਵਾਹਣਾ *vāhnā*, *v. a.* To plow, to plough.

ਵਾਹੀ *vāhī*, *s. f.* to ploughing, agriculture.

ਵਾਕ *vāk*, *s. m.* Word, speech.

ਵਾਂਗੁ *vāṅggu*, ਵਾਂਙੂ *vāṅṅgū*, Like, similar, resembelling.

ਵਾਚਣਾ *vāchnā*, *v. a.* to read.

ਵਾਰ *vār*, *s. m* a blow.

ਵਾੜਾ *vārā*, *v. m.* A sheepfold, an enclosure, a place with a hedge about it.

ਵਾੜੀ *vārī*, *s. f.* An enclosure, a garden an orchard, a small melon patch.

ਵਿਆਹਣਾ *viāhnā*, *v. a* To marry, (a wife,) to get (son or daughter &c.) married.

ਵਿਘਾ *vigghā*, *s. m.* A measure of land varying in different places, (as fixed by British law, 120, feet), square.)

ਵਿਚਾਰਾ *vichārā*, *s. m.* helpless, forlorn .desolate.

ਵਿਧ *vidh*, *s. f.* space, distance, separation

ਵਿਨ੍ਹਣਾ *vinnhnā*, *v. a.* to perforate, to bore, to pierce.

ਵਿਰੁਧ *viruddh*, *prep.* Against, contrary to.

ਵੀਹ *vīh*, twenty.

ਵੀਰਵਾਰ *vīrvār*, *s. m.* Thursday.

ਵੇਰਵਾ *vervā* *s. m.* Distinction, difference

ਵੇਲਨਾ *velnā*, *s. m.* A sugar mill.

ਵੇਲਾ *velā*, *s. m* Time, awhile.

SOME OPINIONS CONCERNING THE "PUNJBI GUIDE."

OPINION OF THE CIVIL AND MILITARY GAZETTE.

We have received a copy of a "Guide to Punjábí" by Bhai Jawahir Singh, R. H. A. Munshi, Umballa. The book is divided into three parts.

Part first contains a Grammar to the Punjábí Language, Part second is composed of lessons with expamples for exercises, and Part third is devoted to Punjábí dialogues in daily used, and Punjábí chits. The Guide should be very useful to those studying the Punjábí language, in the preface the author hopes in future editions to improve the book largely and make it a real self-tutor to students.

MY DEAR MUNSHI SAHIB,

Thank you for the copy of your "Guide to Punjábí" you have so kindly sent me. It seems thoroughly practical and will no doubt be very useful to Officers and others learning the Language.

I have only had time to glance through it as yet.

CALCUTTA, 27th July 1898. — (Sd.) G. RANKING, *Surgeon Lt.-Col.*

About a month before going up for the H. S. Punjábí I saw Munshi Jawahir Singh's new Guide to Punjábí advertised and procured it at once. It is not only the "Guide to Punjábí" Extant but it is for the best help to any Oriental Language, I have ever seen. The gramatical out line is very clear, the system of arranging words in groups is excellent, and the exercises and chits are very well chosen. I had been working in the dark before, but this book cleared away all difficulties at once, and was of the greatest assistance to me in passing.

DALHOUSIE, *7th July 1896.* — (Sd.) DALME RADCLIFFE, LT., *1st Hampshire Regiment.*

MUNSHI JAWAHIR SINGH,

I am much obliged to you for sending me a copy of your "Guide to Punjábi," It contains much valuable information, and I am sure that all who study the Punjábi Language will find it most useful.

SIMLA, *11th August 1898.* — (Sd.) SYDNEY SMITH, *D. S. Police.*

DEAR MUNSHI SAHIB.

Having successfully passed the Punjabi Examination, I feel it a duty to thank you for the great help which you have indirectly afforded me through your Punjabi Guide. I had studied for 2 months when I got it, and one month was left to the Examination. In this month I learned twice as much out of your Guide as in the previous 2 months.

SIALKOTE,
18th September 1898.

Yours faithfully,
(Sd.) T. HABER, SERGT.,
Commissariate Department,

Munshi Jawahir Singh, whose reputation as a Munshi is so well established, has embodied his experience of teaching the Punjabi language in his Guide to Punjabi. The book is most practical, clear and concise, and having found it most useful when preparing for the Punjabi Examination of July 1896, I feel sure that in recommending every student of Punjabi to purchase a copy they will not be disappointed.

SIALKOTE,
25th October 1896.

(Sd.) E. Q. HOWELL, LIEUT.,
D. A.C. G.

JAWAHIR SINGH, MUNSHI,

I am glad to be able to certify as to the usefulness of your Punjabi Guide and Vocabulary, and I can thoroughly recommend them to any body desirous of studying the language.

MULTAN CLUB,
7th March 1890.

(Sd) H. W. NORKET, LC.-CPL.,
1st Hants Regt., Multan.

I found Munshi Jawahir Singh's Guide to Punjabi most useful when working for the H. S. Punjabi Examination, and the small price of the book is imply repaid by the time saved through studying it.

CAMP ALI MUSJID,
16th March 1898.

(Sd.) A. WARD, LIEUT,
30th P. I.

DEAR SIR,

I received a great deal of help from your Guide to Punjabi which is a very useful book, the 2,000 words were also of great assistance, when this little book is revised it will be a great help to candidates.

Yours faithfully,
C. B. PRALL, SURG.-CAPT.

I strongly recommend Jawahir Singh, R. H. A. Munshi. Umballa, to any one booking up for Punjabi Examination, I consider his Punjabi Guide an invaluable aid one I think any one could pass the Punjabi obligatory by reading it himself without a Munshi to teach him.

UMBALLA, 28th October 1899. (Sd). A. GILBERT CAPT, *34th Punjāb.*

Munshi Jawahir Singh, whose reputation is well known has embodied the result of his teaching in Urdu, in his "Urdu Teacher." The book is practical easily understood in all its detail, and is exceedingly useful to any one preparing for either the Lower or Higher standard examination in Urdu.

The rules are specially good and the book generally was of great assistance for Lower Standard Urdu.

CHAKDARA, 25th July 1899 (Sd.) S. ANDERSON, LT., L. M. S. *Medical Officer 30th P. I.*

I derived great benefit from the H. S. Exercises at the end of the "Urdu Teacher" which I thought were especially good for teaching idiom &c.

UMBALLA, 16th July. (Sd.) NICOLAS, LIEUT., *34th Pioneers.*
